AF478658

The Dialectic of Creativity

by Hermann Vaske

HATJE
CANTZ

WHY ARE WE NOT CREATIVE?

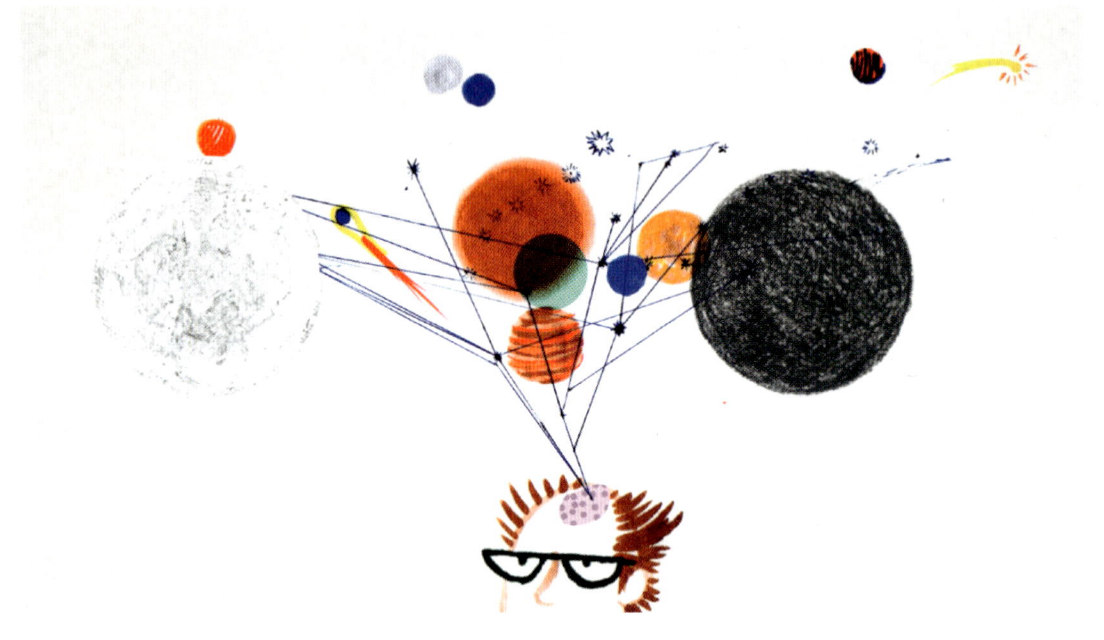

INTRO

When Jean Genet was interviewed by the BBC, he said: "Do we have to do this interview face to face? Me here, you there, camera over there? Can't we do something different?"

The interviewer said: "What do you mean?" Genet said: "Can't we stand on our heads or let our hands talk?" An idea should turn people on their heads.

WHAT IS AN IDEA?

An idea is a solution to a problem. What kind of people have ideas? We all have problems. We all have to solve those problems. Therefore, we all have ideas. A mason makes nice stonework. With every stone he has an idea. Scaffolders erecting a large construction are having ideas. A florist arranging flowers has an idea. A person making a cake has ideas. A hacker thinking up scams to make money has to have ideas. Every time a footballer makes a clever move to outwit an opponent, he is having an idea. Incidentally these people are wonderful mathematicians. But not one of them knows it.

Ideas are not the exclusive domain of the fancy few who like to describe themselves as creative people. Ideas are what we all work with to make our lives practical.

WHAT IS A GOOD IDEA?

It's often a matter of taste. What is a good idea to some can be a bad or boring idea to others. To me, a good idea is a clever solution to a problem that I have never seen before.
Like new the Tyne Bridge. The bridge is a curved road across the river that swings up to become a bridge. A road across a river becomes a bridge. Problem solved. If an idea is not taken up and used as the solution to the problem, its value as an idea is useless. That's not to say it's a bad idea, probably quite the opposite. It has to happen, it has to be executed for it to be recognized as a good idea.

The idea of the Eiffel tower is not strong. What counts is the monument in Paris. The second criterion of whether an idea is good or not is the proof of history. If something withstands the test of time and is still considered to be useful, it passes into the realms of classicism. We can safely say that was a great idea. The Egyptian planked wheel is an old idea that's stood the test of time. It was followed by a spoked cartwheel, followed by the bicycle wheel, the modern car wheel, the wheels on the lunar rover. Probably one of the greatest ideas still in use.

Probably the greatest idea ever.

WHAT IS A BAD IDEA?

Without the execution of the idea, there is no idea. An idea lying in a drawer is not useful. It is a dead, forgotten thing. Not to say that a bad idea executed is better than a great idea, undone. But there are a lot of great ideas that didn't make it.

Ingenious. Yes. Clever. Yes. But how are we to know if they're good ideas or not; they were never made. They will always remain non-ideas. That can't be a good idea.

Great ideas are built on the willpower and human resolve to see an idea realized at whatever cost. Like the lightbulb, the radio and the horn gramophone. All these got made; that made them good ideas. They are still around today over one hundred years later. That in itself makes them great ideas.

The determination and guts to eventually make this a reality is what turns it from a non-idea collecting dust in a cupboard to a very good idea.

THE "I COULD HAVE DONE THAT" SYNDROME

Someone said to Damien Hirst in a recent interview: "Your pictures and things, I could have done that." And Damien Hirst said, "Yes, but you didn't, did you?" And that's all there is to it. Ideas are the property of every individual. The only difference between so-called creative people and non-creative people is that creative people just get on with it.

So, without the execution of the idea there is no idea. Or, as Henry Sobel, Rabbi of São Paulo, said: "An idea sitting on the shelf is betraying the idea."

Everybody has ideas. If you don't have many ideas, you have to make those ideas you do have work in your favor. Sometimes the solution is hidden inside the problem. As they say, if you ask the right question you get the right answer. Maybe the solution comes from doing exactly the thing you shouldn't do simply because it breaks the train of logical thought that bogs you down. Maybe it's divine intervention. Maybe dumb luck. I don't know. But I do know the golfer Arnold Palmer was right when he said: "The more I practice, the luckier I get."

IT'S THE RIDICULOUS WHO CREATE THE SUBLIME

Many of history's greatest innovations have been created by people who are beyond reason. People who are out of line with their contemporaries. It is because they are out of line that makes them think differently. They are not interested in being popular, social animals. All they care about is seeing their ideas through from an abstraction to a reality.

"When Stravinsky performed his 'Le Sacre du Printemps' in Paris, it was an absolute scandal," Yello frontman and artist Dieter Meier explained. "People got up, booed, whistled, felt totally threatened. And that's part of it. Every true innovation is a disruption of the status quo and therefore a disruption for the people who believe in the status quo and not in the future and change."

THE DIALECTIC OF CREATIVITY

I continued reflecting on creativity. Questioning the question. Asking what every creative person should always be asking: "Why?"

For over forty years, as part of a personal quest, I have been exploring the genius behind the world's most intriguing artists and thinkers. My interview partners included over 1,000 luminaries, Academy Award and Nobel Prize winners among them, from the fields of visual art, music, acting, philosophy, politics, business, and science—posing to each the questions, "Why are you creative?" and "Why are you NOT creative?" From that wealth of material I made the first two movies of my film trilogy, *Why Are We Creative* and *Why Are We Not Creative,* which were shown in almost every country of the world. In *The Dialectic of Creativity,* I am embarking on a journey of exploration in conversations with some of the greatest artists, activists, and thinkers of our time. Together, we try to seek out and identify not only creativity's critical stimuli—Spirituality, Sex, Money, Fear, Nurture and Ambition—but also the killers of creativity—Censorship, Self-Censorship, Bureaucracy, Compromise, Distraction, and the dreaded, lethal "Gatekeepers"—the oppositional forces that act as beta-blockers to creative energy. It's an existential clash between creativity's angels and its demons. The assassins of creativity are many and they lurk everywhere.

And ironically, reasons for NOT being creative are often the triggers that motivate us to even greater creativity! Today, for example, the Anthropocene period threatens our very survival. This existential threat, however, is also inviting us to explore new and disruptive ideas if we want to avoid disaster. Creativity may be under threat, but often that threat is exactly what makes it thrive. A dialectical synthesis of opposites, as Hegel would have said.

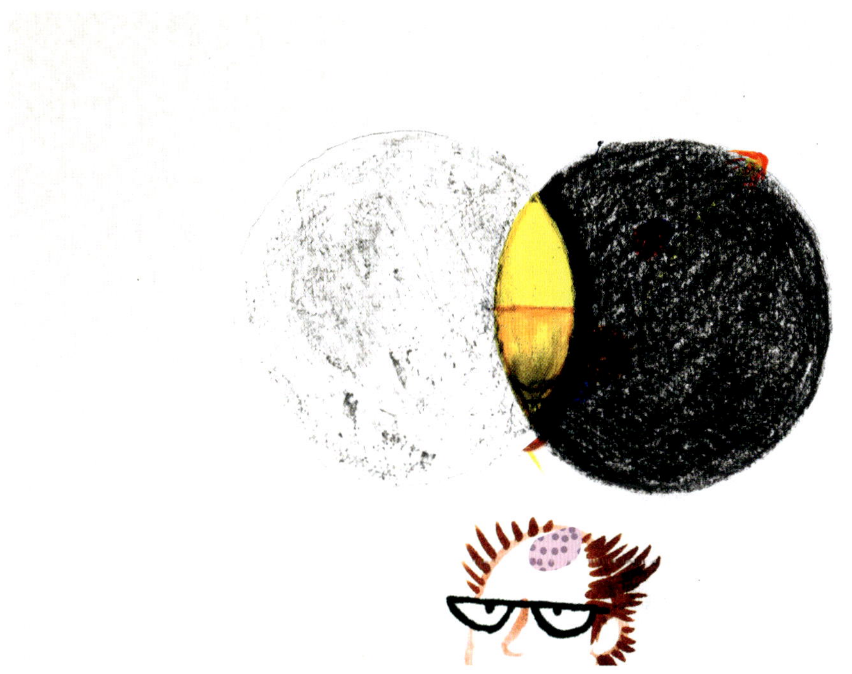

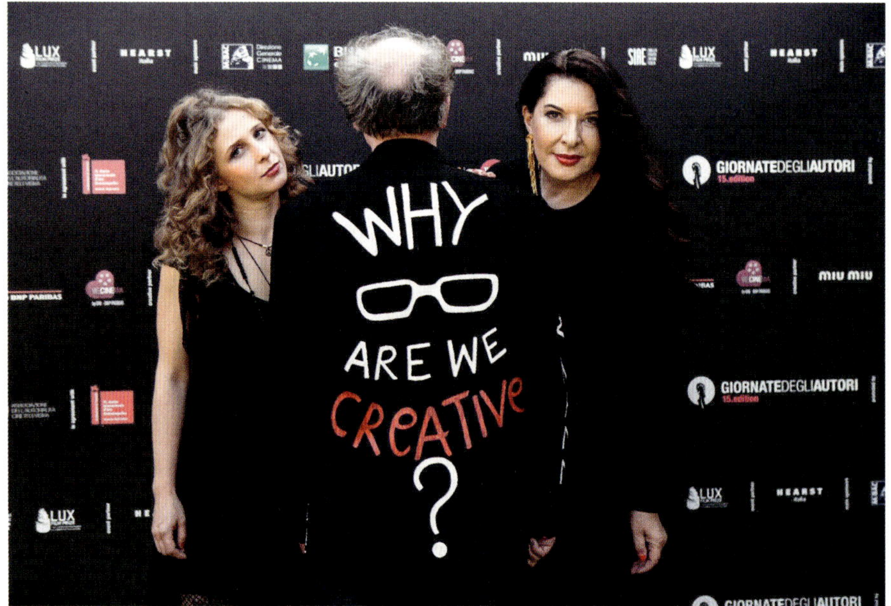

Premiere of Why Are We Creative *at the Venice Film Festival with artist Marina Abramović and Masha Alyokhina from Pussy Riot.*

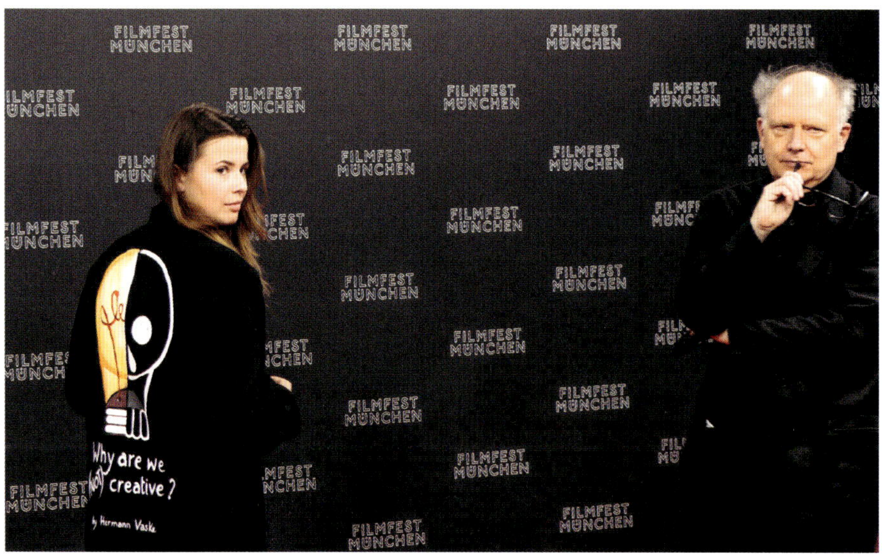

Premiere of Why Are We Not Creative *at Filmfest Munich in the presence of climate activist Luisa Neubauer.*

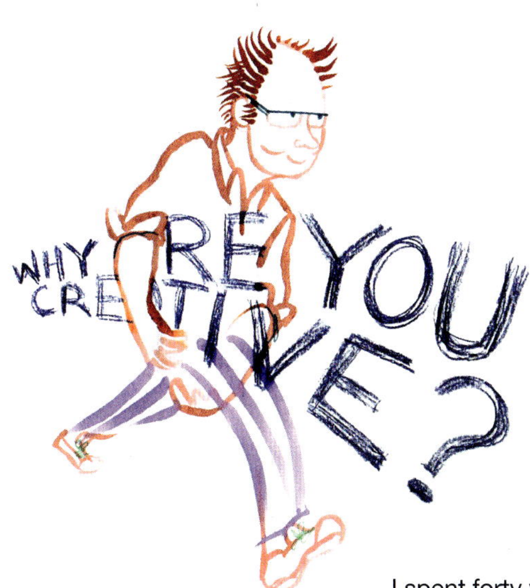

I spent forty years making this chronicle, meandering the roads of postmodernity and surfing on the tidal wave of creativity where ideas are king. My hope is that this book offers up the highlights of my conversations and is an interesting reflection on the killers and boosters of inspiration. A visual and aural document of what is after all our primal culture: creativity.

So, a creative as well as journalistic investigation. An enquiring and intriguing documentary on art, alternative and mainstream culture. A provocative debate that informs and entertains while also exploring the crucial and extraordinary power of imagination and creativity and its potential for solving the existential problems of the world.

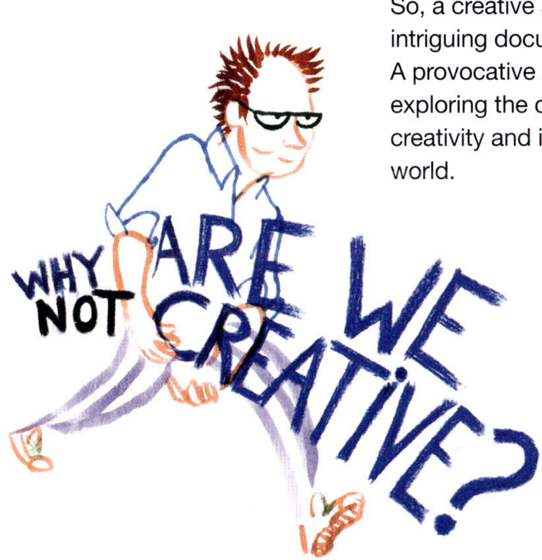

As Malcolm McLaren said: “Hermann’s conversations should find a place in the libraries of every university available to all students.” And I hope that this Dialectic of Creativity, gives them and the reader. in Malcolm’s words, “ideas to simply know what to do and what not to do, where to go and where not to go, or perhaps be inspired by it.”

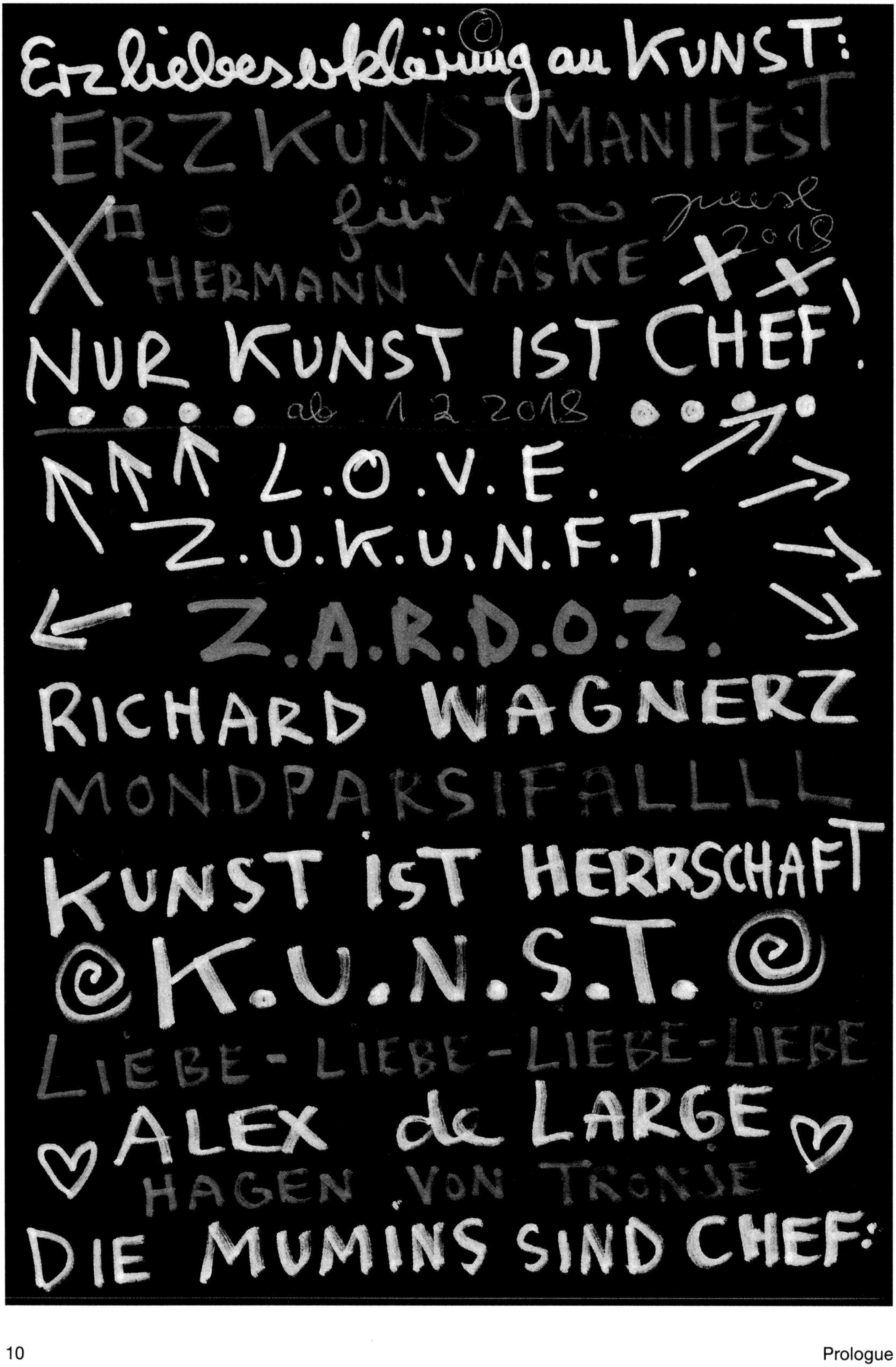

Erzliebeserklärung an KUNST:

ERZKUNSTMANIFEST

für A ∞ meese 2018

HERMANN VASKE

NUR KUNST IST CHEF!

ab 1.2.2018

L.O.V.E.

Z.U.K.U.N.F.T.

Z.A.R.D.O.Z.

RICHARD WAGNERZ

MONDPARSIFALLLL

KUNST IST HERRSCHAFT

K.U.N.S.T.

LIEBE-LIEBE-LIEBE-LIEBE

ALEX de LARGE

HAGEN VON TRONJE

DIE MUMINS SIND CHEF:

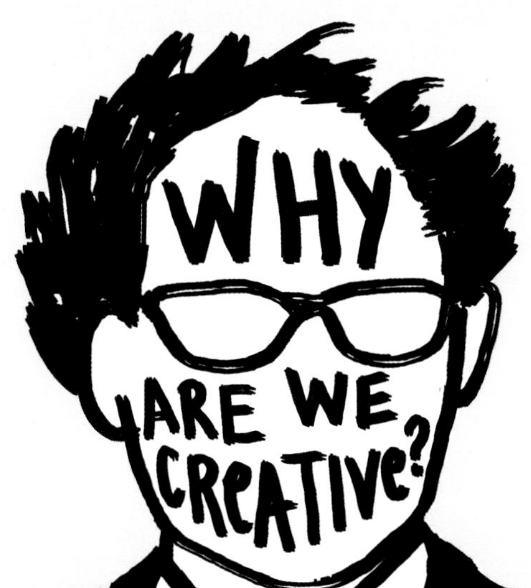
WHY
ARE WE
CREATIVE?
DAVID BOWIE
AI WEIWEI
BJÖRK
WIM WENDERS
Oliviero TOSCANI
YOKO ONO
John HEGARTY
David LYNCH
Yohji Yamamoto
Damien HIRST
Angelina JOLIE
Nobuyoshi ARAKI
Quentin TARANTINO
BONO
NICK CAVE
Isabella ROSSELLINI
Stephen HAWKING
the Dalai LAMA
PETER USTINOV
Marina ABRAMOVIĆ
Diane KRUGER
Julian SCHNABEL
John CLEESE
JIMMY PAGE
Vivienne Westwood
TAKESHI KITANO

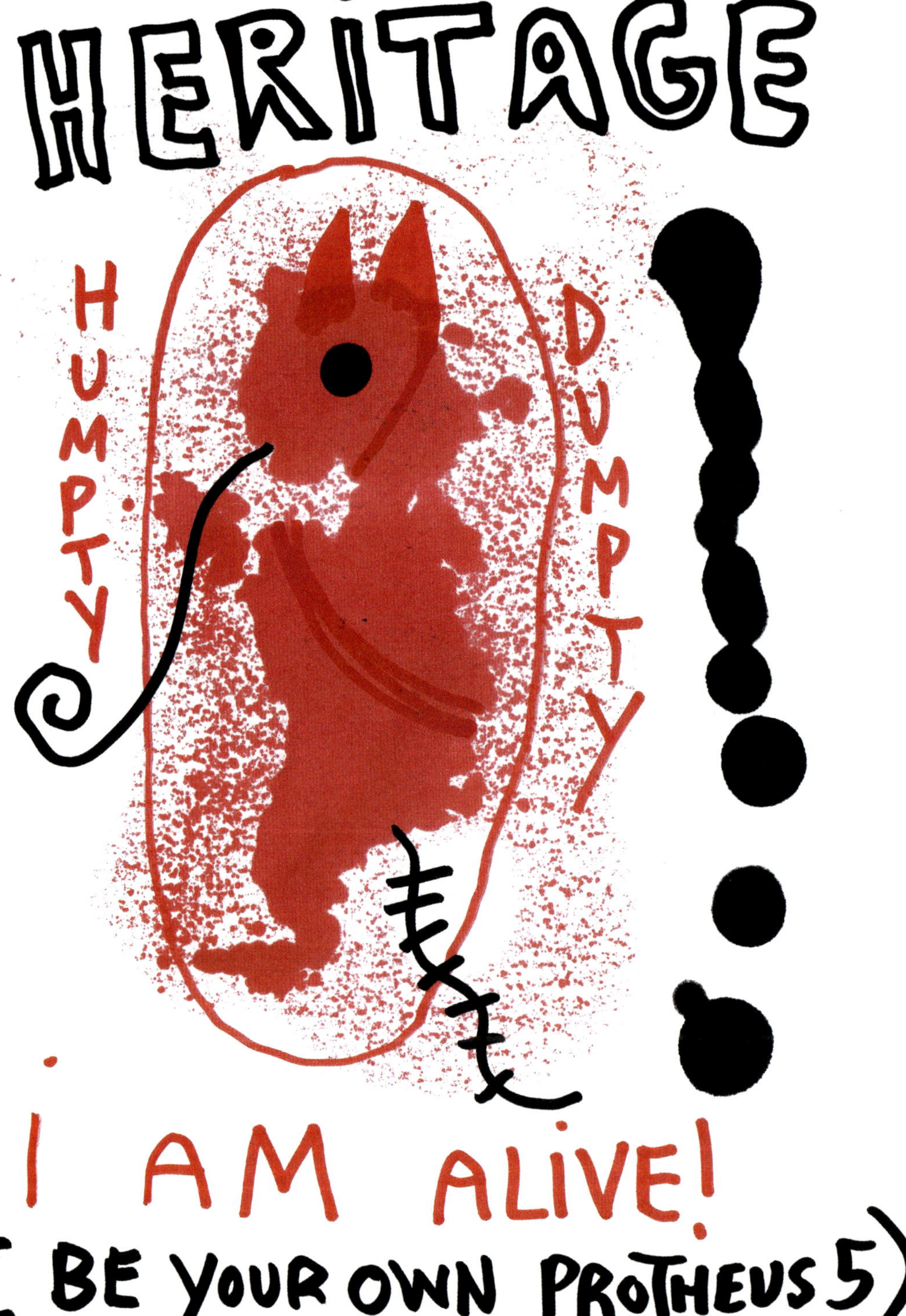

MOTHERZ MEESI IS IN TOWN!

Our greatest, our first influences are our parents. But not everyone who has creative parents is creative. And some of the most creative people on earth came from parents who'd never dream of making the things these people make. No parent could conceive of the things their child creates. And why do we choose what we choose to create? We have to ask ourselves: Nature? Nurture? Neither? Heritage. Are we creative because of it? Is creativity in our blood? Does it come from the culture we grow up in? Are we creative to honor our heritage? Or do we do it in spite of it?

MARINA ABRAMOVIĆ

My mother was extremely strict. Everything was, you know, everything I was doing, I was always like a black sheep, I was always punished, you know? And she would write me notes in the morning how many sentences of French I have to learn, what I have to read, what I have to do, and, you know, how many times I have to wash my hands, everything was like controlled. And I was already doing performances at that time but I had to be home. ... You know, I was twenty-nine years old and I have to be home by ten o'clock. And I didn't know that somebody had called her and told her that "your daughter is hanging naked on the wall in the gallery." So, she was waiting for me and she looked at me and she took a very heavy ashtray, it was the one of the presents for the, whatever, twenty-fifth anniversary of unhappy marriage she got when they celebrated my father and her—and she takes that ashtray and she is looking at me and she is telling me, "Taras Bulba," you know, the sentence from the, you know, the Russian book of Gogol, and she said: "I gave you life and now I'm going to take it from you." She takes this ashtray and she throws it at my head. ... And the ashtray is flying toward my head and I'm saying to myself: "Okay, I'm not going to move the head. She's going to splash my head all over the place but then is she is going to prison and then she is going to pay for it." But then I moved my head and the ashtray just went toward the glass door and smashed into the glass door. I think that I could never do the work I am doing right now if I didn't have this kind of upbringing because I need an enormous amount of self-control and an idea of purpose and sacrifice. So it was actually this kind of genetic code in me that made me to what I am now.

"I THINK THAT I COULD NEVER DO THE WORK I AM DOING RIGHT NOW IF I DIDN'T HAVE THIS KIND OF UPBRINGING."

ISABELLA ROSSELLINI

I stayed in the same metier as my parents. My mother, Ingrid Bergman, was an actress. My father, Roberto Rossellini, was a director and often wrote scripts. So, I'm an actress, I write my scripts, I direct them—of course they are very short films, and they did big masterpieces and, you know, won Oscars and all sorts of awards. So I can't really compare myself to their career ... well, I liked it since I was a child. I liked going to the set, I liked the people in the film business, I liked their creativity, their playfulness. I like it more than the undertakers.

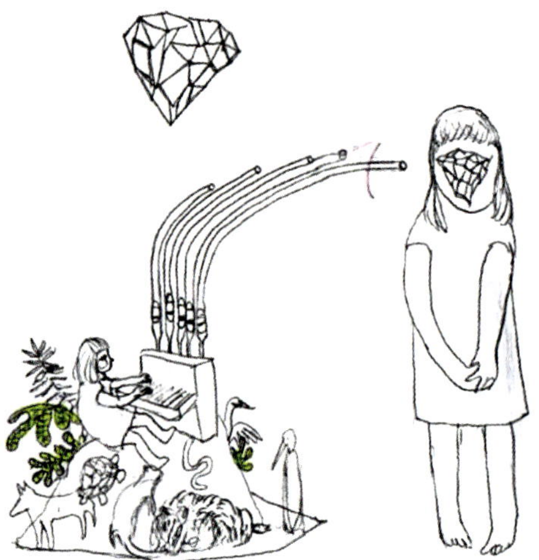

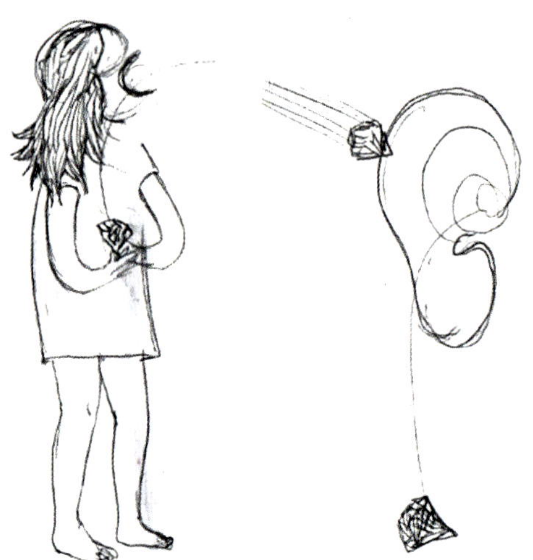

SEAN PENN

I grew up in a very creative home. My parents were involved in the theater and painting and writing. So I'm sure that had an impact and now, I think as I've gotten to be able to do things creatively, it's turned out that it's in movies mostly. I find that the things that are occupying your experience at the time fuel what you do creatively. You know, and the things that you question … you're looking to find, not answers, but some kind of hope in, are worth pursuing creatively.

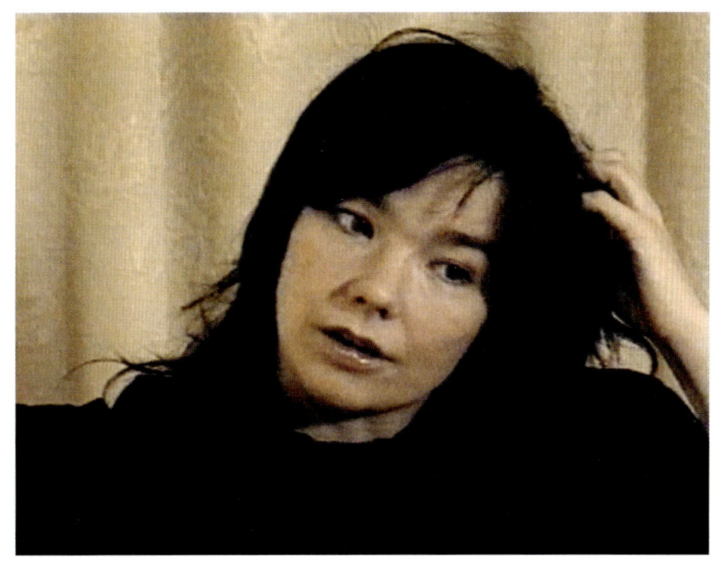

BJÖRK

Creativity, it is a funny word. Maybe because I was brought up in with such a working-class situation—and with the people I admire most, like my grandmother, my grandparents, and my family. If you would look at their passport, not one of them says artist. But for me, they have all been very brave, and completely stood by what they are made of. And sometimes just to take care of a lamp shop is a very creative thing, or to feed eight children can be a very pro-life statement, with all the hindrances and everybody wanting to stop you. My grandfather, he would show me a fireplace he had just made, a Polaroid of it, just as proud as I was playing my song.

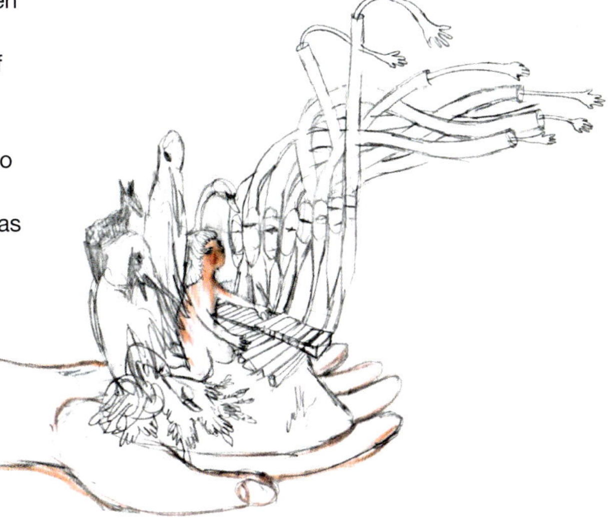

me go to Prague, because my aunt was there, so it was like, one coincidence after another, that I would one day look back into my private biography and fit into the world of art as the newcomer who was discovering the beauty of art when he was twenty-one, twenty-two, twenty-three. And when I was twenty-five, I made my first feature.

Why Are You Creative?

"I BECAME A FILM DIRECTOR THANKS TO MY PARENTS AND MY CURIOSITY."

Myself specifically, I don't know because this is a really difficult question. It might be the mental characteristics that I inherited from my ancestors coming from the mountains. Being very, at the same time, tender and barbaric, being very violent and, as I said, being very tender, combining all these elements, there was just the question when in our genes there will be a time to project this definitely into cinema.

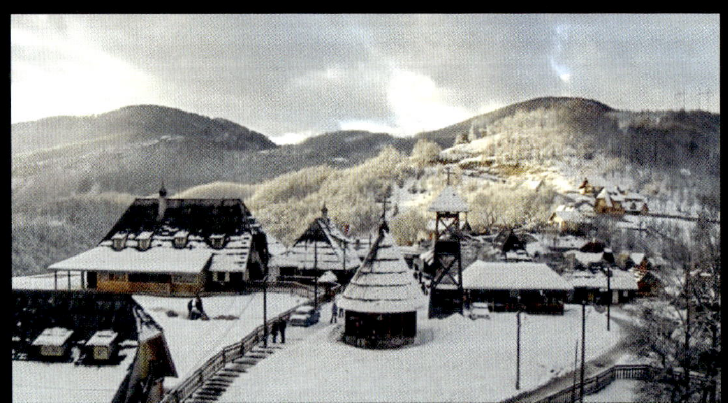

In Aschersleben, the artist Neo Rauch organized an exhibition in memory of his parents. Neo's parents were both artists who died in an accident when he was a few months old.

NEO RAUCH

How much is your father the reason for your creative development?

Creativity is probably in the genes, because there was no direct influence. I was only four weeks old when the big farewell took place. Of course, in my grandparents' house, where I grew up, there was this or that work by my father on the wall. Most of them were portraits of my mother. It was the grandparents' household on my mother's side, and yes, they always looked down on me. And of course, I knew that Hanno drew that, Hanno being my father. So it was suggested to me from an early age that my father and also my mother were artistically active. But that probably only had a limited influence, because I somehow got on track myself. So, I set out in this direction for me, in a genetically predetermined way.

"CREATIVITY IS PROBABLY IN THE GENES."

That is what you describe as genetic disposition. Can you explain this genetic disposition?

You get things added and given by your parents, which also have an effect on or influence your life path, although you may never have had contact with your parents. That even goes as far as gestures. Somebody who knew my father told me that I have his gestures, his habit is on my back and that's amazing. If something as seemingly incidental as habit is communicated genetically, why shouldn't something as profound as my artistic disposition be conveyable?

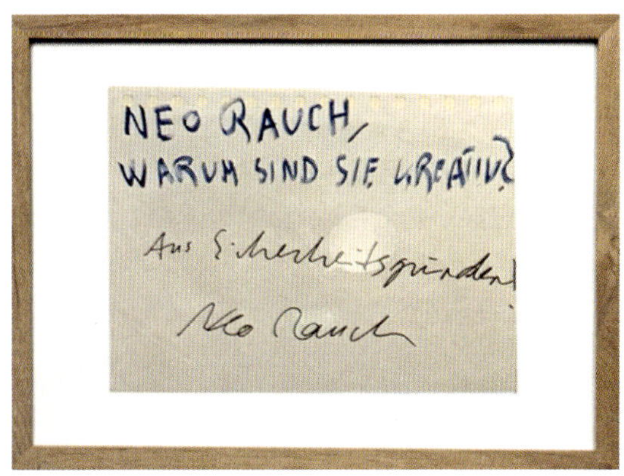

Spike Lee's answer is also heavily influenced by his heritage of basketball and jazz.

Spike Lee

IT'S ALL BECAUSE
OF MY PARENTS.
BLAME THEM.
MY MUDDA JACQUELYN SHELTON
LEE TAUGHT ART AND MY
DADDY BILL LEE IS A
GREAT JAZZ BASSIST/COMPOSER.

WHY IZ YA
DO CREATIVE?

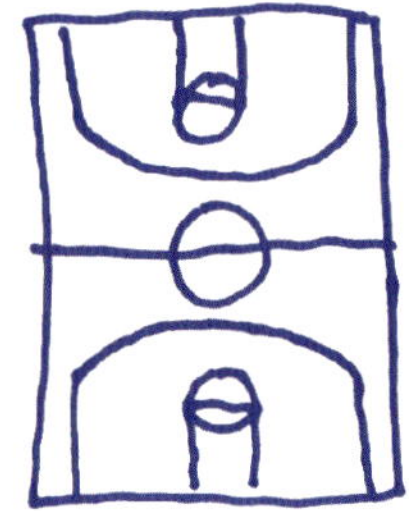

① ②

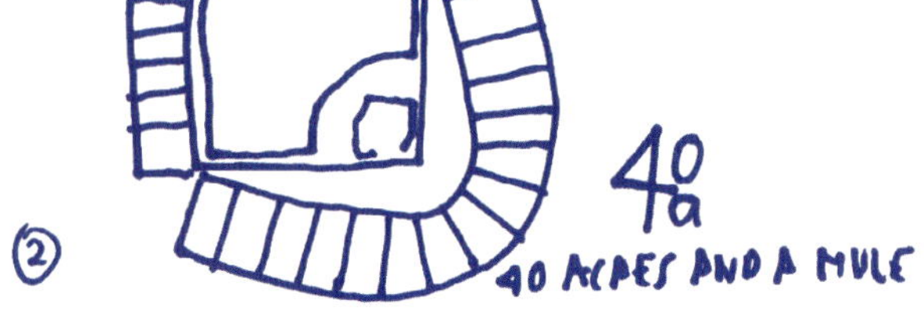

SPIKE LEE

I'm creative because that's why I was put in this world: to make films.

To tell stories.

To tell stories. And a lot of stories I heard from my parents.
Creativity enables me to do what I do and that is to direct. Doesn't have to be films you know, I enjoy directing commercials and music videos. We try and put a narrative in our, in our thirty-second spots and our four-minute, four-minute music videos. I look at commercials and music deals as a shorter form of narrative films.

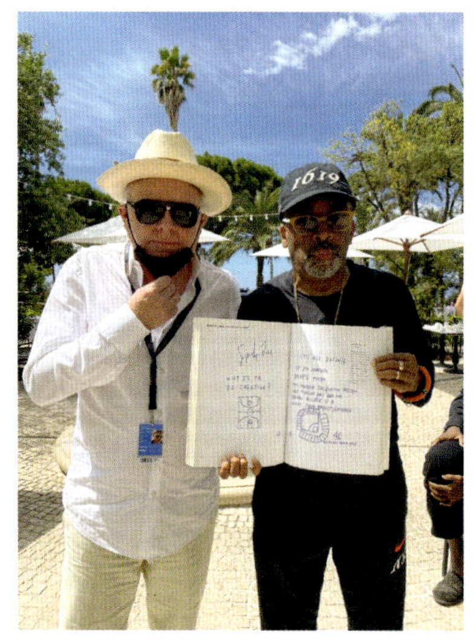

Director-supremo Steven Spielberg sums up his creative influence in one sentence: "I was born that way because of my father and my mother."

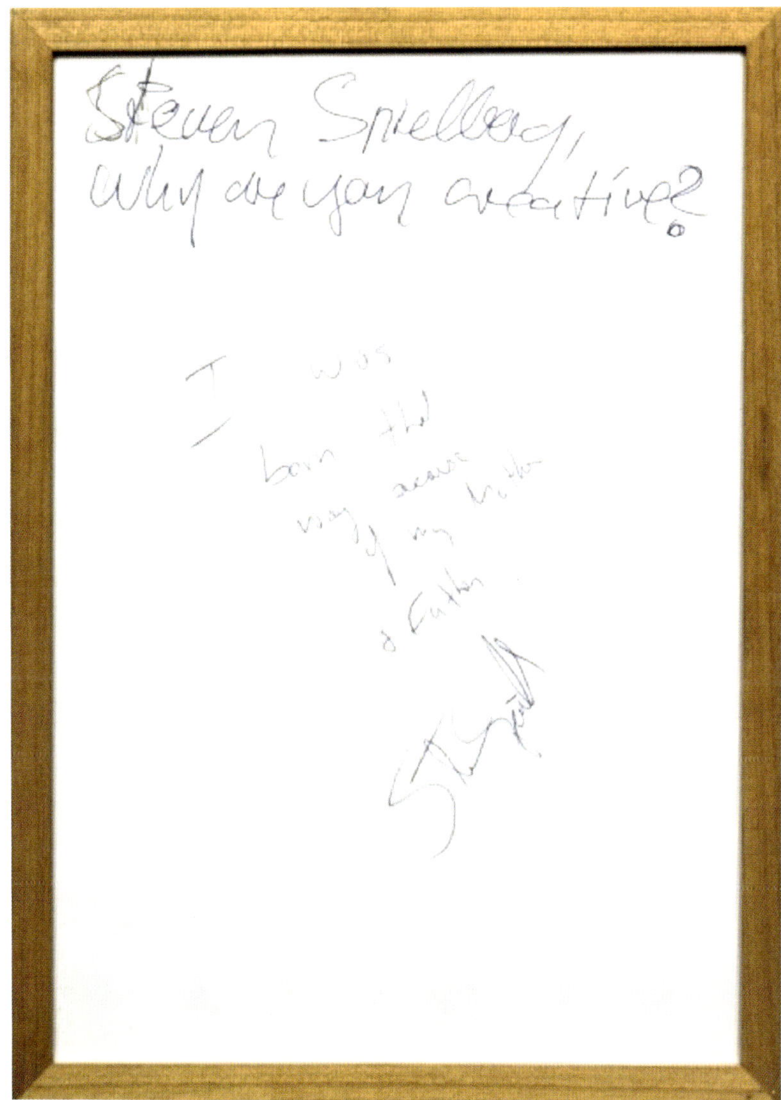

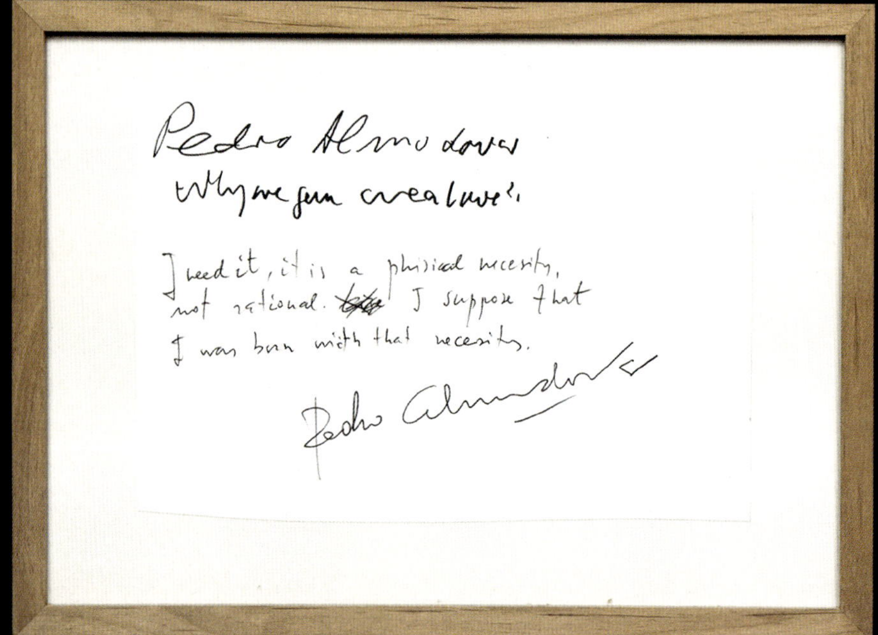
Pedro Almodovar
Why we [illegible]?

I need it, it is a phisical necesity, not rational. J suppose that I was born with that necesity.

Pedro Almodovar

PEDRO ALMODÓVAR

You never know if you are respecting your mother in the way that she wants to be respected, because you have your own life and sometimes, you know, I don't know, if sometimes she felt offended by me, I don't think so. Because of course I was a very peculiar boy for a mother, for a brother, for … and not making movies, also about my personality and so on, but I didn't have any problem with her, and actually, I mean she was the origin of many of my male/female characters. I didn't talk directly about her in the movies, but she inspired all of the strong women in my movies.

So, it's all about your mother?

Yeah, I mean without realizing, just listening to her. There are many lines in my movies that they came directly from my mother's mouth. Anyway, she didn't give it much importance, it was no big deal for her that I was directing movies. But you know, I mean my mother and also, you know, the people, I mean the women of her generation, they were, or they are, if they were alive, some of them, very strong women. I mean they had to face an awful postwar … almost all of them were survivors, but also, you know, the men are more like conservative than women, I don't know why, in a natural way. So, they were strong. I mean all my generation, we survive because we have very strong mothers in every sense. So, you know, of course, I mean in my case, that I wrote and made movies after, I mean these types of women inspire many, many women. My women have developed in their lives, and they are now in this period, they have a sort of autonomy and a freedom and lack of prejudice that I saw in my mother and the women of her generation.

JEFF KOONS

What about your parents? Were they an influence?

My father was an interior decorator and had a furniture store. So, I realized at an early age how manipulating objects in your environment, colors in your environment, could really affect the way that you feel. So I go to my father's store and one day, maybe a room in the front would be like a dining room, everything would be like this, maybe red and brown. And I'd go back the next week and it would be a French provincial bedroom and everything would be a gold or turquoise, and that had a very big impact, and my family was also very supportive; I started taking lessons when I was about seven years old. Every weekend, I would take lessons, et cetera.

"I THINK THAT MY DESTINY WAS ALREADY MADE BEFORE I WAS BORN."

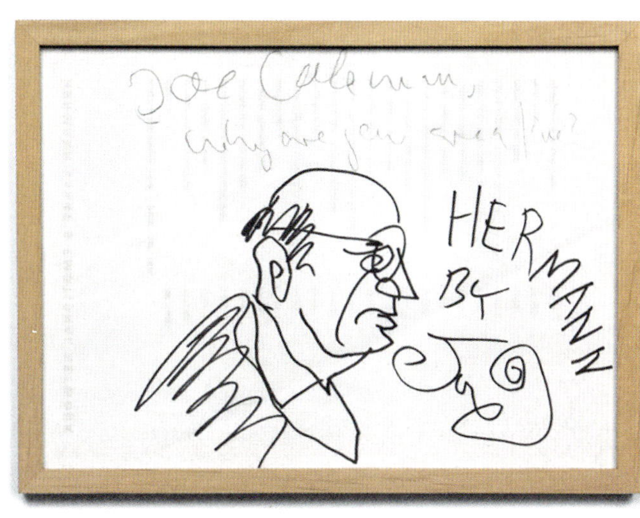

JOE COLEMAN

My mother was an aspiring actress, and my father painted, what you would consider almost flea-market art, like paintings of lighthouses and New England landscapes, and he traded them at the bar that he hung out in for drinks and that always paid his tab. So, I had kind of an artistic influence from childhood, but I think that my destiny was already made before I was born, you know, that I was born into that family for a specific reason. And it wasn't necessarily just that they taught me about, you know, drama and, you know, and painting, they also taught me nasty lessons too because they were a pretty twisted bunch, and it was the combination of the two with my own genetics that created in me something that society needs, a prophet. A prophet for a society that needs someone to express their rage, their pain, their, you know, their attempt to articulate what can never be articulated.

I think it was already written that I was going to do this, and I'm following ... like it's almost the reverse, you know, of history, like it's already been written, you know, and I'm following this. That doesn't mean that I made all my choices in life myself, I made all those choices, but at the same time, you know, I'm a very specific creature in the world. Like I have these other siblings, and they have the same parents, the same environment, you know, the same influences of, you know, of the media, but only I did what I did, only I react in the way that I react to all of this stimuli, and I think it's because that's the way I was made, and so I don't even have a choice, I can't be something else, you know, I'm stuck with this. If there's nothing else, you know, like the only thing that would stop me from creating is, you know, somebody blowing my brains out, otherwise it's not going to stop because it's like breathing, eating.

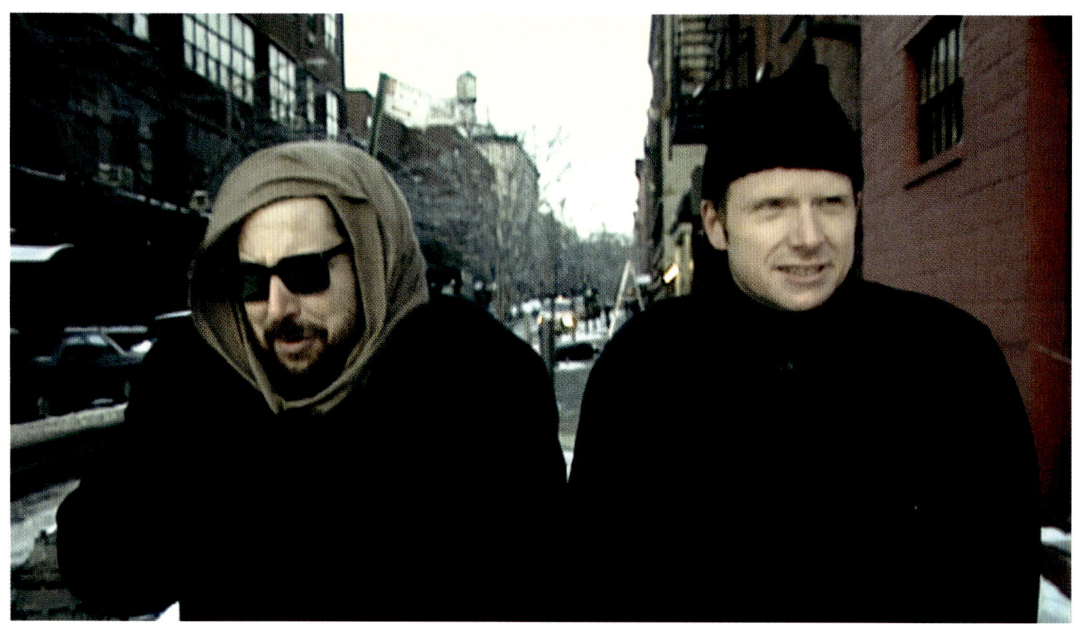

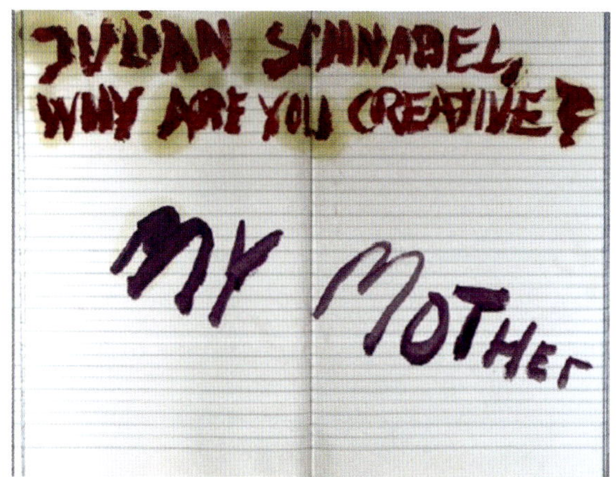

JULIAN SCHNABEL

My mother encouraged me to paint and that's how she had the greatest impact on my creativity. It's funny because I didn't know I was creating anything. Everything seems to sort of be a part of the world already and maybe I just kind of pulled it out of something that already exists, in a way. I've always made things or that's just the way that I've always behaved from the time I was a child, so I never thought I was being creative; I just thought I was passing my time in the world. I guess I had a talent for drawing when I was a child, and my mother was very enthusiastic, so I continued because that was the only thing that I could do well. Later on, I got more philosophical about it, maybe, but I think I had a very Pavlovian beginning.

So creativity can come from many sources. It's inherited. It's instilled in early childhood. It's a rebellion against childhood. And sometimes an attempt to regress back to an idealized childhood, to see the world once again through the eyes of a child.

CRAIG VENTER

"THERE WON'T BE GENES FOR CREATIVITY."

I don't think there is a genetic creative code. That's in fact one of the things I argue against quite strenuously. That's thinking of life in genetically deterministic fashions. So, I don't think there is anything in the genetic code that would code for a creative mindset. I think you take the same individual and two different environments, in one environment that person could be very creative and very successful, in the other environment that person would fail. I think we see that over and over again in society. I think it is a tremendous mistake for people to try and take reductionism biology back to human behavior. There are so many complexities in just our brains alone with billions of neurons, all the connections, all the cells are formed way after the genetic code. We have maybe 26,000 genes, maybe 300,000 proteins. Those neurons develop independently based on the environment, based on the cell-cell interactions, based on independent stimuli, so we are very adaptive creatures. I think most animals are, that have a common physiology. You and I share 99-plus percent of our biochemistry, our cellular functions. Yet we have different personalities, as do identical twins with the same genetic code and very different outcome. So, I am clearly against genetic reductionism. It is a long answer for saying: no, there won't be genes for creativity.

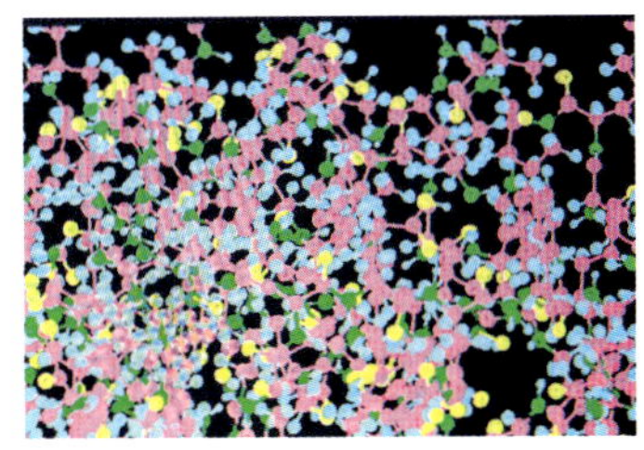

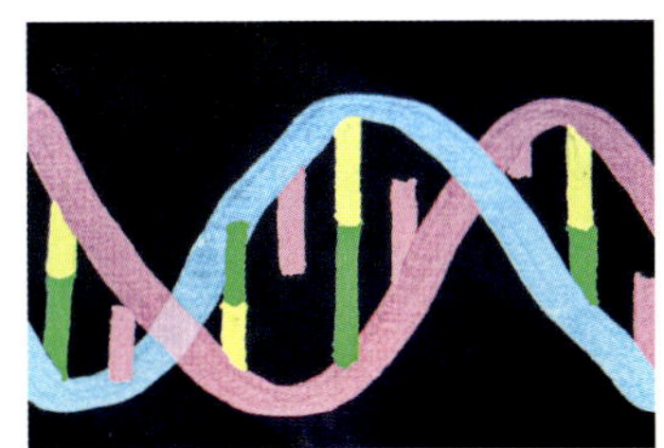

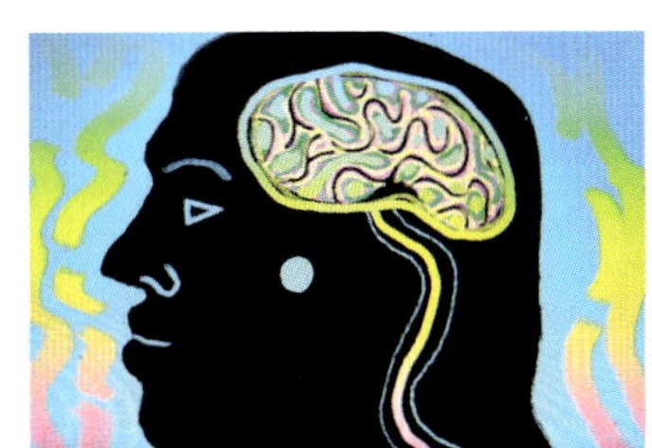

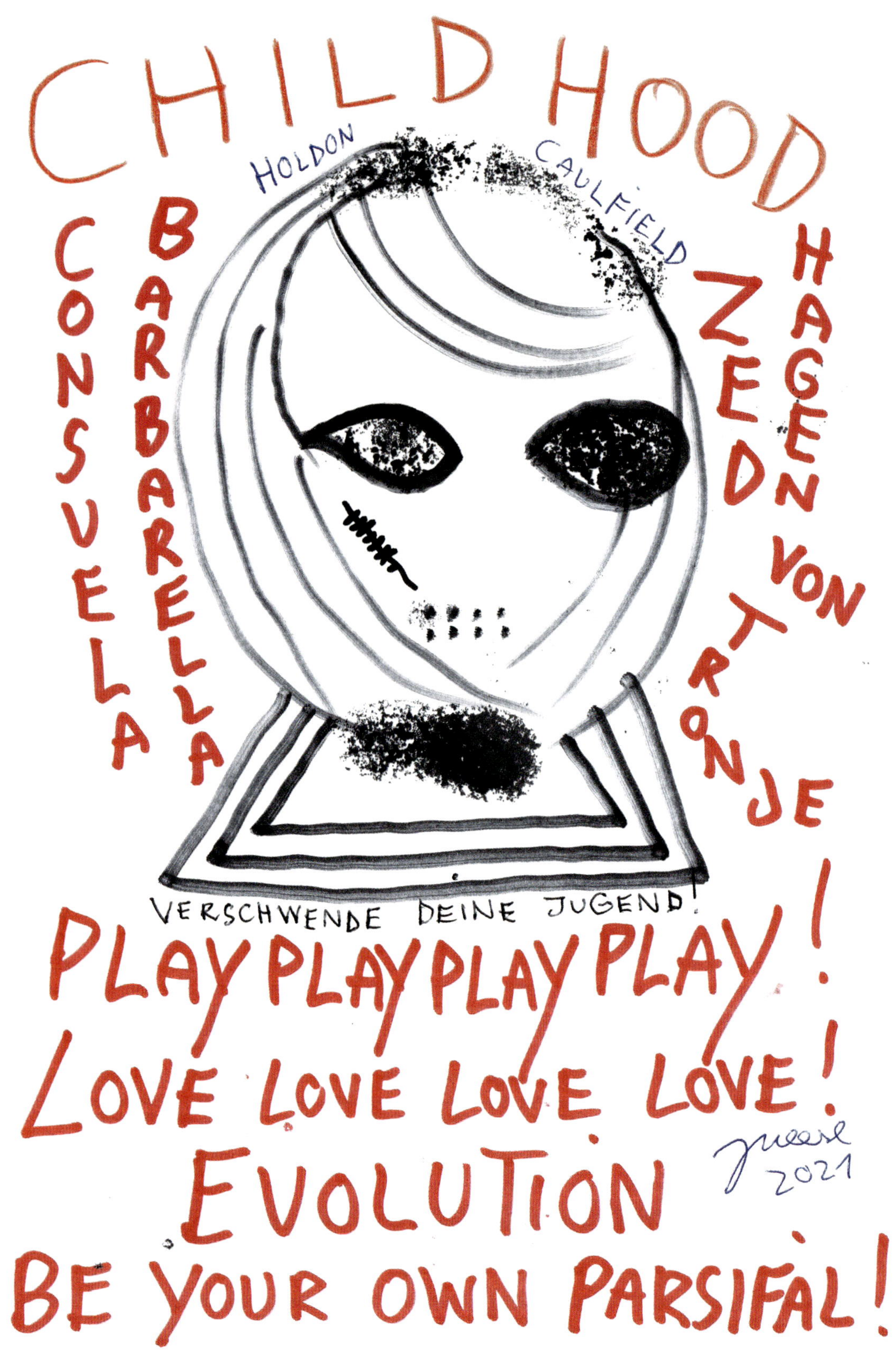
CHILDHOOD
HOLDON CAULFIELD
CONSUELA
BARBARELLA
ZED
HAGEN VON TRONJE!
VERSCHWENDE DEINE JUGEND!
PLAY PLAY PLAY PLAY!
LOVE LOVE LOVE LOVE!
EVOLUTION
BE YOUR OWN PARSIFAL!
2021

As children, we're uninhibited. We need to play to release our twisted minds. Staying in touch with the child inside you keeps your creativity alive. Childhood. That's where many of us return to free what might be our innate power to be creative.

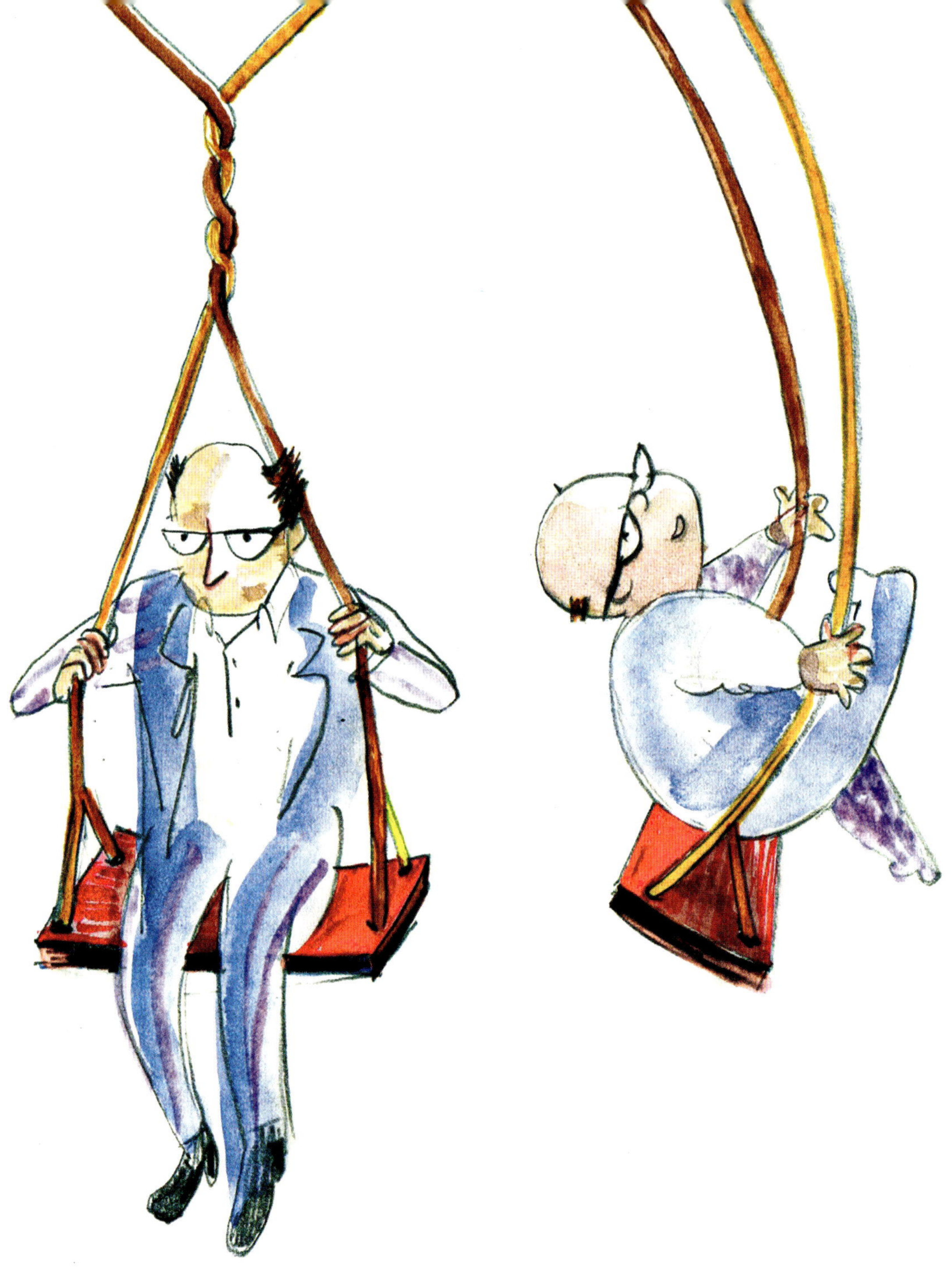

In response to the question of what drives creativity, director Wim Wenders drew a bear. I was surprised and amused by his drawing, an almost childlike feeling.

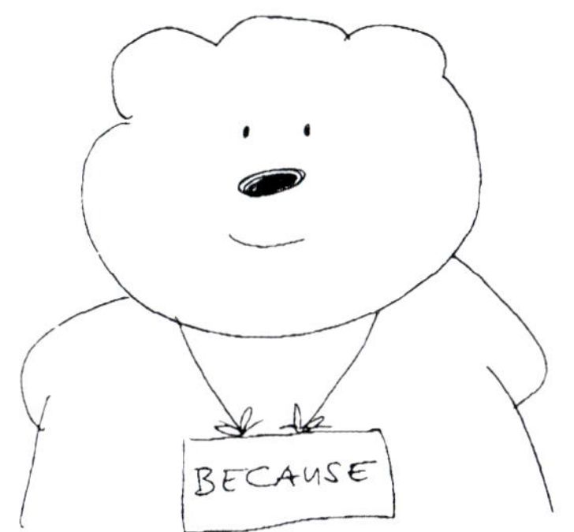

"I THINK LIFE IS PRETTY UNBEARABLE IF YOU'RE NOT IN TOUCH WITH THE KID YOU HAVE INSIDE YOURSELF BECAUSE THAT KID WANTS TO PLAY."

WIM WENDERS

It's a funny question because I think life is pretty unbearable if you're not in touch with the kid you have inside yourself because that kid wants to play. And I think the tools that we have at our hands, cameras and stuff, are really incredible toys. Filmmaking and in advertising even more, it's a lot related to wanting to play. Hey, because. My father and mother encouraged me and did a lot to ensure that my creativity was not blocked. I wouldn't say now, "My father was creative" or "my mother encouraged my creativity," but they gave me courage, and that was a lot.

It has got a lot to do with creativity that in an early phase as a kid it was appreciated. I think it's very difficult to be creative if it wasn't appreciated. Sometimes, of course there's people who are creative because it was never appreciated. They had to be rebels. Actually, if you are parents, I think you can help your child to be creative immensely. Not by, sort of, pushing it to be creative. I mean, there are these terrible parents, too, who see that their son is Michelangelo just because he's drawing.

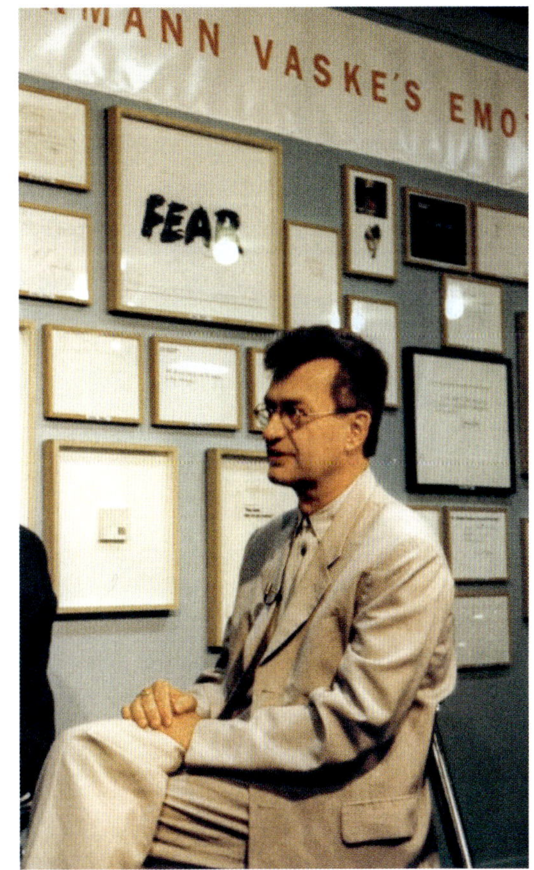

What are the similarities between children and actors? James Mangold, who took the baton from Steven Spielberg shooting Indiana Jones, shares his observation.

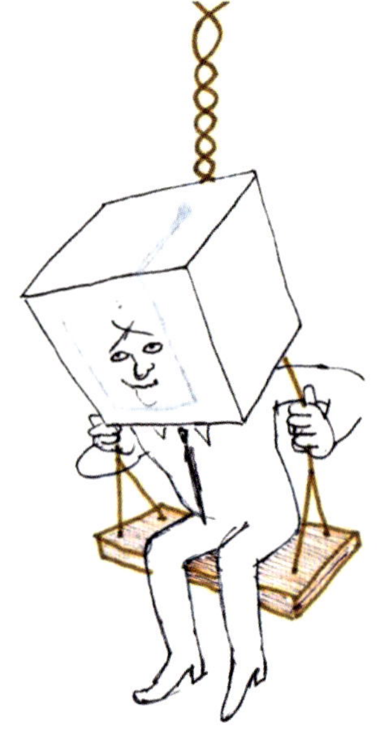

JAMES MANGOLD

One of the things I feel like I've learned is that play, child's play is the home of imagination and creativity. And in essence some people learn to drop and close the door on that part of their lives. And in a sense, they are learning not to be creative. Someone once told me that when you watch children play and act that they laugh hysterically from the sheer joy of realizing they'd become someone else.

"CHILD'S PLAY IS THE HOME OF IMAGINATION AND CREATIVITY."

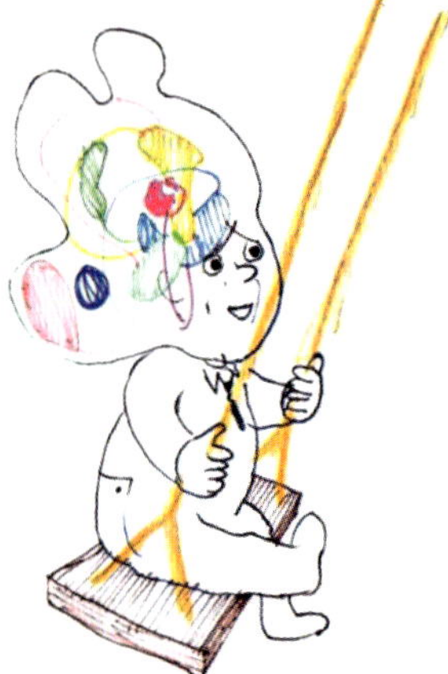

I can't think of a child I knew growing up who didn't love to play and act, who didn't love to play a cop or mother or father or play movie star or gangster. What they are doing is playing roles. They are enjoying the act of imagining themselves as a gangster hitting the dust or as a cowboy or an Indian or whatever, a king or a Queen. That ability is lost by most people as they go through puberty and grow up. Then they learn to stop playing and pretending to be someone else.

Very often you learn as a director that sometimes when your own actors, grown actors, are laughing or can't stop laughing in the middle of a scene, that it's a similar energy. It's actually. … They're really quiet, almost brilliant at this moment. And the reason is that there is almost something spontaneous and quite childlike happening inside them that they're prone to almost giggle or step out of it. Because it's a little thrilling, the act of being someone else. Your body almost wakes you up as a protective act, like you awake from a dream.

Sarah Wiener is a multitalented creative person. A chef, an author, an entrepreneur, and a politician. How are all her creative talents connected with her childhood? I visited her creative kitchen to find out.

SARAH WIENER

Either I'm creative because of my difficult childhood or because of my genetic material. I was very creative as a child, like most children are likely to be. In a way, I was unimpressed by physical laws and patterns and doing things along "comme il faut" simple interpersonal laws, and that's why my imagination was bigger and more colorful.

"I'VE ALWAYS JUMPED, AND I STILL DO THAT TODAY."

I invented a lot of books, invented a lot of toys, and things like that. It all fell into the act of primitive creativity, the somehow animal-like, the, I want to do it that way now and I want to try it out now and that should be in there now, because it makes me feel good. But these were not deliberate considerations. I was not a child who, like many other children, could move through their brains as stringently and clearly as on a banister. I've always jumped, and I still do that today.

TOBIAS REHBERGER

As a child I kind of knew Van Gogh from books, there were these art books lying around at our place and so I'd look into them from time to time as a child, and somehow I liked that, and I always wanted to own a Van Gogh. Of course, I never got one, but I would have liked to have one. Not to hang on the wall of my room, but my idea was always to sleep on it, to sleep on a Van Gogh cheek to cheek.

And that is one of these empty spaces, something you wish for, something you would like to have. And this is probably somehow connected to how I do my work nowadays. There are many things which are more intended to be dealt with than just to be hung up or placed. These are things, even sculptures, that are nevertheless often functionally related. And I could imagine that it somehow manifested itself, so somehow it at least has similarities to the way I deal with art and my own work today. But sleeping on a Van Gogh still didn't work out.

Dr. Ruth Westheimer was born in Frankfurt, fled the Nazis, and became the most famous sex therapist in the world.

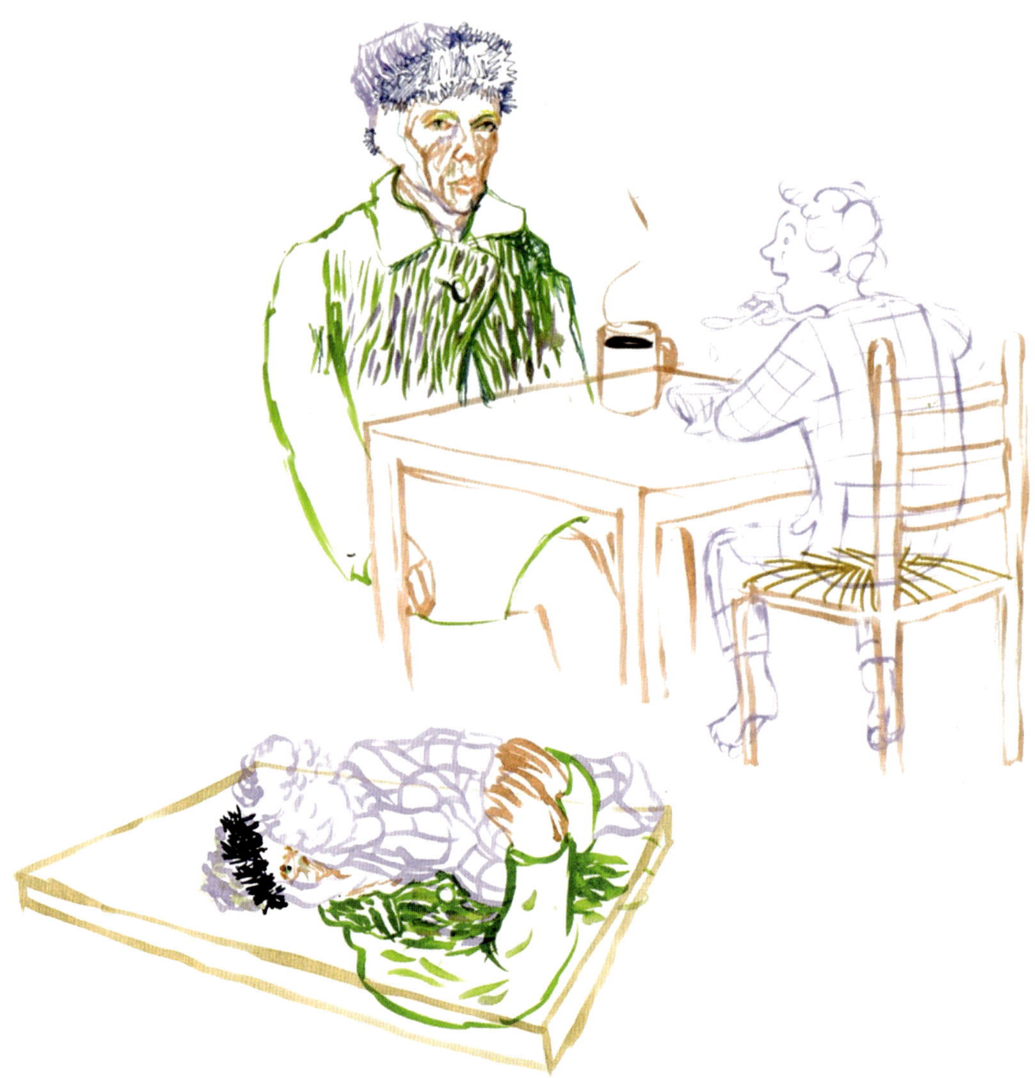

DR. RUTH WESTHEIMER

In the Talmud, in the Jewish tradition, it said that "a lesson taught with humor is a lesson retained." When I was a little girl I certainly had a theater, a puppet theater. So talking about creativity, our children, for example my children do have a puppet theater because one has to encourage creativity. I don't want them to just sit in front of a television set and be entertained, the creativity has to come from the soul, it has to be something that is nurtured. It is not something that is just given.

Björk discovered this situation less in her outer world than in her inner world.

"I FEEL AS IF MOST OF MY IDEAS, THE CORE OF THEM, I'VE HAD SINCE I WAS A LITTLE GIRL."

BJÖRK

I feel as if most of my ideas, the core of them, I've had since I was a little girl. And it's more finding … first of all working through the fact how interesting it is for other people or if it is self-indulgence. And then, once I crossed that one, then actually it would be cowardice to keep it to myself. … Then it is more a question of trying to find occasions where it is suitable to open up and sort of empty oneself, you know, to sort of synchronize with the world around me. I used to think as a child that the most wonderful life one could have is to be alone on an island with a pipe organ and with the animals and nature. As I got older it became obvious that the real challenge was to communicate with people. And it is really tricky sometimes. I'm a quiet solitary sort of person. I want to be on my own and just write a lot of music. But it seems to me that the older I get, that it is more and more about communicating. After that, I made a conscious decision to go away and try to define my own sound better. And first I would start with the extrovert side in me, which was homogenic, and then I wanted to do the introvert side of me.

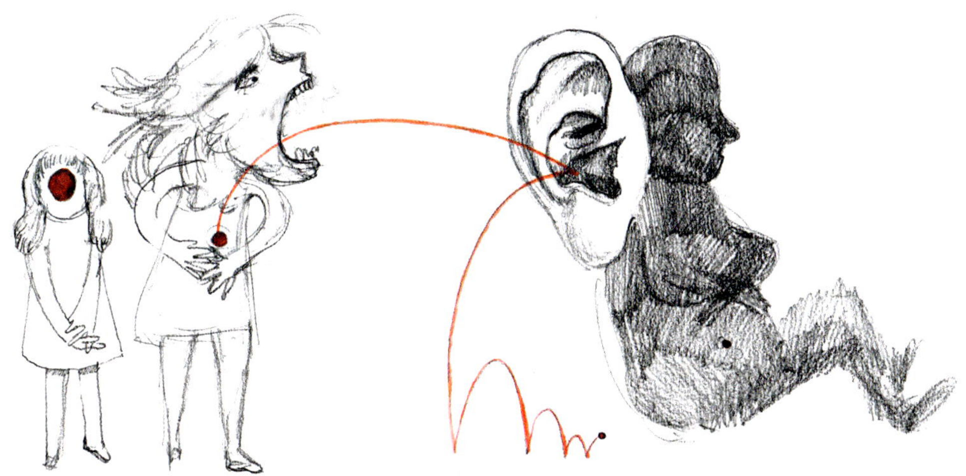

Where does Nordic creativity have its roots? I met with Ingmar Bergman actress Liv Ullmann. Did she really talk with the trees and the stones when she was young?

LIV ULLMANN

As a child I always felt that I was alone but not alone in a frightening way. Alone because I was creative and everything I created was something I did when I was alone. The fantasy I have, you know, at night I would lie in my bed with all my little animals. Then when the light went out and my mother had said "goodnight," my bed and my animals, we would float out of the window and have incredible experiences together. A day when I came from school, I had less of an urge to meet with friends. I had more of an urge to be alone and write and draw and cut pictures out of magazines and make them be in a world that I made or in nature. To take things from the trees and from the earth and make something. I think I got it very much from my grandmother because when I was little, we would always walk in nature in the woods and she would tell me that the stones talked and the trees talked. When I painted something the other grown-ups never understood it, but my grandmother always understood it and said it was wonderful. There is a child within me that will never stop asking me questions. This is the time when we are the most creative and unfortunately, people stop it because the grown-up world kind of stops it in people. We are lucky, we who still have this little thirteen-year-old questioning, crying, wondering why are you doing this?

"I THINK I GOT IT VERY MUCH FROM MY GRANDMOTHER BECAUSE WHEN I WAS LITTLE, WE WOULD ALWAYS WALK IN NATURE IN THE WOODS AND SHE WOULD TELL ME THAT THE STONES TALKED AND THE TREES TALKED."

For actor John Cleese the instinct for play is also a defining motivation. In his answer to my usual question, he wrote, "Because I know how to play." He had his playfulness on full display in our film *The Art of Football*.

JOHN CLEESE

The key to it is play. Being creative is play. And when people play, they are being spontaneous. And when people are spontaneous there is always fun. There might be laughter, there might just be fun. But that's the mood you have to create and in that mood you have much more creative ideas than you would if you are working under pressure. And this is why with most people who are working under pressure most of the time, they have to learn how to create this space where they can begin to play.

"BEING CREATIVE IS PLAY."

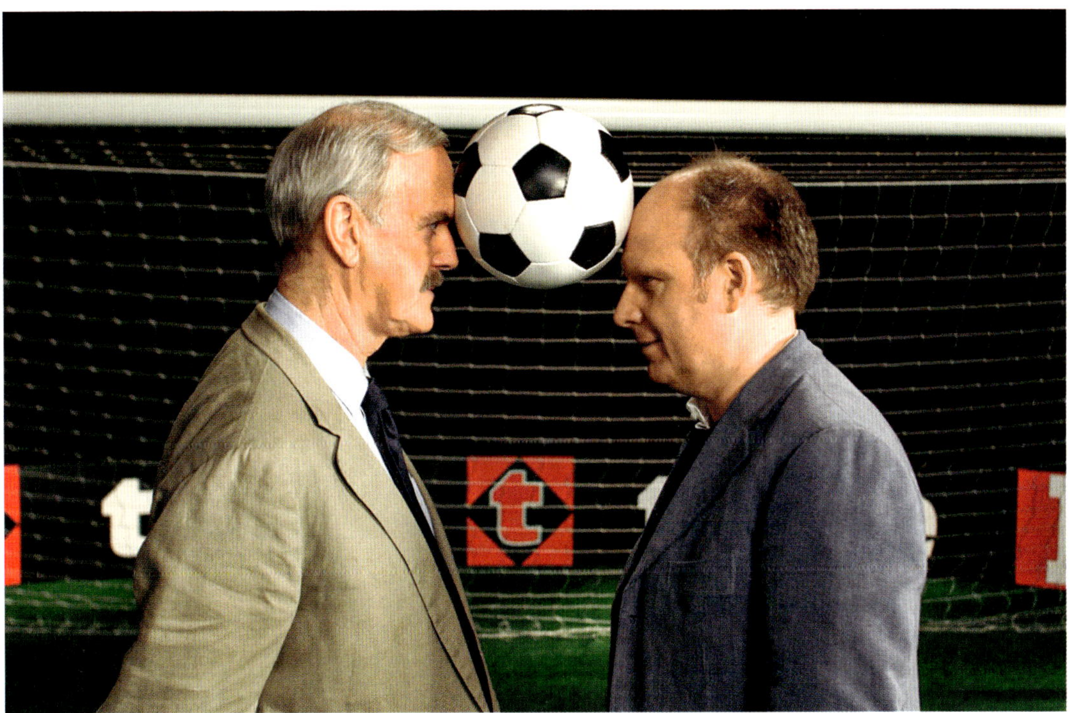

So, where creativity comes from varies from individual to individual. Maybe that everyone has a different reason for being creative is a fundamental feature of creativity. That life can be an expression of individuality in a uniform world.

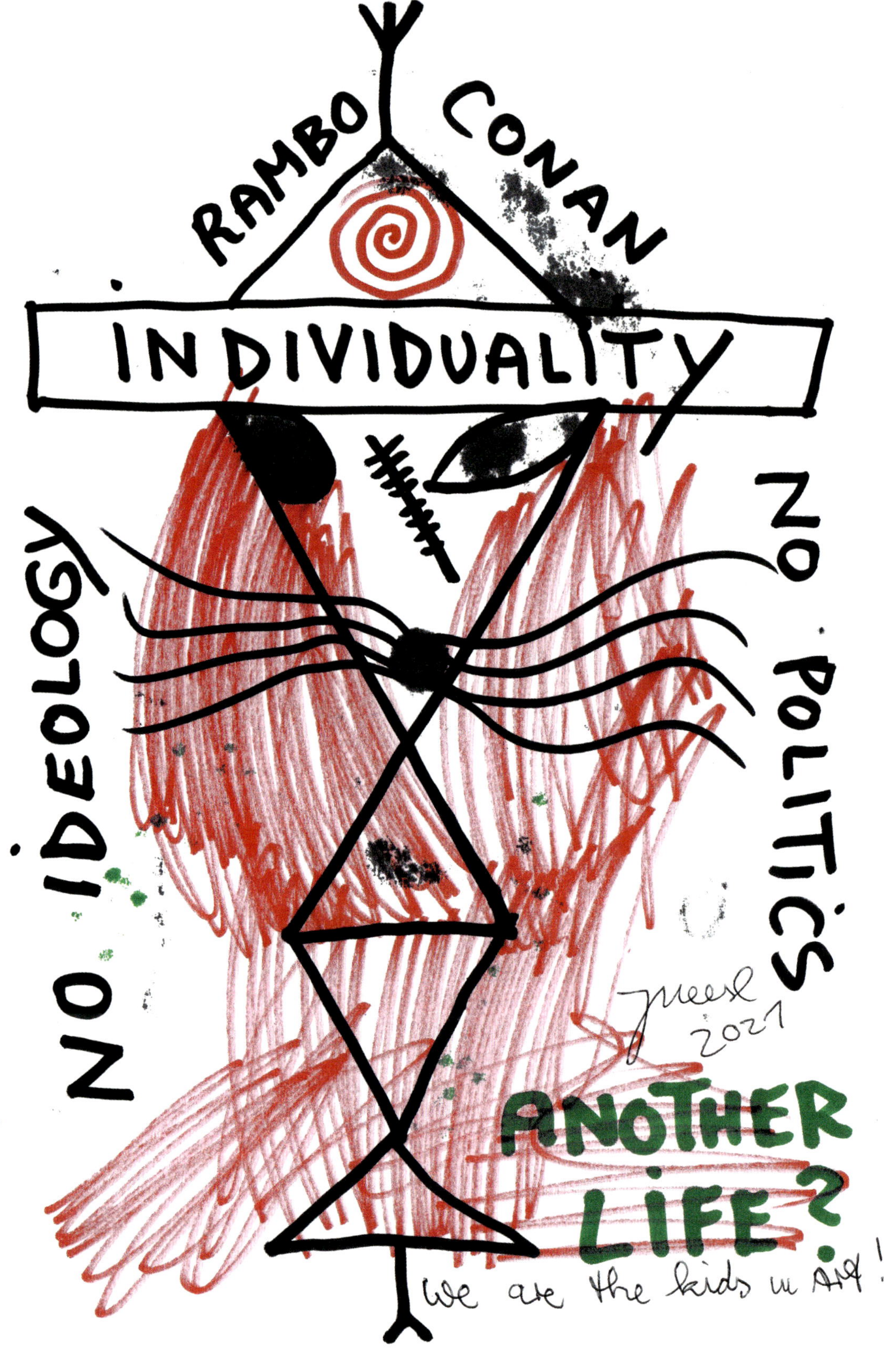
RAMBO
CONAN
INDIVIDUALITY
NO IDEOLOGY
NO POLITICS
2021
ANOTHER LIFE?

Andy Warhol once said: “I think it would be terrific if everybody was alike.” The irony is: it’s that unique point of view that made him famously creative. We all see things differently. So maybe individuality makes us creative. Or maybe we’re creative to express our individuality. Otherwise, we’re just doomed to repeat ourselves. And each other.

Andy Warhol also said: "One day, everyone will have their fifteen minutes of fame." Perhaps I had my fifteen minutes of fame discussing Warholian Creativity with the legend that is Bono.

BONO

Andy Warhol blew out the old-fashioned ideas about authenticity. He just blew them out, and he not only enjoyed the contradictions of being an artist in a commercial world, he mined them. And because there's an honesty, that's, that was the world he lived in.

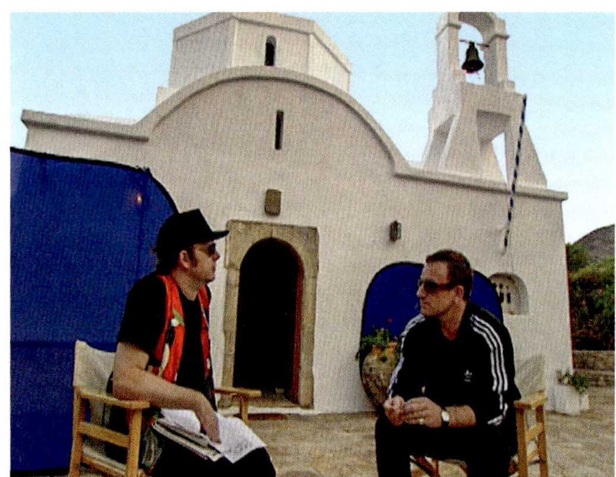

KOFI OFOSU-YEBOAH

My cinema is a river running through a thousand villages reflecting our image. It's almost that we forgot who we are. So, when I look in the river, maybe I see myself. And so, if that is the case, once I have seen myself, I think others see me already. But now there's a way in which I exist with a setting, self-knowledge, a setting, self-determination, visually and aesthetically. And so, I'm a fan of making sure that this work is seen beyond African film festivals to engage in other places.

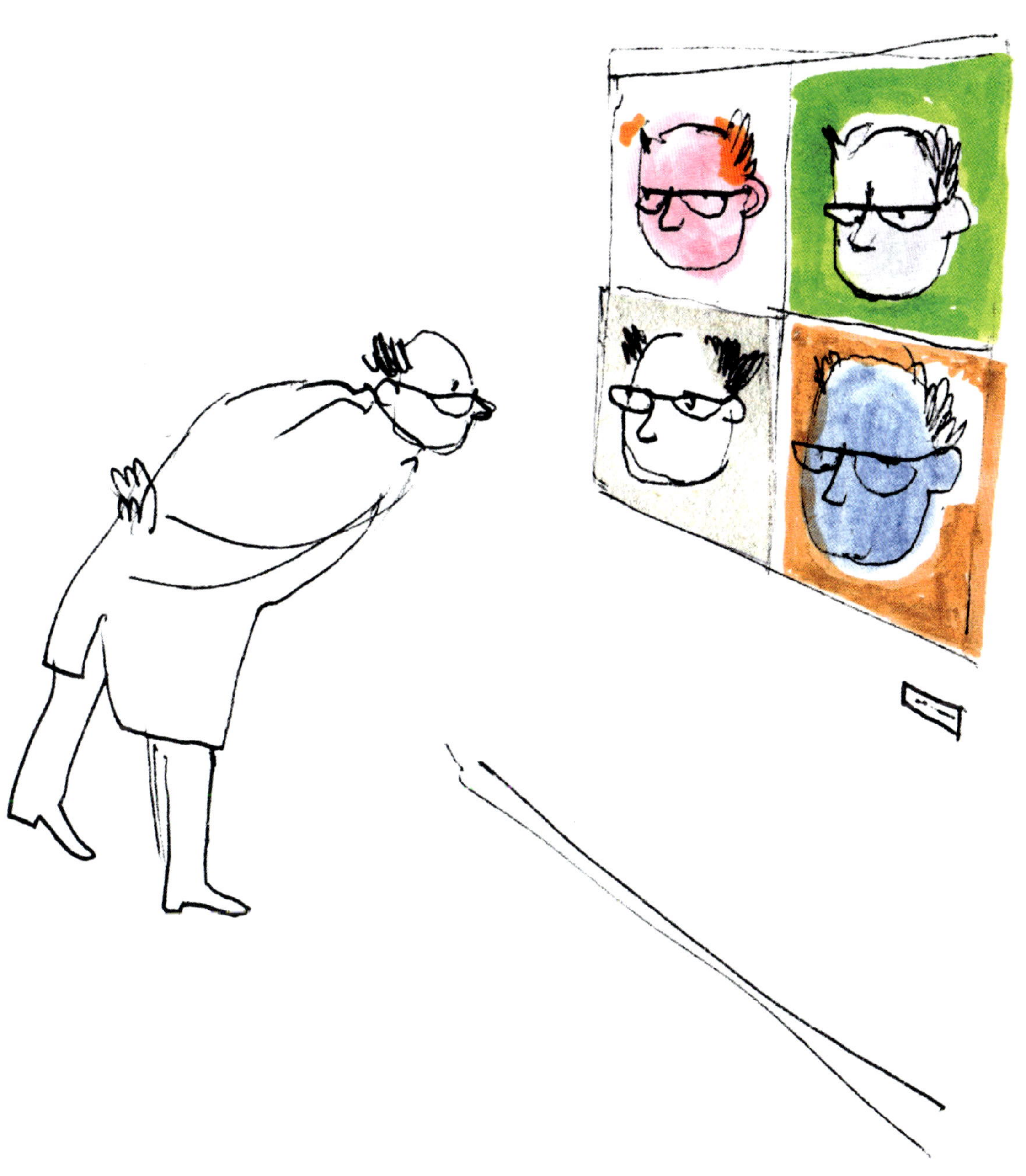

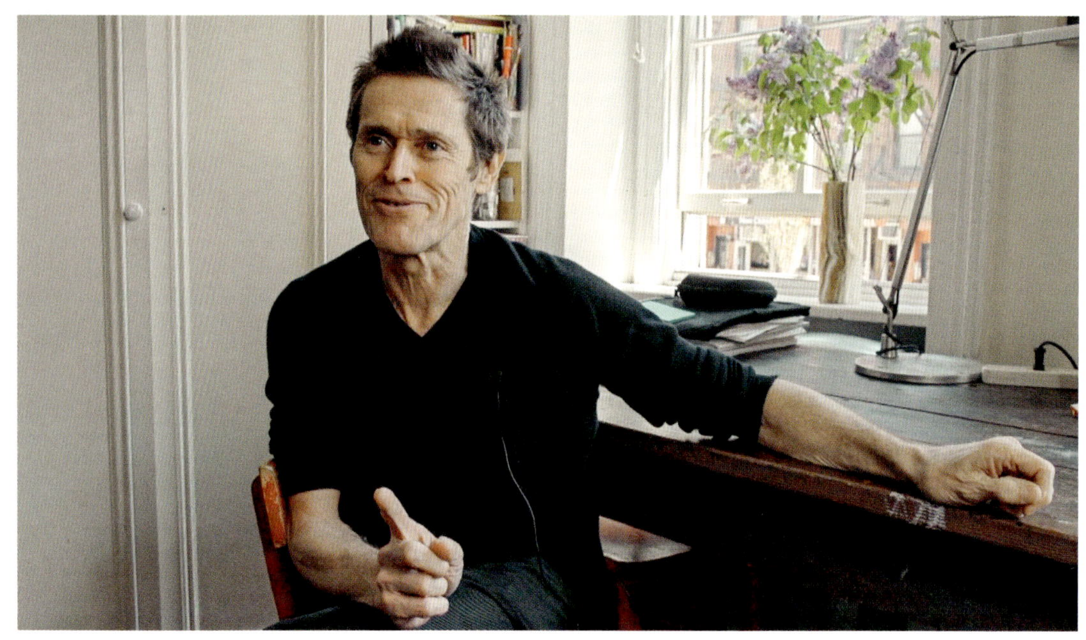

WILLEM DAFOE

Why are you creative?

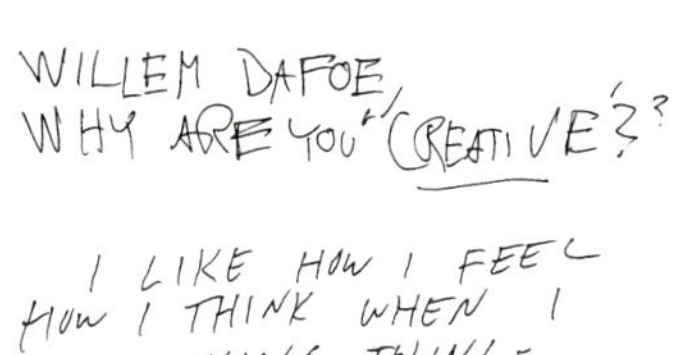

I anticipated this question. Creative is a funny word. I think I do what I do … you know, I don't think of myself so much as an actor as I do as someone that makes things. Someone that collaborates with others to make things. And I think I like making things because I like how it makes me feel.

I think better when I'm in movement I … you know, I'm more generous, I'm more free thinking and I'm taken away from kind of big eye consciousness that I have day to day. I'm always looking for opportunities to get at that place where I work with other people making things. I work with other people because I am a performer and I use myself as material, and I find I feel free-est when I am doing what I do for other people. And I don't mean an audience, I mean … I'm not motivated by my ideas to express something or to explain something.

I'm like … much more being a doer and I find myself more engaged with kind of a pure presence and a clearer mind when I have to go toward someone else's idea and inhabit it. And that's a liberating feeling. So, it's kind of sad to be a performer because … you don't necessarily but I feel like I need other people to do what I do. To make things. But that dependency also ironically frees me from myself.

“I HAVE TO GO TOWARD SOMEONE ELSE’S IDEA AND INHABIT IT. AND THAT’S A LIBERATING FEELING.”

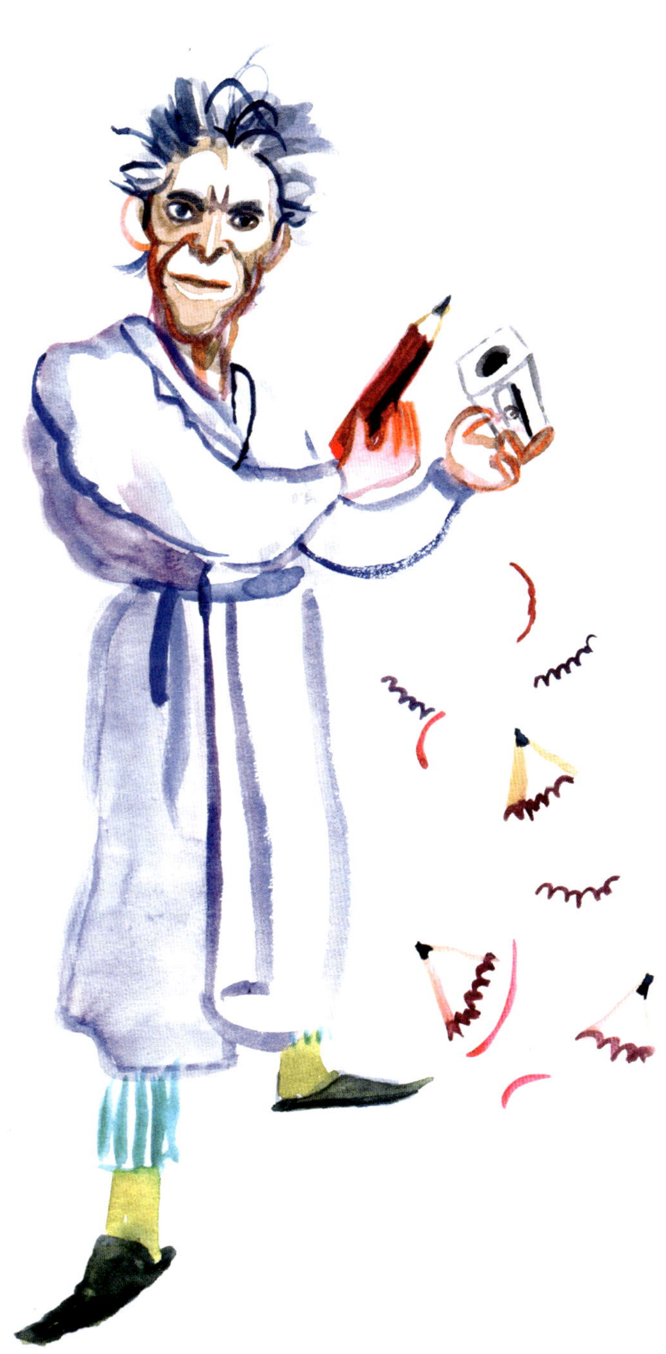

The surprising element interested me when I shot in Rio de Janeiro. I was supposed to meet world-famous architect Oscar Niemeyer to talk about surprise and creativity. On the day before, we went on a recce to the stadium that he had built for the carnival called the Sambadrom. When we were standing on the tarmac, I heard TAC TAC TAC TAC TAC TAC nearby. When I asked my Brazilian friend about it, he said: "This is coming from the Favelas next to the Sambadrom. It is the drug lords firing M16s in the air, indicating that a new delivery of cocaine has arrived. In fact, more people get killed in the Favela through the falling bullets than through actual gun fights or cocaine use!" Wow, that was a surprise. In the evening, we went to the Sambadrom, protected by our bodyguards, and the drums of the Samba replaced the M16s. Ronny Wood from the Rolling Stones, Grace Jones, and Carlos Alberto were in the VIP section and out of their minds, celebrating their creativity. A surprise party too! I guess Oscar had a point. Surprise is a big aspect of creativity. I jumped as a display of fireworks exploded over our heads.

OSCAR NIEMEYER

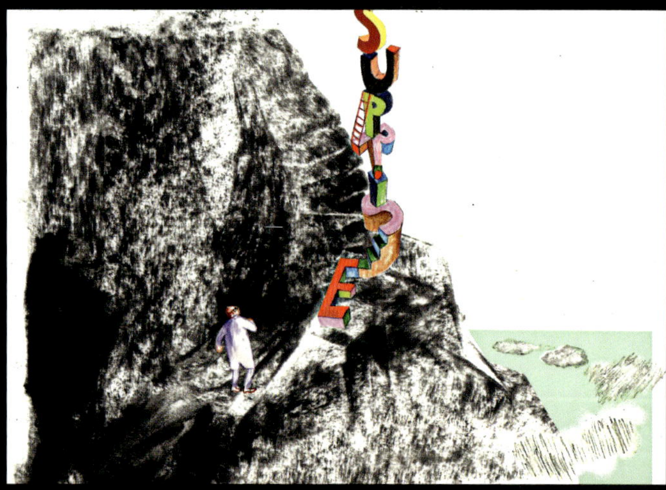

The thing that fascinates us about football, how do you call it … a drop kick. That's a fantastic move. And the fascination about architecture is seeing something that you have never seen before, something which creates a true surprise. For me, surprise is the basis for everything.
Art is emotion and surprise. For me, architecture is an invention. It's not enough to be pretty, it has to be different. When you go to Brasilia, you can like the buildings or not, but you can't say that you have ever seen something comparable before. And that reassures me. The cathedral of Brasilia, for example, the people who see it might not like it, but they have never seen a cathedral like it before. When Le Corbusier climbed the ramp of Congress, he said: "Something new has been invented here."

Sir Peter Ustinov was individually creative in a Warholian sense. For my film *The Ten Commandments of Creativity* I couldn't decide whether to pick a great writer, a great speaker, a great director, or an Academy Award–winning actor. So, I picked them all and shot with Sir Peter.

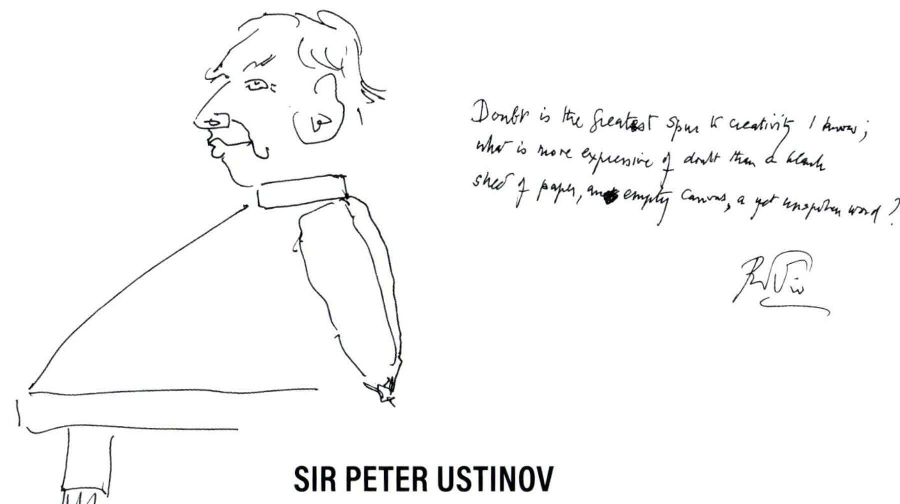

SIR PETER USTINOV

Creativity is really not believing entirely in what you see or hear, but finding another angle and seeing it as truth—in that, that is very much a part of creativity. Because it means taking yourself out of the shell. I remember the case of Einstein, who belonged to a yachting club in Zürich, and those days there was no wind. And everybody went into the restaurants, started eating, and they suddenly saw Einstein pass by on the way to his small boat and they said: "What's he doing? There is no wind today!" But Einstein, when everything was reduced to a fact that there was no wind, began to notice things that he would not have noticed had there been a wind. And therefore, for him it was most important to go sailing on an unpropitious day. He never won any regattas in his time, but he did notice all sorts of things.

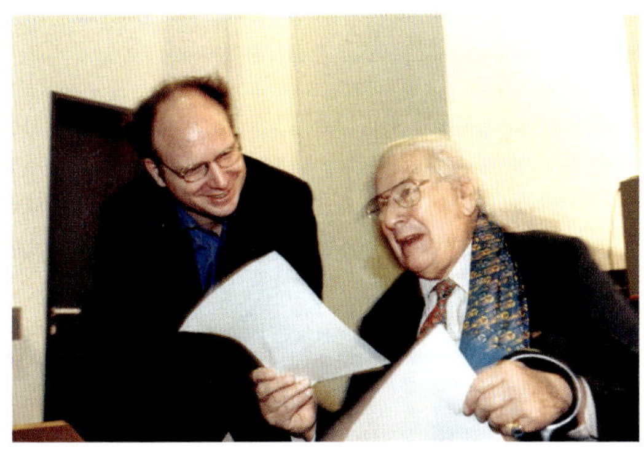

MILLA JOVOVICH

I think there's something really interesting that John Frusciante said, "I learned to play guitar before I took drugs." So that's really important to be able to learn to do something and then forget about what you've learned and just go crazy. It's amazing to have crazy people creating wonderful things because they break our definitions and make us go, "Ohhh wait a minute, where have I been for the last twenty years, what have I been thinking?" I thought my ground was so stable but suddenly I realized I'm flying and floating and I like that feeling of sort of losing all your conceptions and then trying to put them back together again. It's like always an ever-changing puzzle that you're just like, oh this used to fit but now somehow it fits too well and I don't want that. I want to put in a piece that doesn't fit.

"I WANT TO PUT IN A PIECE THAT DOESN'T FIT."

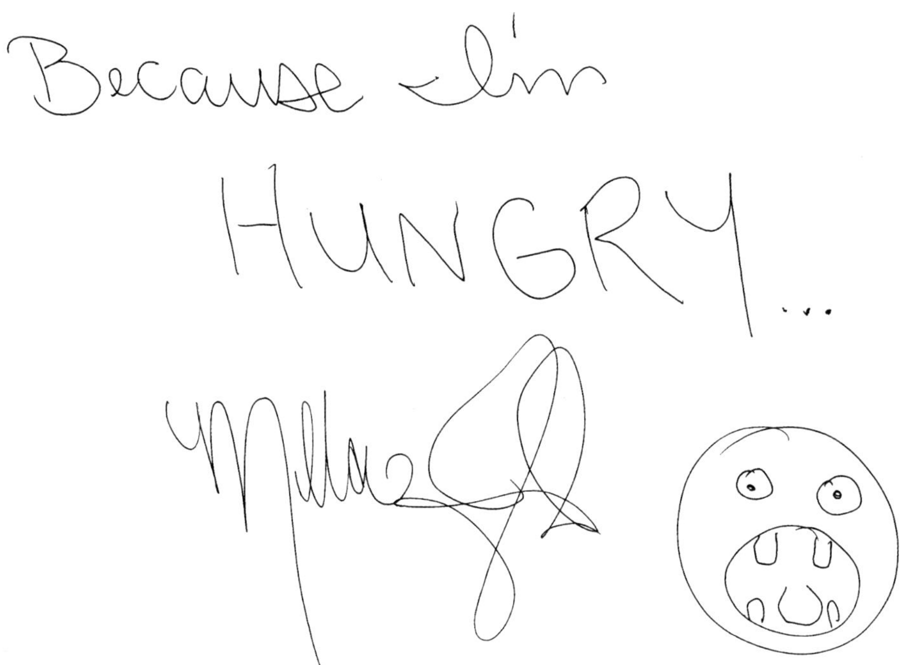

BJÖRK

My creativity is about my friendship with myself, and definitely where I had my happiest moments. It is a very safe world like this. But also, I did try, because I am quite an extreme person, so I would like to do that very very well, you know, to have a really interesting relation with myself. But also, once I started communicating I wanted to do that nine hundred percent. So the collaborations I've had have been very deep and very sort of … I think I can say with my hand on my heart, that in the collaborations I've had … I have merged with the other person truly. It has not been an artificial handshake. It really felt like chemistry … sort of a complete mix.

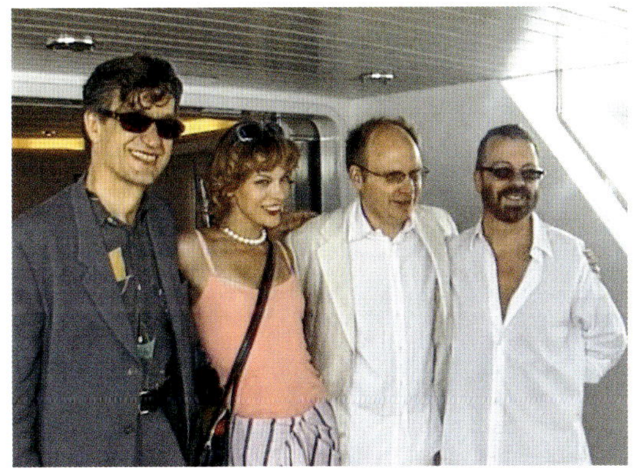

DAVE STEWART

I think that everybody is looking at the world, and some people are looking at it with different lenses, right? And if you are somebody who was born and started to realize you felt different and didn't quite know how to fit in, it is as if you got like different lenses on and you see not the same pictures everybody else sees, you tend to keep wanting to show the pictures that you're seeing, to see if there's anybody else there. You know, like, I mean obviously in rock music or pop music the end result is 100,000 people in a stadium singing along and then you go, oh yeah, they must feel the same. But the trouble is it can be a bottomless pit. Like, everybody has a hole that needs filling and depending on, I suppose, how, what's happened in your life and you know, at a certain age, some people have a much deeper hole that needs filling. So I think … you know, being creative is a way of constantly getting your balance in the world. And soon as I'm not being creative, I don't feel like I'm fit at all into the world that's being built around me. So I'm constantly having to sort of do the stuff that makes me feel at ease.

Often, a demonstration is the most effective way to prove what you are saying. Let's move on to Anton Corbijn's shortbread principle. Anton broke a Scottish shortbread in two parts to demonstrate why he his creative.

ANTON CORBIJN

Why are you creative?

I think, now you have this, now you have this and maybe you, I like this piece better, but you have choice. You know in creativity you can eat it. You can do many things. I think creativity makes, for me, life full with a lot of options.

How does this relate to your creativity and to your life?

Well, I come from a very strict Protestant background where my father was a minister and the church we went to had absolutely no imagery at all. Actually, totally devoid of any imagery and we didn't have a television until I was nine. And my parents only bought a TV because we were always at the neighbors' watching it. So a pretty imageless youth. I was always very jealous in later life of a lot of friends that were Catholic, and they grew up with incredible imagery. And when I started to take pictures, I started to take pictures of people in pop music. Of course, that is full of imagery. But it is funny how I come from this totally nonimage background and I create so many images.

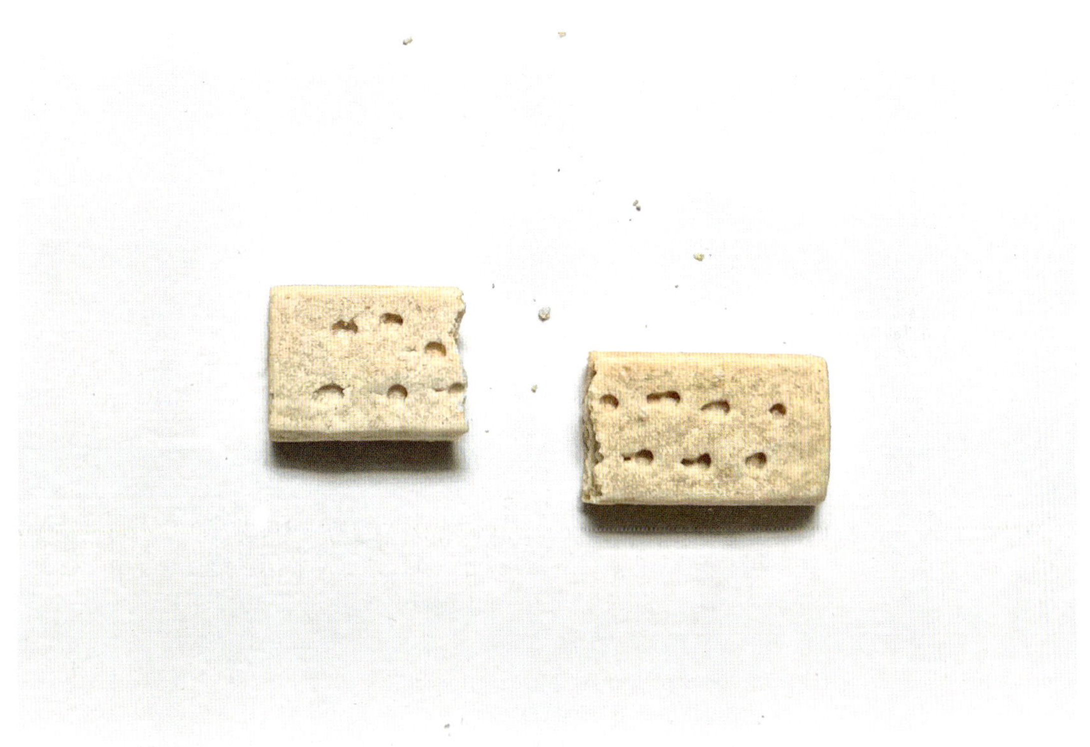

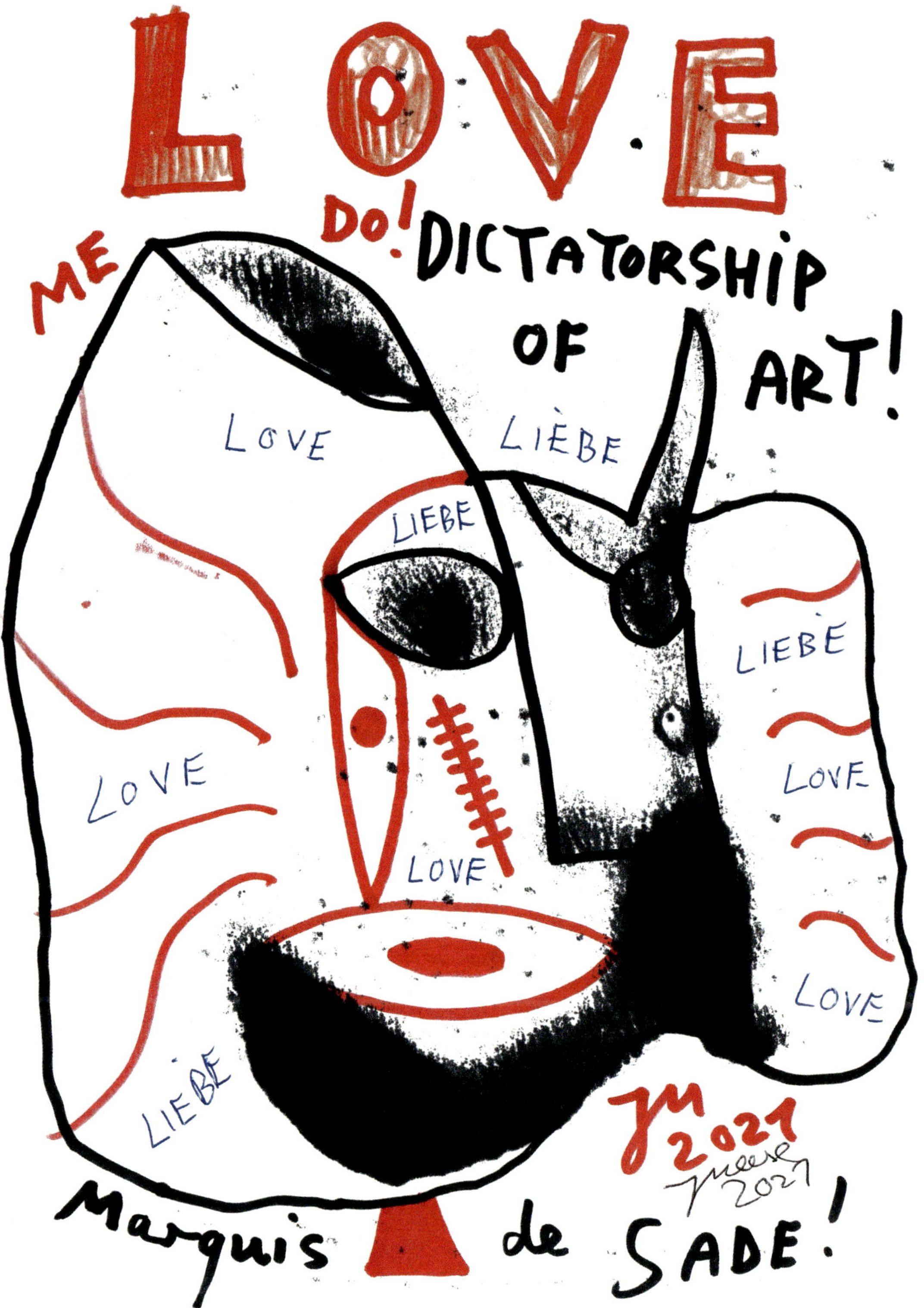
LOVE
ME
DO!
DICTATORSHIP
OF
ART!
LOVE
LIÈBE
LIEBE
LIEBE
LOVE
LOVE
LOVE
LOVE
LIEBE
JM
2021
2021
Marquis de SADE!

Many insist that it is love that drives them that they are never more creative than when they are in love and they love what they are doing. All you need is love. Love is all you need. Without a muse, a rose has fallen dry. Without passion, we are nothing. Just ask these giants of men brought down by a thing called love, from Anthony and Cleopatra to Johnny Cash and Dolly Parton, the love ranch is full to bursting as Heartbreak Hotel echoes with the weeping of millions. As the philosopher Hegel once said: “Nothing in the history of mankind has ever been accomplished without passion.”

What is the significance of the great emotions for our creativity? Love? Friendship? Passion? A Freudian hydraulic understanding of emotion that is at the core of so many works, from novels to films to sculptures to digital artworks. Can the energy of these emotions be released and channeled to produce extraordinary works?

MARINA ABRAMOVIĆ

I would like to quote Bruce Nauman who said: art is the metaphor for death. Sounds maybe very melodramatic, but it is very true. And that's what I think. Because I really think that whatever you do, you have to do 100 percent for the complete inner belief, with total passion. And that's the only way, absolutely. There is no different way. So it is for me. Artists live like that. In fact you have to give more than 100 percent just to be good enough.

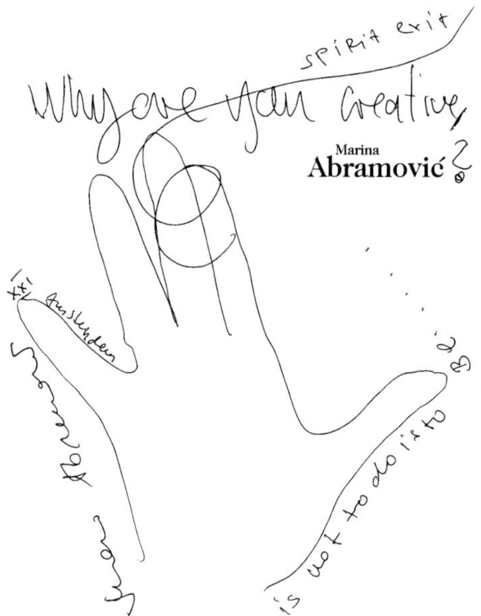

ISABELLE HUPPERT

It's a privilege to have passion, of course. It's a great luck to be so much in love and dedicated with what you do. It's a luck. And it's very lucky of course to be able to live with your passion. Sometimes you don't have passion and sometimes you have passion but you don't know what to do with it. Or you don't have the tools to express it so … when you have both, it's nice.

ANGELINA JOLIE

"IF YOU CAN COMBINE ART WITH SOMETHING YOU CARE ABOUT, YOU CAN EDUCATE YOURSELF AND MAKE FRIENDS AROUND THE WORLD."

Why am I creative? You know, I got into the film business when I was younger and it was always a good way to learn about different worlds, whether it would be a fantasy world or something you can explore, I always liked that. But in the last few years I have been less comfortable with what I've been doing. I haven't been as happy. And this is why I need to do films more like *Blood and Honey*. I think creativity can help bring forward discussion and debate. And without that we don't move forward. We have to have that to move forward. So, if you can combine art with something you care about, you can educate yourself and make friends around the world—learn about other lives and other peoples and that's a different kind of art, that's the best art.

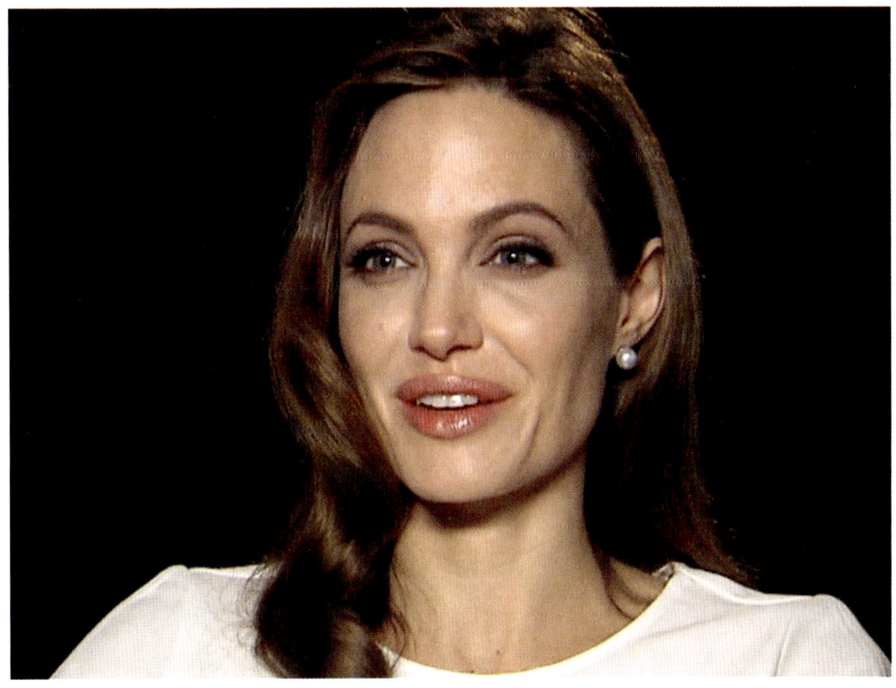

DANIEL BARENBOIM

Every day when I wake up, I want to create something. I love having new ideas, reworking old ideas and learning from one thing for another. There are too many people, unfortunately, who wake up in the morning and ask themselves: "What can I do with myself?" That's not true of me. You really have to wake up and accept life without conditions. Develop the wisdom to accept what you can't change and have the courage and creativity to change what needs to be changed and what doesn't suit us. I can very rarely achieve that, but that's what I strive for every day.

BERNARD STIEGLER

The word amateur comes from *aimer*, which means love. Love the life. Pablo Picasso once said that if there would be no longer be a market for his pictures, he would continue painting not to earn money, but because he loves his work. And if that's a true amateur, every artist, every philosopher, every human being that does something in his life that makes sense is an amateur. There are amateurs like Charlie Parker, who started as an amateur and then became a professional musician. Frederic the Great, King of Prussia, was an amateur when he played the flute. Jean-Luc Godard, Francois Truffaut, they all started as amateurs.

"THE WORD AMATEUR COMES FROM *AIMER*, WHICH MEANS LOVE."

NICK CAVE

I love the power that singing actually has. Being able to get up on stage and sing a song and it's a moment that exists in history that is three minutes long and disappears and perhaps lives on in the bloodstreams or in the hearts of the people who hear the song or perhaps it doesn't; if it's unsuccessful it might be meaningless. But if it works, if it actually has the magic, or once again that duende that Lorca talks about, it is something that lives on within people, and that is a rare and beautiful thing.

JEAN-PAUL GAULTIER

I love cinema and I started to want to do fashion because of cinema. The things I did with Luc Besson were incredible, because *The Fifth Element* was a science fiction movie, which was very different. Also, I worked on *Bad Education* with Almodóvar. And with Peter Greenaway I did *The Cook, the Thief, His Wife & Her Lover* and with Jeunet I did *Amélie Pulain*. I do what I love, which is the most important thing and I love that, you know. I don't think that doing couture is art, but I think it is very exciting and very beautiful. And for me it is perfect.

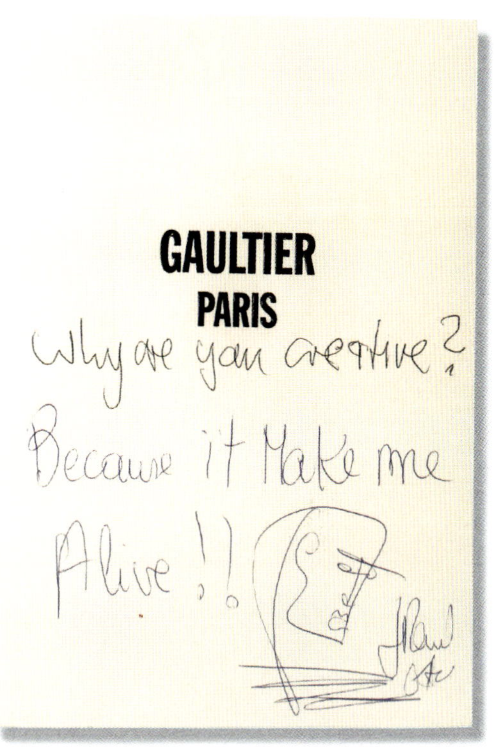

"I DO WHAT I LOVE, WHICH IS THE MOST IMPORTANT THING AND I LOVE THAT YOU KNOW."

BRUNO GANZ

Why am I creative? It's a way of life, a pretty good one. Somehow you have the feeling that you stay awake. But to really answer why I became an actor, I still can't. But I love my job, and I know that somehow, it's good that I do, and that it keeps me going in a way that makes me happy and also satisfies me—drives me and keeps me alive. If that's creative, yeah then. … It's a wonderful way for me to spend my time, my lifetime. Creativity is something that maybe makes the world richer.

"CREATIVITY IS SOMETHING THAT MAYBE MAKES THE WORLD RICHER."

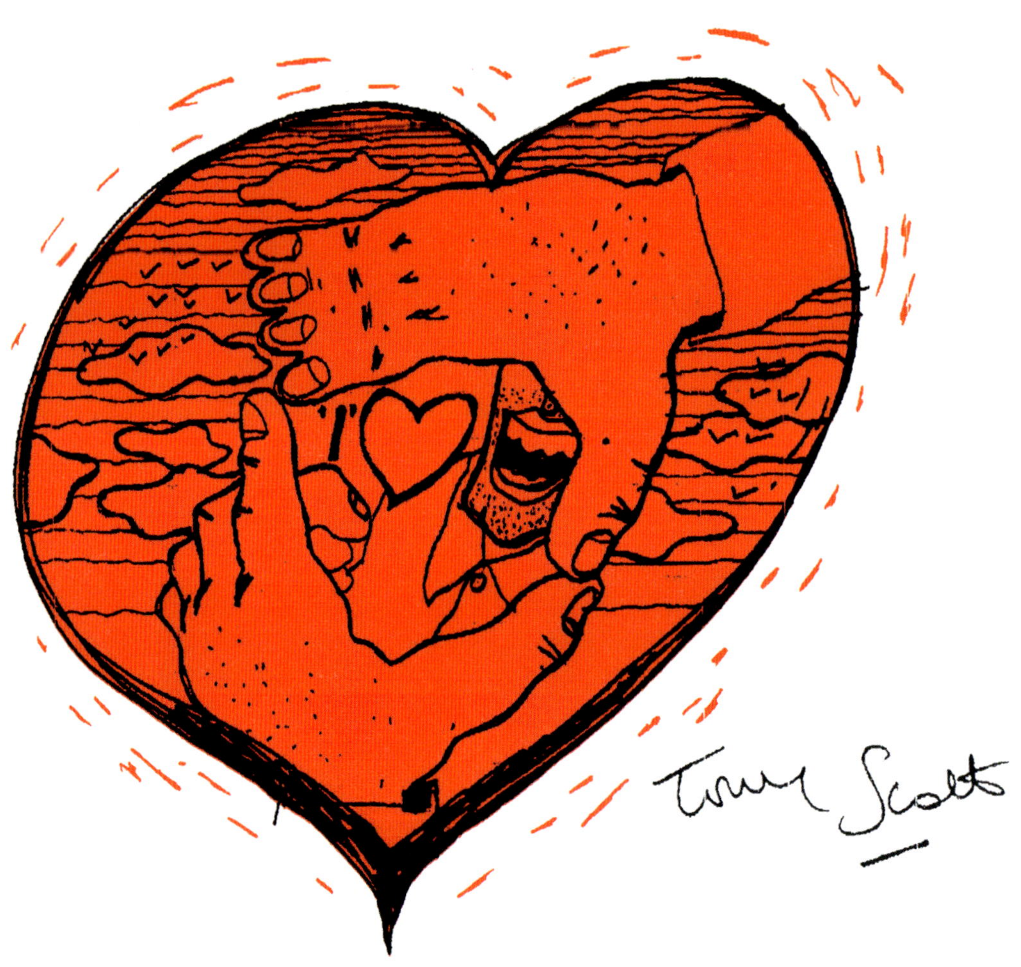

TONY SCOTT

Being creative is just a brilliant way, because no two days are the same. That's what excites me most. You know, I always pursue something that I'm creating as well. And I can create with $60 million, so it's a bit like being President of the United States. I used to create on a canvas, with a paintbrush, but now I bring that same process with $60 million. I get actors and cameras, people, things, and toys—and I bring my painting process. I've adapted that to the process of moviemaking.

Oscar winning composer Hans Zimmer worked many times with Tony Scott making soundtracks for "Days of Thunder", "The Fan," and "Crimson Tide." I met Hans in Los Angeles when he was sitting with Tony brainstorming about a score at Ridley Scott Associates. Hans supported the thought that his ideas are driven by love.

HANS ZIMMER

The ideas have to come from yourself and in a way, the place my ideas come from, is because I actually truly adore and love people.

DR. RUTH WESTHEIMER

The question here is why am I creative? I think it has a reason. That by my being creative in talking about contraceptives and talking about issues of sexuality, in talking about different positions, in talking about making life more enjoyable. In English it's like a zest for life, a joie de vivre in French. And I think that I always try not to become boring to myself. So any lecture I give or anything I do in life, I passionately think to add something that will make it interesting for me. Because if it's interesting for me, then I know that it's interesting for people who watch me on television or who listen to me.

out of passion

Dr. Ruth Westheimer

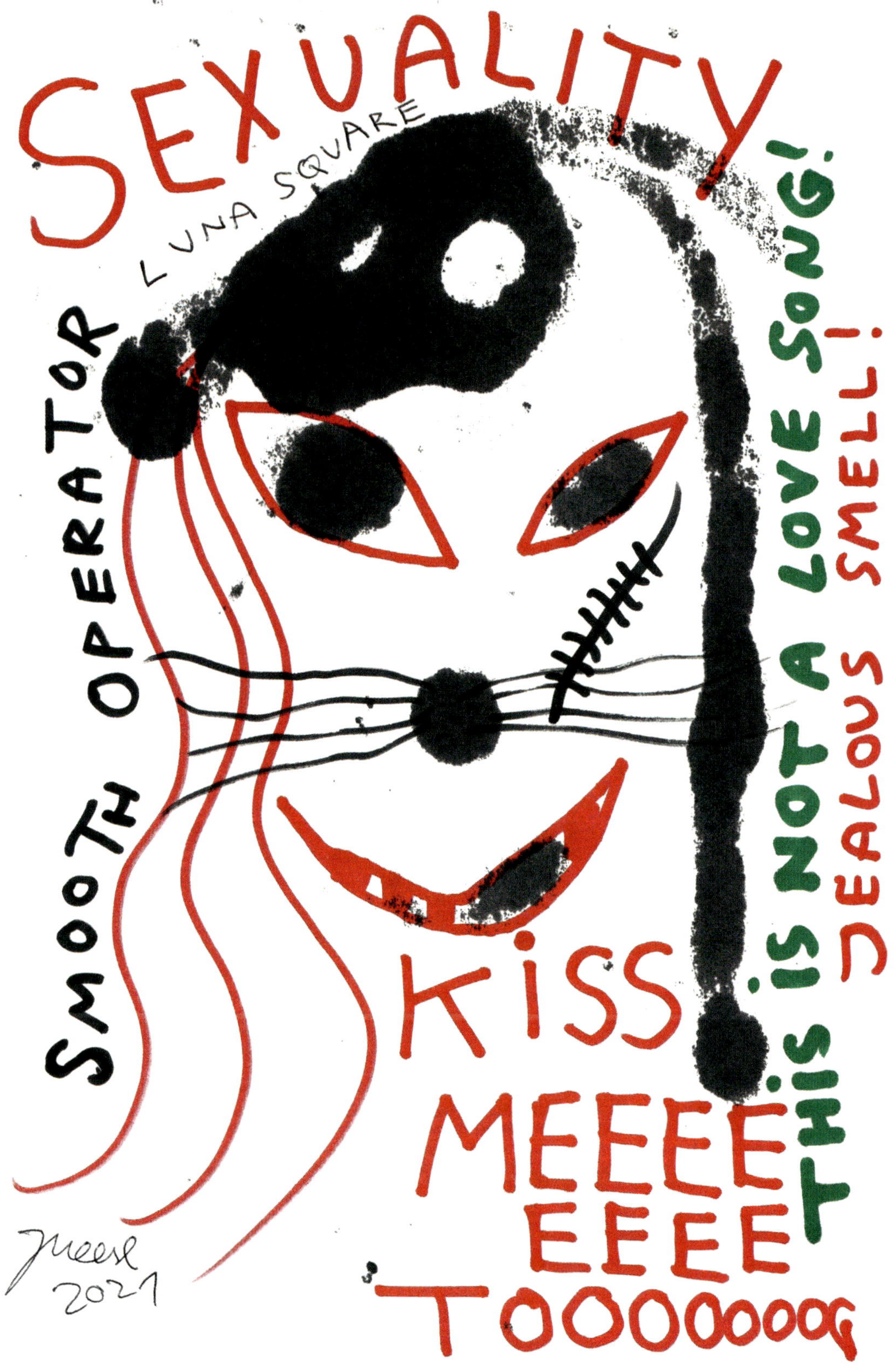
SEXUALITY
LUNA SQUARE
SMOOTH OPERATOR
THIS IS NOT A LOVE SONG!
JEALOUS SMELL!
KISS
MEEEE
EEEE
TOOOOOOG
meese
2021

Are people creative in order to make themselves more attractive and desirable? Freud assumed that the sublimation of primitive drives was a creative force. It seemed inevitable that sex was going to take center stage. Is procreating a substitute for being creative? Or is being creative a substitute for …?

Some say it's love that drives us. The driving passion that inspired the romantic works of William Shakespeare … and Lord Byron … and Anaïs Nin … and Russ Meyer.

KITTEN NATIVIDAD

I'm creative because I love sex. I have big boobs and you know what? You can do a lot of creative things with big boobs.

RUSS MEYER

Where do you get your stimulus from?

Tits.

Is that a one-word answer to everything?

That's right. That's what it's all about. See right here, this is what it's all about. The breast. Cleavage. That's the thing that I'm known for. That's why it's successful.

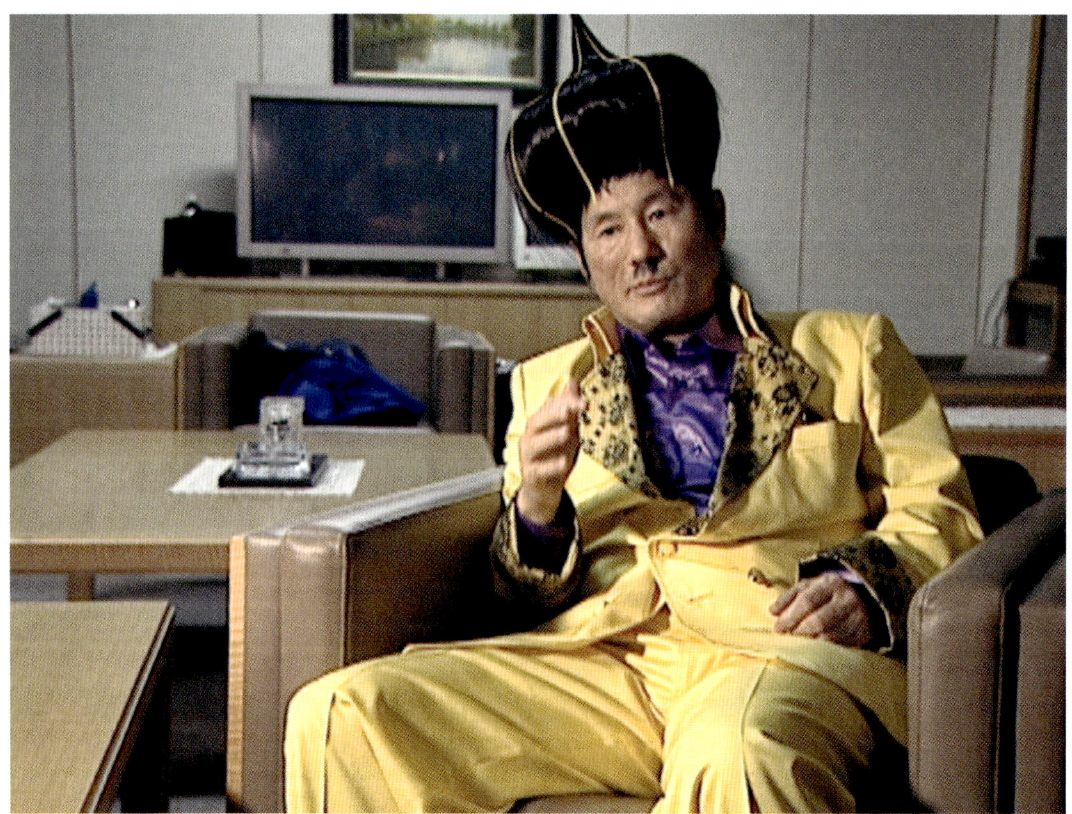

Mr Kitano,
Why are you
creative?

← これがあるから。

TAKESHI KITANO

You are an actor, director, entertainer, and author. A man of ideas. If you hit a good idea, creatively, do you get an erection?

I think that comes after the erection. Good ideas tend to come when I'm not conscious of any of the basic bodily urges like sex and hunger. There seems to be no link between getting a good idea and having an erection. I don't think there's any connection with sex. I actually think that like in Zen or with any basic human desires, the outcome is decided by how much self-control one has. I feel it's a cultural thing and I don't really think it's got anything to do with what you said. I think that when a great idea appears, it's like an erection itself. But you can't have two erections at once. The moment I get a good idea, I feel like it's an erection.

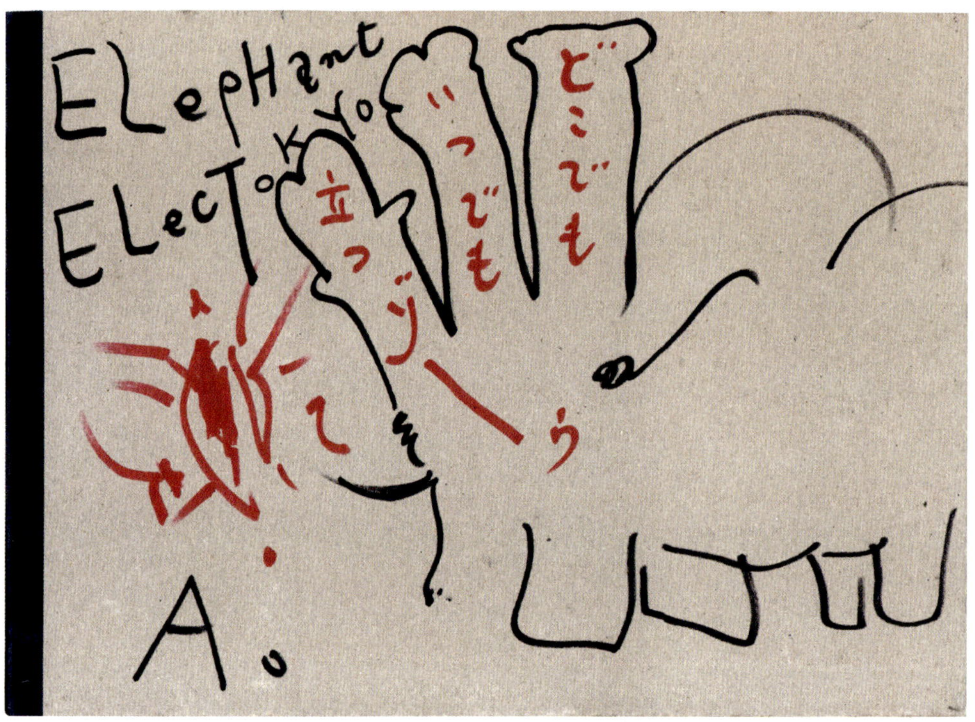

NOBUYOSHI ARAKI

When I'm shooting, when I'm taking the photos, I do get an erection while I'm doing it. But when I show them, exhibit the photos as that's quite important, my mind just turns to that and so I don't get erect. In other words, showing my photographs the act of doing it, I first get the subject to sort of die, temporarily, I kill them, and then when I show the photos I bring them back to life, that's what it's all about. That's why it ends up this way. Deviation from the norm is one of the basic principles of creative work.

"DEVIATION FROM THE NORM IS ONE OF THE BASIC PRINCIPLES OF CREATIVE WORK."

JEFF KOONS

Many of my works function through sexuality, that it has almost all forms of sexuality within the piece, that the public automatically when they look at it, hopefully they enjoy the piece because they find the form of sexuality they're interested in. It's a tool. In any kind of creative field there are certain vocabularies you have to work with and sexuality of course is one. I don't know if it's so much motivating but it's a tool. It's part of the language to use to be able to kind of manipulate or at least communicate with somebody. Sexuality is a strong one. Because it affects everybody in their lives.

"SEXUALITY IS A STRONG ONE. BECAUSE IT AFFECTS EVERYBODY IN THEIR LIVES."

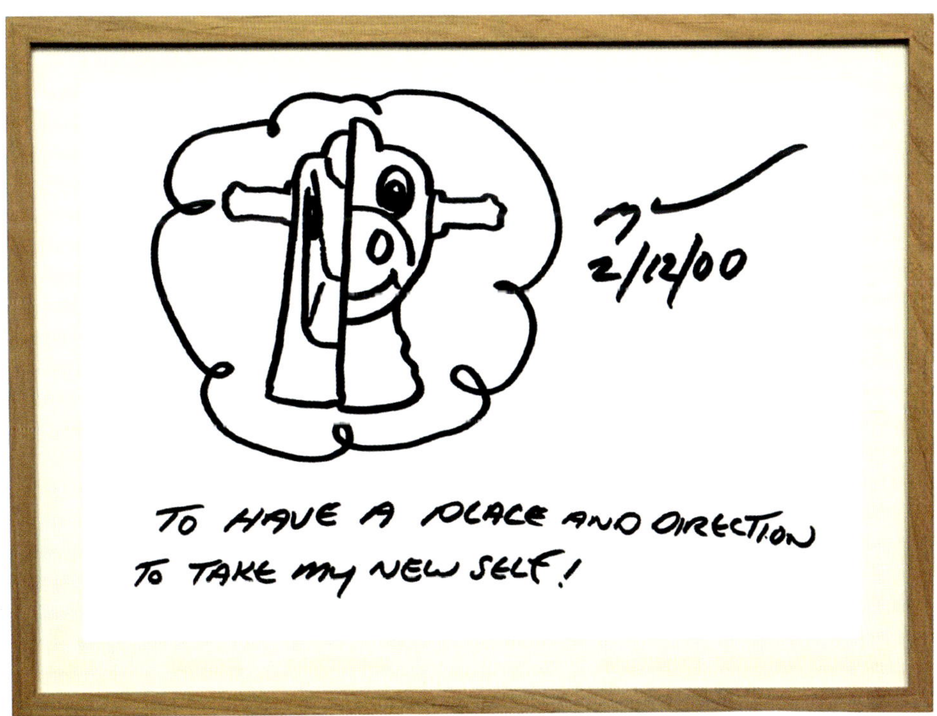

Damien Hirst's answer to the question "Why Are You Creative?" supports Freud's theory.

Why are you creative Damien Hirst?
I don't know, I always made things, it's like collage
if you give me two objects I would move them around
to see how they looked.

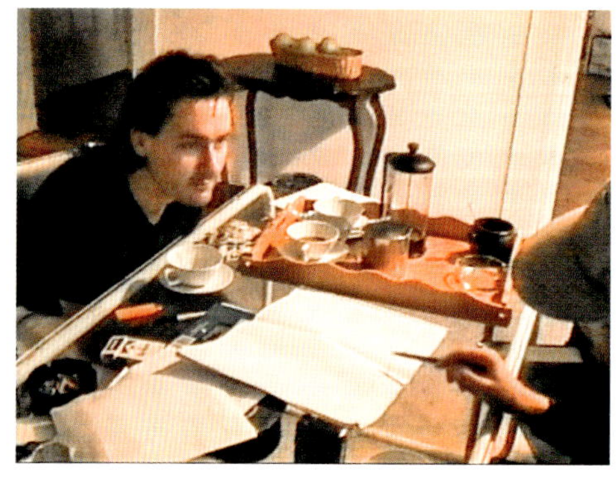

Years ago, I was supposed to meet Michel Houellebecq at a hotel in Frankfurt. Before the meeting his wife came down and checked us out. We passed the test and went upstairs where Michel talked about the correlation between sex and creativity. I pressed play as he was leaning against the pillow, smoking one cigarette after another.

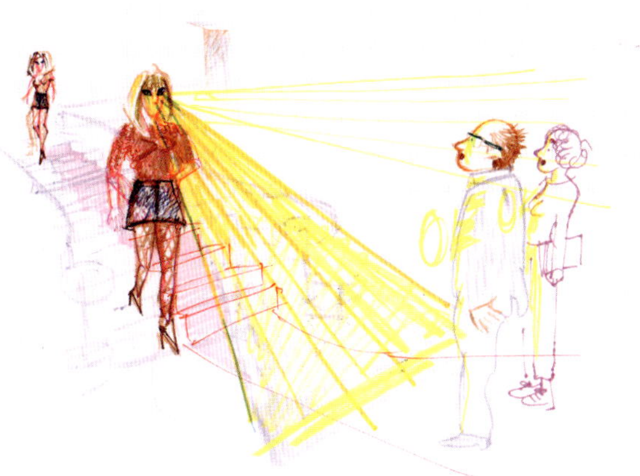

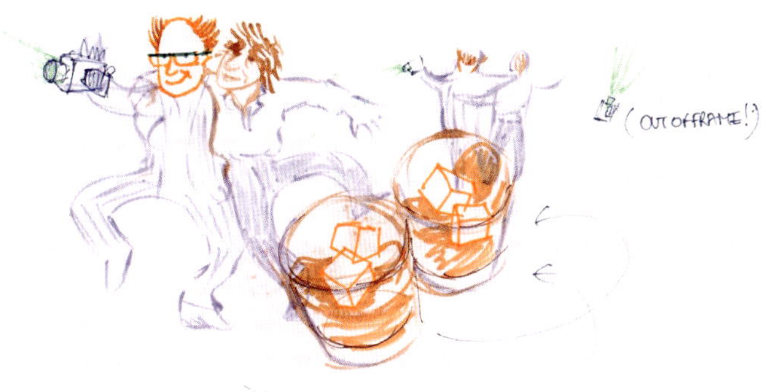

MICHEL HOUELLEBECQ

You're toying with the idea of making a porno. Is there a creative porno?

Yes. Filming men is difficult. When their penis is inside, you can't see anything at all. Fellatio is therefore a good subject. When the penis is in the pussy, you can't see the sex. Then it's very difficult to make a good movie. Pussies are impossible to film. You can write them a little better. But it's more interesting when you see them. Lust is creativity. It's really an interesting subject.

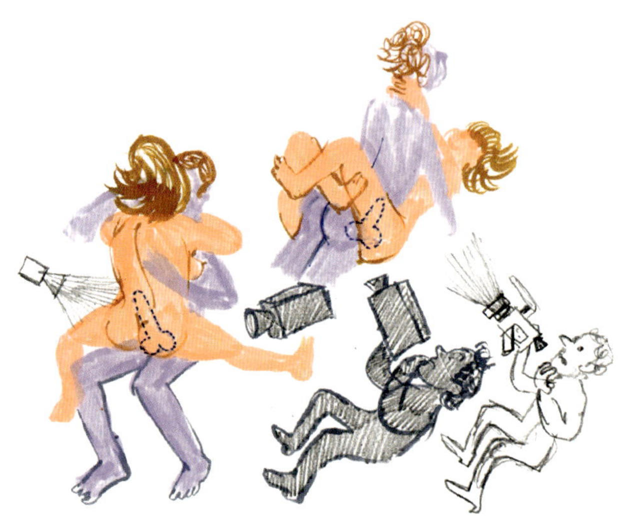

Why are you creative?

I'm creative because I'm not happy. And somehow, it's also a way to be able to control situations. The situations may not be happy, but I have control over them. And that's different, different from ordinary life. I don't know if what I do is creative, it's just a reconstruction of life. I'm not inventing anything, except maybe in some places. What I really invent are my dreams. I write books to have a clearer vision of life. I think that's my only motivation. I don't want to create anything; I just want to escape. For me, it's pure "escapism" and creating another world. Sometimes another imaginative world is useful to understand the real world.
I never had the impression that I create things. I find these things within me. I suppose I am there like everybody else. So that's the main reason: what I think, everybody can think. What I feel, everybody can feel. And that's the only thing I'm sure of.

To what extent is sexuality a motivation for your creativity?

Well, it is a very good motivator. Because when one writes books one can have girls. Sex, death. These are the great powers.

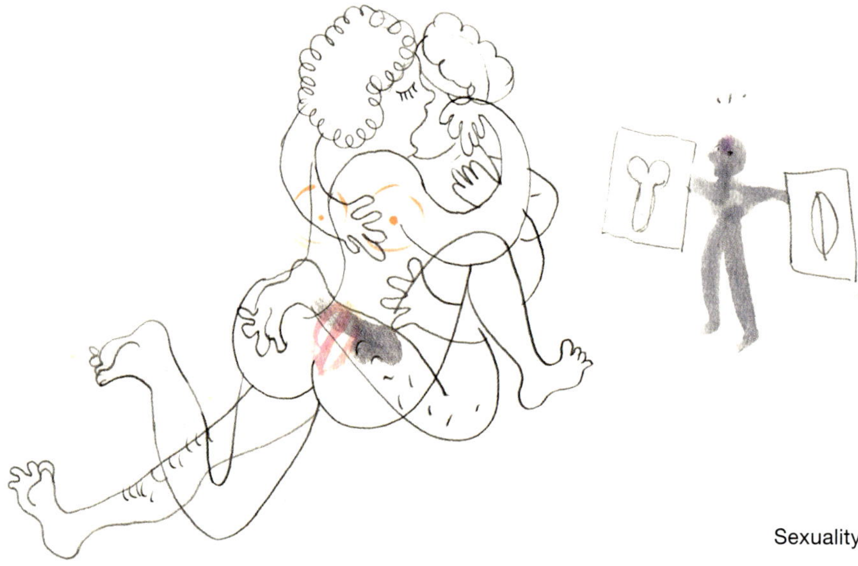

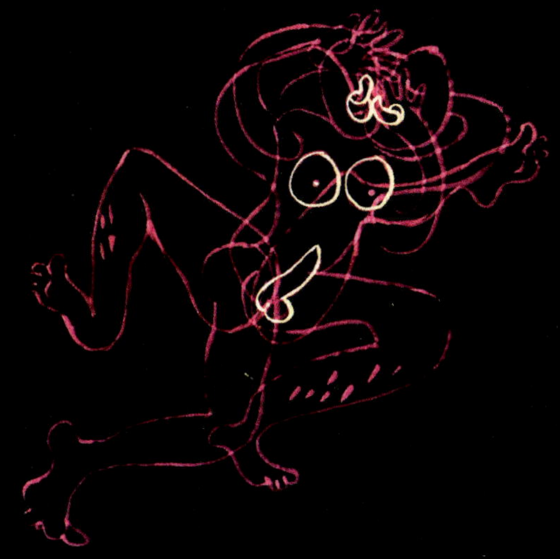

One artist who did pull off the difficult task of making a porno was Isabella Rossellini.

ISABELLA ROSSELLINI

I did *Green Porno* because I was always interested in animals, and so as I became older and didn't work as a model anymore, and also film roles started to be scarce, I had time. And I went back to university to study animal behavior, which is always something I wanted to study. And then, while I was studying, I started writing these funny stories. And then, I come from films, so I made these films, but it was completely experimental. But it became really successful. And so, in the end, I made forty short films, I made a monologue that I've toured the world. So, it became a career. So, why am I creative? It's storytelling for me, you know, principally, for me, as a filmmaker, is to tell a story. And I thought. … Though I completely admire David Attenborough, *National Geographic*, especially David for the films that he makes on nature and animals. But sometimes, especially in the *National Geographic*, there is a lack of humor. And animals make me laugh. And so, I thought, you know maybe I can tell, what is it about an animal that makes me laugh? And, of course, sex is a subject that everybody is interested in.

In 1971, Yugoslavian filmmaker Dušan Makavejev made a film called *WR – Mysteries of Organism* The film played with the theories of notorious Freud student Wilhelm Reich and was enhancing the view that sexual and political liberation can't be separated from each other. But what about sexuality and creative freedom? I went to Belgrade's Professor Square to talk to Dušan Makavejev.

DUŠAN MAKAVEJEV

"SEX IS THE BASIC MATERIAL FOR DRAMA."

Sex is important everywhere, and people are clumsy with sex everywhere. And I think that both things are natural. I think that sex is natural because that's how we stay alive but clumsiness and difficulties are also natural, because if you have something as important as sex, it has to protect itself in all kind of troublesome moments. Sometimes it's peoples' incapacity to stay loyal. And sometimes it's about some people who are too possessive, so you have all kind of extremes, that happen in sex, and it happens because sex, the nature of sex, is that it needs extremes. You have to either be in a great love or be terribly disappointed because like otherwise you can't have these great historical suicides. You know from the desperation of lost love. So basically, sex is the basic material for drama.

Many creatives that I met have claimed that we are creative so as to attract the opposite sex. "Look at me, look at what I have made," like a peacock shaking its tail feather. ... We use creativity like others use a flashy sports car as a penis extension. Within primitive passion, there is a fount of potential creativity energy. According to Freud, artists produce creative work as a way to express their unconscious desires in a publicly acceptable fashion. Get out there, get on down, shake your tail feather.

GORAN BREGOVIĆ

How important is passion in sexuality in the Balkans?

I started as a striptease bar musician, so at the age of seventeen, I saw more naked girls than all the kids in ancient Yugoslavia together. So it's connected somehow. Like God sent a sign: you have fun, you have passion. Passion is obligatory. I don't really rationalize this, I don't know how other people do that. But I started playing music because of the girls. Then I started composing because we were sitting with electric guitars and someone has to invent something, it was me. This is how it started. Then at the beginning you play just for fun and you study ...
There is one famous sentence by one of the richest men in history, Aristoteles Onassis. He says: "Only the money that I spent on women was worth spending." I started to play guitar because I wanted to please the girls. My father wanted me to be a piano player. But because I was a clever boy, I started to play guitar.

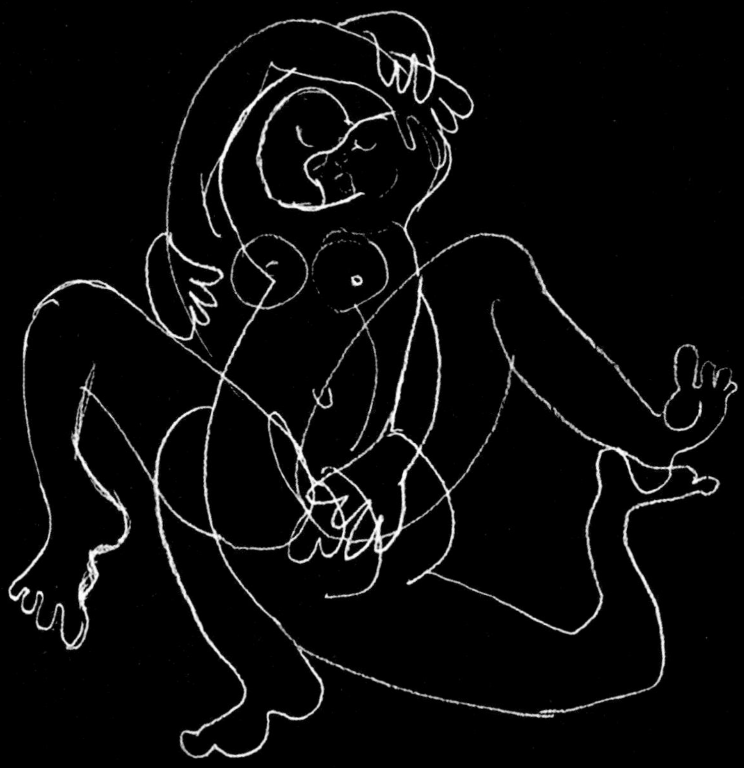

SLAVOJ ŽIŽEK

For Freud's *Psychopathologie des Alltagslebens* the key is that old Bosnian guy who brings together death and sex where he says, "If I'm no longer able to do sex, the only thing remaining is death."

When sex comes into the room—death is never far behind. They go together like ... well, like sex and death.

So it's no wonder that many creative people try to cheat death with their works.

They're indisputable. They exist. Forever.

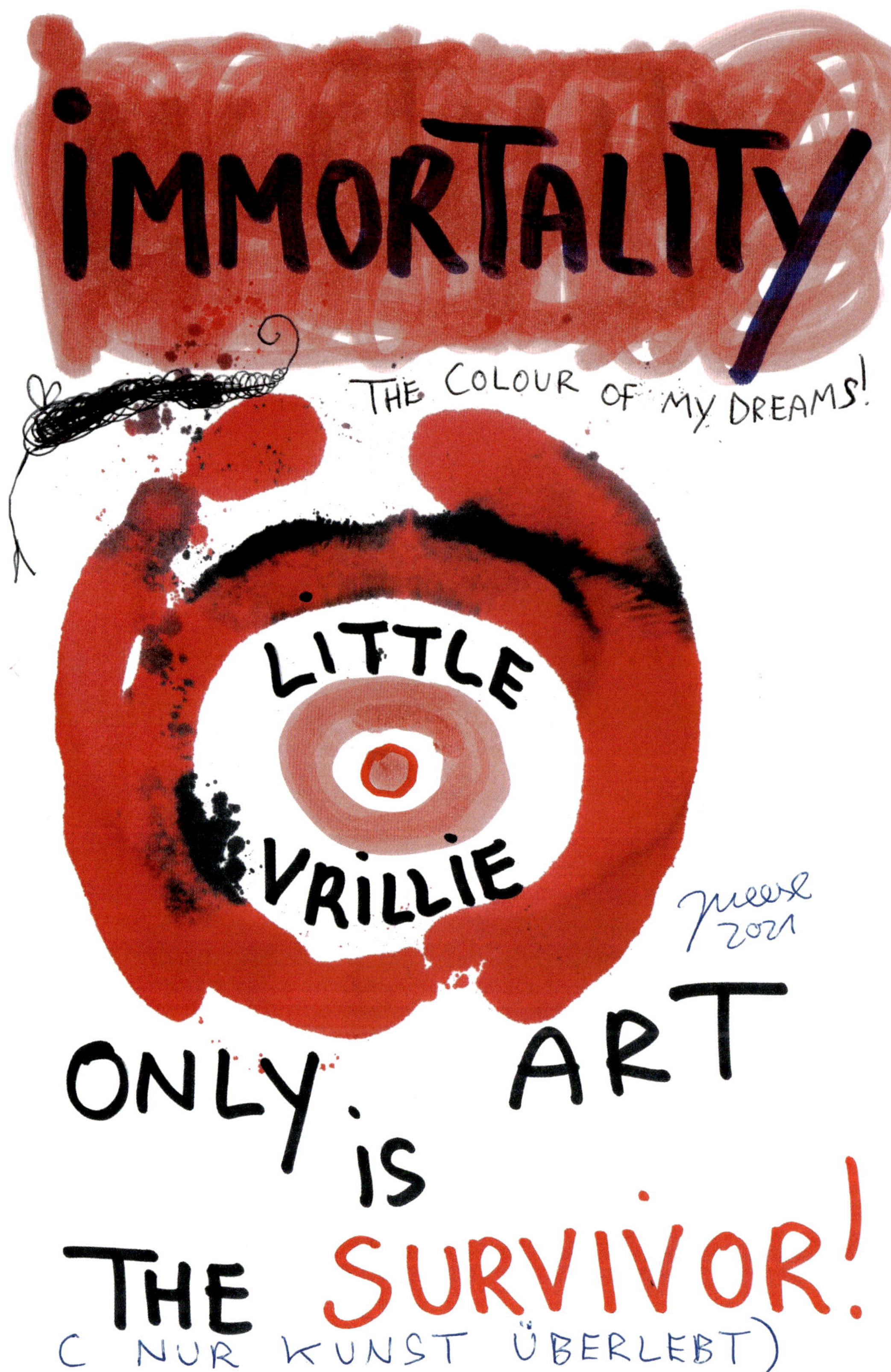
IMMORTALITY
THE COLOUR OF MY DREAMS!
LITTLE
VRILLIE
meese
2021
ONLY ART
IS
THE SURVIVOR!
(NUR KUNST ÜBERLEBT)

Maybe being creative is a way to become truly immortal, in a way of our own doing. To cheat death, to create ourselves anew, in our work, to leave a body, yes, a body of work, that exists beyond the dictates of our mortal existence.

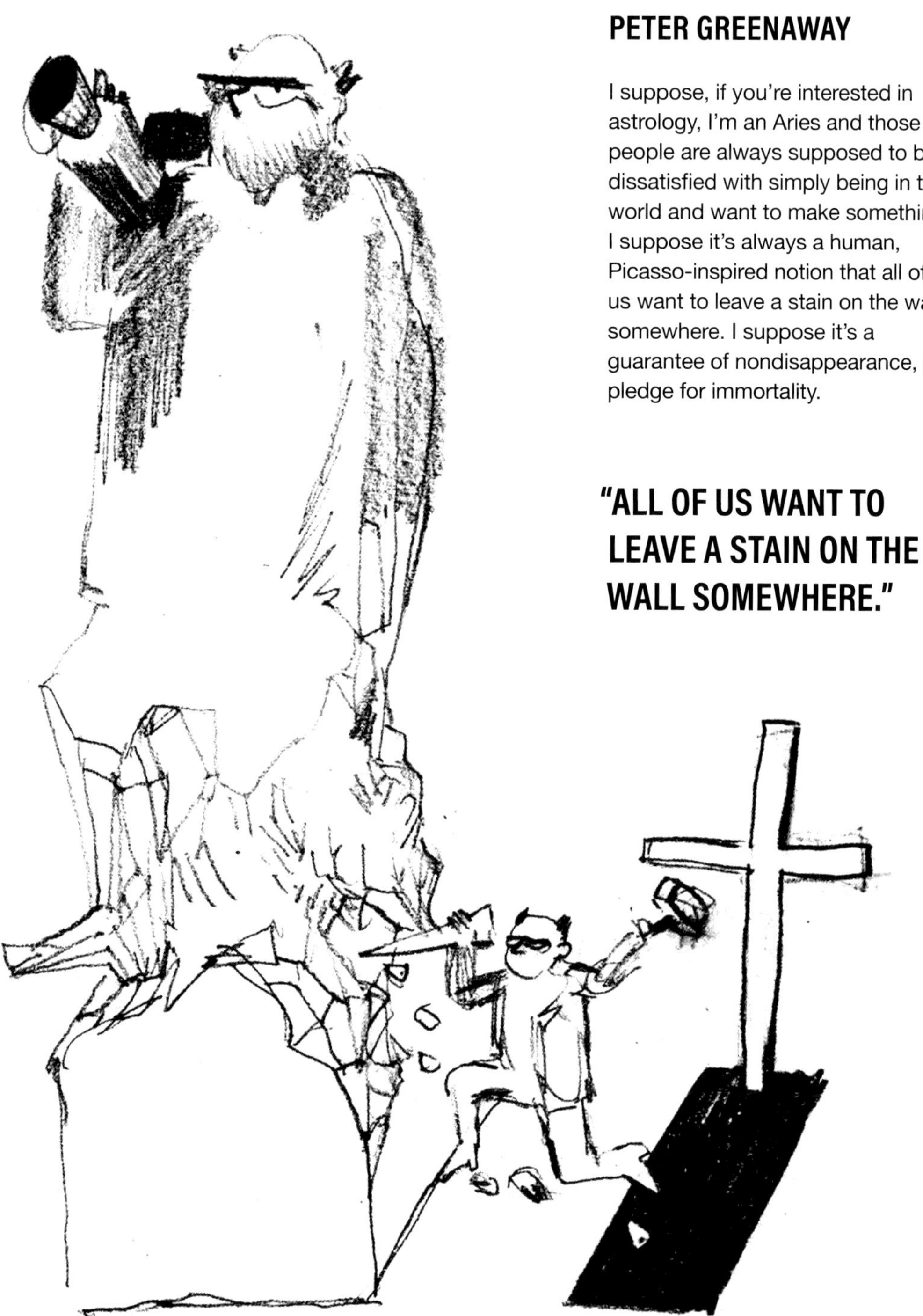

PETER GREENAWAY

I suppose, if you're interested in astrology, I'm an Aries and those people are always supposed to be dissatisfied with simply being in the world and want to make something. I suppose it's always a human, Picasso-inspired notion that all of us want to leave a stain on the wall somewhere. I suppose it's a guarantee of nondisappearance, a pledge for immortality.

"ALL OF US WANT TO LEAVE A STAIN ON THE WALL SOMEWHERE."

The biggest fear in life is the fear of death. Creativity is ultimately seen as a chance to cheat death. We meet American Creative Director Jeff Goodby, who addresses the idea that creativity can achieve a permanence in the face of death. But can the creation outlive the creator?

JEFFREY GOODBY

So, Jeff, why are you creative?

To cheat death. I think that the reason why people are creative really is to make more of their time on earth. Instead of just to have things happen to you, you know, you have breakfast, and read the paper, you go up for a walk, to have things happen in that linear way, I think people try to get beyond that by being creative, to mix those things up, and to try to make them into something greater than just the sum of the parts, and give themselves this more time and more quality on earth.

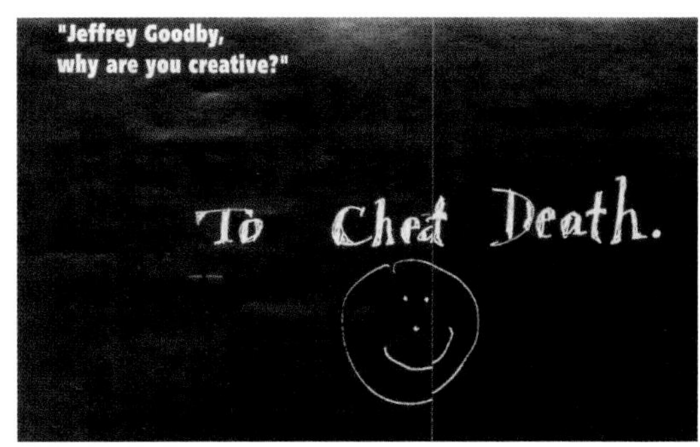

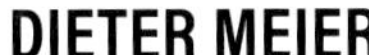

DIETER MEIER

Immortality as such does not interest me at all. My life is walking through a couple of tens of thousands of days that I'm present in this little body, and part of it is that I leave footprints. But whether they are washed away or not, I don't care. I never look back at these footprints. I'm walking through my life.

KATHARINA THALBACH

I think it started when I was five, in some way, and it always had something to do with dying. Somehow, my sister died at an early age, and that's when I started playing, and somehow wanting to understand life—and I don't think that's changed until today. It's always somehow a form of survival. But how exactly it works and why it works—it's always fear, actually. In some form, I think it has something to do with fear for me. Fear of not being noticed. Fear of not being left with something. Fear of not being loved. And sometimes it has something to do with wanting to memorialize people I like, that too.

It's a bit like cheating death, isn't it?

Maybe a little bit, yes.

LILITH STANGENBERG

People forget that you actually want to create something. A work of art, which can actually only arise from an intimacy, and not if you do it in such a civil servant–like way. I think you'd have to shoot much faster. You'd have to cut things faster, and they'd have to be put out faster. And there you have to shoot the next film already. And yet we work five years on a script and then three years on the funding and then it takes two more years until the finished film comes out. There's something sick about that. Fassbinder worked fast, another new film every three months.

Why are you creative?

Um dem kurzen Leben einen Funken von Ewigkeit zu stehlen

Lilith Stangenberg

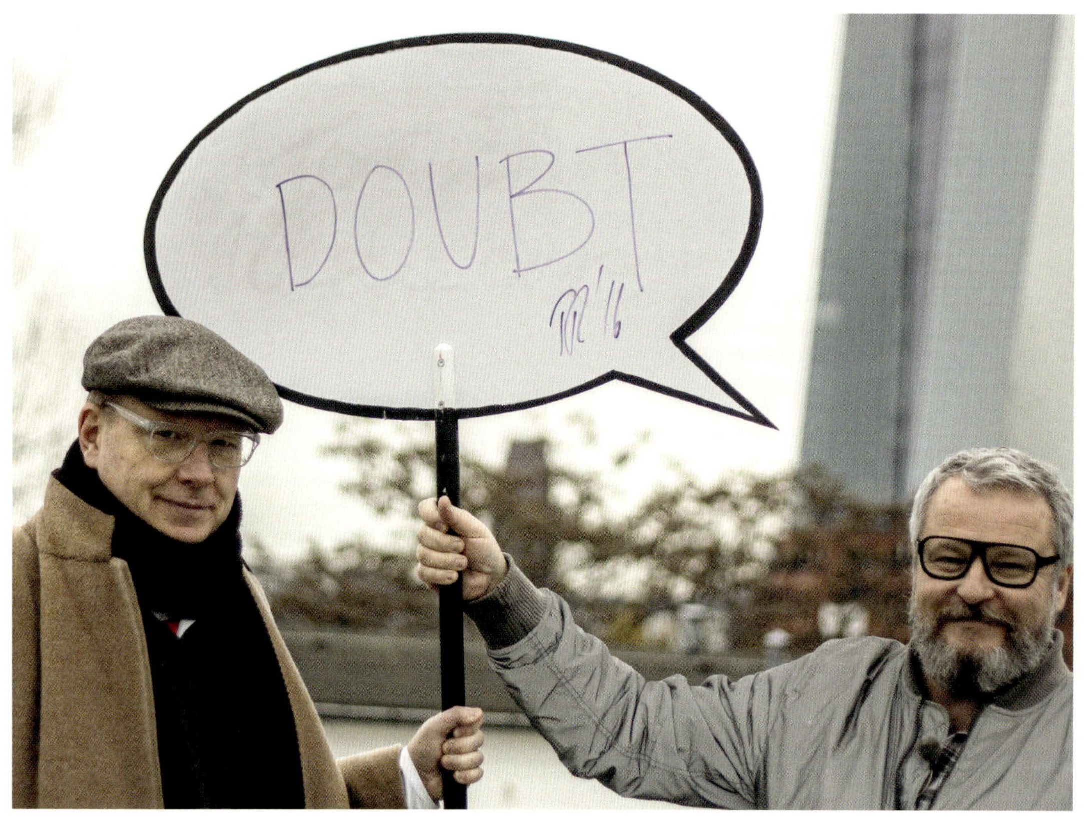

TOBIAS REHBERGER

I do believe that the topic of immortality has a relevance. And sometimes I've heard that a little bit from colleagues, although the thought is actually a little embarrassing. I don't think it's really because of that, but it's a moment of being able to leave behind what remains of you, even if you have died physically, so to speak, and that something spiritual is still left, so to speak. I think that can also be a certain motivation. It's more like an underlying, wafting motivation—not from the individual work or so. … There's something somehow reassuring about thinking that you're somehow not completely gone.

"THERE'S SOMETHING SOMEHOW REASSURING ABOUT THINKING THAT YOU'RE SOMEHOW NOT COMPLETELY GONE."

Creativity and mortality are common threads throughout the creative disciplines. Character actor Armin Mueller-Stahl taps the energy of mortality in film, art, and music. What is his inspiration? I went to the Baltic coast to meet him.

ARMIN MUELLER-STAHL

Where does my creativity come from? My ideas actually come from the material I deal with. So it's a different kind of creativity when I paint, for example, or when I write, or make music. These are all things that are related but a bit different. I think if one day I'm not creative anymore, then it's also time to leave this planet. Creativity is what keeps me going, anyway. It's a force. You know, ideas often change when you sit down to the material and suddenly start. You can take an idea that is quite common. An idea that is not original at all. But the moment you work on it, the moment you sit down, it starts its own life. You know this story of Dostoyevsky who cried terribly while writing it. Yes, why are you crying, someone asked, and Dostoyevsky said, "Just now my main character died, I didn't intend it."

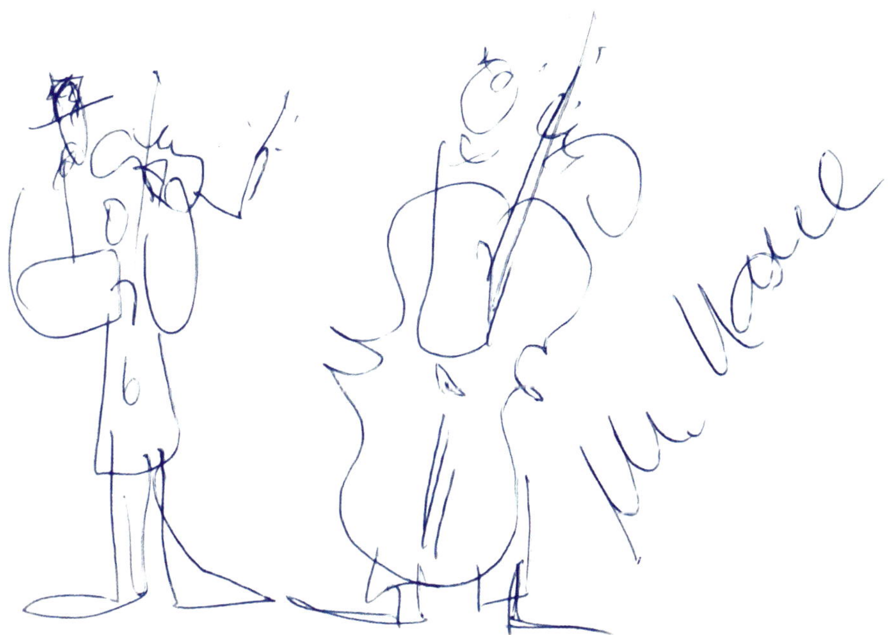

We hug the Baltic Coast and go further East. The Latvian capital Riga is where Anton Dolin fled to escape Russian oppression following the first war with Ukraine. Anton was Russia's most important film critic, running Europe's oldest film magazine. How does he see the relationship between creativity and immortality?

ANTON DOLIN

After Roland Barthes wrote in *The Death of the Author,* the creative process in every reader goes on, goes on and goes on and goes on. Never stops, never stops. And if you're interested—even though the author is dead—you're still part of this process.

Or, as Dylan Thomas put it so well, before he shifted off this mortal coil, long before his time: "Do not go gentle into that good night, Old age should burn and rave at close of day; Rage, rage against the dying of the light."

MARINA ABRAMOVIĆ

You can't treat death with your physical body. Your physical body dies. Look at the example of Maria Callas. Yes, she's dead, but the voice is absolutely immortal. They never die. And in every century, in every different generation, people and young people discovering Callas over and over again because it's the voice of what you leave behind, this is forever. So, who cares that the bodies die. We are all going to die, but what you leave behind—that's immortal.

OLIVIERO TOSCANI

"THE ARTISTS GO DOWN IN HISTORY!"

It's an artist that goes down in history. I mean, when you come to Italy, you don't go around to see which Pope made the Sistine Chapel! I mean, yes, it's written there. I don't even know. Pope Leono Secondo? But Michelangelo made it! And Bernini, Boromini, and not who commissioned this work. I mean this: the people with the money didn't go down in history. The artists go down in history!

Why are you creative, Oliviero?

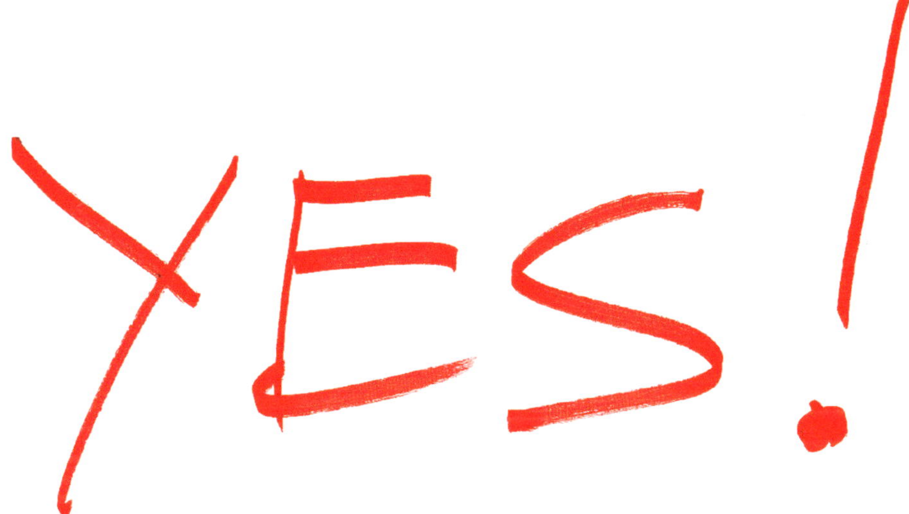

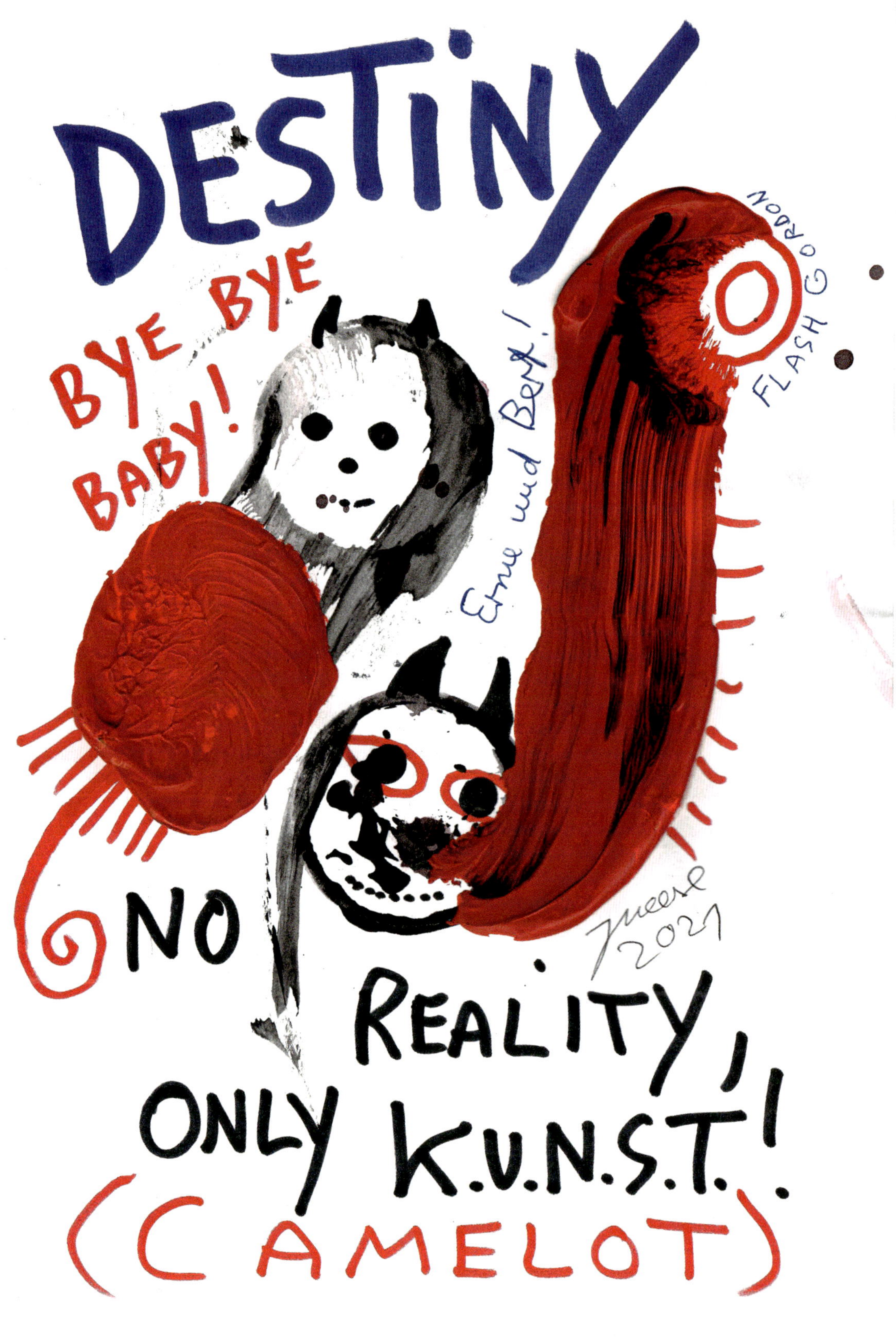

DESTINY
BYE BYE BABY!
Ernie und Bert!
FLASH GORDON
NO REALITY,,
ONLY K.U.N.S.T.!.
(CAMELOT)
2021

Some people say that creativity is destiny. That we have no say in the matter. Compulsion pulls our strings. Fate is our master, and we are condemned to perform our destined, demented, delirious dance.

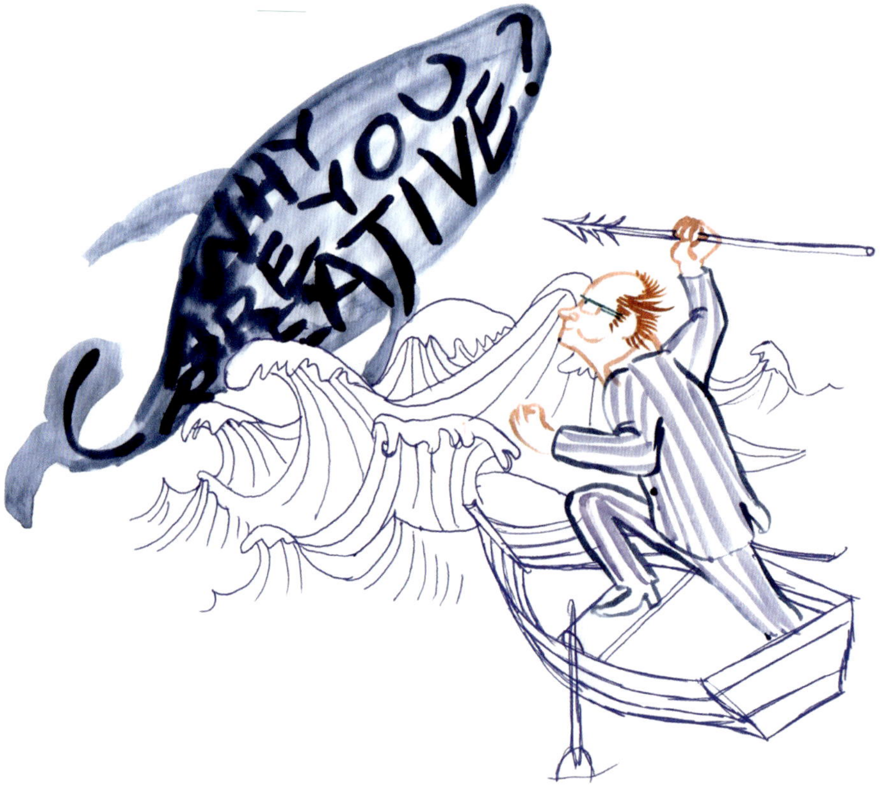

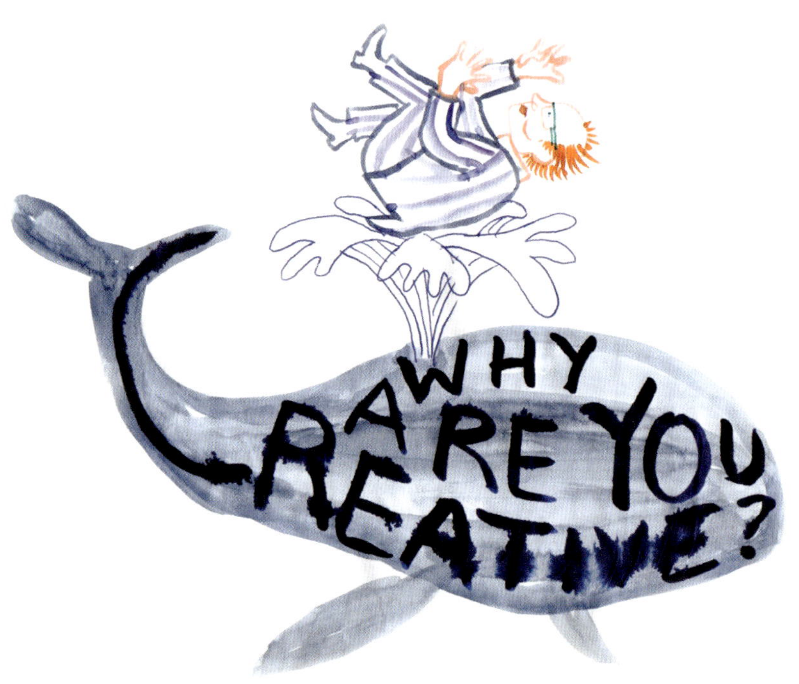
WHY
ARE YOU
CREATIVE?

I began to feel like Captain Ahab from Moby Dick where it had become my destiny to hunt the white whale of creativity for all eternity, endlessly compelled to make the journey between the shores of the familiar and the birthplace of the barely imagined.

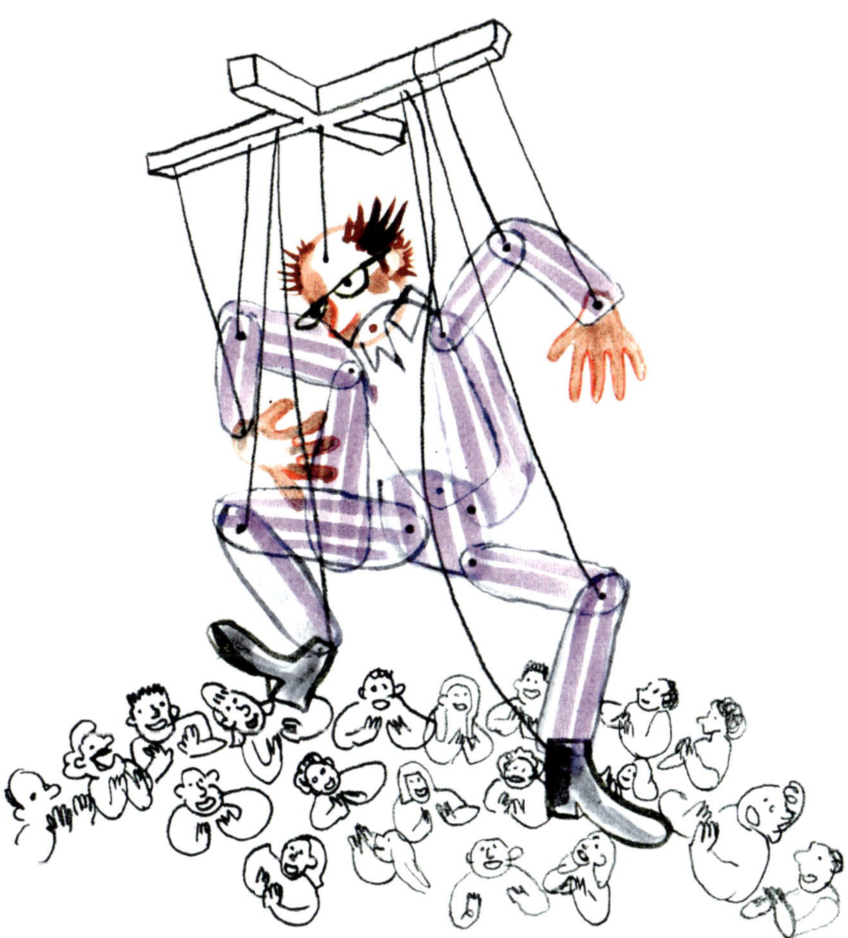

Once upon a time,
I met Quentin Tarantino in Hollywood.

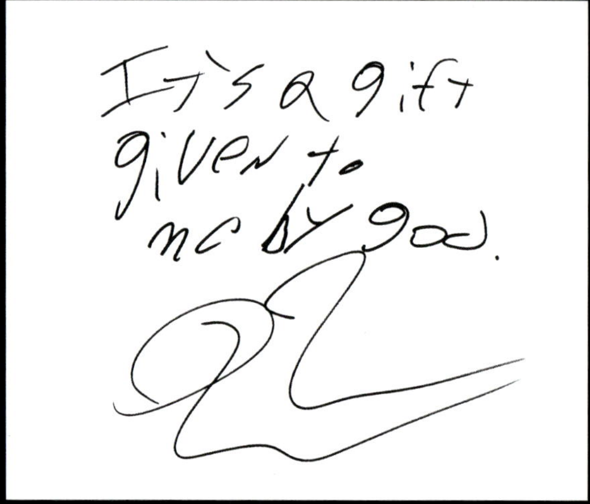

QUENTIN TARANTINO

With all the great movies you did, why are you creative? What drives you?

Alright, I really actually—at the end of the day I do believe we are born with things that we do a little better than most of the people that we know, or that we meet in our daily lives. And … I think that's where it comes from. Whatever I. … If I have anything, it's because someone gave it to me before I was born.

It's like a gift?

It's extremely like a gift, and the part about it, it's a lucky gift, I get the part about it that makes us worthy of it is we got to now do something with it. And that's not predestined.

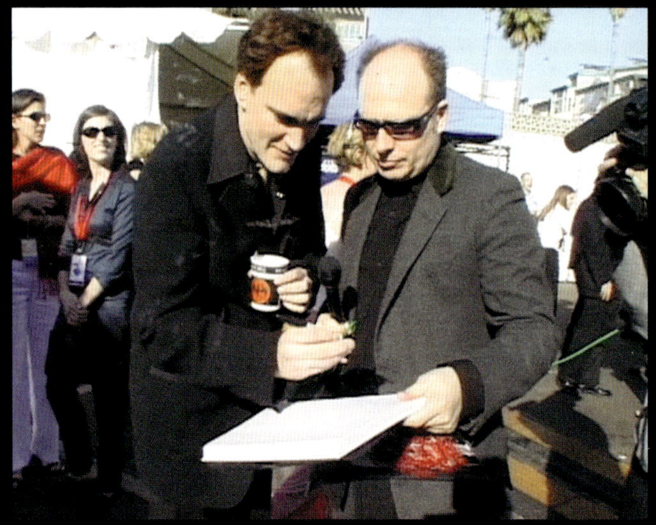

"IF I HAVE ANYTHING IT'S BECAUSE SOMEONE GAVE IT TO ME BEFORE I WAS BORN."

On my journey, I met a lot of people who are compulsive creatoholics. Those who are addicted to the creative process. They feel they have no choice in the matter. They are compelled to create, addicted to feeding the creative impulse. If a day, or even an hour, passes without them feeling that they're enhancing our world, they are unfulfilled.

FRANK GEHRY

Well, you start out, you don't know what you want to be when you're a kid until you find out something you enjoy doing. Luckily, I found something I enjoy doing. It's like a disease or habit. I can't stop it. I really enjoy doing it. You could say that I am addicted to the creative process. A creatoholic, yes.

But no one was as compulsive as George Lois—the crazy Greek of Advertising, one of the original Mad Men of Madison Avenue.

GEORGE LOIS

When I was a young, a very young kid, I was drawing from the time I was four or five years old, drawing, drawing, drawing, drawing everything. … I was drawing everything in sight, you know. I'd stay up … I'd stay up at night and draw. My wife … my mother would come in and say, "Go to sleep, go to sleep", I was six, seven years old and not sleeping. But I did notice, I did know that when I was going on I was reading books and looking at things and I loved art, I would go to museums when I was a young kid. … I loved Cycladic art, I loved Brancusi, and I loved some things that people didn't know about. But I also loved and enjoyed posters like Cassandre. I liked seeing design that communicated something specific. I knew before I went to a high school of musical art when I was twelve, I guess, I knew that somehow that I was going to be, I think, a graphic designer. I mean, I loved architecture and I loved product design but somehow I knew I was gonna do it. I don't know how people can exist without drawing, to tell you the truth. It's as if they can't see.

"I DON'T KNOW HOW PEOPLE CAN EXIST WITHOUT DRAWING, TO TELL YOU THE TRUTH. IT'S AS IF THEY CAN'T SEE."

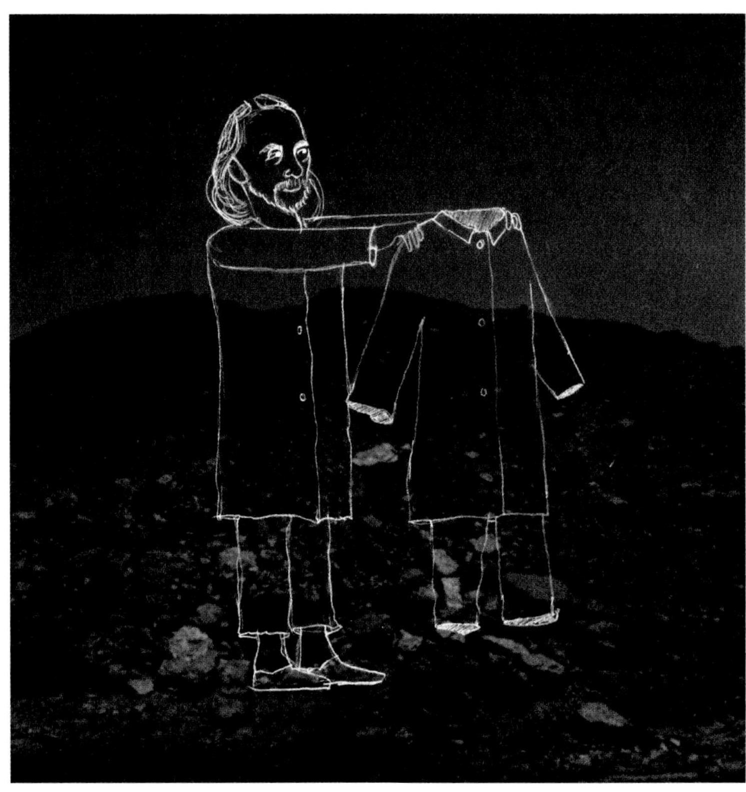

YOHJI YAMAMOTO

You know, it's always the same for everybody that you want to be understood. That's why people keep on going doing something or making something.
But there is naturally a difference between ordinary people who want to be understood or artists who want to be understood. An artist has very deep motivation to continue to make something until the end, but ordinary people don't have it. This is not very fair.
The people called artists are sometimes unlucky. They have something, something given. Their life is to make something—they can't stop. It's like a nonstop train. It is so uncomfortable sometimes, so rushing. I don't know why. This is the fate of artists or creators—to look for something new, fresh, exciting.

NICK CAVE

Why are you creative?

It is the only thing that I know how to do properly in my life. My creative side of me works extremely well, it is extremely rich and it is not balanced properly with the rest of my life. The rest of my life suffers very much because of my rich creative side. Friendships suffer, relationships suffer, my relationship with my family suffers because I have a very rich creative side and a side that is constantly drawing me to it.

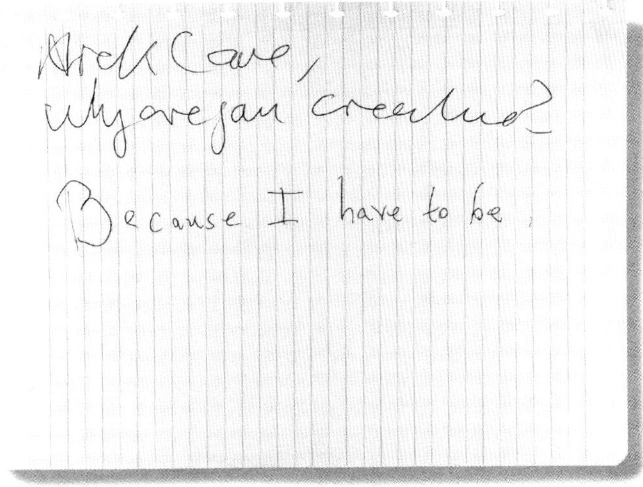
Nick Cave,
why are you creative?

Because I have to be

SALMAN RUSHDIE

I was interested to note that in the answer to your "Why Are You Creative" question, Günter Grass and I, without conferring, gave exactly the same answer—which is that we have no choice. You do it because you have to. And I've always felt that there are enough books in the world and if you are going to add a book to that, it has to be because you have no choice in the matter. Because the book insists on being written. And those are the books that I've always tried to write.

Because I seem to
have no choice in
the matter.

GEORGE R.R. MARTIN

I've asked myself and I've asked other writers when we sit around in bars late at night discussing this: "What would happen if you could no longer get any money from your writing, would you continue to write?" And different writers give different answers to that, but I think I would still be compelled to write up my stories even if no one but me wanted to read them. And indeed, of course, as a child no one paid me for those stories, I was writing just for my own amusement, no one ever saw these little notebooks, and then, in high school, I was writing for comic book fanzines which were amateur publications. They printed twenty-five copies on a ditto machine … so it was … the idea of telling a story to an audience. I mean, I think, if need be, you know, I might just gather a bunch of people around the campfire and say: "Hey, here's a story!" Yeah. I think it is a compulsion in that way. The frightening thing about it, because I don't understand where it comes from, is always the fear that it will stop coming. That one day, the muse will be silent or the left brain will stop talking to the right brain or whatever, and these things won't come anymore and then I will go silent. Certainly, I see that with other writers and artists, you know. You see, as I studied the history of my field, science fiction, fantasy, you know, you see many writers who are very prolific and then at a certain point in life they just stopped. And it's like they spend their last twenty years rewriting one thing or struggling on one novel and never completed anything. That hasn't happened to me yet and I hope it never does. I hope I'm more like Jack Vance or Nigel Tranter or some of the other writers who kept writing well until their nineties, in which case I still have another thirty years to go or so. But … that's all I understand about creativity and it's not much. It is a mystery.

"I THINK, IF NEED BE, YOU KNOW, I MIGHT JUST GATHER A BUNCH OF PEOPLE AROUND THE CAMPFIRE AND SAY: "HEY, HERE'S A STORY!"

CHRISTOPH SCHLINGENSIEF

My creativity is compulsive. One is tied to a chain and then one creates one's own chain. Yes, it is compulsive. Murnau for instance followed his dream of a movie. He went to the South Sea and lived an eternal movie there. With me it is quite similar because I don't want to be necessarily in the movie that I was born in, I am building my own movie. And you necessarily do not find creative stimulus when you are feeling well, but feeling bad often makes you stronger. Doubt and self-destruction are reasons that drive me to do things. That's why I am not doing necessarily glossy things but trashy things. I make use of leftovers.

"MY CREATIVITY IS COMPULSIVE."

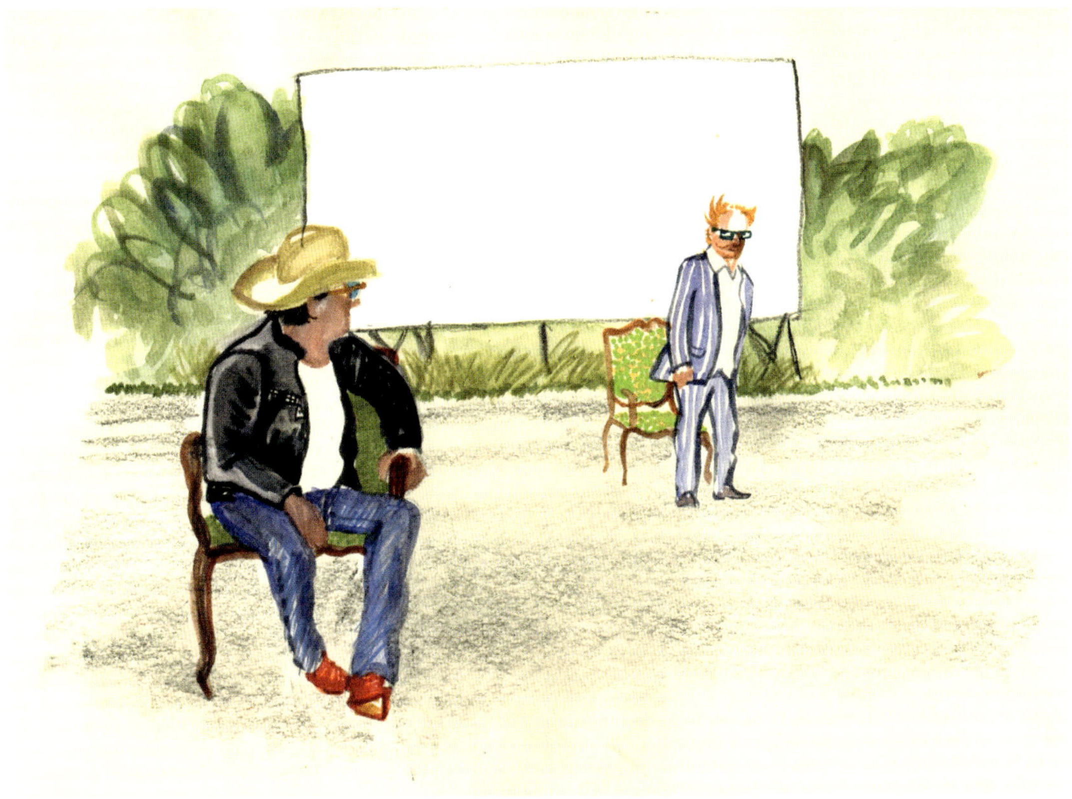

When *Reservoir Dogs* actor Michael Madsen had no paper to hand in a New York cab, he wrote a poem unceremoniously on his knee.

"AND I PULLED UP MY PANTS, AND I WROTE IT ON MY LEG."

MICHAEL MADSEN

If I have to play a character in the movie, they give me a cigarette and a pistol, and I am ready, I can do it, and even if I don't feel like it, I can be believable. But if you're going to write something, you can't just take a piece of paper and say, okay, well, I'm going to sit down and write now, it just doesn't really come out that way, it doesn't work that way. If you don't have the notion of something that you suddenly see and you go "Oh man!" Or you can hear it in your mind. And if you don't write it down right away, you forget it. I wrote a poem on my leg one time, in the back of a taxicab in New York City, I didn't have a piece of paper. I didn't want to forget it. And I pulled up my pants, and I wrote it on my leg.
Here's some compulsive ideas for working from New York's finest Parisian.

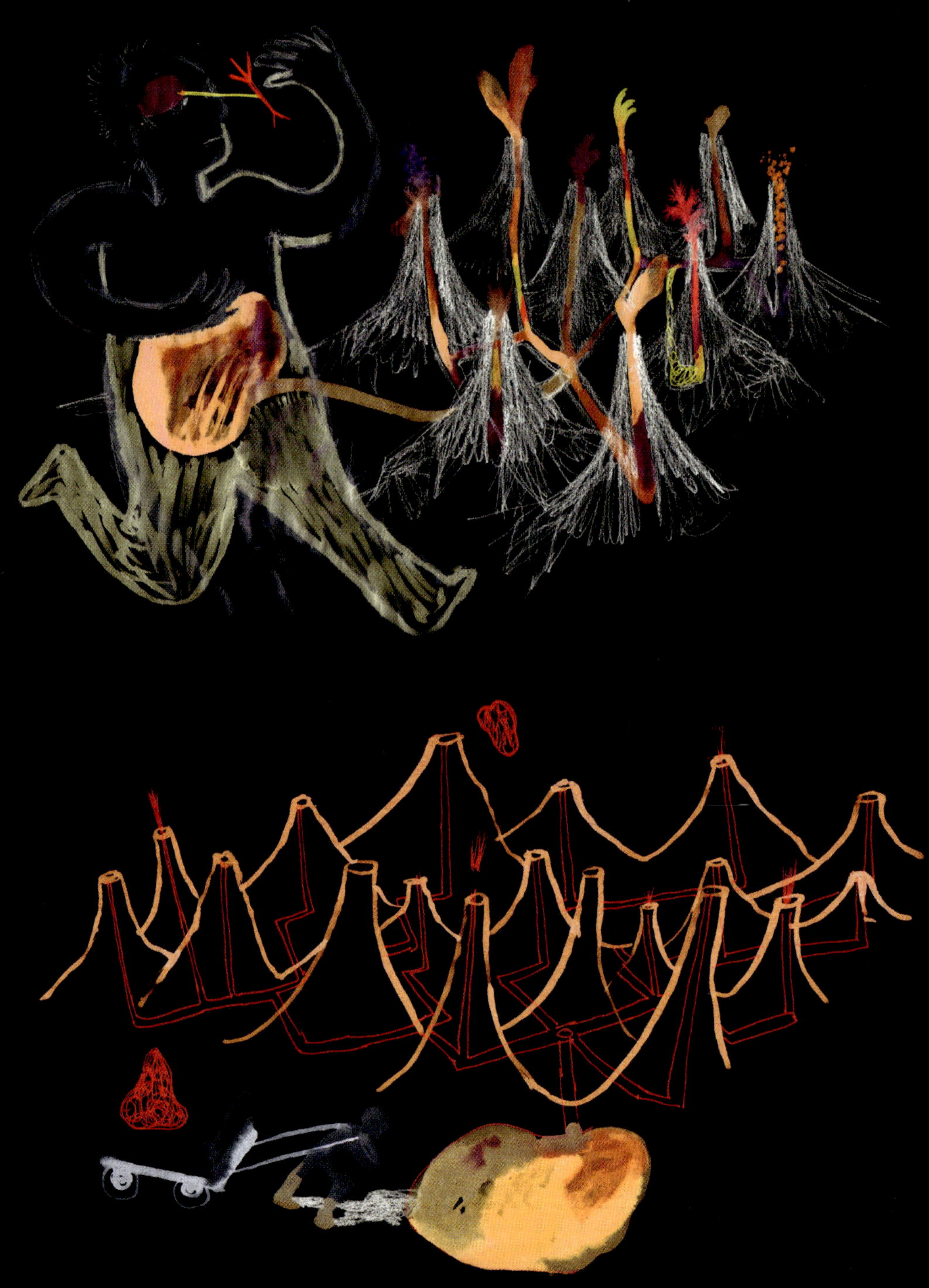

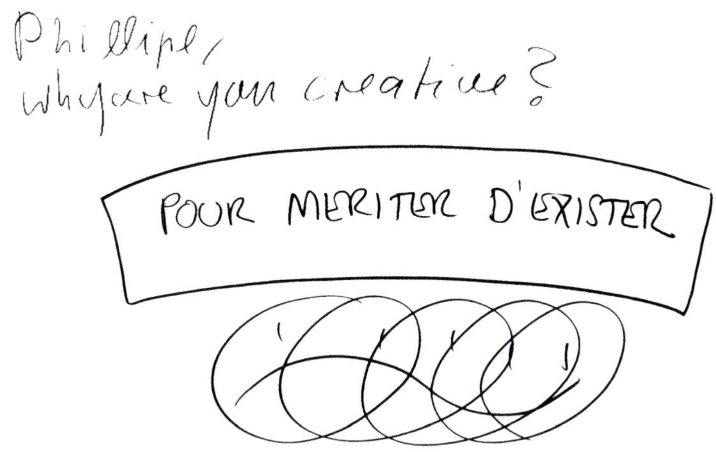

PHILIPPE STARCK

I work on about 250 projects at the same time. Meaning I am doing all of it by myself and that there is a computer, which works on many projects simultaneously. But, paradoxically, I am forced to leave a kind of permanent magma. Actually, I'm a farmer and I work on magma. All of those projects you can see need years or of development. After the development, the magma gives me a complete image. My mental exercise is simply to see a hologram, a tridimensional representation. If it's an object, I make it turn around to see all of its details, and if it's a room, I explore it to see it in its entirety.

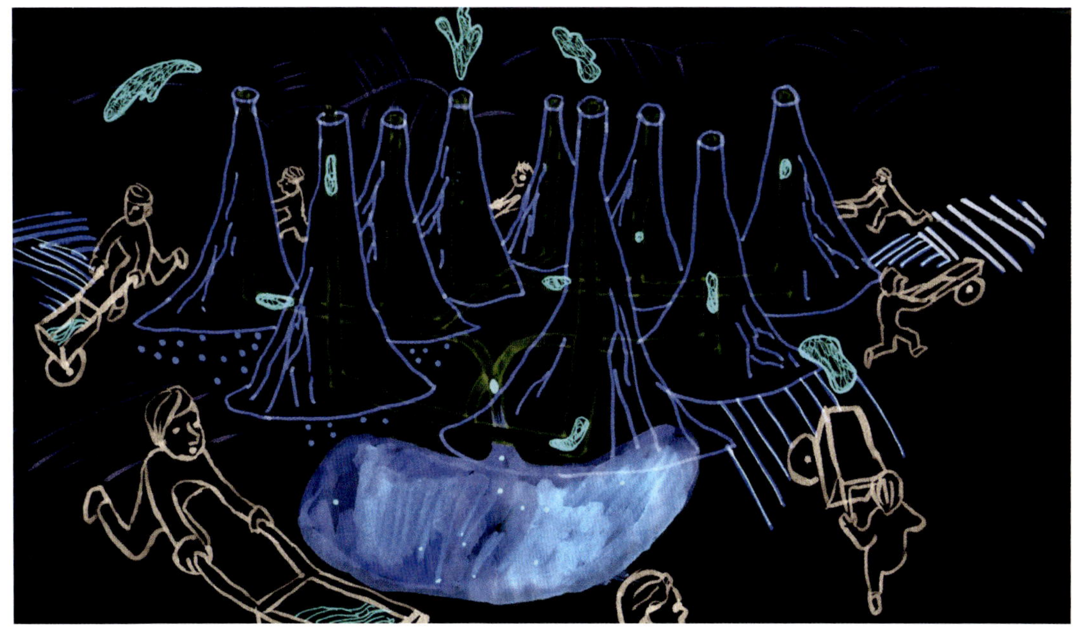

I live in a complete physical autocracy, in a complete cultural autocracy and also in a spiritual autocracy. For me creativity is only gymnastics of the brain and of concentration. And my bed is my fitness studio and my office. That's why I have a bed in my office. If I have to think about something I just go to bed. I lay down and spend my time dreaming and waiting until my software has downloaded the program. That's why I have a table standing right next to my bed, so that only a minimum of seconds gets lost between my bed and my table. And if it's ready and accomplished, I'll sit down at my table and print.

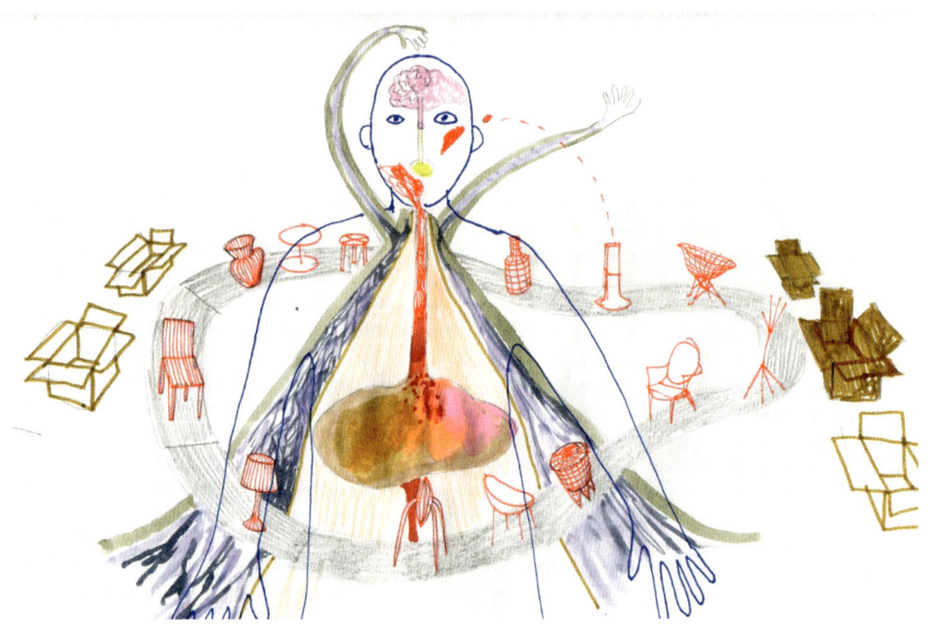

"CREATIVITY IS ONLY GYMNASTICS OF THE BRAIN AND OF CONCENTRATION."

This brings to mind Salvador Dali's method of half-sleeping on a couch while holding a spoon. He maintained that the moment he drops the spoon and wakes from the clatter, his thoughts are at their most perceptive.

NEO RAUCH

What pushes me to create are these zones of trouble inside me. These are moments that make me nervous, these are also visual attractions that spark me from the side, from the studio floor or from a mortar structure on a weathered wall. And that can really put you in a state of panic, that can rush you, this overabundance of material that wants to be shaped, that demands creative effort for your attention. "Paint me!" it screams at me from the studio floor, and where I mix my colors, the craziest things come into being. And, of course, these seem to be outward appearances, but there are nevertheless also these inner zones of uniqueness, from which springs the impulse to want to create, to create my own worlds, in which I set the tone, in which I can rule and rule, in which I reign, without restriction. I set the boundaries myself, no one else. And that is a highly satisfying but also permanently unsettling state.

Are there any limits for you?

Yes, they are set by me. Those are the limits that are set by me, in my possibilities. And one must arrange oneself within these limits. We must follow our own tone, which we perceive within ourselves.

Is creative work now, when something screams at you, is that based more on chaos or on discipline?

These are states of chaos in which I have to intervene in a disciplinary way.

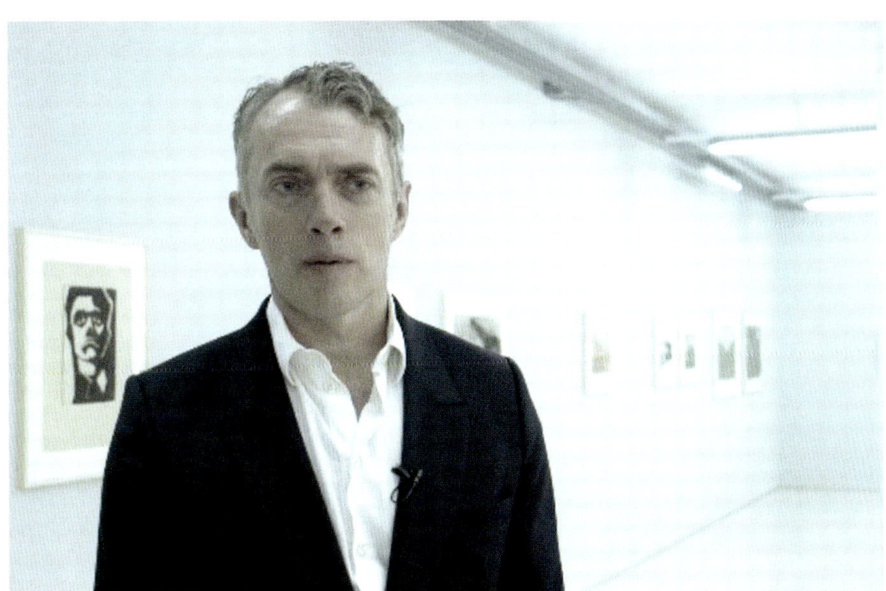

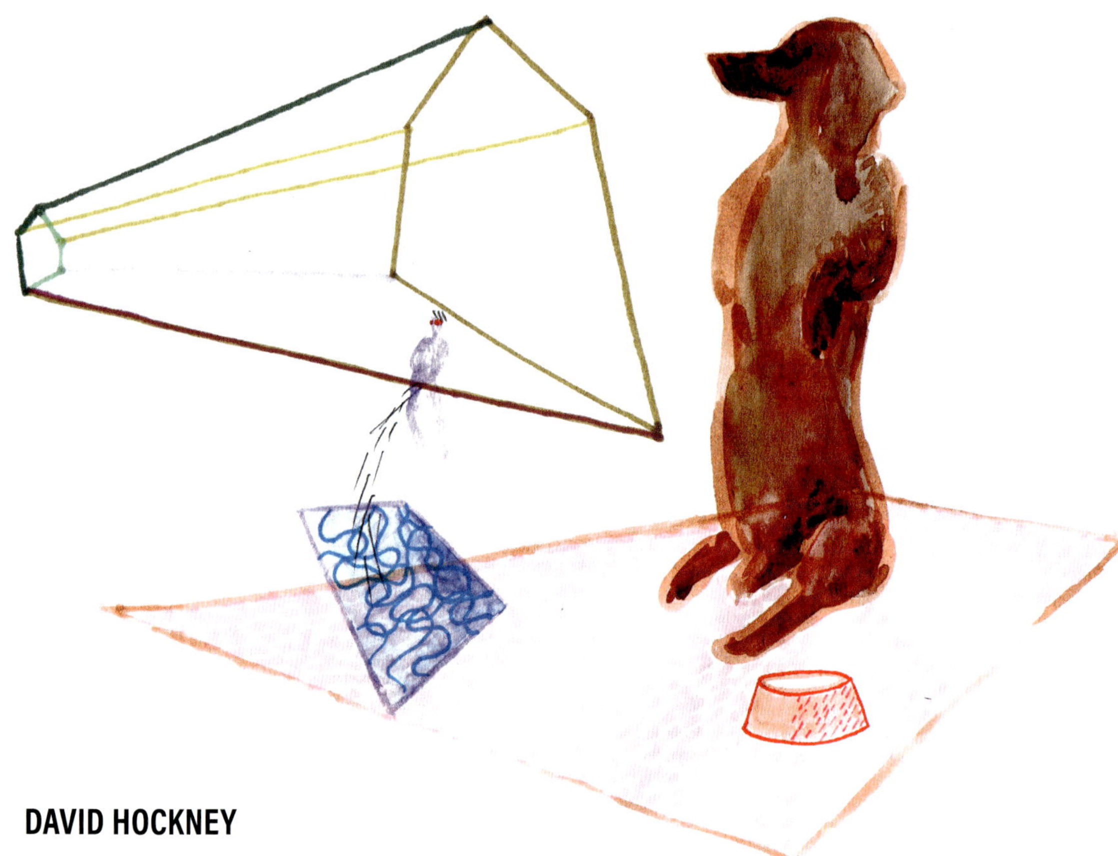

DAVID HOCKNEY

I can't help it. I'm forced to be creative. Otherwise I don't think I could bear life that much, actually. My friends tell me that as well. I realized, compared to other people, I'm driven to it, meaning I'm using the word "drive," meaning you're forced to do it in a way, you are. I'm not sure I'd use that word. I certainly need to do it. And I expect to do it in some ways until I fall over. I think all artist do that, don't they?

You're obsessed about painting dachshunds, your dachshunds—do you think dachshunds can be creative?

I'm not sure they'd actually care about it. I assume they had two desires: food and love, in that order. Maybe that's a lesson for us all, actually. They took no interest in my pictures, wouldn't care less; they'd pee on them, actually.

David Hockney,
Why are you Creative?

I need to be.
I love life.

TONY KAYE

Hermann sent me a blank piece with that question on the top: Why are you creative? I took a knife, cut my face, and rubbed some of my blood on the piece of paper. I wake up and I'm driven by these things that make me want to create things. Fortunately, these sort of angels that are driving me are always telling me that I need to get better and so that's what I spend my time doing. When I'm not doing it, I'm trying to get better at doing it, so that when I do it, it gets as good as it can be.

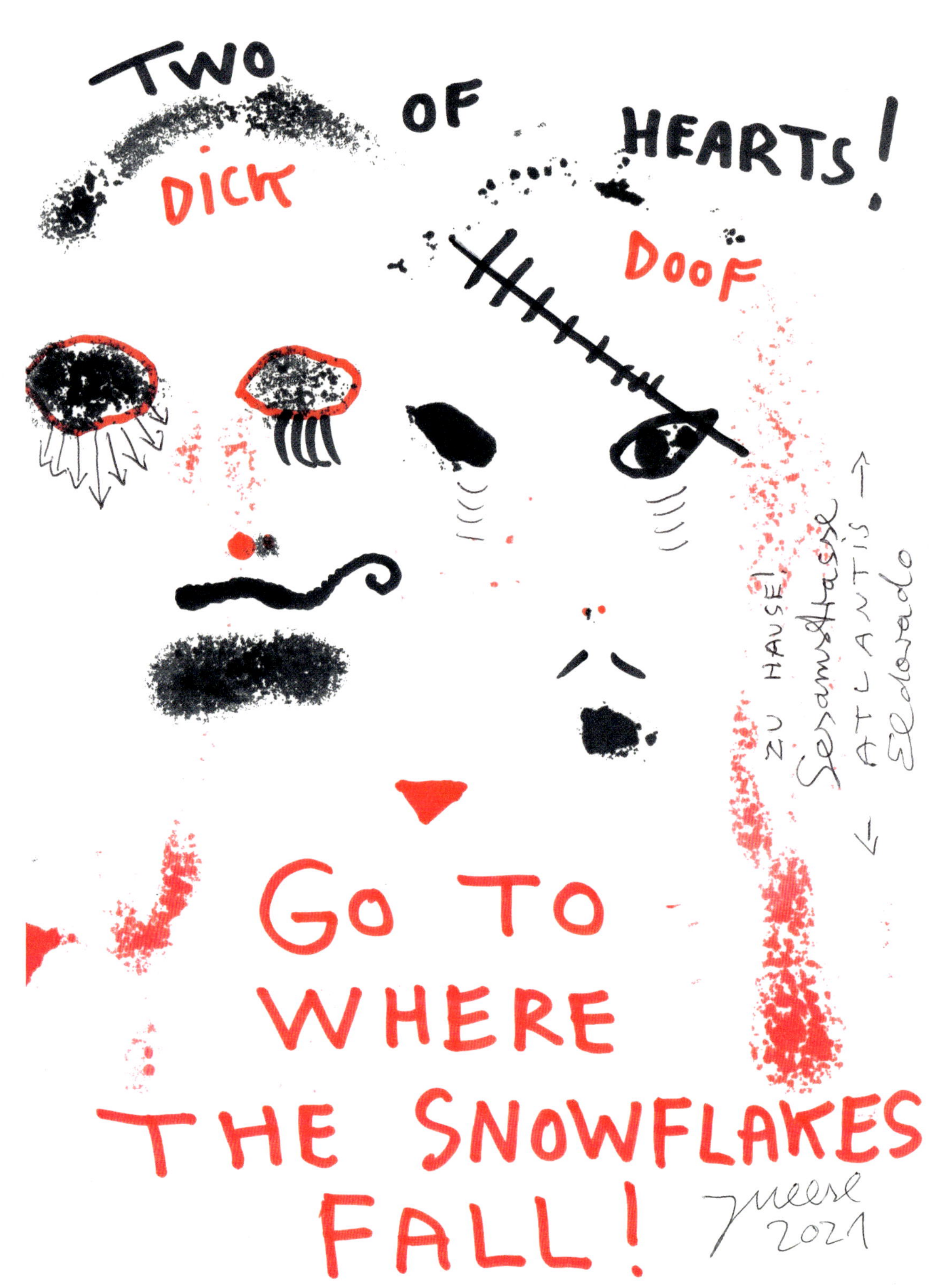

TWO OF HEARTS!
DICK
DOOF
ZU HAUSE!
Sesamstrasse
ATLANTIS
Eldorado
GO TO WHERE THE SNOWFLAKES FALL!
Meese 2021

It is said that we don't have ideas. Ideas have a life of their own, floating by out there in the ether. We just have to put ourselves in the right frame of mind to pick them up. Put another way: ideas are like snowflakes floating in the wind ready to fall on anyone who stands under them.

WOLFGANG TILLMANS

"IF I SUSPECT THAT A PICTURE MIGHT HAPPEN, THEN I HAVE THE CAMERA WITH ME."

I don't separate planning from chance, because nothing happens without chance and nothing happens without planning. By planning I mean knowledge, being ready with one's abilities. In this respect, I go through life with a mixture of being open to the events of life as they happen to me, which one might call coincidence or fate, and on the other hand a certain readiness to take it in. But this readiness does not interfere so much technically in my life that I am no longer able to take anything in. In this respect, I live without a camera, I experience the world with my eyes, but in this case, to come back to the image. I know that when I fly, I always ask to sit at the window, and not to sit above the wing. So I have exact rows, rows of seats, where I just ask, can I sit the second row from the back, on the left, because I know when I fly from Germany to London, I can just see who knows what on the left, or on the right I can see Hyde Park. These are just experiences, I know that, and it doesn't cost much to ask once, can I sit there. And then every time on such a trip I also have a camera lying next to me, a real camera with SLR, lens and everything. It just lies there, and sometimes I sleep the whole flight, and sometimes I just look out. And sometimes I wake up briefly, see something, take a picture and go back to sleep. So, I'm asleep, but I know that it's possible that there's a picture happening. And I think that's how I deal with the camera. If I suspect that a picture might happen, then I have the camera with me.

Why ARE YOU creative?

Um Orangenhaut zu vermeiden

Hamburg 27.9.2001

PETER GABRIEL

What encourages creativity? I noticed, for instance when I travel on the train, I get more good ideas than other times. My theory is it's because there is peripheral motion, which you sometimes get in the car as well, if you can get to zone out, so it's maybe a little dangerous sometimes, so your eye goes straight to the brain. It's sort of got this little surface action of moving things, so it knows it's in motion, peripheral motion sort of sets it in gear, and somehow this seems to create a space for thinking and for new ideas.

DANIEL KEHLMANN

"CREATIVITY IS A KIND OF CONTRACT WITH THE SUBCONSCIOUS."

There's this phrase by Norman Mailer that I often think of. Norman Mailer said that "creativity is a kind of contract with the subconscious." And the contract is you say to the subconscious: "You're going to bring things out of the depths, out of your depths, out of the unfathomable darkness, and I'm going to be there when that happens." That's the contract. I'll be there every day, being there. By that I really mean sitting there and trying. I can't exactly do that every day yet. But being at your table and trying to do the work, I think that's the essential thing.

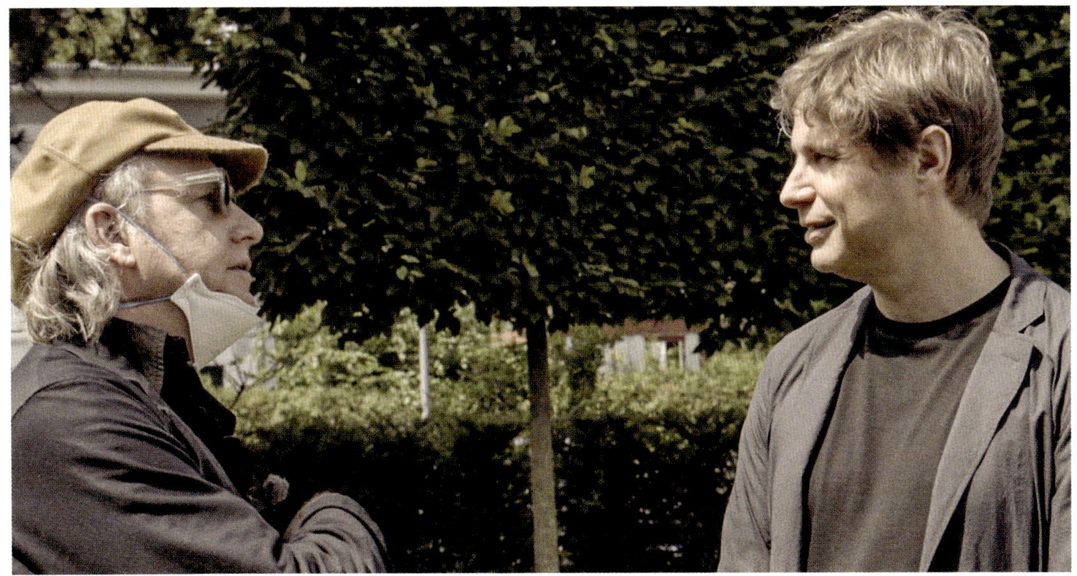

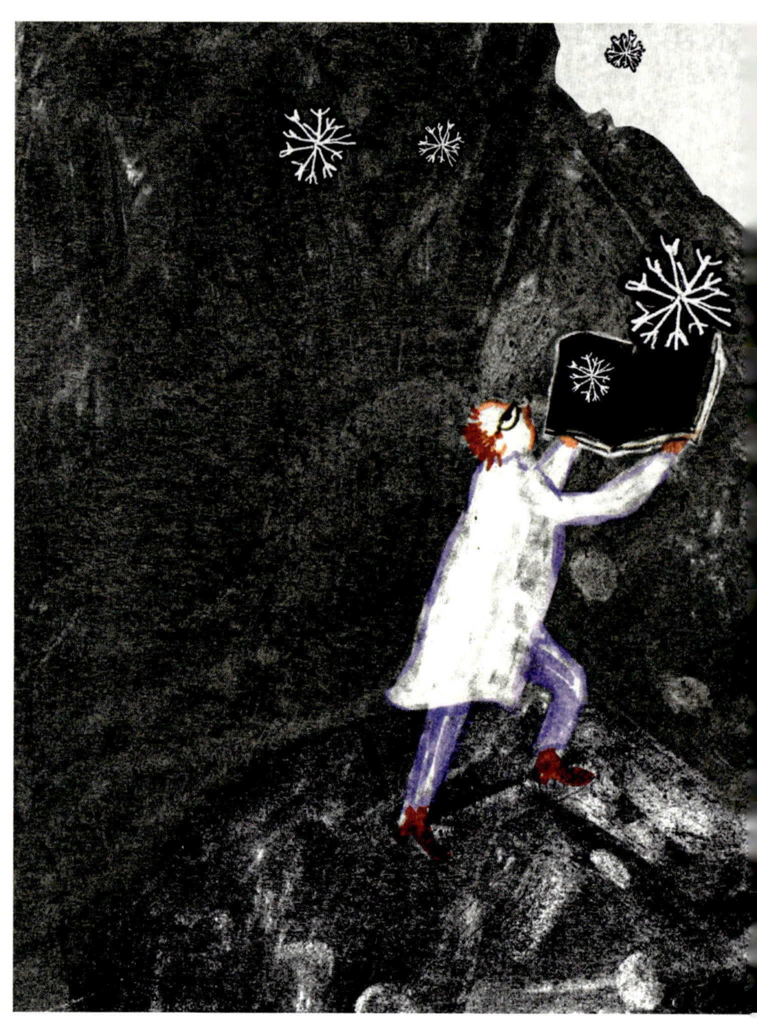

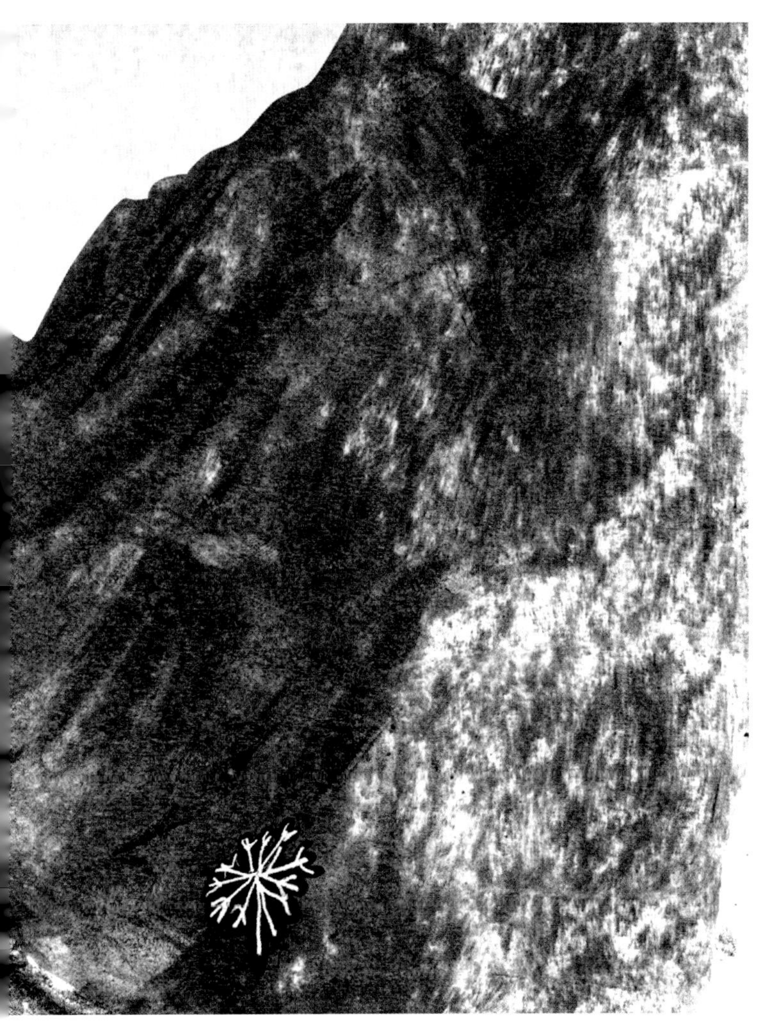

MARINA ABRAMOVIĆ

Where do you find the snowflakes?

In myself. There isn't anywhere else. You know, snowflakes come and go and every single snowflake is different. And every time you, you look at yourself, you'll find another one different and something to learn about.

FRANK GEHRY

How do you get your stimulus?

From everything in life around me, that I've seen or witnessed or experienced. You know: paintings, sculptures, the city, the people. I gave a talk in Turkey a few years ago, and I was asked this question, "Where do you get your inspiration?" and I had just been to the capitol of the Hagia Sophia, and I said to the students at the university that if you looked at those forms in that capitol, there are enough ideas in there for you to last a lifetime of taking those ideas and discovering and playing with them. And I really believe that everything is very rich if you see it that way.

If you look at the space between, if you look at the just accidental pile of books, if you look at paintings and stuff, but then I find, years ago I went to the Oracle in Delphi and I cried when I saw it.

If I feel like I'm stuck creatively and I don't know where to move, I just go to the museum and look at paintings. It takes the clouds away and makes everything good.

DANIEL LIBESKIND

"TO BE CREATIVE MEANS TO PUT YOURSELF AT RISK, TOWARD THE METEOR, TOWARD THE UNKNOWN."

I think you have to be struck by an idea. It is kind of not one's own idea even, it is something that hits you, sort of like a meteor falling on top of your head. And it is an unexpected encounter with something real which again is not communicable at first stage but maybe through a drawing or a model or through some color that takes articulated form. So I would say it is more like that, and then of course, it grows and it has its own voice, its own physiognomy. And if it is a good one, if it is truly creative, then it can resist and interact with all sorts of processes. Of course, one has to compromise but if the core of fire is in it, then it lives. And if it did not have the fire, if the fire is extinguished, then it was not a creative idea in the first place.

To be creative means to put yourself at risk, toward the meteor, toward the unknown. And then of course it happens all the time because every second of the world something incredible is happening. It is not as if there is a lack of possibility.

I was invited by Keith Reinhard to give a talk in Barcelona. It was a great event because the other guy he invited was Sir George Martin, the legendary creative producer of the *Sergeant Pepper* album, and I had the pleasure to sit next to him during our dinner and modestly listen to his stories. He was known as the fifth Beatle. When we finished our meal I confronted him with a piece of paper and he wrote down where he found his snowflakes.

SIR GEORGE MARTIN,
WHY ARE YOU CREATIVE?
BECAUSE I AM . .
I LIKE DESIGN
I LIKE MAKING THINGS
I LIKE MUSIC
I LIKE SCULPTURE .

AND I LIKE BOATS & PLANES
& TENNIS & SNOOKER
& GARDENS
I LIKE LIFE!

George Martin

We can find creativity in all walks of life. We can find our snowflakes everywhere. Life is a long learning process. I found my snowflakes and learned about creativity. All of these people had something or made something that motivated me creatively. Wow, their ideas surprised me and blew me away. The cover of *Sergeant Pepper's Lonely Hearts Club Band* by The Beatles is a good example. They put all of their creative influences into one photograph.

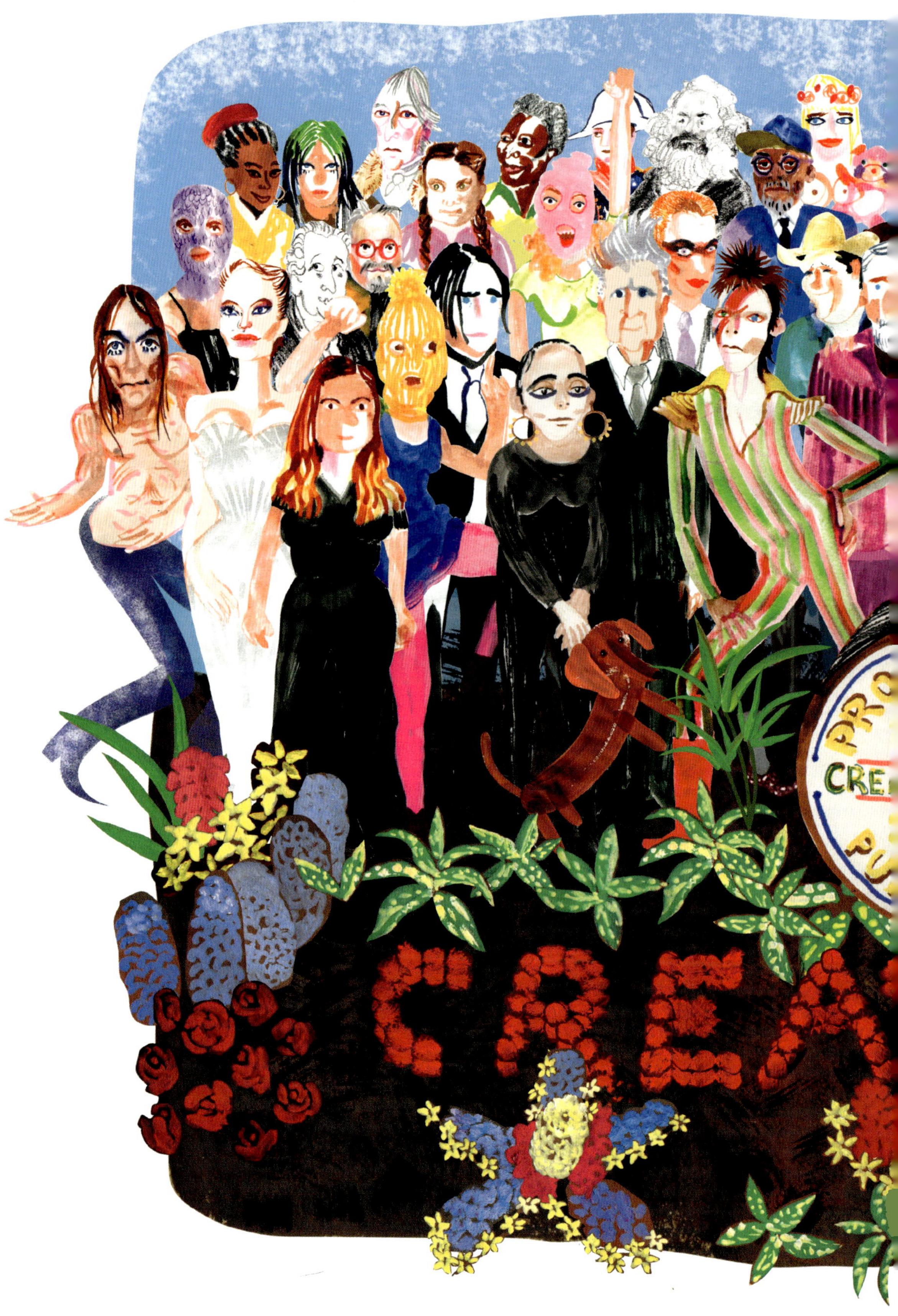

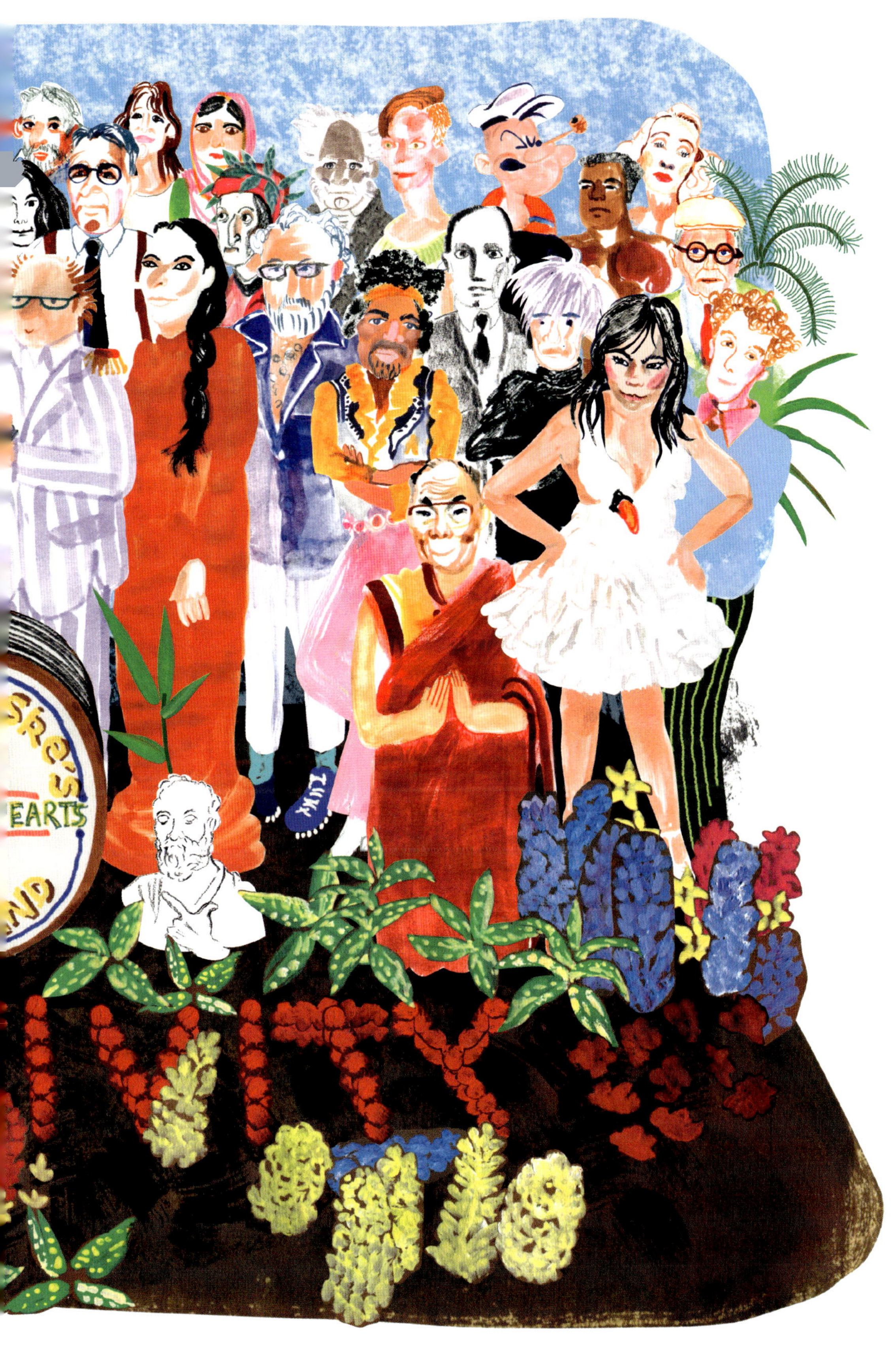

DAVID BOWIE

For some people creativity is life blood, and far more than a purely decorative thing. I think in a way that was unforeseen as a career opportunity now, more than it ever was. But I think that for some, it still is virtually as necessary as eating and breathing and sleeping. I mean, I do it naturally, I create naturally. I can't conceive of having a life where I wasn't writing or painting as naturally as I do anything else.

"THE LANDSCAPE IN TEXAS WHERE I GREW UP IS IN ALL MY WORK."

Robert Wilson

Robert Wilson,
why are you creative?

ROBERT WILSON

What are your creative influences? Where do you find your snowflakes?

My creative influences are … I think where I am, if I'm in Hong Kong or if I am in Waco, Texas, or if I'm in Salzburg, that always has an influence on the work. I think also the landscape in Texas where I grew up is in all my work. I think the first time when I've seen George Balanchine in New York City or Los Angeles, it's a tremendous influence; in this cool, classical way of structuring space; the formality of it; the distancing of it.

But then if we look at the more conventional idea of creativity, so art: art is the journals and the diaries of our time and we learn by history. When we look back 5,000 years from now on, what do we look at? The culture of the Chinese, and the Mayans, the Egyptians, and we look at what artists did. And they're influencing us today. So … things remain up in the culture but usually art does. Well, I think that creativity is always—it's like a tree. And sometimes the tree is in a storm and it's broken, and sometimes it's in the winter and the leaves fall off and spring comes back and there are leaves again. It's like a river that's always flowing around and going on and going in different directions. I don't think one can stop being creative.

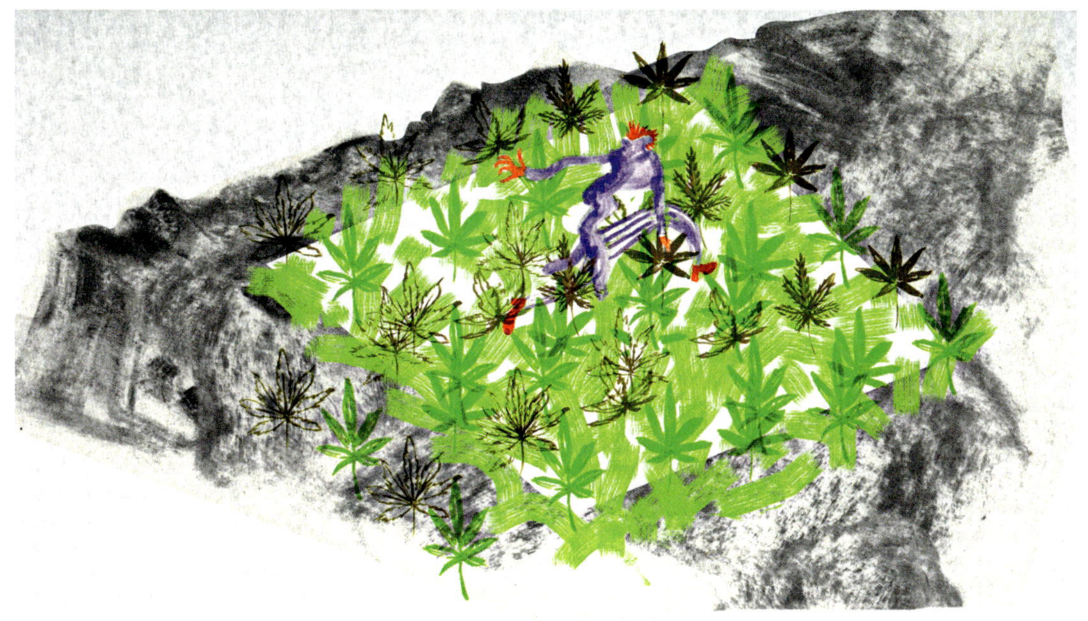

JOHN CLEESE

I never believed that alcohol or something like cannabis makes you more creative. I do know one philosopher who literally used to have two (Cleese imitates sucking a joint twice) inhales of a spliff to review his work. He felt that under that influence he sometimes was able to put ideas together better than if he would not have smoked this. People often said regarding Monty Python, what were you on? The answer was "No, no, it was much more a matter of precision and technique." You get the crazy ideas but then you use your technique to get your crazy idea up there on the screen in its right form. So you have to have the crazy idea but you have to have the technique too.

RABAN RUDDIGKEIT

Creativity is the most natural way for me to live, work, and connect with people. Growing up in an artistic household, ideas and their realization were everyday life. Every attempt to earn my money with anything else failed.

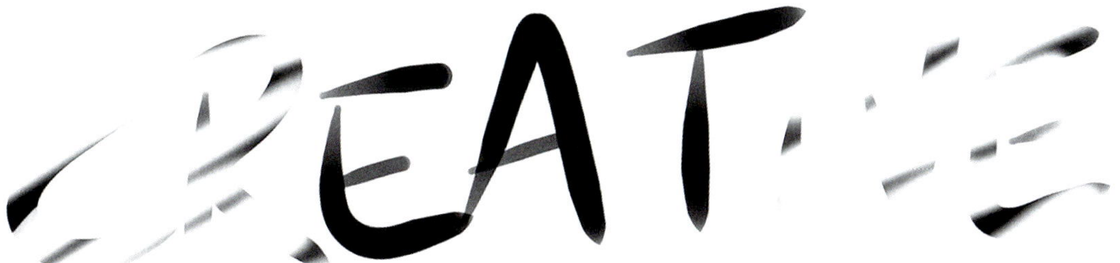

In New York, I talked to Shirin Neshat, winner of the Venice Film Festival's Directing Award. We talked in her Brooklyn studio, surrounded by large-format black-and-white photographs.

SHIRIN NESHAT

I always think that there's always a fire inside of artists that you have to keep alive. And if that fire goes out, if it's extinguished, then what you are left with is stagnation and repetition. But to take that fire, you are like a kind of a servant to it, you don't really know where it's taking you, how you should protect this fire to keep it going. But you have no option but to follow it and follow your instinct.

What you're also saying relates to the Roman philosopher Seneca, who said, "There is no favorable wind for the sailor who doesn't know where to go."

"THERE IS SOMETHING EXTREMELY THRILLING ABOUT BEGINNING NEW CHAPTERS AND REALLY GOING TO PLACES THAT ARE SO UNKNOWN."

It's the element of risk, I think it's a really important one to me. You know, and I sometimes worry that I'm taking too many risks and just to be more specific. You know, the way that I've sort of moved on between smaller photographs to video, to movies, to opera, and making movies for theatrical release and yet going to opera where I'm not known at all.

And you know, it is like sailing to these unknown territories, and the uncertainty of it is so vast. But there is something extremely thrilling about beginning new chapters and really going to places that are so unknown. And could I add to that that maybe that comes with being like a nomad. Where I am perhaps more fearless about taking the steps and risk where someone who is more fixed, like a painter, or someone who lives at home in the same country, wants to be speaking the same language, and all of that; it's more difficult for them to expand or flex their muscles. But for me, it just comes naturally, and I'm constantly adapting to new things and new places anyway.

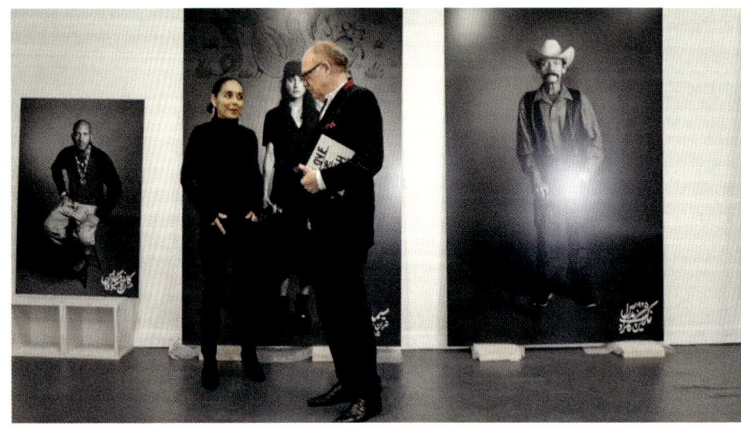

The Nomad Concept offers a great opportunity to remember Christo and Jeanne-Claude. Two artists who had a dream. After many years of talks, discussions, and preparation, they wrapped the Reichstag in Berlin, which became an unforgettable moment. I wanted to know how nomad life was influencing their creativity.

Jeanne Claude and Christo
Why are you Creative?
we can't help it!
creativity is
our life!
Christo and Jeanne-Claude

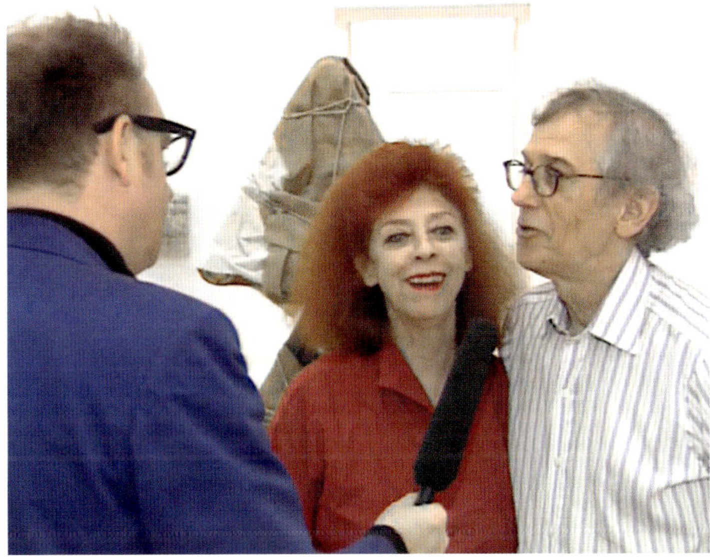

CHRISTO

Our art has a nomadic quality, it's very nomadic, it's not heavy, it's very sensual and not routed to some special place.

Nomadic means travelling. Is that an inspiration for your work?

Yeah, the nomadic tribes in the Sahara and Tibet are moving. It's the moving, it's the passing through. That feeling is very deeply demonstrated with our temporary works of art.

JEAN-CLAUDE

It's very typical for the second half of the twentieth century and the twenty-first century. There have never been so many people going from one place to the other. Moving is very important and essential. It also transforms the culture. When people come from one country to the other, the country that welcomes them changes little by little.

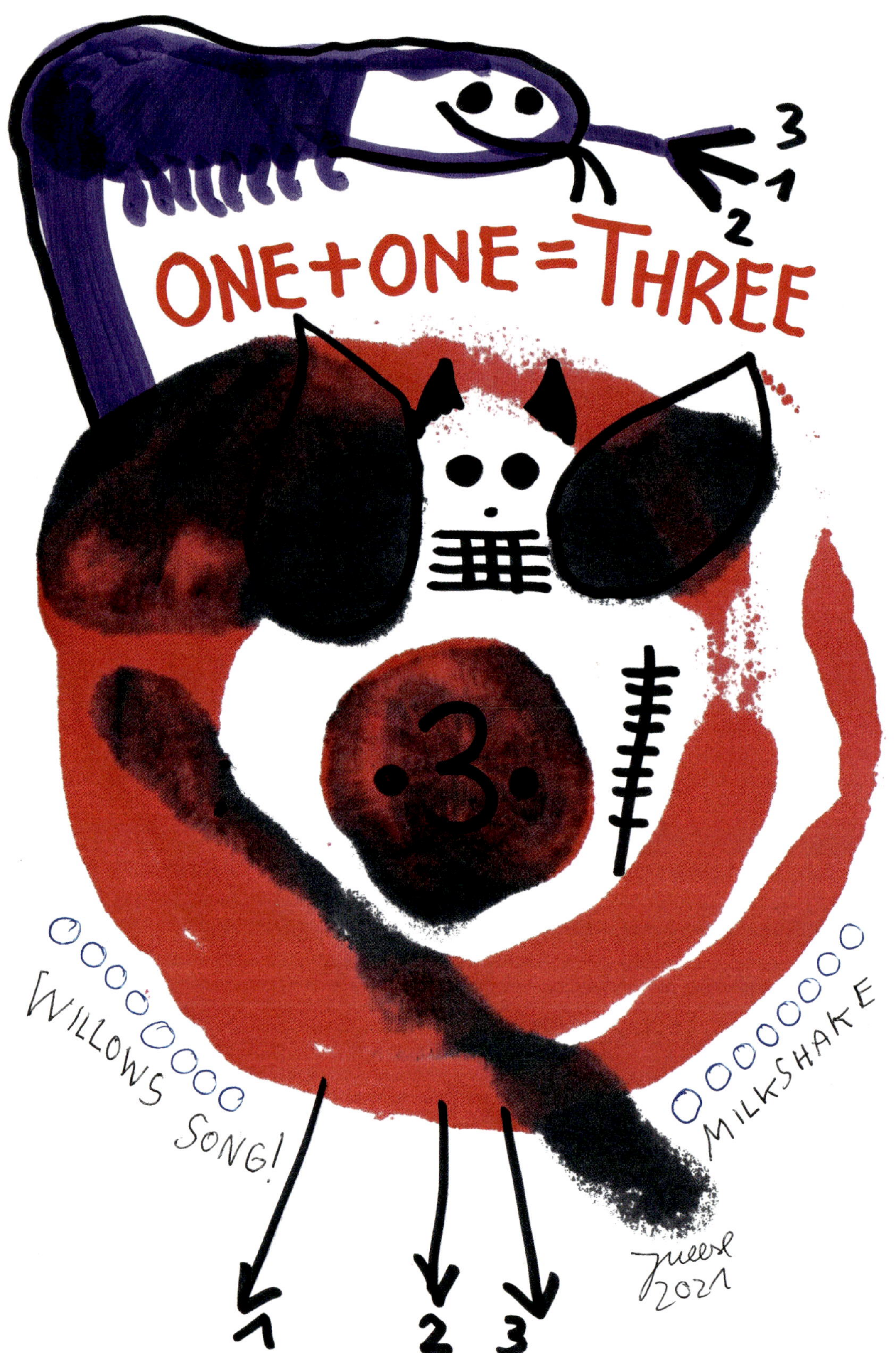

3
1
2
ONE + ONE = THREE
3
WILLOWS SONG!
MILKSHAKE
1
2
3
2021

Russian Director Sergey Eisenstein defined creativity as bringing together two things that do not belong to each other to create a third. David Bowie tells us how he mastered this creative technique.

DAVID BOWIE

Is content or style more important for your creativity?

Content is one thing and packaging or style or framing is another. It's an interesting thing, but if you see a lot of young artists' new work, they'll pull out things and just throw them on the floor and stick 'em up on the wall and they'll all be lying on each other and you'll say to them, is this how you wish them to be perceived by the public or when you show them?
And they'll say, oh no, we'll put them in proper frames and things, or sellotape them up on the wall, and they're immediately aware that you have to consider some kind of framing device for the work to refocus people's attention on it and I think that's what packaging becomes.
Some guy in advertising said something that product plus personality equals brand. I thought that was really cool. And I think maybe I try and apply that to what I do. So once the work is done, you then create a personality for it and hopefully, then it becomes a kind of Bowie-ism afterward.

"PRODUCT PLUS PERSONALITY EQUALS BRAND."

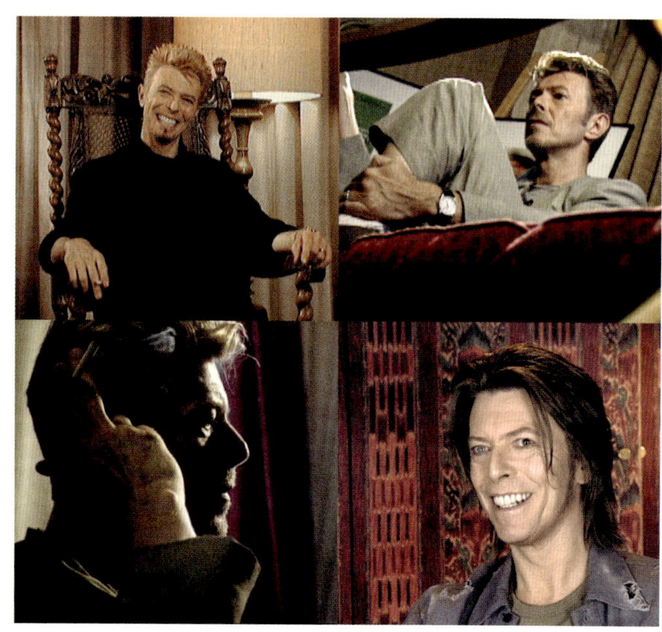

And what applies to music production can also be a productive approach in the fight against the climate crisis, Luisa Neubauer, main organizer of Fridays For Future in Germany, supports the synergies of "connecting the people."

LUISA NEUBAUER

We regularly try to question ourselves, which I think is quite helpful. We allow people to have a "say" in what we do, regardless of age. It sounds banal, but creative thoughts often come at the point where you're not stuck in a lot of "we've always done it this way" inevitabilities. And that means that all of our ideas come from people who have never done anything before and can therefore throw ideas into the room without reservation.
When you do and create extraordinary things that did not exist before, people then take it for granted that you don't need help. Help is always possible. There are always people who know more, do more, and have more thoughts and ideas than yourself. Often great ideas fail because you don't turn around at the right moment and ask for help, for an opinion, for an evaluation, take advantage of thinking in networks. How can we make a good idea even greater? Build a network and maybe ask someone from a totally different discipline. We have a great idea. How can we make it even better? Maybe engage with someone from a completely different field.

Connecting the dots.

Connecting the People.

"PEOPLE WHO HAD IN THEIR YOUTH TO PUT TOGETHER TWO DIFFERENT FRAMEWORKS TENDED TO BE VERY, VERY CREATIVE."

JOHN CLEESE

I wrote a couple of books with a psychiatrist about the mind in general. And what we felt about creativity was that people who had in their youth to put together two different frameworks tended to be very, very creative. And that sometimes meant if they had travelled a lot they had to put together where they like live this year, you live that year ... and you have two different frameworks or more that you have to try to integrate and make sense of, and if you have two identical parents with a very, very similar "AHH," you know what I mean, then you are not likely to be so creative. And if you live in a community that is very, very conformist then you don't have different frameworks that you have to put together, just one framework and then people that do not belong together tend to be less creative.

The brothers Dardenne are a congenial directorial duo. So I asked them how One Plus One Equals Three relates to their way of working:

LUC DARDENNE

Maybe one plus one equals three, that's the dialectic. Yes, but sometimes also minus two, minus three even. It all depends on the moment. But in fact: we are the same and we are different, so naturally we produce more than two, at least I hope so. I hope that in the end it's someone else who ends up making the film, that is—that it's a result of exchange. We discuss a lot, we talk a lot, but there is an intuition that unites us and keeps us together when we work. An intuition that made it possible for us to work. We make the same film thanks to the fact that we talked so much. This fact that we have talked so much gives us a common intuition, or we create it at the same time, I don't know. In any case, there is something in common that allows us at a given moment, during a shoot, when one says, "I can't be there, I'm sick," that the other then continues the film for the three days when the other is sick. And yes—we then, before making the film, felt, rehearsed, and wrote things in such a same way that everything works like that.

ISABELLA ROSSELLINI

The scenes that you did with Dennis Hopper in *Blue Velvet* are so remarkable, you know … you two—one plus one equals three, you know, perfect.

Yeah, that's why it's so great to work with films you know. And I have to say, even when I direct my own films, they're not only mine. I share them with the other people that I work with. Because one plus one does make three. Or four or five If you select the right people. You know, David's films are enhanced by the actors and I'm really glad to be one of them, they are enhanced by the music, by the cinematographer, by the scenes, the sets, the costumes. With my film, my little *Green Porno*, I owe so much to Andy Byers and Rick Gilbert, who created the costumes. I gave hints of what I wanted, but they created so much more. And then I said to the cinematographer: "I don't know anything about technology. But Georges Méliès's films make me laugh. I don't wanna deal with camera moves and editing. So let's do film like Méliès." And Sam Levy, my cinematographer, understood completely.

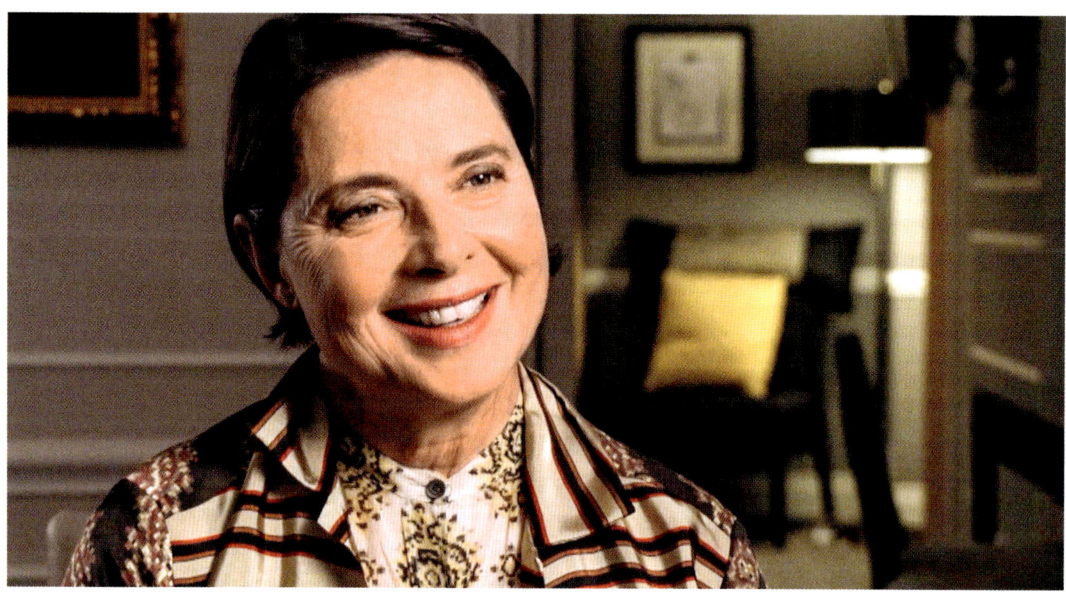

MARINA ABRAMOVIĆ

Eisenstein said basically one plus one equals three to bring two things two together to create a third. You brought together your performance art and the art of Maria Callas.

If someone would have said to me five or ten years ago that I would do an opera, I would have replied, "Are you crazy?" I come from hardcore radical performance art. But then I became interested how to deconstruct opera. How to add performative elements, acting, film, singers, orchestra, and electronic music into that kind of structure to really create something that a young audience can relate to, not a classic old audience, and turn it into this new discipline. So, it was really the most creative moment this time of my life to do that.

So one plus one equals three or five.

Yeah, absolutely. You take one element, you mix it with another one, and you get many different outputs of that.

"YOU TAKE ONE ELEMENT, YOU MIX IT WITH ANOTHER ONE, AND YOU GET MANY DIFFERENT OUTPUTS OF THAT."

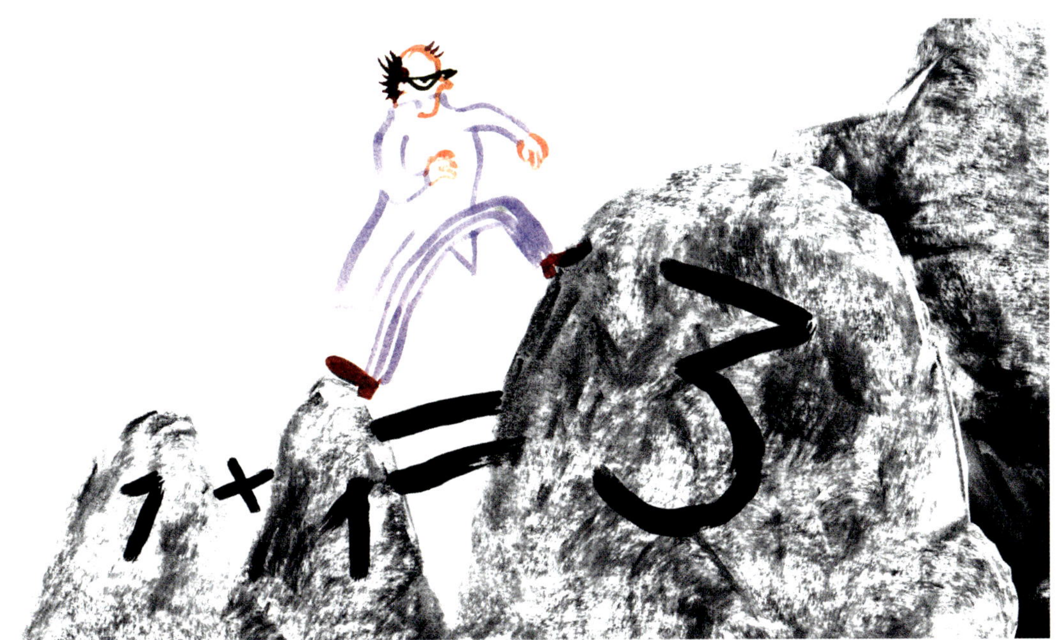

SHIRIN NESHAT

I see my work in some ways, so Western, so much grounded in art history of conceptual art and the whole history of self-portraiture. And, representation, identity issues, and the film work that I'm doing are so rooted in, let's say, Eastern European influences. From Kieslowski and Tarkovsky to people that I've been fascinated by. At the same time, my work is so truly rooted in Persian Islamic culture, and it's poetic and has kind of a mystical nature. I'm not really all Iranian, I'm not all American or Western, so I become this representation of what comes as a result of one plus one equals three, not two.

Malcolm McLaren determined the norm as the great enemy of creativity. After all, deviating from the norm was the tried and tested program for the pioneer of punk.

MALCOLM MCLAREN

Could your elaborate how you combined different elements in your work?

My projects, from the Sex Pistols through to managing other groups, such as Boy George or Adam and the Ants and Bow-Wow-Wow and thereafter. The most important point was always to come up with something that had confrontational abilities, and I think the way that happened for me was by making sure that everything I did had a degree of subversion to it. It had a degree of, I suppose, of style in order to sell it and hoping I was also able to make it very sexy. I think it's those three things which are like the three S's: sex, subversion, and style.

"THE THREE S'S OF SUCCESS: SEX, SUBVERSION, AND STYLE."

And if you had those three ingredients correct, then whatever interpretation was made, it would always work to your advantage because it was that juxtaposition, you call it, that provided, I think, its motivation for success.

If I take work that I've personally been involved with as an artist, then the interesting thing for me was to take those ingredients, say from a song like Madam Butterfly, and to transpose that into the context of a song that could ordinarily be played on a pop radio station as a brilliant ballad implying love and its tragedy. You have ingredients again for doing something that is on the whole subversive, because it's deconstructing culture that's been put into a precious box and spitting it out into another arena.

MIRE LEE

What did you think when the Schinkel Pavilion had the idea for an exhibition that brings together your work with that of *Alien* designer H.R. Giger?

I've known Giger's work since I was nine. Probably it was the first book my father ever gave to me. First art book that I've ever had. And I really love Ridley Scott's *Alien*. Wow. I really love the scene where in *Alien One*, it bursts out from your belly. It totally blew me away. Yeah, something very primal. A twist that is very cruel. Simple. Strong.

As a sculptor, I almost serve my sculptures. I labor a lot to make them exist. Liquid circulates the whole thing. I started to use water and then I started to use soft material right next to hard material. And then I saw it deforming because soft materials are being like pushed against the hard ones.

Soft and hard. You bring two things that do not belong to another to create a third?

Yes, definitely. Two things against one another. I love dichotomy, like two things that belong to a completely different direction, two different extremes. And you always get something just by putting them together in one place.
Yeah, material, people, situations. Whatever it is, it's exciting. You know, this, I really love it. Yeah.

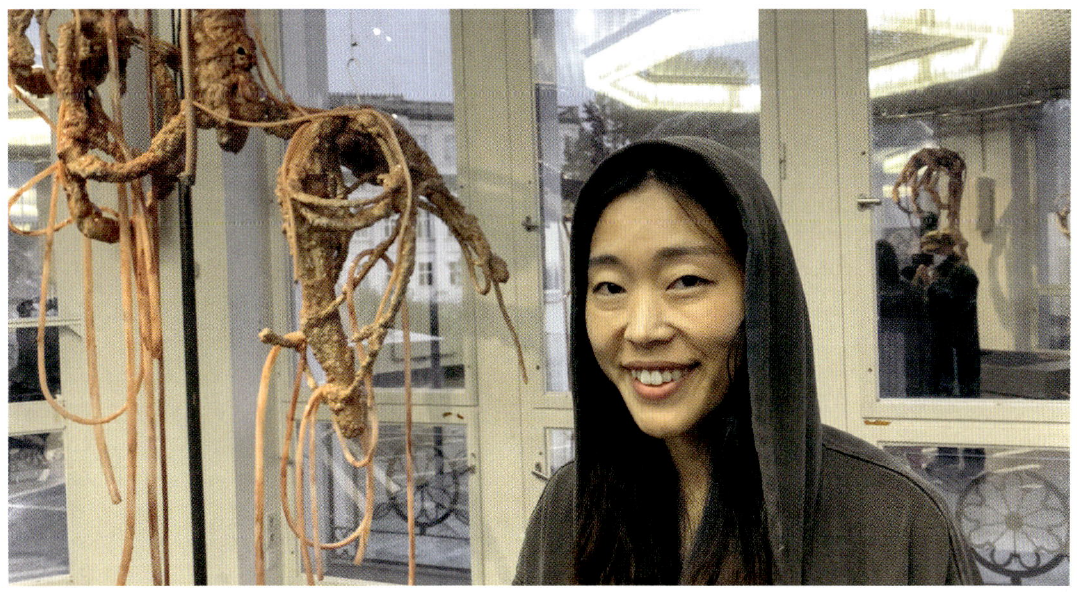

BRIAN NEWMAN

You brought two things together that do not necessarily belong together to create a third. What you did with Gaga and Tony Bennett is one of these things where you amazingly created a third. Does one plus one equal three?

Yeah, I think so. I mean, I think what we did with Tony and Gaga in a sense with the jazz standards that we did with them, we never really, I never really changed the formula from what I did with my own band since the 1990s, since 1999 I've been playing with my guys, and we built this style up where, you know, it's in your face but it's not that New York Swagger but it's still a jazz standard, it still has that timeless ability but it just has a little more like punch, a little more something else for, you know, for everyone. For the young kids, for adults, for every age group and I think that's important with jazz music, because you see it nowadays and it's faltering because so many people are playing for the audiences. They are playing for themselves or they are playing for certain cliques that hang out here in New York, or wherever that is, and I think it just needs to be more of a team and more of a, you know, we are trying to make jazz music. We're not trying to reinvent the wheel. It is just entertainment, you know.

PIERRE BOULEZ

Counter influences are very important for me. And you can't stay isolated only on your level.

Can you give an example of what you found in literature that you transferred to music?

Well, the poems of Mallarmé, influenced me a lot, not only by the sound of the words or by the meaning, because of course you have to understand what a poem means; but it was also the structure of Mallarmé, his sonnets especially, that influenced me a lot. And I transcribed that directly into the music, in a form that was exactly consistent with the structure. In painting, also, I have had very many influences from Klee, for example—and not only from the paintings themselves, but also from his teaching, his teaching at the Bauhaus. That was really very interesting to see, because he generally thinks widely enough to really have an influence over other art forms.

1+1=3

Actor Michael Douglas described the magic of One plus One equals Three in his answer. As we say nowadays "synergy." As we used to say "The whole is greater than the sum of the parts." And perhaps that in itself, is the best summary of creativity.

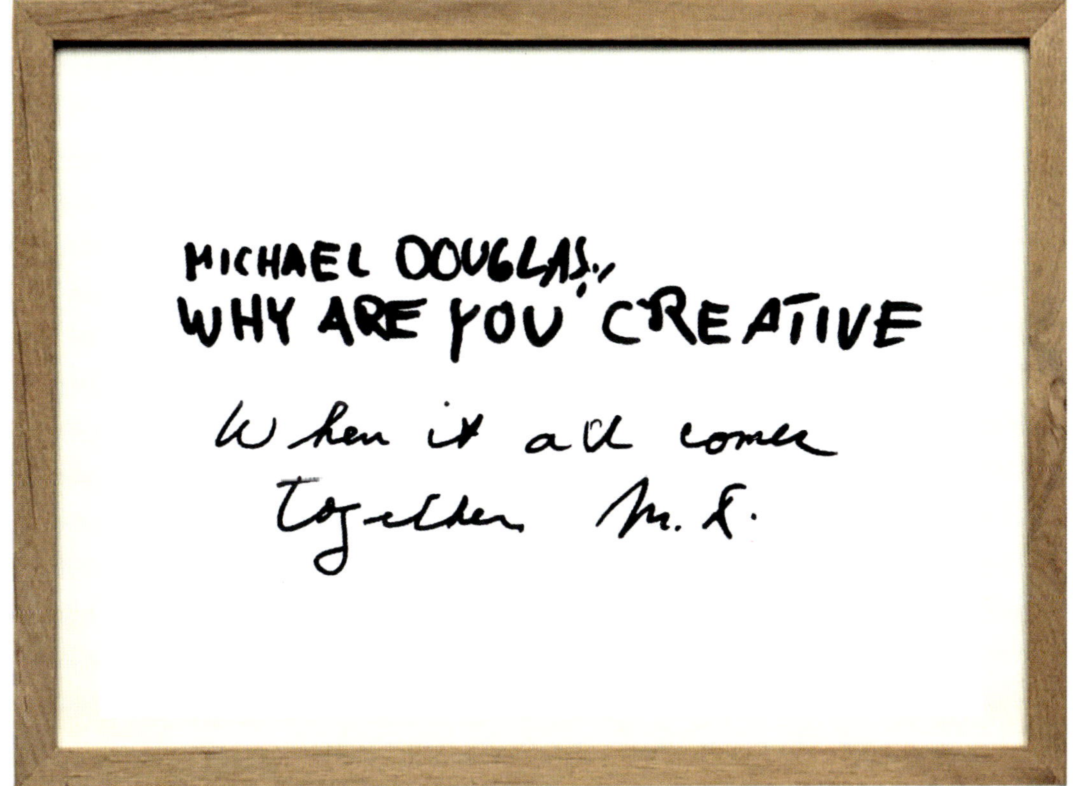

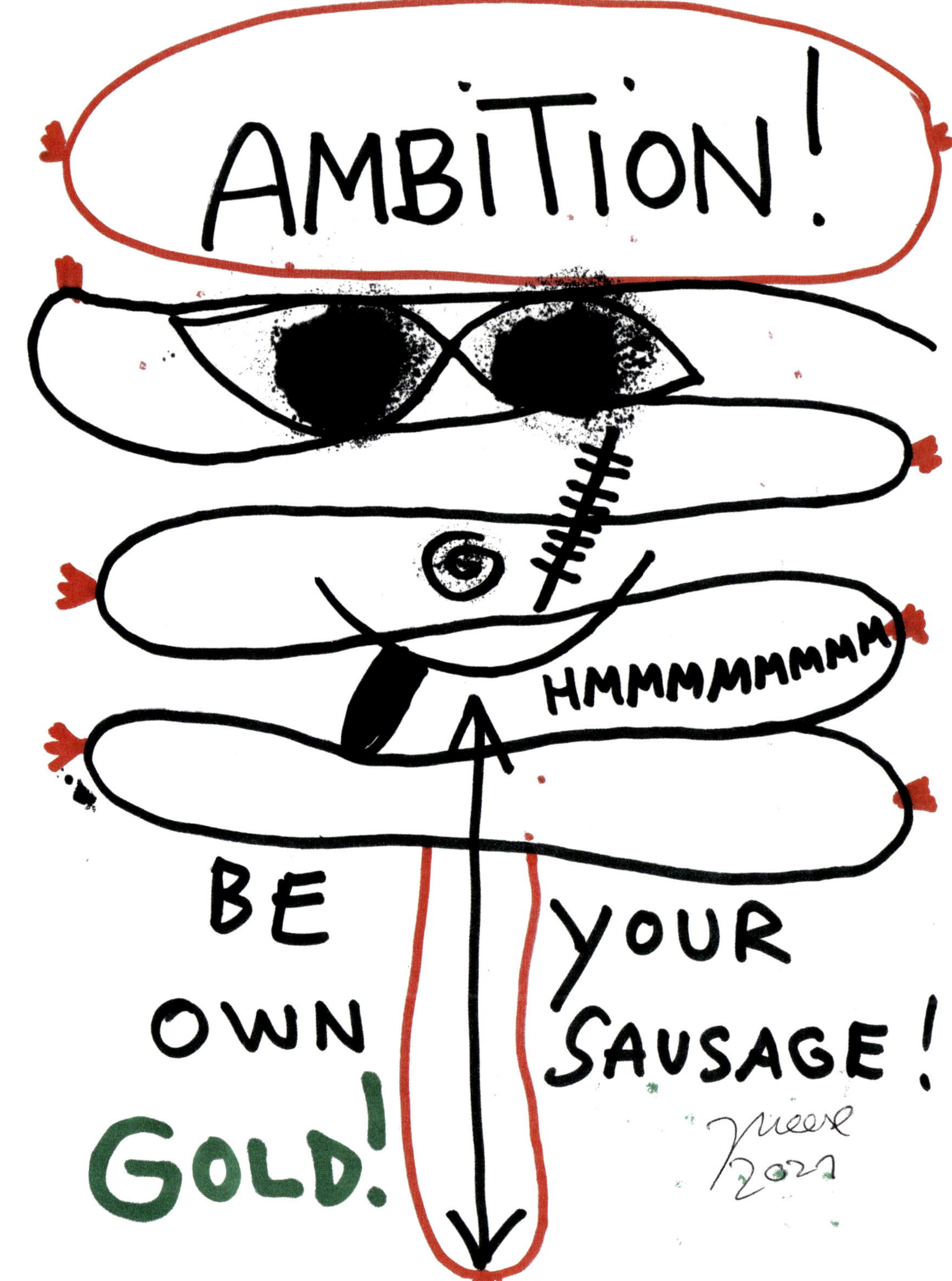

AMBITION!
HMMMMMMMM
BE
YOUR
OWN
SAUSAGE!
GOLD!
2021

Attempt the impossible. A lot of people believe that ambition is what drives us to be creative. Like a racehorse with blinkers, so it can't be distracted from its aim to win. Ambition drives us away from distraction to follow a path to powerful, single-minded achievement.

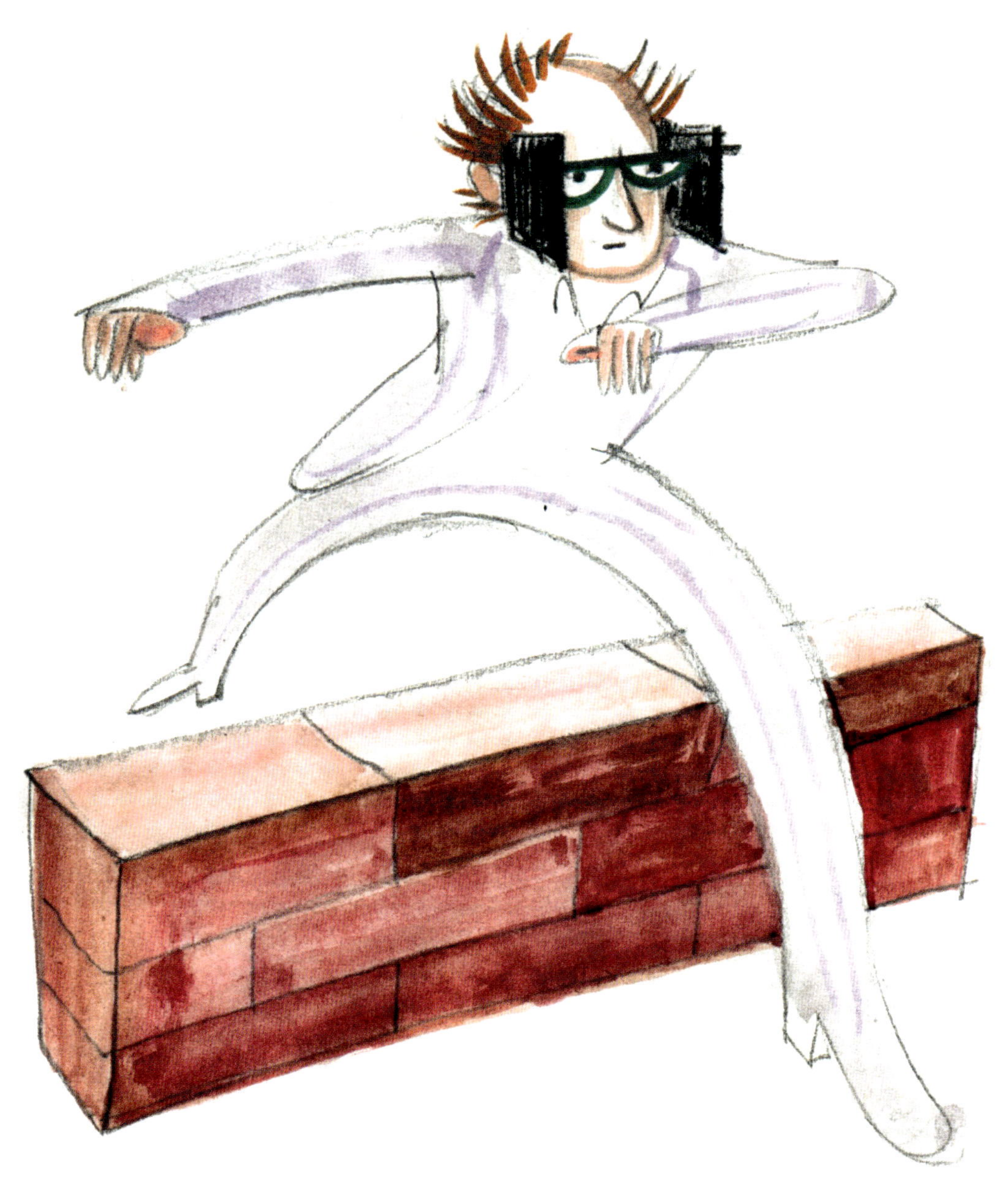

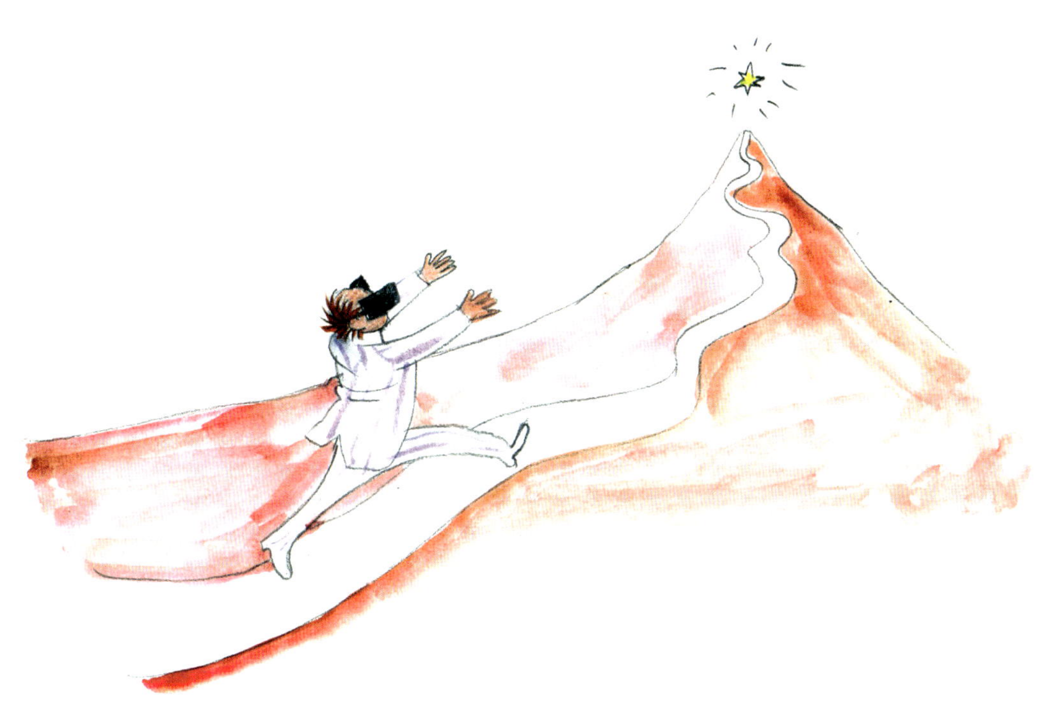

Paul Arden was the Creative Supremo of Saatchi and Saatchi when the agency was the most creative in the world. He then became a director and won countless awards. As an author, he wrote a bestseller with the beautiful title: *It's Not How Good You Are, It's How Good You Want to Be.* I went to Paul to ask him how we can become as good as we want to be.

PAUL ARDEN

I think that the better people are obsessive about what they do. And the truly great people have tunnel vision, they only see it their way in one way. And that's what makes them unique, because they close out everything peripheral, everything everyone else had to say, and they only go their way. I mean Carl Theodor Dreyer is a classic example. So you're thinking about your work all the time. Your vision of where and who you want to be is the greatest asset you have.

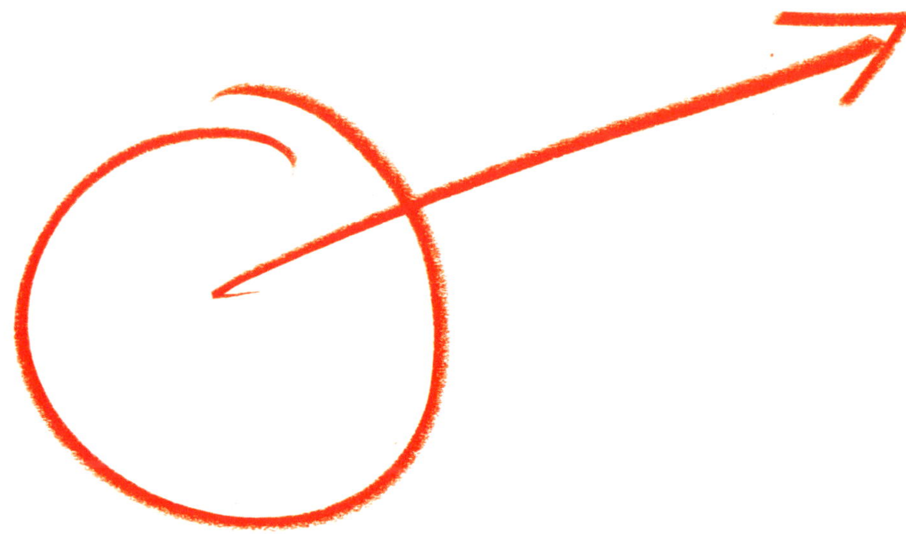

Let's stay in the world of commercials. In his ironic answer to the question, "Why Are You Creative?," Sir John Hegarty describes the ambition of an art director in the advertising world: "To use the typeface Franklin Gothic Extra Bold without making it look too bold is an ambition to be proud of and one that makes you attractive." John Hegarty has written a book titled *Hegarty on Creativity: There Are No Rules.* His ambitions are never in question. Except perhaps by him.

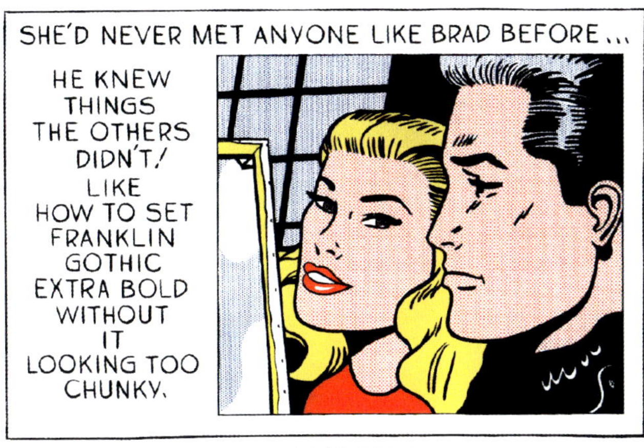

With apologies to ROY LICHTENSTEIN and MARVEL COMICS

SIR JOHN HEGARTY

Tell us about your ambition.

I get terribly disappointed when something isn't as good as I think it could be. I get terribly depressed. And it's got to be much, much better. We've got to kind of somehow improve standards. We've got to do that without really being compared to anybody else. I think we've got to set our own standards.

OSCAR NIEMEYER

When Brasilia began, it seemed that a better time had dawned for all Brazilians. I remember, workers ran from all corners of Brazil to help build Brasilia. I remember people were driving on dirt roads and the trucks were full of workers coming from other states. That was a hope. Brasilia was built and they remained poorer than before. Months before I had a meeting with students, I said to them that when life deteriorates and hope disappears from people's hearts, only revolution helps. They clapped enthusiastically. The following day they went to the beach. What is missing is the knowledge, the will, the ambition to make things better.

Ed Ruscha is one of the most important representatives of the West Coast art movement. His works, with their roots in commercial art and billboards, are iconic images which have created the topography of Los Angeles.

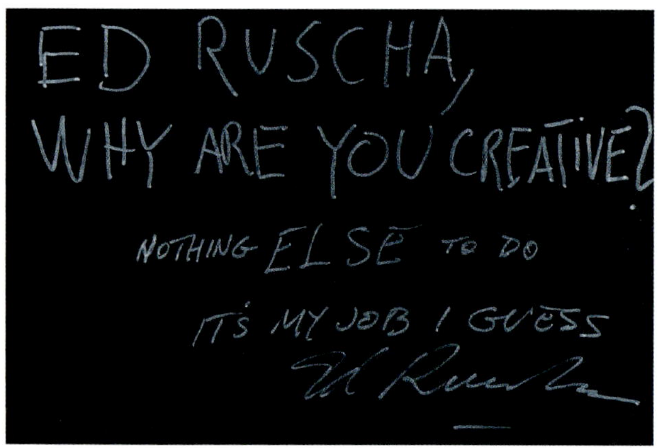

ED RUSCHA

That's a good one that can almost never be answered. I don't know, it's just like putting things together, putting two or more things together that don't usually go together. It's like a boxing match or something. And also at the same time these people that you're sparring with, these people that are your opponents are also people that you want to impress. You know. You want their respect. So having the respect of other artists was a prime motivating reason to be an artist. It certainly wasn't to make a living. I mean, we never had that. Today is much different. Today, I mean the artist, there are more artists making a living today than there ever was, I think.

"SO HAVING THE RESPECT OF OTHER ARTISTS WAS A PRIME MOTIVATING REASON TO BE AN ARTIST."

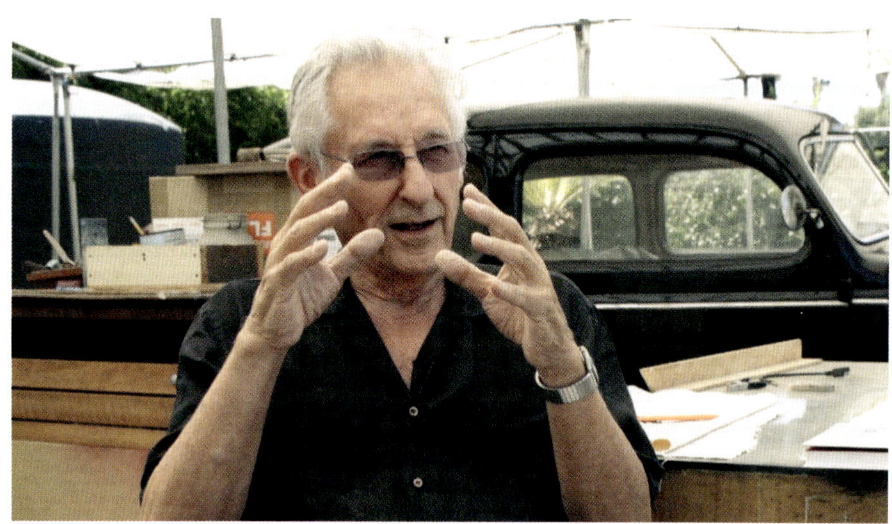

"I WAS ABLE TO DO SOMETHING, WHICH OTHERS DIDN'T DARE TO DO."

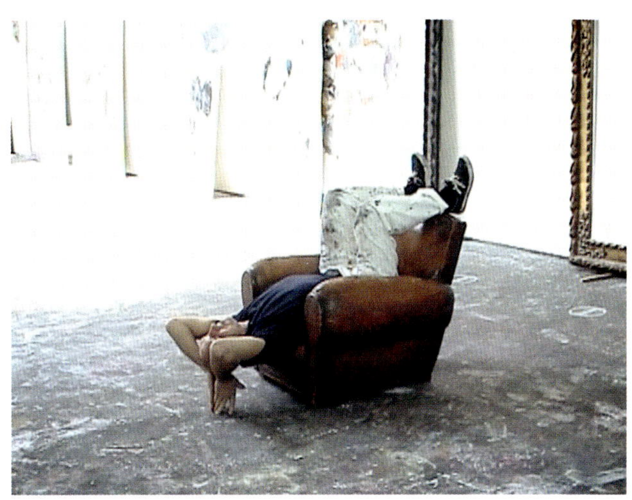

Painter Georg Baselitz is famous for creating upside-down paintings. I turned his world upside-down by asking him: "Why are you creative?"

GEORG BASELITZ

You take me by surprise! When I started out, I didn't think about what it meant to be creative. That was many years ago. It had something to do with showing off. I was able to do something, which others didn't dare to do. And it still remains that way.

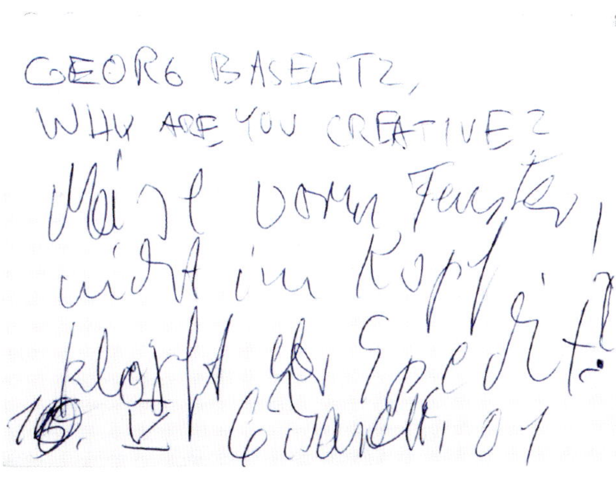

I went down to Geneva to meet with solar flight pioneers Bertrand Piccard and André Borschberg. They were the first men who flew around the world with their solar airplane, Solar Impulse One, which is totally powered by solar energy.

ANDRÉ BORSCHBERG

The mission to fly around the world is a very clear mission. There is no discussion about it. If you want to succeed in the relationship, I think you should not try to be the best, you should try to help the other one to be the best and then the other one will do it also for you.

BERTRAND PICCARD

We are creative when we have a goal.
And our goal is to fly around the world in
our Solar Impulse Airplane.

There will always be people like Piccard and Borschberg. The human pioneering spirit is based on ambition, curiosity, and self-confidence. Without a goal, you cannot score. Good isn't good enough. You have to have the will to push beyond that. Like award-winning director Mark Williams, who answered the question, "Why are you creative?" by highlighting the word "will" in his last name with a yellow magic marker.

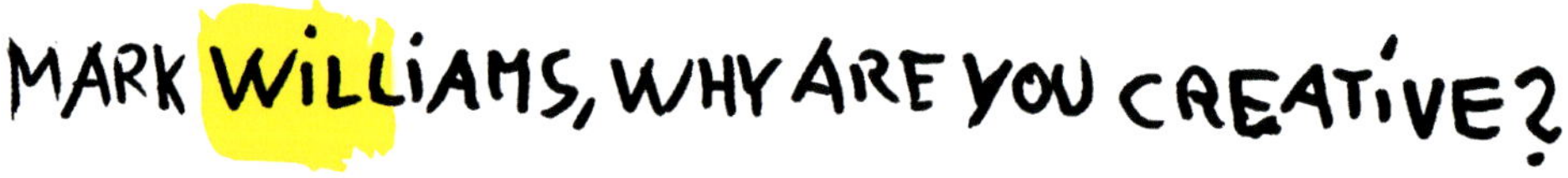

MARJANE SATRAPI

When I have to do a project, I wake up at a certain hour, I eat a certain thing, I do things at a certain time. Because when you have a project with so many people you cannot just go to sleep. … You have to be on all the time, and for that you have to be very, very strict. But then I also like to be completely distracted.

DENIS IVANOV

In Ukraine, we have our classical director, his name is Alexander Lukashenko and he is famous for saying that creativity is an act of will. And during the war, when you're denied your usual way of living, it's takes a lot of effort to still be able to do something, to still be focused on something and still find out what the mission is. It's a crash test for your will and your ideas.

Onward and upward. We meet mountain climber Reinhold Messner, who mentions Friedrich Nietzsche.

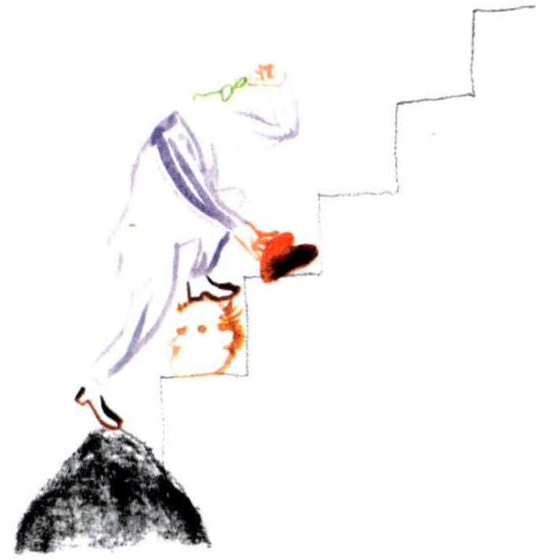

REINHOLD MESSNER

In *Zarathustra* Nietzsche claimed a human being that makes the highest possible demands upon himself and that keeps on climbing higher and higher. And if it's not possible for him to climb higher, he should climb on top of his own head.

In our interview some years ago you said: "Why not, if he can climb further that way?"

No, of course you can't climb onto your own head. You can do a handstand on a mountaintop, if you wish, but that's not necessary. Nietzsche's *Zarathustra* story is a strong mountain story because it uses the mountain as a metaphor for the whole, for the fact that humans can generally achieve self-determination.

For what you do, how important is ambition and willpower? How much ambition does it take to climb mountains and cross ice deserts?

I have a clear goal in mind and the goal is not the summit. So the normal alpinist or the layman from outside thinks that we are only climbing up there to reach the summit. In reality, the summit is only a turning point. When I'm talking about these walls, I go up anyway on this difficult route that I've come up with, on the so-called climbing route, and then I go down on an easy route that may have been climbed one hundred years ago. But if I climb the really big mountains, then of course going down is a problem again, then the summit is a kind of turning point. Before that I go up and then I go down, and I don't stay up there for long because I want to get back to safety.

For me, ambition is not necessarily a negative value. I know that in Europe it's viewed with more skepticism. In America, it's not. And it's not that way for me either. So I stand by the fact that I have ambitions, especially ambitions for myself.

The philosopher Arthur Schopenhauer concluded: "Will is more basic than thought in man and nature." He felt that great ideas are built on willpower and human strength. But when I met the philosopher Slavoj Žižek, he concluded that boredom is a great motivating factor.

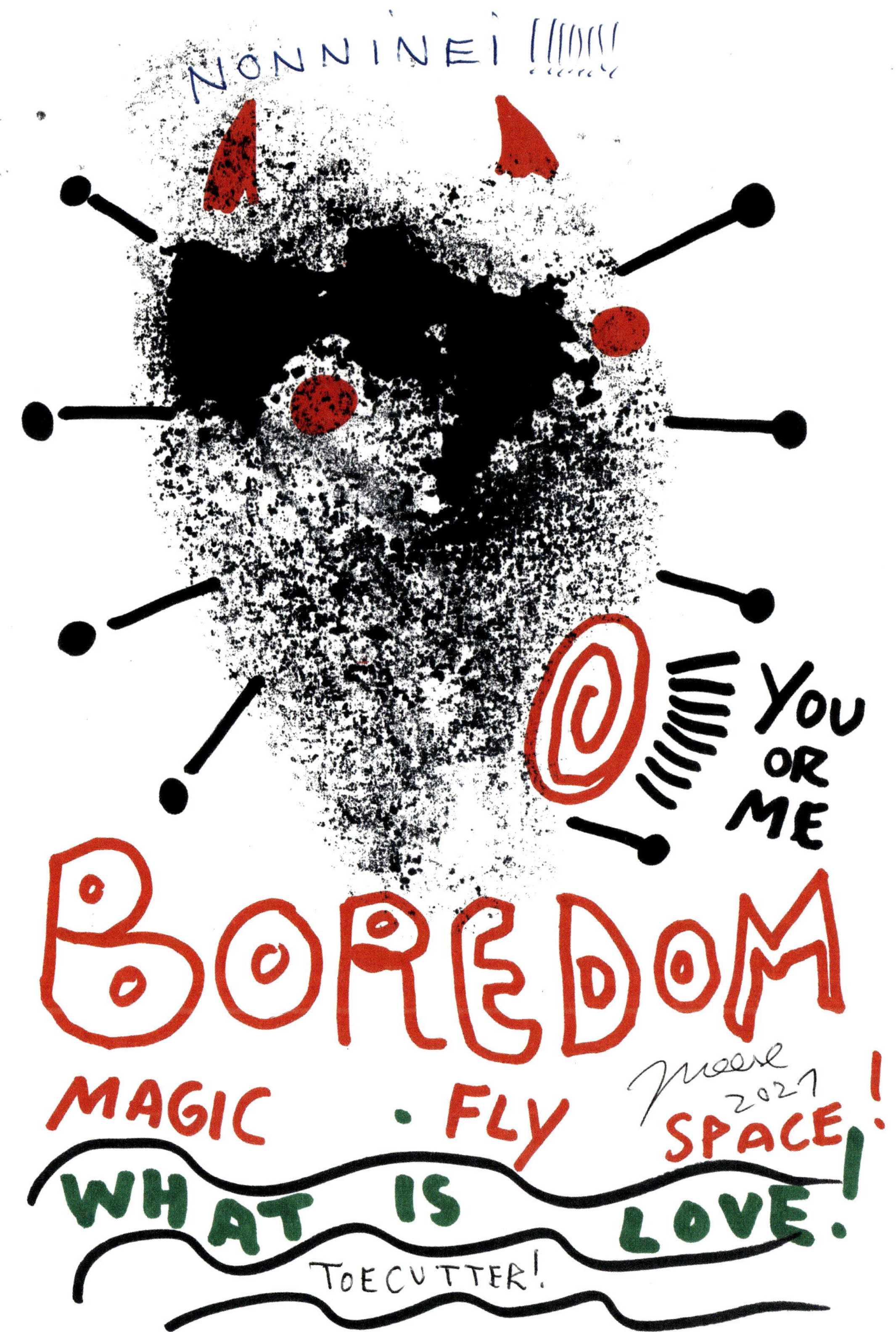
NONNINEI !!!!!!!
YOU
OR
ME
BOREDOM
MAGIC
. FLY
moore
2021
SPACE!
WHAT IS LOVE!
TOECUTTER!

It’s tedious to say that we all suffer from boredom. But don’t we? And is that a clue to why we do what we do? So, for some people, maybe creativity is a reaction against boredom.

LAURIE ANDERSON, WHY ARE YOU CREATIVE?
1) THE ALTERNATIVE IS WAY TOO BORING
2) I LIKE TO BREAK RULES
3) I LIKE TO LAUGH.
und so weiter

LAURIE ANDERSON

Why are you creative?

Why? It makes me laugh … that's really simple: it just makes me laugh, it makes me feel like I can change things … like I can change things.

The most efficient way to escape from boredom is to create: if only just to relieve the boredom of our humdrum lives. After all, they do say time flies when we are having fun.

SIR BOB GELDOF

I have a very low boredom threshold. And when I get bored, I get very depressed because I'm melancholic by disposition and I'm afraid of that state of being, so my mind just stops getting bored. Work, work, work. All the time thinking of things. All the time. And if it's not there then I must be reading things and it's frantic, it's frantic activity. It's not creativity and out of all the things I think of, out of all that frantic creativity, if I don't do something then it just blocks up my head. So out of all those things come all these extensions of the idea, which you make into reality. Maybe you try a hundred things and ninety-eight of them fail. That's me.

"TO BE CREATIVE, YOU HAVE TO WANT BOREDOM. YOU NEED BOREDOM."

Frédéric Beigbeder

KLAUS STAECK

One day, I realized that I grew up in a strict family. But soon, I realized that I saw things differently. My uncle Oswin was a photo freak. And whenever we visited Uncle Oswin, I dived into his bookshelves. And he had a couple of photographic magazines from the company Voigtländer. That magazine had a special section where amateur photographs by readers were published. One of these photographs showed a very tall man and a somehow smaller woman, and the man had a strikingly high skull. And the caption read, from a photographic standpoint, that that photo is not really interesting, but maybe from an anatomical one. I went around and showed it to everybody. Isn't that great? And nobody understood me. The photo was basically useless, but they presented it in order to put that caption. And suddenly, I realized what kind of people I wanted to have fun with and that I was different.

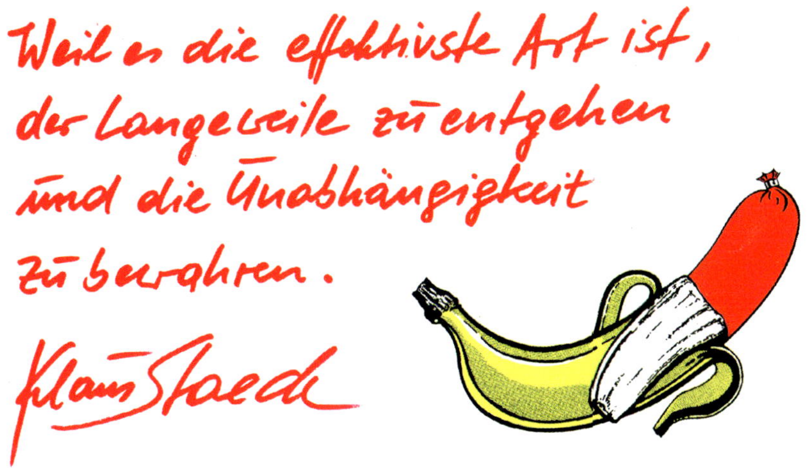

FRÉDÉRIC BEIGBEDER

I think to have ideas you have to live. You must not stay at home, you have to go out, you have to, and also, I often noticed that boredom is good for creativity. I think you have to stay alone in a silent and quiet place for a long time and suddenly you have ideas. I think what kills ideas is precisely the noise. When you are with too many people and too much noise it prevents you from thinking, it kills the thought. So I think you have to go out a lot, look at everything, and come back home and then get really, really bored, and then you might have an idea. It's the change of speed. Very speedy at first and then you slow down. And then you don't move. And when you don't move, first of all you think, "I'm going to die, it's terrible," you think of all your problems and then maybe you can have an idea.

Creativity is a reaction against boredom.

Yes, I think so. So, it means also that to be creative, you have to want boredom. You need boredom. Creativity is a reaction against it, so you need it. That's why I'm worried about the way we are living now. Because everybody wants to escape from boredom, all the time. Going to the cinema, listening to music, reading, playing with the PlayStation, making telephone calls all the time, just to escape boredom. But boredom is necessary, boredom is important. Boredom is creative.

Slavoj Žižek is the pop star among philosophers. Žižek owes his creativity to the political realities in Eastern Europe, and he gave me the clues to how boredom can be used for creativity.

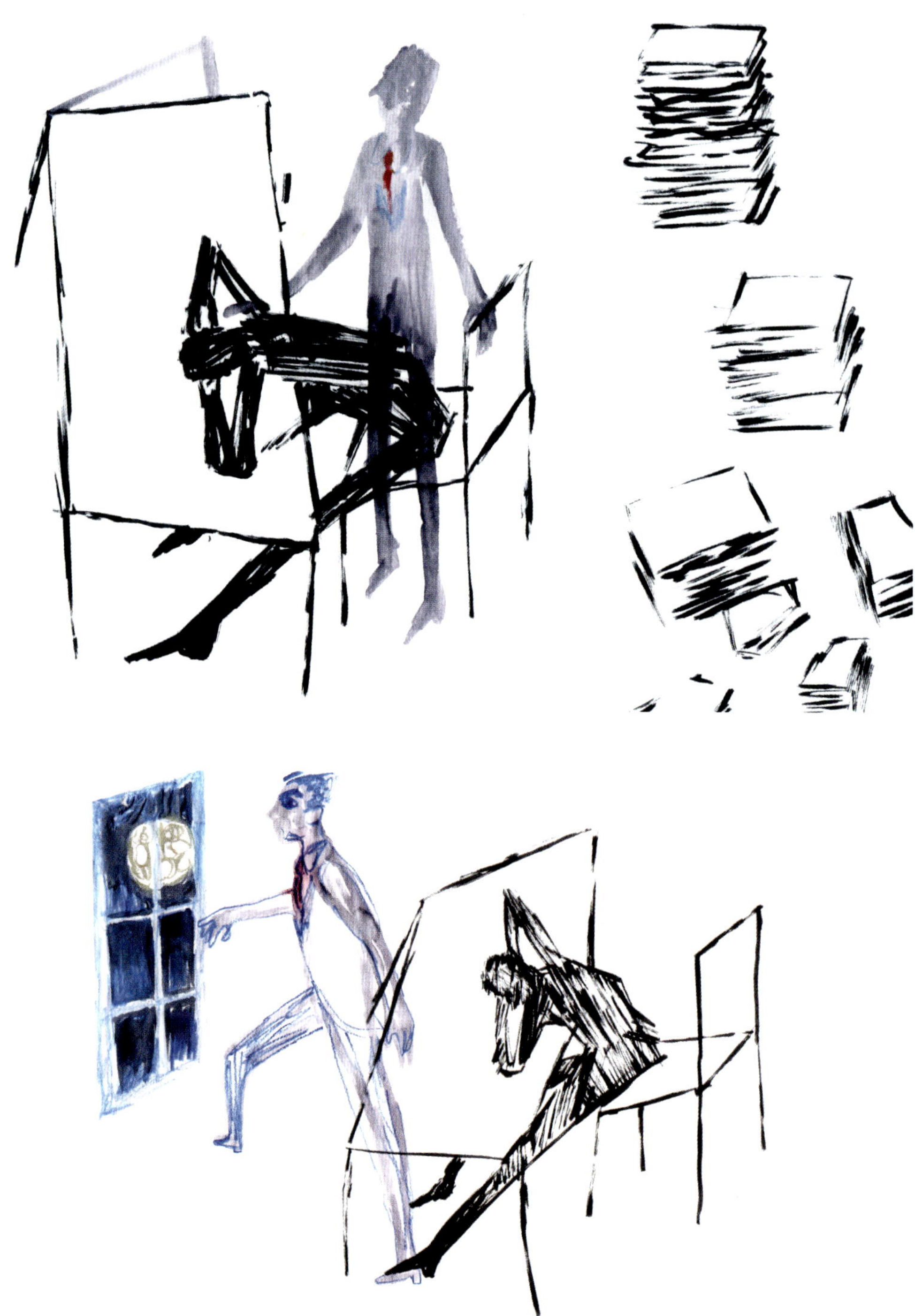

SLAVOJ ŽIŽEK

Why are you creative?

No deeper thing, because I was happy. The greatest, my greatest gratitude, of course this is meant ironically, is to ex-communists, you know why? Because in 1973, after I finished my postgraduate, my masters, this was the last Indian summer of hard-line communism, so I wasn't allowed to teach, so for four, five years I was unemployed, but they put me in a research institute. I am there now. And then I was pushed, myself I decided to start to get contacts abroad and so on and so on. So if you were to ask me, and this is literally true, not some kind of a metaphoric provocation, exaggeration, if you ask me where would I have been without communist operation today, I would have been an unknown stupid professor in this city, Ljubljana. The irony of history. This is what Hegel called *List der Vernunft*, probably.

You know, my notion of creativity is not what people usually think precisely that Balkan cliché, some crazy artists who provoke. Creativity is for me something deeply connected with boring administrative work. Like did you notice how many great, great people, and by great I mean great great great, poets or writers were banking administrators or whatever. To say that in English, Kafka's legal writings, you have that in German, his report to that workers' insurance company that he worked, my god, it's formidable. All of Kafka is there. My idea is that one hundred years from now, Kafka should be redefined. Everyone should read Kafka's great legal theories. In his free times he also wrote some important books or whatever, literature. T.S. Elliott worked in a bank. My god, you will be surprised how precisely some great poets apparently had the most boring bureaucratic jobs.

"CREATIVITY IS FOR ME SOMETHING DEEPLY CONNECTED WITH BORING ADMINISTRATIVE WORK."

And Bukowski was a postman.

Because you know, we are all creative, maybe even too creative. In the sense of exploding with crazy ideas. The problem is to put these ideas into form. True creativity is order. Every idiot can have explosions of genuine madness, I don't care about that. The problem is order afterward. Creativity is not about great ideas, it's about the hard patient work of putting it into form.

Can creativity motivate us to find out what's going on behind the walls of boredom and, as Jim Morrison used to say, motivate us to break on through to the other side? I talked to Asian-American film pioneer Wayne Wang, who immigrated to the Bay Area from Hong Kong when he was eighteen.

WAYNE WANG

My family is basically very boring, so to speak, very middle class. And I grew up always trying to be different from that, I think. I was always trying to understand what else is going on—maybe what are the secrets, what are the mysteries behind this sort of boring façade? I think that's the main reason why I am creative. I was left alone as a kid a lot with my grandmother, you know, who was always sticking things up her ass because she couldn't go to the bathroom. And I think that was the beginning. She was very religious. She was always listening to the radio, religious programs and I didn't know what that was. I was always trying to understand something more beyond just this very wholesome middle-class background family that I grew up in.

"WHAT ARE THE MYSTERIES BEHIND THIS SORT OF BORING FAÇADE? I THINK THAT'S THE MAIN REASON WHY I AM CREATIVE."

I met Lee Clow, the communications guru in charge and creative partner of Steve Jobs in Venice Beach. Lee, whose credits include Ridley Scott's legendary 1984 Apple Macintosh Superbowl Commercial answered the question, "Why are you creative?" with a drawing:

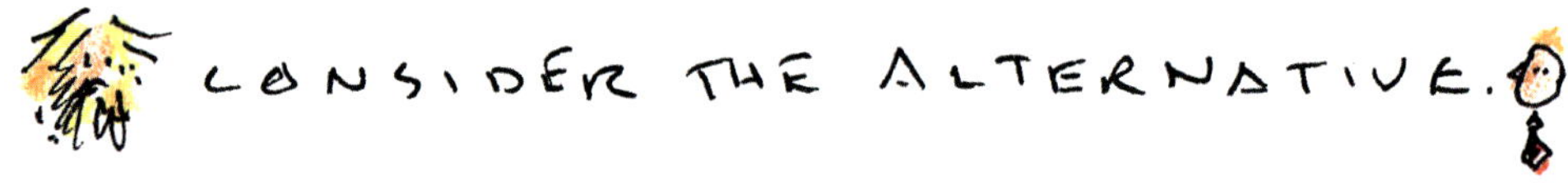

LEE CLOW

I have now been in this business long enough that being around the people who don't want to approach whatever their job is creatively is just empty and hollow to me. It appears to be the most unhappy way to go through life. To not be approaching what you've got to do every day creatively and with the idea that there's a way to do it better or smarter or different or more fun? The alternative sucks.

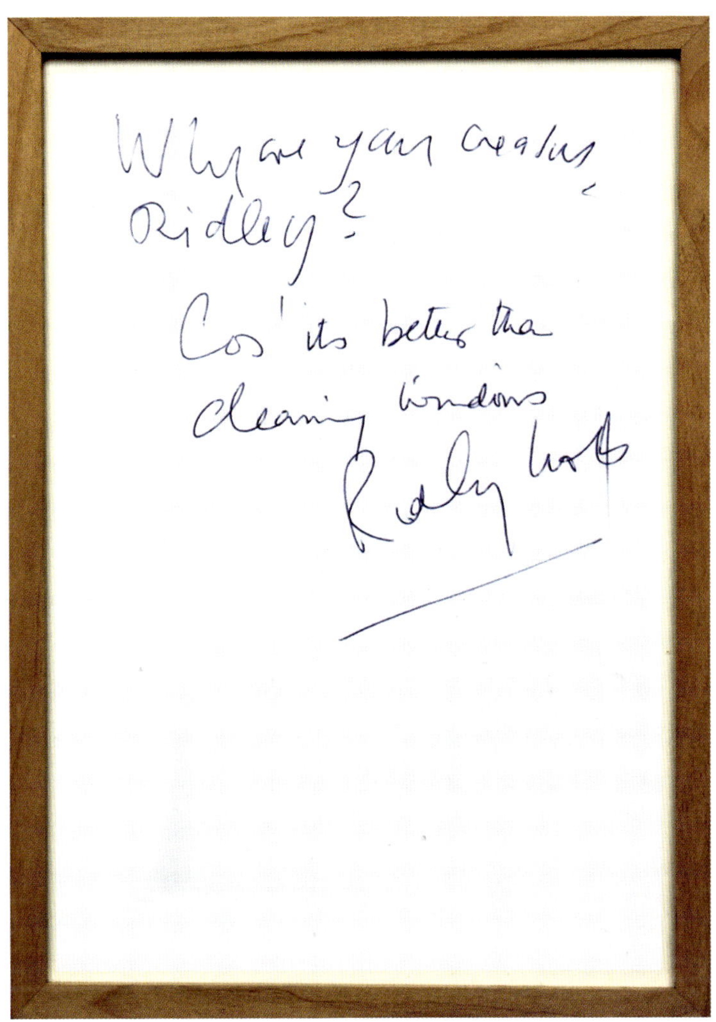

RIDLEY SCOTT

What should an idea have for you to get involved?

I take ideas on from advertising for the same reason I take on a film. The nut, the idea, the encapsulation, whether it's a film or a commercial, is very important.
And very often my interest will be got simply by a phrase in terms of what the film is about. Like, someone said to me, "Well, this is going to take place in the Roman Empire at the German front and ending up in Rome." That was enough. I was immediately interested in what was to become "Gladiator." And what came second was, "Oh, what's the story?" But it doesn't always happen that way. Normally, it's all about story, story, story. And at the end of the day, it has to be about story … well great stories and great characters.

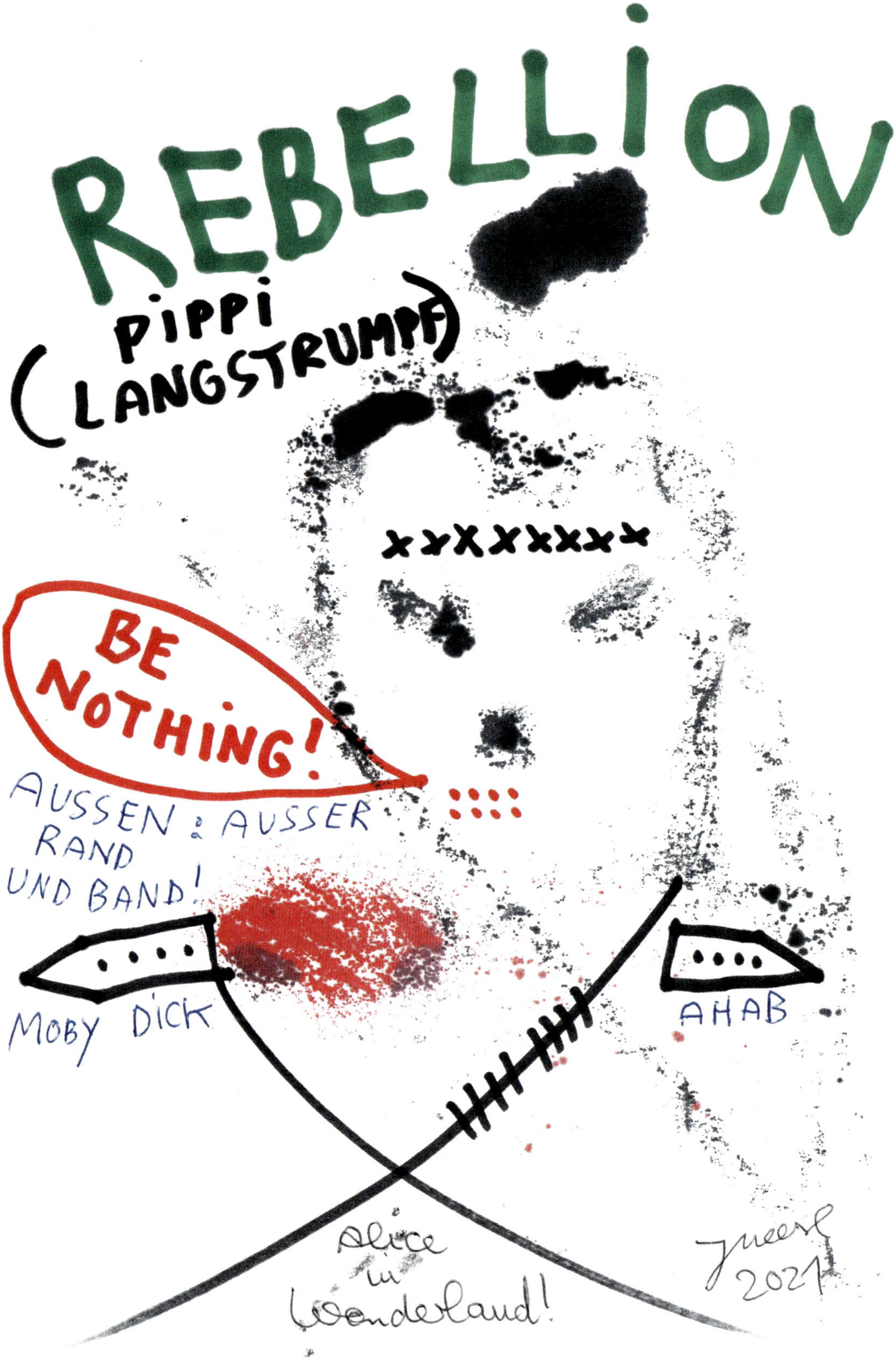

REBELLION

PIPPI
(LANGSTRUMPF)

BE
NOTHING!

AUSSEN & AUSSER
RAND
UND BAND!

MOBY DICK

AHAB

Alice
in
Wonderland!

2021

Convention is the enemy of creativity. To rebel. To break the rules. To do what you're told not to. Anger is an energy, as John Lydon from Sex Pistols and Public Image Ltd used to say. Like the French Nouvelle Vague and Italian Neorealism, rebelling against the restrictions of Hollywood—or any activist rebelling against the restrictions of totalitarian regimes and censorship—or indeed any artist rebelling against the formal constraints of what we call acceptable art. Is the need to rebel an irresistible urge that forces creativity on certain people?

T.C. BOYLE

Look at rock n' roll music, you know, rock n' roll … some angry guys or girls living in some industrial town decide: hey, fuck everything, let's have a band. And they present themselves, and they do it and it's delightful and it's great and it's revolutionary. For instance, you know, the evil empire of the Soviet Union in the past, before the wall fell, well, it was brought down by rock n' roll, you know, in large part.

I talked to Masha from Pussy Riot in front of the very church where Pussy Riot started their rebellious creative journey. After Russia attacked Ukraine, Masha undertook a spectacular and daring creative escape from her house arrest, on which she finally reached Lithuania. The chilling stuff of spy thrillers, if only it wasn't so horrifyingly real.

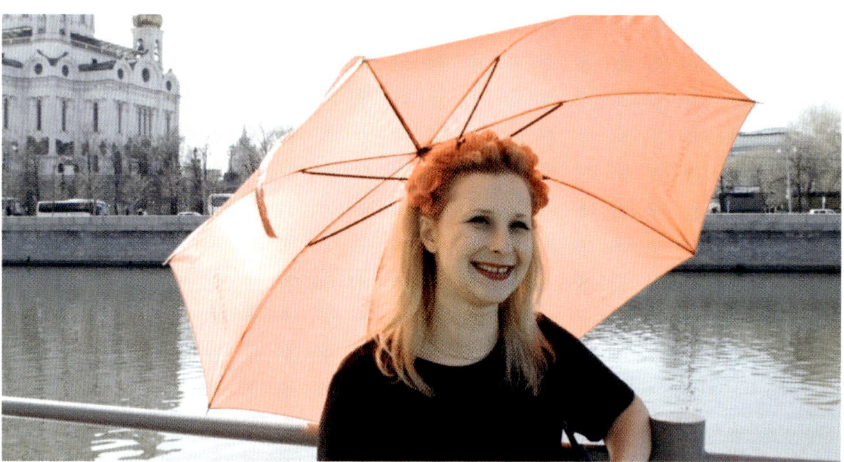

MASHA ALYOKHINA

We're fighting against hypocrisy, and hypocrisy has a lot of faces. And our government always produces new ones. So, they're killing people in the center of Moscow. They started two wars. They occupy all the media and all those people are totally corrupt and dishonest. Of course, our protest was planned. You cannot do something spontaneous with these actions. You need to spend a month of preparing for a single day of protest, because when you're going somewhere, you don't have time. You have about one minute,usually less. So, you have to be ready. You have to. … Because you will not have a second chance.

"WE'RE FIGHTING AGAINST HYPOCRISY."

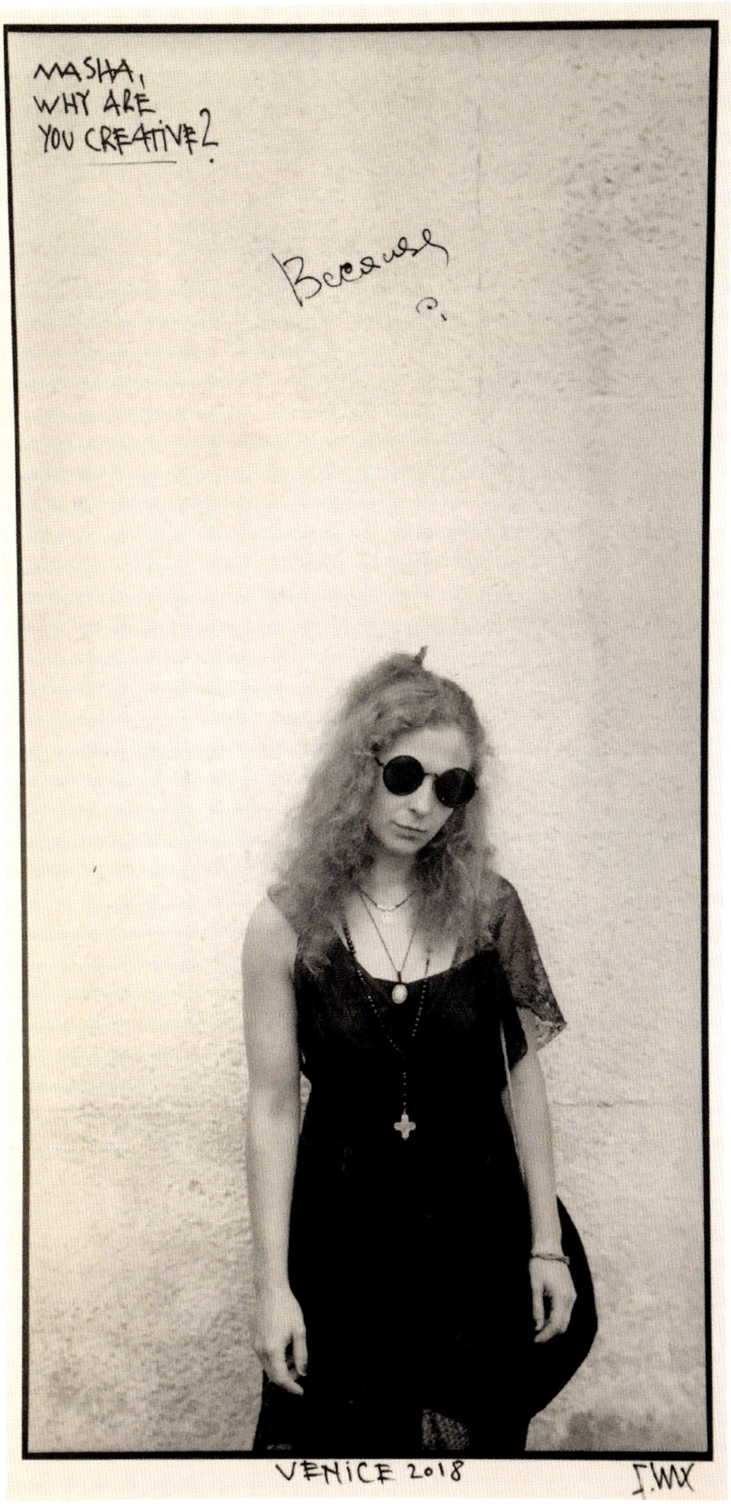
MASHA,
WHY ARE
YOU CREATIVE?
Because
VENICE 2018

Nadja,
why are you creative?
(!) RIOT.
Nadya

NADESCHDA TOLOKONNIKOVA

Who and what is killing ideas? Why are people not creative?

All sorts of fun stoppers. And you know, mostly cops are doing it and governments are doing it because they're afraid of change. So I am just trying to … recreate what has happened in 1968 and imagine what does it mean today in 2017. You cannot make political changes without that spirit, because otherwise it is made from politics that we got today and that brought us Donald Trump and other European fascist politicians who are coming up, because you need to make political changes with passion and love.

"I AM JUST TRYING TO ... RECREATE WHAT HAS HAPPENED IN 1968."

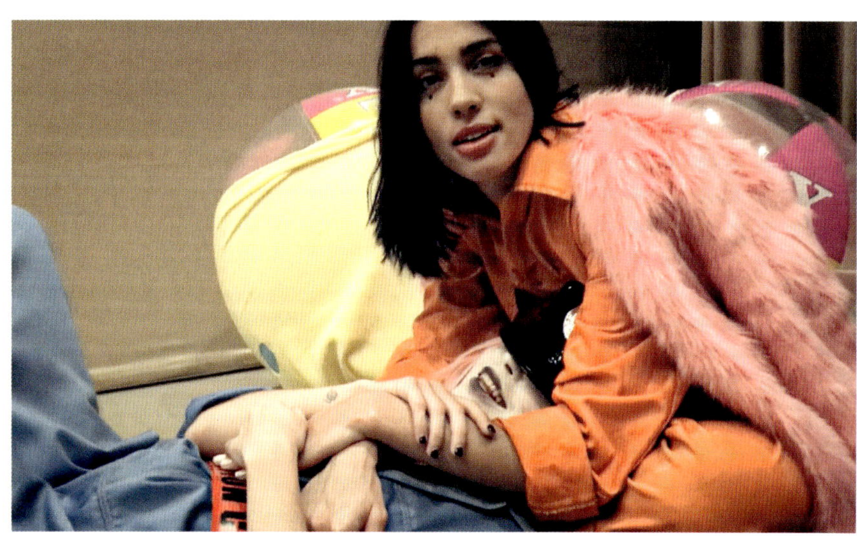

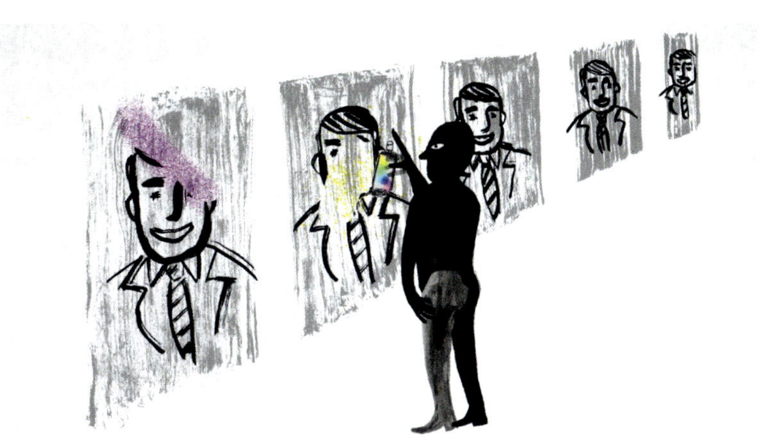

PETER VERZILOV

We originated as artists from the school of Moscow Conceptualists. There was this movement in the 1960s and the 1970s and the 1980s. And they basically produced a method to tackle various questions. The early conceptualists in the 1970s and 1980s, under Soviet times, they were mostly working with existential matters, matters of personal freedom, etc. … Whereas, in our case, since the time has drastically changed, we tackle various political issues with the use of creativity and art.

"WE TACKLE VARIOUS POLITICAL ISSUES WITH THE USE OF CREATIVITY AND ART."

In a chaotic and totally unexpected way, Peter Verzilov and members of Pussy Riot, dressed as policemen, stormed the pitch of the Croatia vs. France World Cup final.

PETER VERZILOV

We said that the World Cup was a period when the Russian police were told to behave much nicer than they usually do, try to abide the law, and at the same time this led to such a big international event as the World Cup, to kind of forget about serious political matters that were happening and affecting Russia. So, since we wanted to connect these two, we developed an action which should both be embedded in the events of the World Cup and have important statements of its own.

Pussy Riot used a globally broadcast event to gain worldwide attention. In doing so, they drew political grievances out of the shadows of repression and into the the glare of the floodlights. It was an offensive but effective tactic. And for New York director and artist Shirin Neshat, creativity can also take a combative form.

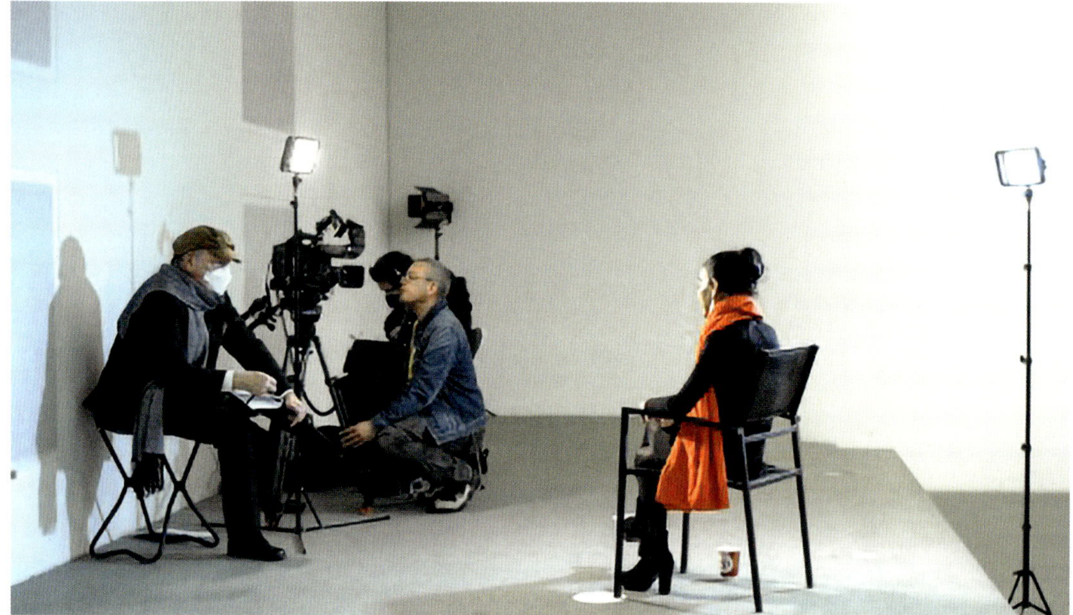

SHIRIN NESHAT

My story as an Iranian woman and my personal circumstances and emotions and political to psychological states have constituted my approach to art. How you can—with absolute poverty of possibilities—make magic happen. We take pain into a weapon. And that's really positive. A weapon for change, not a weapon to destroy. But a weapon to resist and talk back to tyranny.

The creative is often also the innovative—new, unfamiliar, but also alienating, unfamiliar, and unpleasant. Confronted with the unfamiliar, art opens up new vantage points while equally challenging the old. Questioning the status quo is a creative act that turns the familiar and comfortable on its head. In her socially critical novel *The Hate U Give* Angie Thomas addresses social inequalities in the U.S. in an original narrative voice influenced by the rhythms of hip-hop. And perhaps it is precisely the provocative that gives artistic expression a particularly effective voice.

ANGIE THOMAS

Is creativity, also for you, a motor for rebellion?

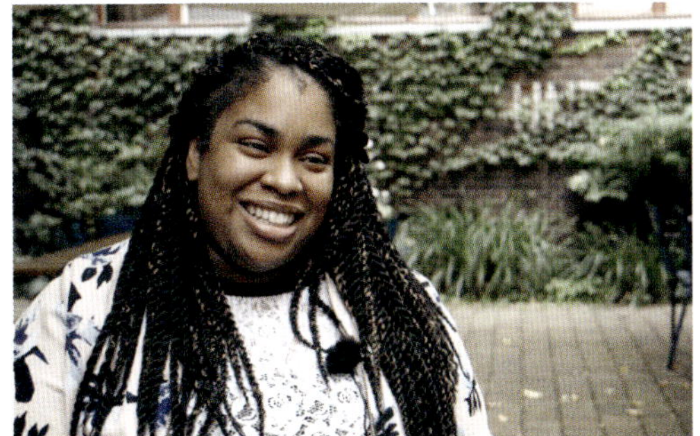

I would say more so a form of activism. But yeah, that is a form of rebellion too. If it makes someone uncomfortable, I'm okay with that. I think true change comes in discomfort. I was angry. And I still have anger about these things because it feels as if black lives don't have any value to some people. Black lives don't hold value in my justice system. Just yesterday another cop in Saint Louis was found not guilty of murdering a black man who he said beforehand he was going to kill. So there's evidence right there that he had intentions to kill this man, but he's found not guilty. So where is the value on my life? It angers me that someone whose salary is paid for with my taxes has the right to kill me and get away with it. And that hurts. Anytime someone speaks up for me, they are seen as the antagonist. Like, Dr. King is up there now and untouchable, but when he was alive, they considered him an enemy of the government. So that's the pain that you have to carry with you as a black American, then and now. And seeing these young men lose their lives and young women lose their lives, it just makes it even worse and it reminds me once again that my country doesn't look after my best interests.

KANIKA FEASTER-GORDON

The only way that I could take out my frustration and anger and hate, really, was to put my words to music. I rebelled to the words of the song: "Who's gonna stop it? Police must stop it. But we, the people, gonna stop it, this is how We're gonna stand up, speak outProtest in the streets as we shout out."

There are some people who use their creativity … for good. And others who use it … for negative. And so, for me, I use my voice, my creativity, and my passions to hopefully tell the story of what's going on, right in my backyard, here in Baltimore, Maryland.

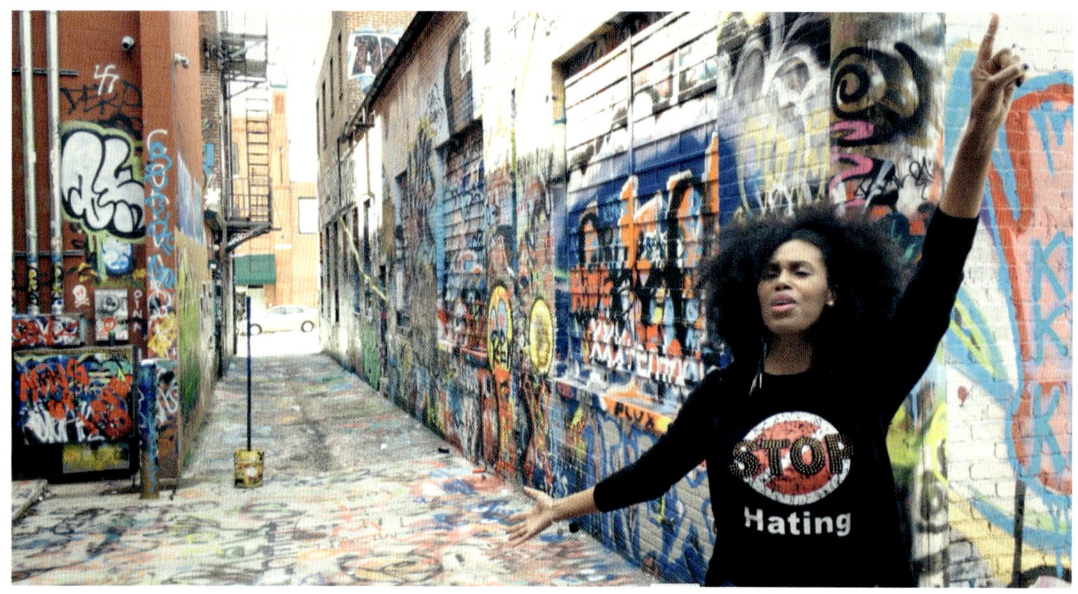

AI WEIWEI

That's kind of normal, if you're in certain society. If you break the rules, if you frighten the foundations of the society, you become very dangerous. Because the establishment means a lot to most people. And that seems to mean that your ideas can be very dangerous. As a result, I was being put in prison. Which actually, I do understand. If they don't stop someone like me, the change will come. And my condition in that cell is very restrictive, a horrible experience, I should say. But still, compared to many people who spent a much, much longer time without any kind of recognition, no voice, nobody even cares, forgotten about. I mean, their situation must be worse than mine. Provocation is kind of like an announcement. It's the nature of art. If it has a new meaning, it's always provocative. Always, in any society, in religious art, in conceptual art, in surrealism, Dada. It's always provocative. It only becomes relevant while it's provocative. Otherwise, it's just decoration or trying to bring some comfort to certain types of emotions. But for me it's very normal. It's absolutely a natural act.

"IF THEY DON'T STOP SOMEONE LIKE ME, THE CHANGE WILL COME."

You have to draw the line somewhere: Ai Weiwei answers the question, "Why are you creative?"

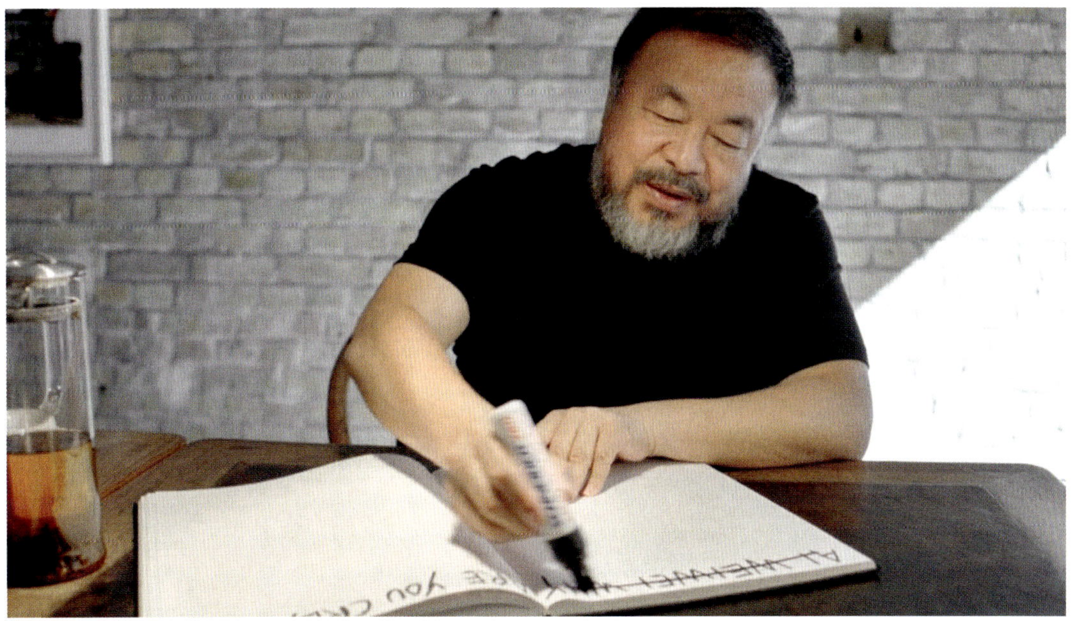

FRÉDÉRIC BEIGBEDER

Like Johnny Rotten, my creativity is a kind of anger. All my books are about different kind of disasters in my life. I did a book about nightclubbing, because I started to hate going out. I did a book about my wife, because she had left me. And now my last book is about advertising, which I worked in for ten years and started to hate. So, I would say my main energy comes from anger and rebellion. I think when you start writing something or creating something it is because you do not accept the world in which you are.

"MY MAIN ENERGY COMES FROM ANGER AND REBELLION."

LARRY CLARK

Well, I started as a photographer and then became a director. I never sold out. I'm a final cut director. I mean, it's my film and you can't fuck with it after it's over. Although they always try to, someone tries to.

Fuck up the idea.

"I NEVER SOLD OUT."

Yeah, my first film *Kids*—they wanted me to cut another version for a blockbuster so it can be more commercial, and I said no. "Oh, there's only a couple of minutes off and there is a $ 100 000 into your pocket for you to cut it." So, I said: "No, you can't buy me."

What are the ingredients of creative rebellion? I went to Milano to meet Oliviero Toscani in his studio. In a performance, Oliviero approaches a canvas. In the middle of the canvas is a square with the sentence, "Do not color outside the lines." Toscani takes spray paint and demonstrates what it takes to be a rebel breaking the rules. You don't be a teenager to rebel.

OLIVIERO TOSCANI

What is this? "Instructions." Ha, "Do not color outside the lines." Do you see that? I mean, I belong to a generation of rebels, rebels, we belong to the rebels. So this probably is written by somebody from the marketing department of course. They tell you what to do exactly inside the line. Because you cannot go outside of the lines. You cannot go outside the rules. So, okay, we stay inside the line because we … we really believe in "politically correct." Well, we gave them a little concession. Just to show them how they can get out. And I hope they can see it clearly that we have been painting inside the line. Never do what they tell you to do when you want to do something new. Creativity cannot be secure. Probably in the moment of most insecurity is when you are the best. So, rebel against what they tell you to do. You have to rebel, that's the principle. Always. Listen to what marketing people tell you, listen very carefully, and just do the opposite.

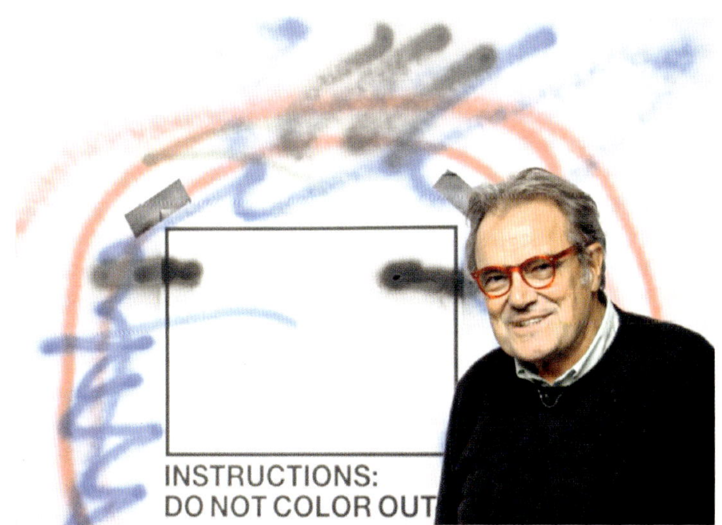

Just do the opposite. That's very helpful. How was this going to get me any closer to my Holy Grail: pinning down a unified field theory of creativity. Think, Hermann, think. What was it that all these people had in common? Let's enter the twilight zone—to the worlds and spheres where creativity and spirituality meet.

Dennis Hopper was a legendary rebel: from his humble beginnings in the dust blown plains of Kansas to the mind-blowing agonies of *Apocalypse Now*. From the A-list glamour of Los Angeles to the constantly high lifestyle of New Mexico. From box office zero to art house hero. From has-been actor to happening artist with exhibitions in Vienna, Amsterdam, Basel, and Los Angeles, Hopper's life was no easy ride. But a hell of a trip.

I was desperate and lonely. There seem tobe no way out

DENNIS HOPPER

I think my creativity comes from a very unhappy childhood. Wanting to … not getting enough approval from the house, from the home. So I rebelled … having to look for it in other places, having the drive to wanna be something, wanna be somebody but really not having the education because of the schooling to be able to do anything, but perhaps play sports, fight a bull, race a car, or be an actor. At twenty-one I was dropped from my contract at Warner Bros. Because I was considered "too difficult to work with," I was considered a rebel, I was infected with James Dean, and I was blackballed by the studio. So I left Hollywood and settled in Taos, New Mexico, where I found free spirits like Mabel Dodge and Frida Kahlo. And I entered it to live my counter- culture dream.

"I WAS CONSIDERED A REBEL, I WAS INFECTED WITH JAMES DEAN."

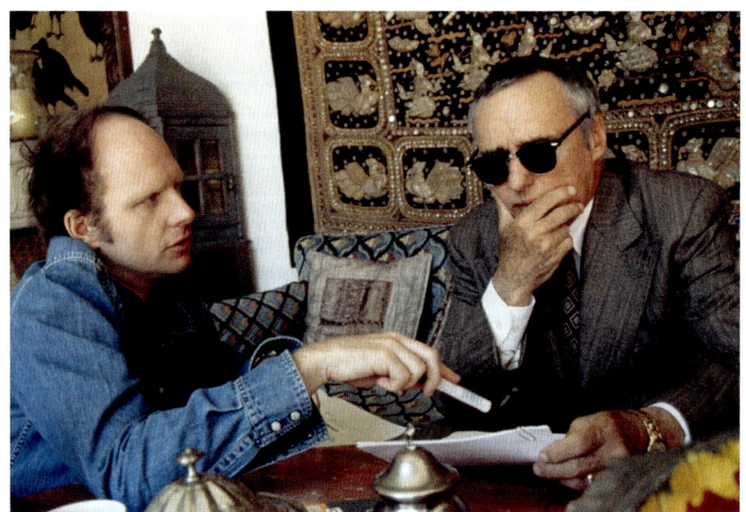

Even as an established artist and Renaissance man, he couldn't shake the rebel image. The chopper from *Easy Rider* became a ghost that constantly haunted him. Dennis saw it everywhere in the world, no matter where he was: in front of the Carlton, at the Vatican, even in front of the Guggenheim Museum.

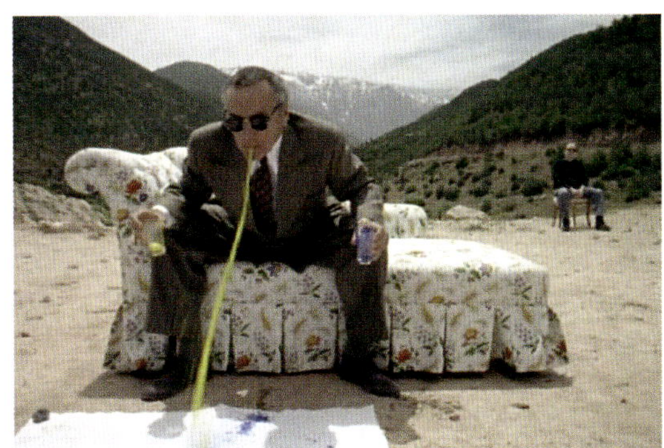

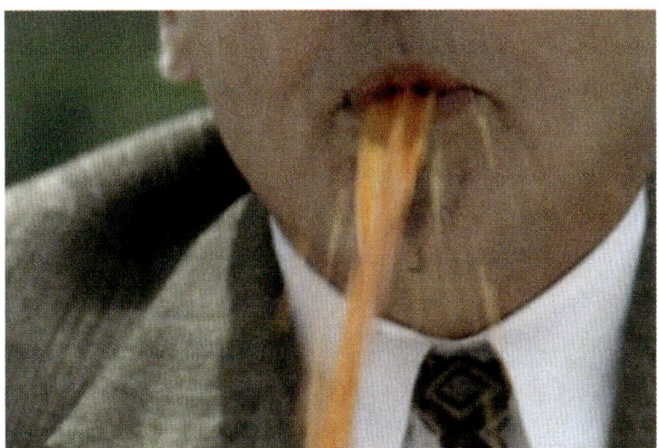

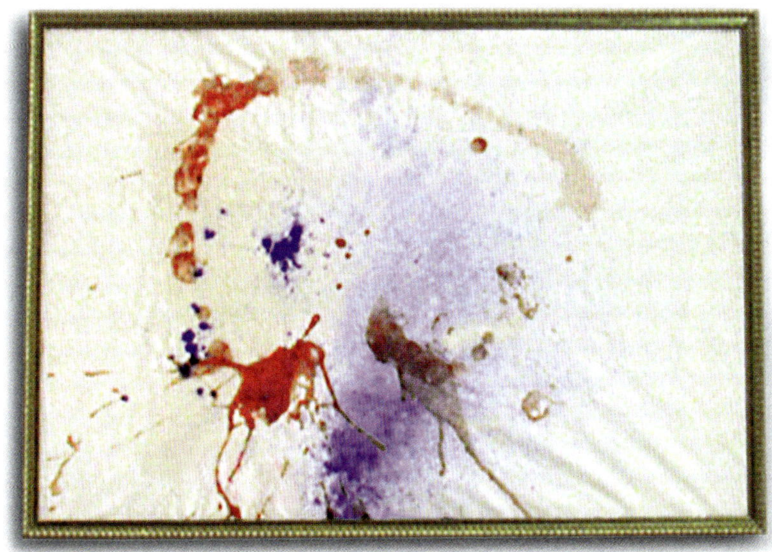

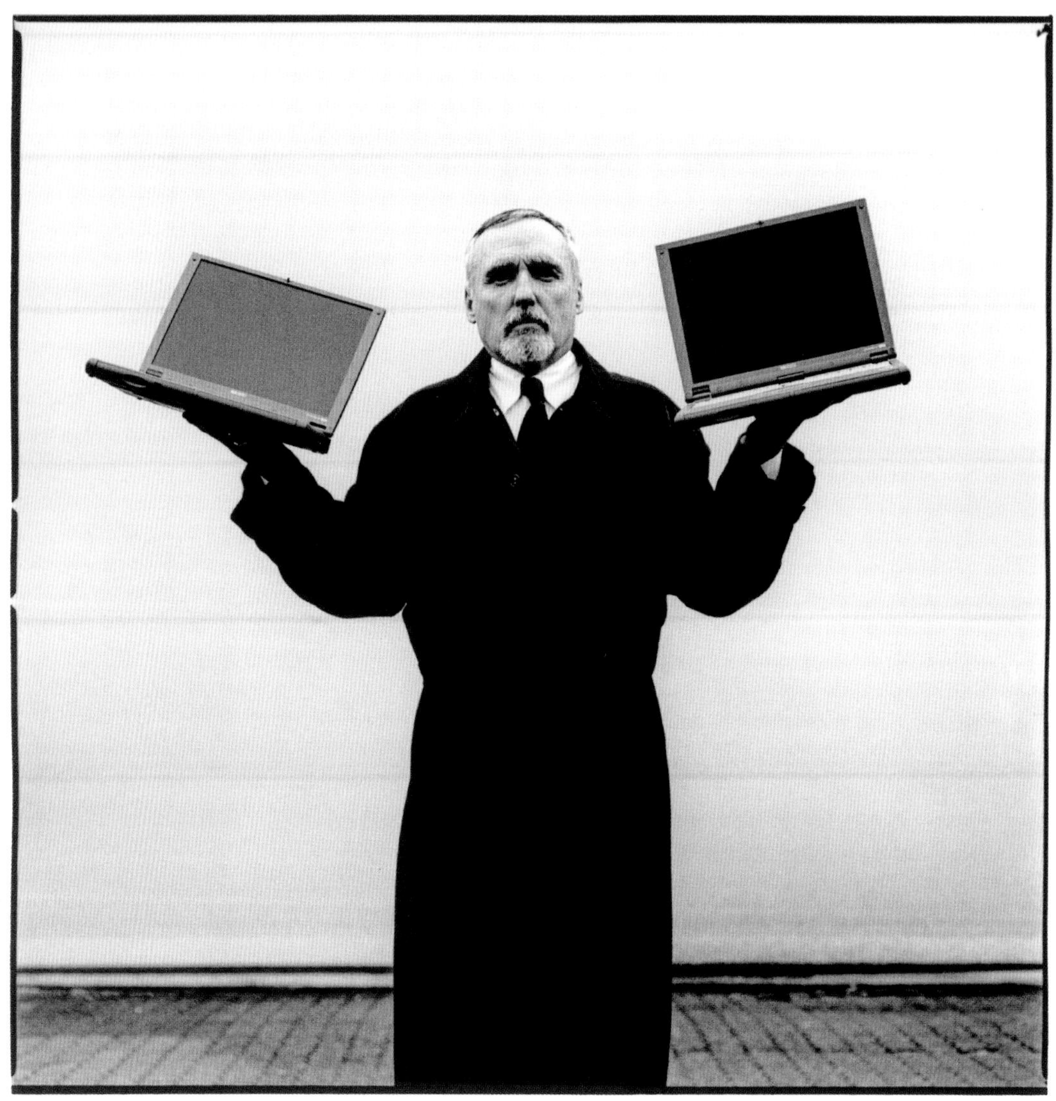

And I had the privilege to go along for the ride. I did four films with Dennis and learned from his creative spirit. In *The Ten Commandments of Creativity*, a film that has a lot to do with spirituality, it aimed to breathe new life into the old rules by relating them to creativity and media today. Dennis plays a modern Moses who receives said commandments on two laptops instead of two tablets of stone.

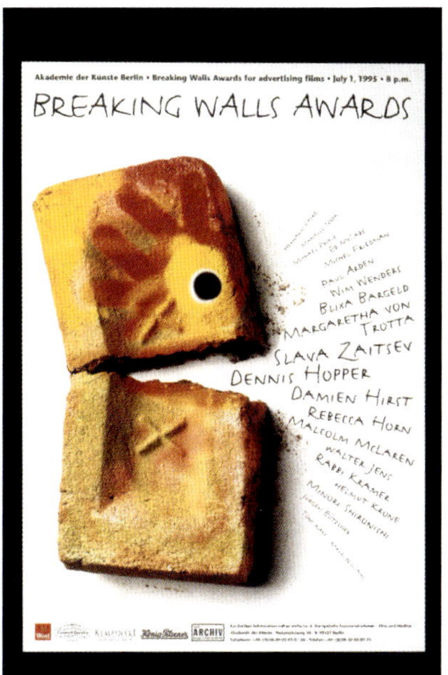

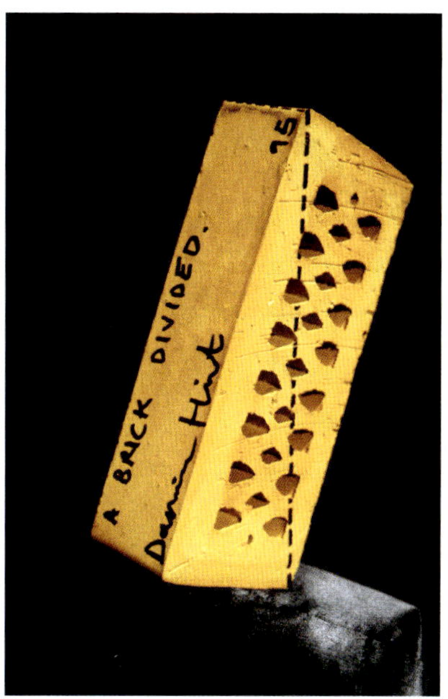

So many stories, so little time. Before Dennis and I went to Morocco, we met with the artist Damien Hirst. Damien was a rebel. He had just won the Turner Prize. He wasn't only putting sharks in formaldehyde, he was also making commercials. At that time, I initiated the Breaking Walls Award at the Academy of the Arts in Berlin. The idea was that the best short films and commercials could win a coveted Berlin Brick. These awards were ordinary house bricks turned into pieces of art by Damien, David Bowie, and other artists. Damien created a very special brick, which he was hoping to knock Peter Lilienthal on the head with.

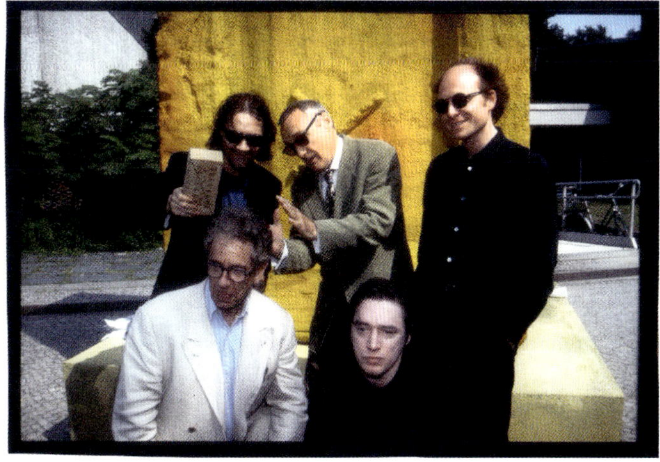

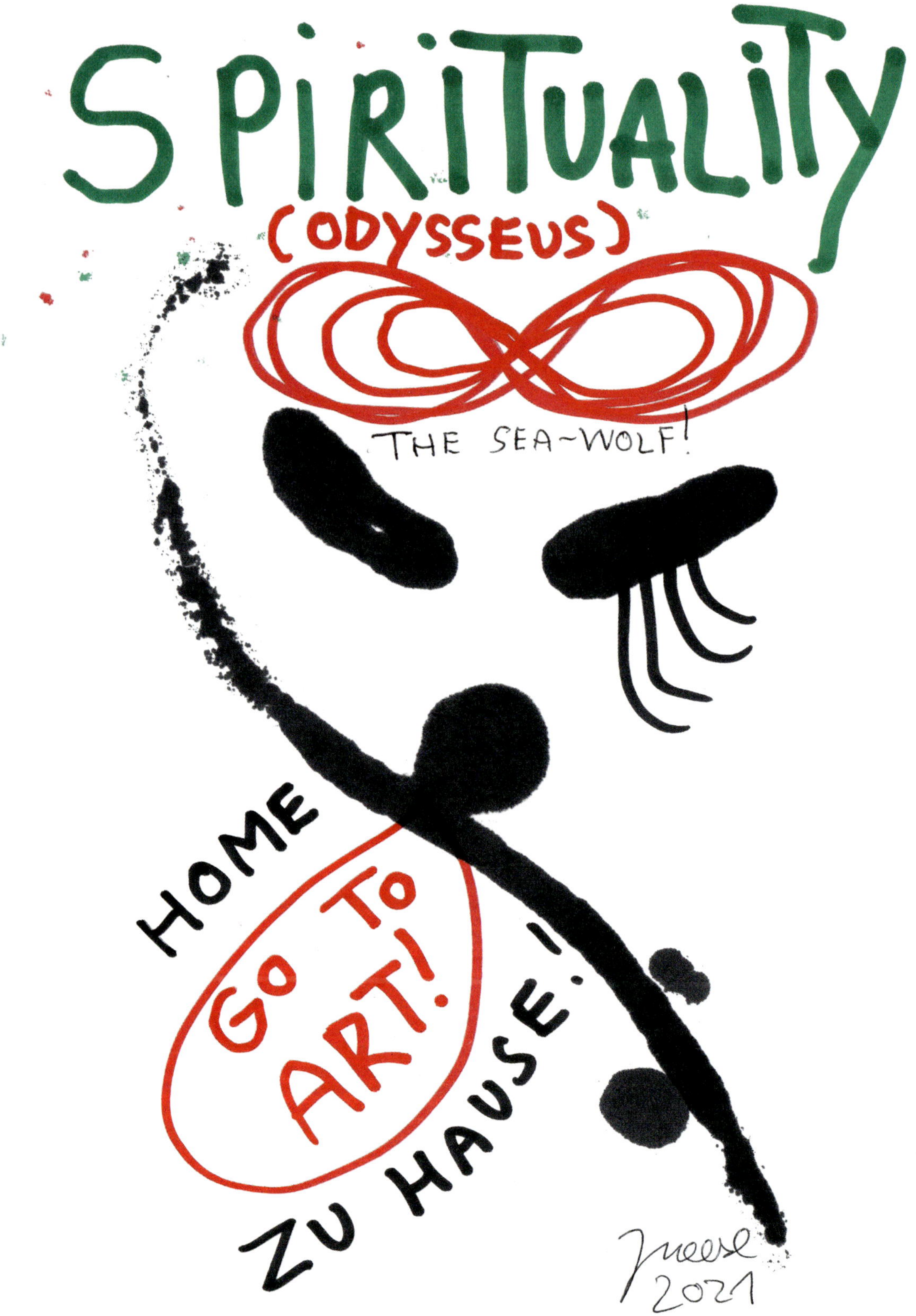

SPIRITUALITY
(ODYSSEUS)

THE SEA-WOLF!

HOME

GO TO ART!

ZU HAUSE!

Meese
2021

Some people believe that what we create is something that comes to us, or through us, but it doesn't come from us. So where does creativity come from? God only knows.

HANS ZIMMER

I think there is a connection between spirituality and creativity. I think for me, on the other hand, there is no connection between religion and creativity. I'm not a religious man in that sense. But I know Haydn was an incredibly religious man und wrote 106 symphonies, you know, because he would get on his knees and pray and be very humble. But I think it was more about the meditative process that, you know, that it gave him. Let me tell you how I write: I sit there for days and I try to think of the idea and I really intellectualize everything, I think everything through, and I write hours of terrible stuff. I mean things that just, you know, notes that mean nothing. And there comes a moment and I'm—it's like I'm not there. And suddenly I look and there's a piece of music and it's like, "It wasn't me that wrote it"—of course it was me that wrote it, but you got into that certain place really deep inside you and it is a spiritual process in a way.

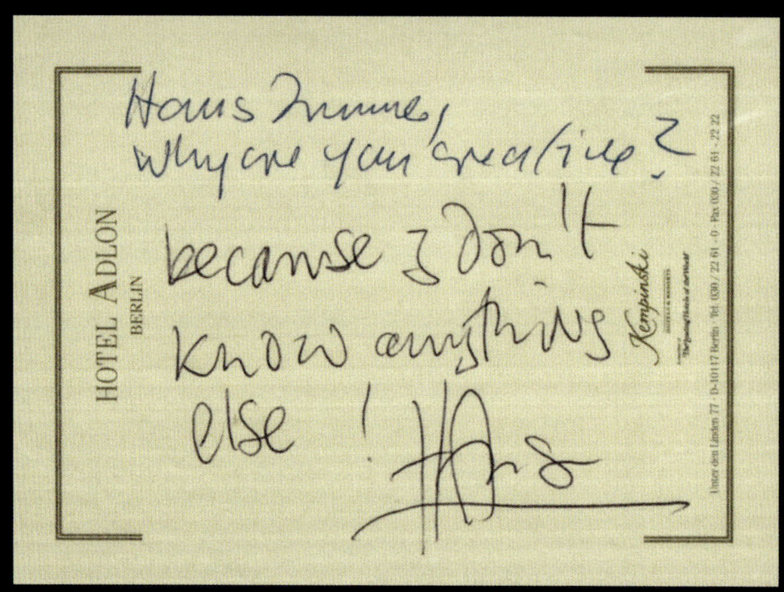
HOTEL ADLON
BERLIN

Hans Zimmer,
why are you creative?

because I don't
know anything
else!
Hans

Kempinski

Unter den Linden 77 · D-10117 Berlin · Tel 030 / 22 61 - 0 · Fax 030 / 22 61 - 22 22

Steven Spielberg came to Berlin to present his Academy Award–winning movie *The Last Days*. In his role as founder of the Shoah Foundation, he was one of the film's executive producers. I talked to Steven for my film *The Ten Commandments of Creativity,* which aimed to breathe new life into the old rules by relating them to creativity generally and the media today in particular.

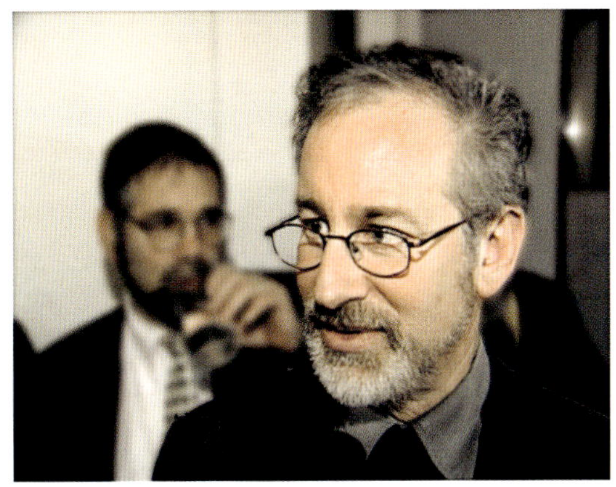

"THE TEN COMMANDMENTS RELATE TO HUMANITY."

STEVEN SPIELBERG

You know, the ten commandments, that's the truth of life.

How do the ten commandments relate to the Shoah Foundation?

Well, the ten commandments relate to humanity. You know, the Shoah Foundation is an echo of humanity, it's an echo of 50,000 survivors' voices and six million voices that never had a chance to be heard.

If there was an eleventh commandment, what would it be?

I think if there was an eleventh commandment, it should be, "Thou shalt listen carefully and closely."

ELIE WIESEL

In the field of culture, art, literature, poetry, music, creativity is essential. There could be no culture, no civilization without creativity. I have written many, many books about so many areas, I still try to find a style, a voice. I believe that the words that we've used until now are still inadequate. We are trying to find a new language. I published over forty books and I try to be creative simply in discovering those words that would be adequate. Sometimes I look and look and look and still go back to Urk, "die Ursprache." the Book of Job, the Book of Jeremiah. They found the words. I didn't.

So, can we say in the beginning there was the word?

In the beginning, there was a beginning.

FOREST WHITAKER

How do you get your ideas?

From my life. From my experiences, from my soul, from my god. I try to keep a center, a center of truth to my work, and I try to be able to take life in each breath, like in a way that it counts as much as the next one. That kind of point of view I'm not evolved enough to have arrived at it, I'm like working on it.

Is there a creative Samurai?

Surely. I think all Samurais should be creative. They should be able to apply the things that they've learned and in the circle, when you go back to the beginning of it, once you've learned it all, to be able to be truly spontaneous. That's what it's all about. That's what studying the martial arts is about. That's what studying discipline is about, that's what studying religion is about, is to find a primordial truth.

ANNE-SOPHIE MUTTER

"ART ARISES FROM THE DIVINE."

Nature inspires me. Every flower inspires me. A ray of sunshine, climbing a mountain, the divine spark that can be found in nature, in every little detail. This is something that always fascinates me anew and that in a certain way is not visualized or set to music in art but is captured in a completely different way. I am also increasingly interested in the connection between visual art and music. It's no coincidence that Klee was the son of a musician and cultivated a strong affinity for music throughout his life, or that Schöneberg, Kandinsky … that there was this parallelism. In the end, art also arises from the divine. There is no other explanation for a genius like Mozart. And this is a circle that closes again and that gives a lot of joy and strength. Without creativity we would not be aware of our spirituality, and I believe that just then one would despair of the excesses with which we have to struggle at the moment. Just then, of course, the reflection on music, on God-given art is, in my opinion, particularly important, because it also gives us hope again, gives us strength to think of spiritual freedom and to believe in humanity for each other and to believe with each other and, in the end, music exemplifies that we can live very well in peace with each other.

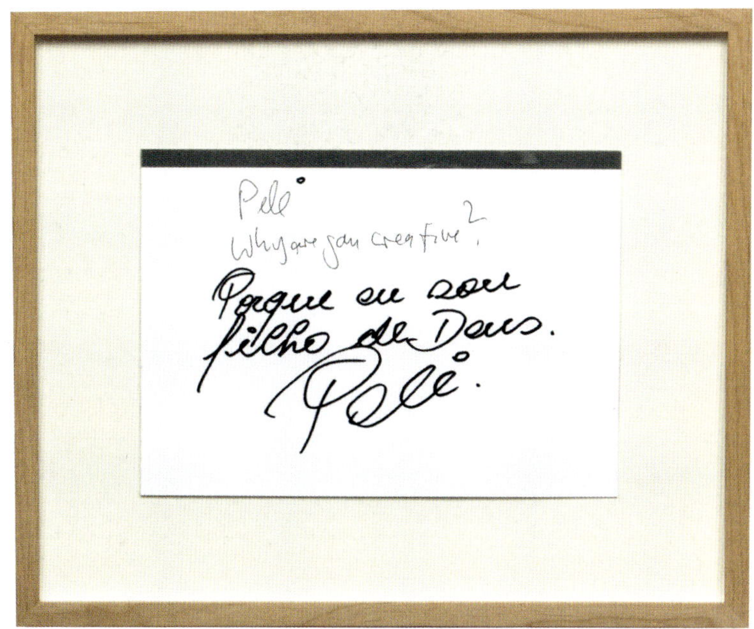

PELÉ

Well, creativity is a gift of God. It is something that comes naturally. And it's a thing that you create in a game move. You have to change your direction and movement, direct the thing. Just in that moment! That is creativity, because you are creating something. When I was a small child, my father told me: "Look, God has given you the gift to play and a natural creativity. But you have to always be physically prepared to create, to improvise." That's why I believe that both things go together. It is better when both things happen, but creativity is more important.

In your answer you described yourself as a son of god. Have you ever prayed for a win?

As a player, I never prayed to God to win a match. I prayed to God to be able to play and to not suffer any injuries. One important thing that I prayed to God for before every game in overcrowded stadiums was the following: "God, please make us not play nil-nil. After a nil-nil, everyone leaves the stadium in frustration. If the score happens to be tied, make it a four-four, a three-three, or a five-five, then everyone will be happy!" I always prayed that the audience would be happy when they leave the stadium. I never prayed for a win.

"CREATIVITY IS A GIFT FROM GOD."

During my quest, I met a few musicans that openly admitted to seeing a connection between creativity and divinity.

BONO

Isn't art an attempt to identify yourself? I, for instance, sing for my life. That's how I sing. I have not figured out and we have not quite figured out what we do. So, we depend on upon that. That's how we live, that's how we work, we operate only on that concept—waiting for God to walk through that room if you like.

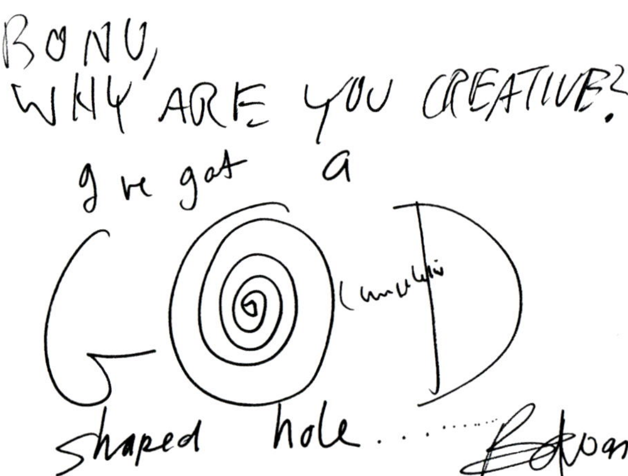

QUINCY JONES

"GOD SENT ME MUSIC."

Probably, since the age of twelve or thirteen, because of something inside that told me that I should stop what I was doing, which was not very good, and get into music. Idle minds with nothing to do in Chicago and Washington, and we would get in a lot of trouble and God sent me music. I'm very grateful, I feel very blessed.

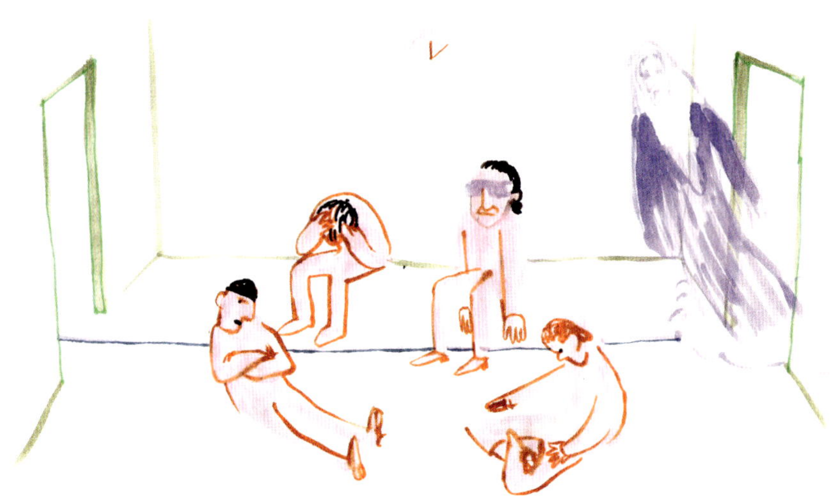

From Bono to Nick Cave, the Evangelist who did Seven Psalms and the spiritual album *The Boatman's Call*.

NICK CAVE

Do you believe in God?

Well, I do, yeah. Of course I do. For me, I use the word almost in the same way as I use the word "imagination." I feel, the feeling that I feel when I look at a particular painting, look at a Goya painting or something like that, and the feeling that I feel is, is, is a God-given feeling.

Do you pray?

Well, I do, yeah. I do.

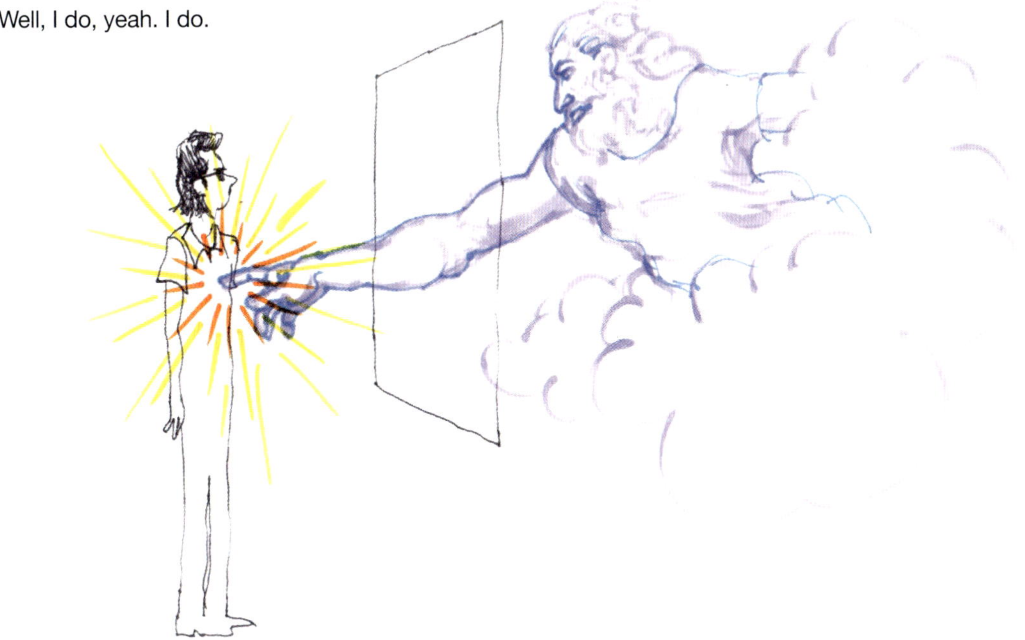

from something else. You can't tell me that an idea comes from you. It comes to you. It's there, something comes to you. You're running, you're standing, you're sitting, you're thinking, you're brooding, you're watching television, you're reading, you're listening to music, and you get an idea. Where does that come from? Did you create that? I don't think so. I think it comes from somewhere else, because if I have a good idea, which is rare, I don't know where it comes from. It's a gift to me. If I have a problem to solve and I put myself in the position of solving that problem and the solution comes, it comes from some place. And that's what I try to do in my work. I try to protect ideas that come to people because they are treasures that are given to people and I try to keep them from corrupting them. In rare instances you'll see a film, piece of music, a book, a play, a poem, a dance, that is perfect. It's beautiful. It's transcendental. A piece of music like the "Moonlight Sonata," perfect. It can't be better. Obviously, Beethoven was given this thing and he protected it and put it down on paper for the world to love forever.

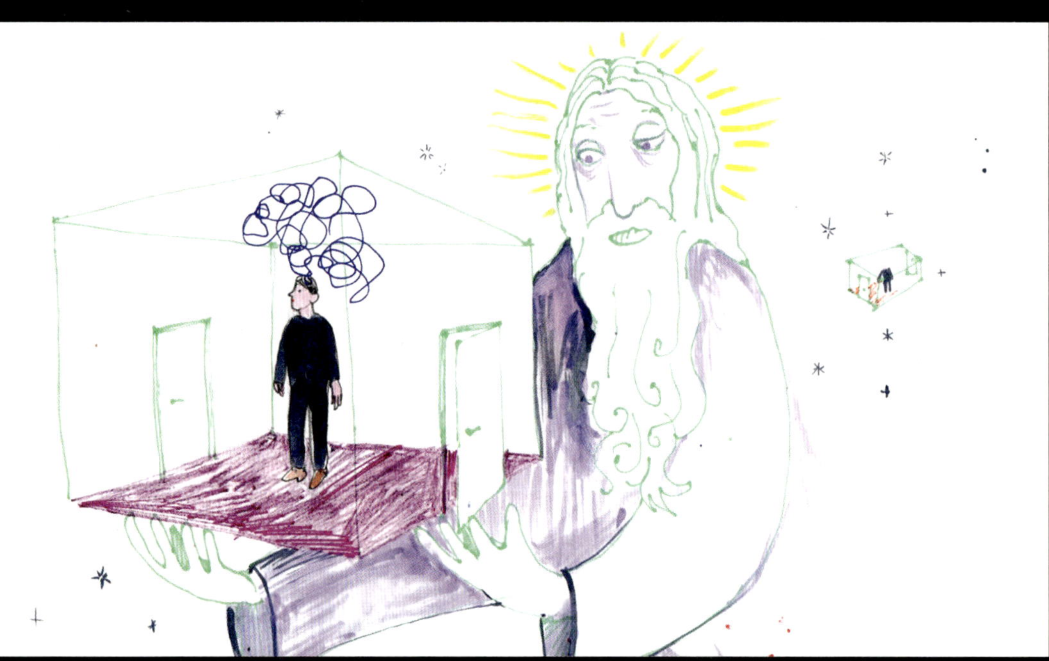

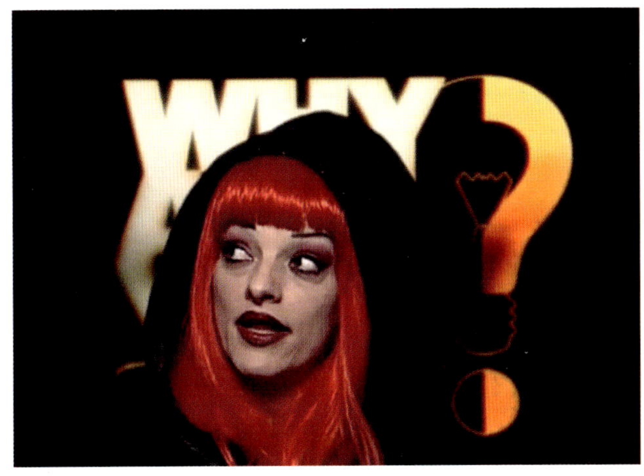

NINA HAGEN

Who is your god?

You and everybody in this room, more I can't see right now. And the air in this room and the light in this room and the life.

Why are you creative?

Because my soul is an eternal highlander, my soul is a highlander, she can't die. She will always be there, and she cannot do anything else than be creative, and so it's the same with all other souls. Actually, for centuries and centuries I have been running around literally on my roller skates and without them, trying to tell people what happened to me. How I started to search for God, and what I've found on my way and how it happened, that I died and went out of my body and could have an interview with God for a whole night when I was nineteen.

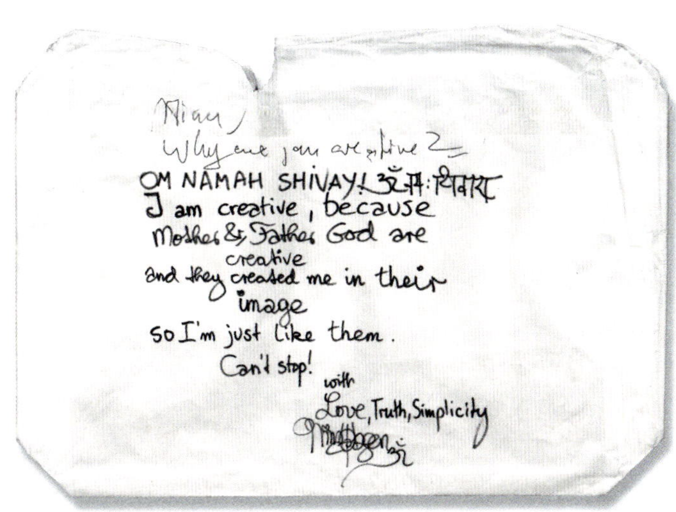

OM NAMAH SHIVAY! ॐ नमः शिवाय

I am creative, because Mother & Father God are creative and they created me in their image so I'm just like them.

Can't stop!

with Love, Truth, Simplicity

Nina Hagen ॐ

JOHN WATERS

I was born almost five weeks too early, so I was premature and I was baptized so many times that I was overly baptized. So all the original sin is gone. That's why. Yes, I don't know how to get real jobs. I couldn't get a job anywhere else, so I thought I better make movies. I'm creative because you are always partially insane and you have to be—to be creative, and that gives you such an outlet. If I had done all the criminal acts that are in my thirteen movies I would have been electrocuted many years ago.

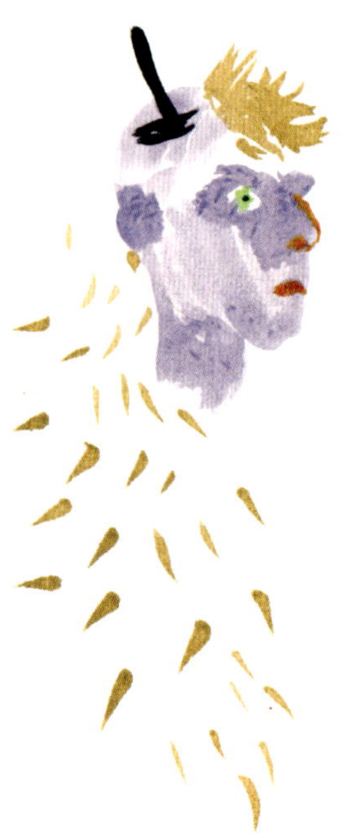

DAVID BOWIE

I had a book that I first read when I was about seventeen years old. It's called *Seven Years in Tibet*, by an Austrian called Heinrich Harrer. I had absolutely no knowledge that there was a country that hadn't been explored when I was a teenager. And that had no existence with any other country or knowledge of any other country, sort of an impossible dream. And having secured the name of this country, Tibet, it caused me to go and search out more information about it. In London at that time there was a society called the Tibet Society. And when I went in there, there was one young monk, lama, called Chime Tulku Rinpoche.

And it became very much my way of thinking at that time as a teenager. In fact, I was so keen to be a Tibetan monk that he had to talk me out of it. He suggested that maybe my métier was music and not an eastern religion. But there were certain things that he sort of … made me aware of about the … I guess the transience of things in life, about letting go of things, about really the basic fabric of life exists flowing like a river that is changing all the time.

ANDREAS DRESEN

There is a nice little booklet, *Zen in the Art of Archery*, which describes how a European tries to learn the art of archery from the monks in a Buddhist monastery. The monks shoot by not actually aiming. They shoot from the movement and let the arrow fly, and most of the time it hits exactly the center, and this European almost despairs that he just can't do it. So then he breaks the bow, gets in trouble with his master, yeah. And at some point in his rage, he shoots and the thing is stuck in the middle and he runs to his master and says, "Here, now I hit it!" And he says: "But it wasn't you who shot. It shot out of you." The decisive thing, the decisive 5 percent perhaps in the production of a work of art, you can't explain that exactly. They are, if you will, a gift from God. That's something very positive, but it's also very frightening. You suddenly find yourself reflected, and many things in the process of making a film are not even clear to you. So, you do things that you don't quite realize the implications of, or where you don't quite know why you're doing them. So you're somehow taken by the hand in a funny way by something that you can't describe at all.

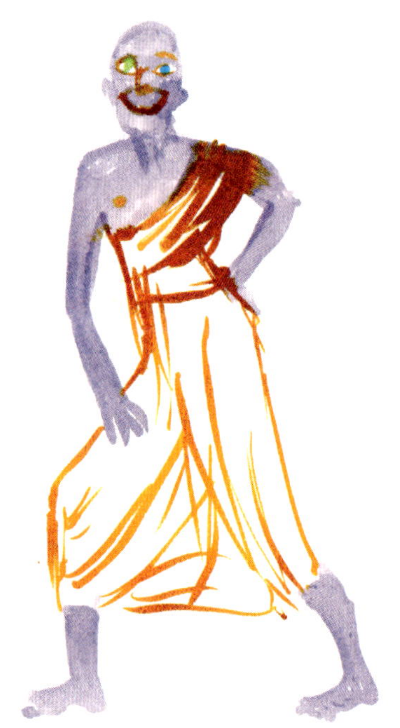

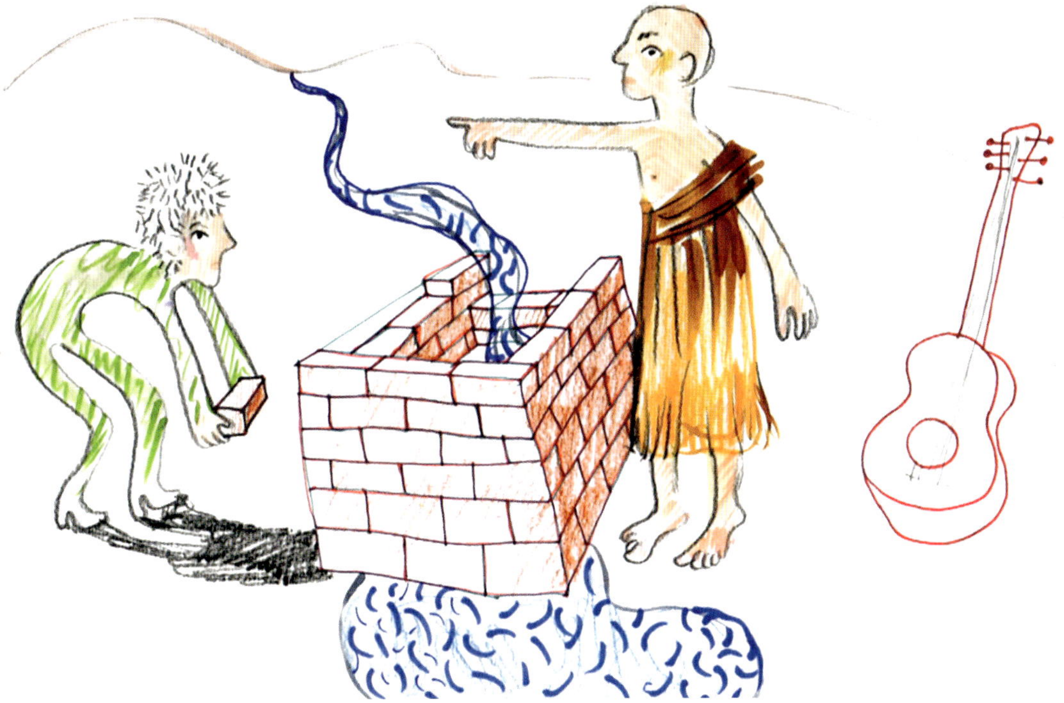

"I WAS SO KEEN TO BE A TIBETAN MONK THAT HE HAD TO TALK ME OUT OF IT."

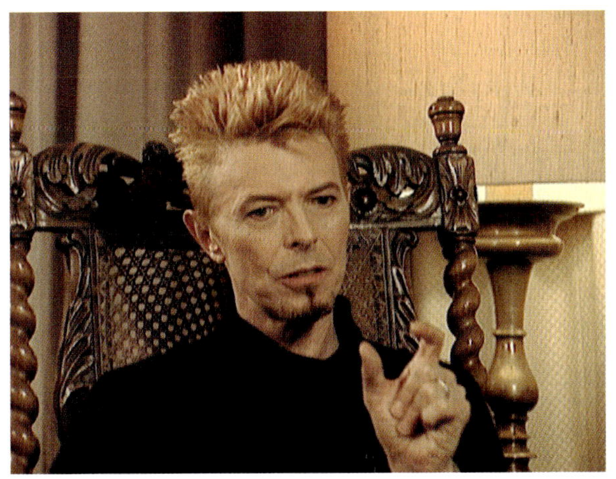

There are only two days in the year when you can do nothing. One is yesterday, the other tomorrow. Is creativity actually part of a deeper, more spiritually significant transaction? Luckily, I was able to go straight to the top.

DALAI LAMA

If the sheer power we are now capable of harnessing is not to have far reaching harmful consequences, there must be an accompanying inner development, a sense of responsibility for our world and the fellow beings with whom we share it. It is time to awaken our positive human potential by making the lives we lead meaningful. The answers to the question, "Why are you creative?" collected in this project are evidence of people trying to do just that. I think that creativity by itself is something neutral: creativity can be destructive; it can be constructive. So, generally, without creativity, there is no further progress. For this progress, of course creativity is very essential. I think because one of the basics for human beings is that we have imagination, and through that we have a creative potential. Because of that the human civilization, or development, is much greater, or faster, than other species of mammals. But creativity used in the wrong direction with negative motivation, creates more disasters. So, I feel creativity can violate human intelligence. But on the other side, with proper values, with warm hearts and a sense of responsibility, a sense of caring for one another and also with a broader, more holistic approach—which means with fully knowledge of the side effects and long-term consequences—through that way creativity can become more constructive.

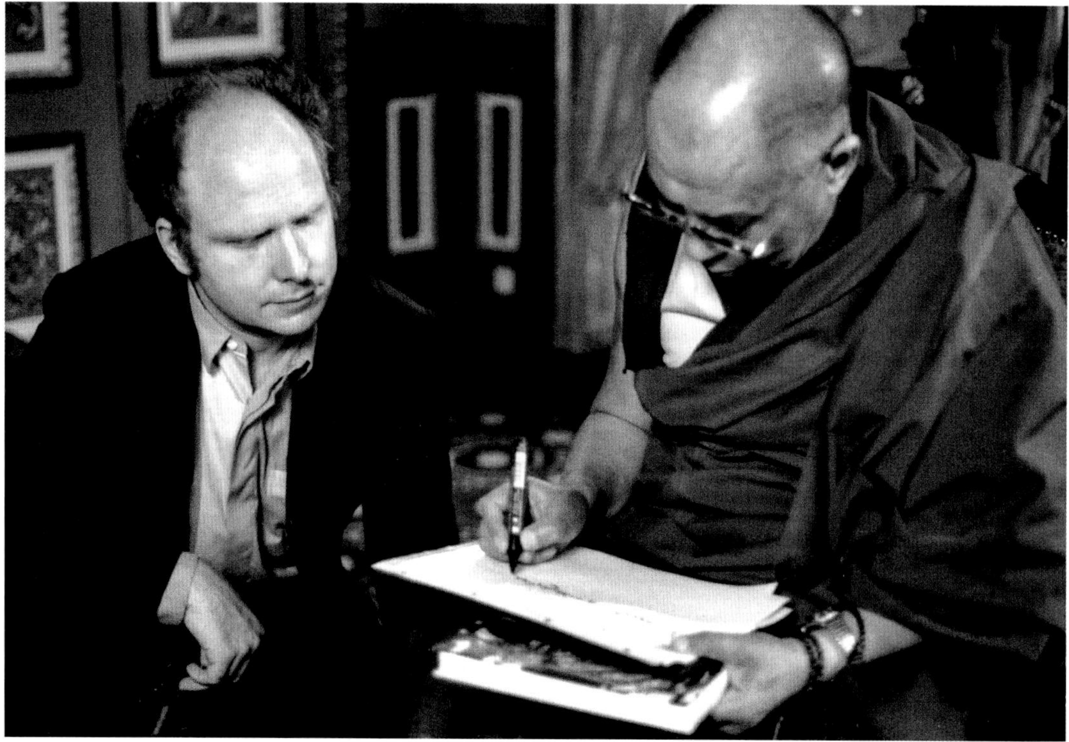

I felt like in Dante's *Divine Comedy*—no heaven, no hell, no dark, no light.

MICHAEL HANEKE

Why are you creative?

I think one should never ask a centipede why it walks because then he is going to fall flat on his face.

"YOU HAVE TO BE CREATIVE TO DO GOOD SCIENCE—OTHERWISE YOU ARE JUST REPEATING TIRED OLD FORMULAS; YOU ARE NOT DOING ANYTHING NEW."

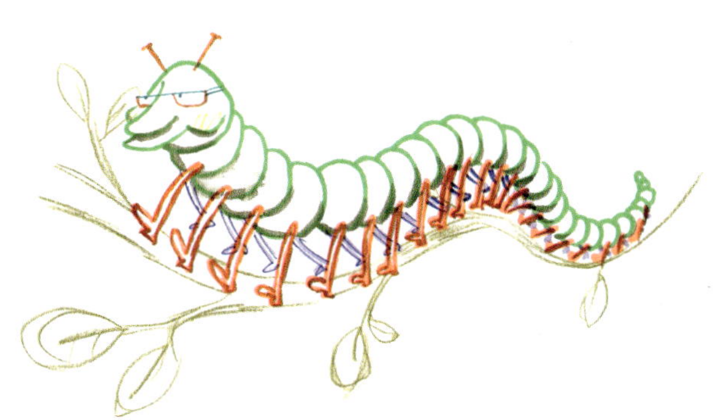

Clearly, I was in over my depth. This needed to talk someone much cleverer than me. So I went to the cleverest man in the world.

STEPHEN HAWKING

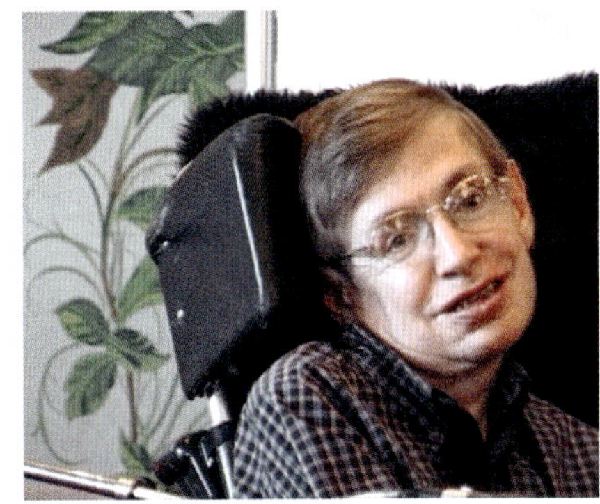

Two questions, Professor Hawking: Why are you Creative? And the second question is: What's more important, creativity or science?

I don't think it is for me to say whether I am creative or not. That has to be decided by other people. And the second question doesn't make sense. You have to be creative to do good science—otherwise you are just repeating tired old formulas; you are not doing anything new. It is much better to travel hopefully than to arrive.

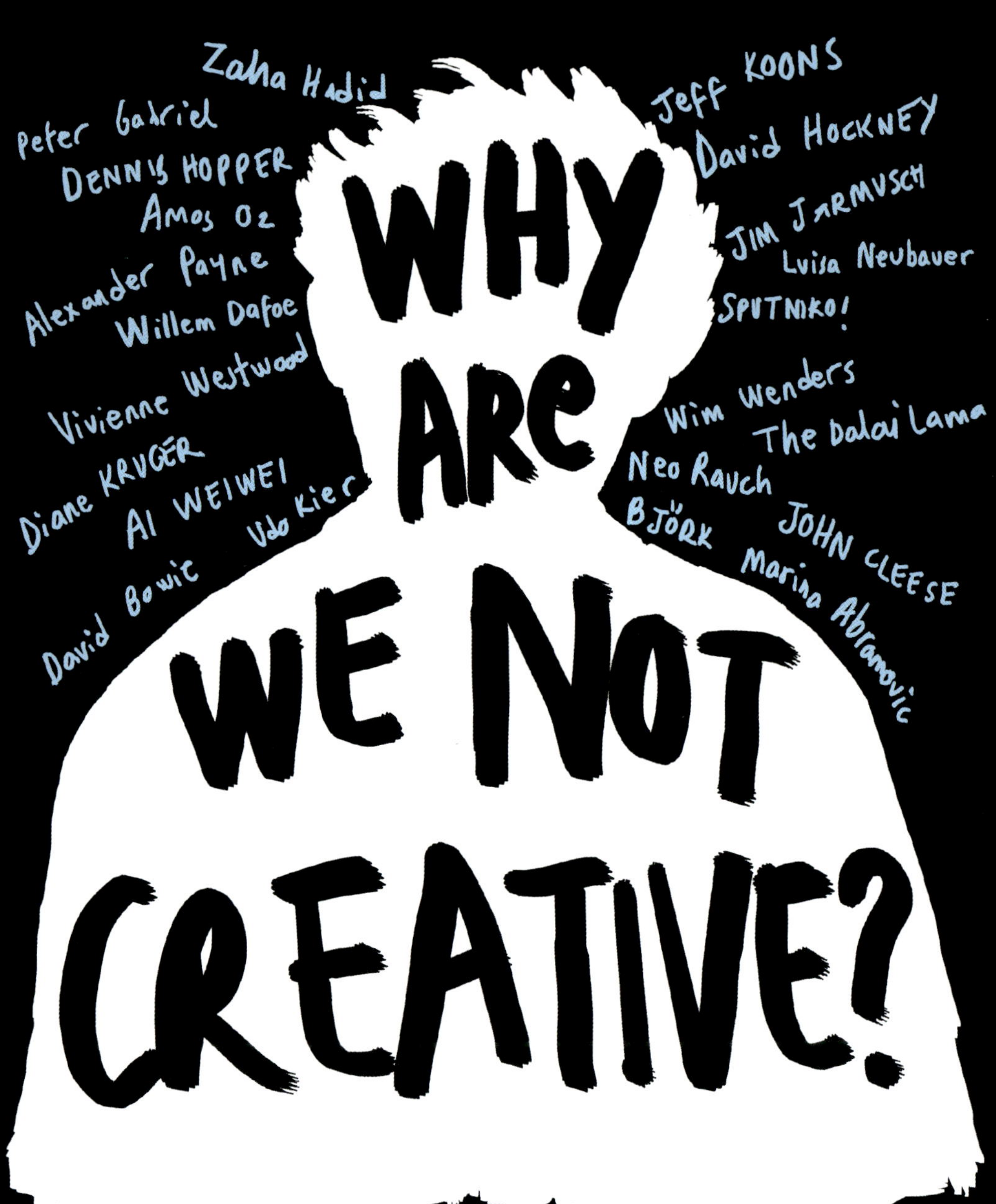

BY HERMANN VASKE

My journey, which started so hopefully, continues. And I am still not in any danger of arriving. It seems that there are as many reasons for creativity as there are creative people in the world. Yet, in all this polyverse of creativity, a common thought can be found: "I am who I am. I'm not afraid to be different and I don't ask for approval."
The one thing that all these people had in common was the ability to imagine something that doesn't exist—and then make it real. And it didn't seem to matter whether you use pencils or paints or film or fashion—or make a real societal change in the real world—that is the powerful magic that flows through you: the ability to bring the nonexistent to life. That's a trick only God's supposed to be able to do.
Of course, we do it. It's the thing that sets us apart from every other species. The thing, as Angeline Jolie said, that connects us. The question we should be asking is, "Why are we so often not creative?" But that's a whole other story. But a much shorter chapter.

In an age of uncertainty, simply encouraging creativity is not enough. Only when we unmask and identify the idea killers will we be able to avoid beta blockers of creativity. What awaits us on the dark side of the moon? Why are we not creative? Who are the real villains? Only if we get to the other side will we see the complete picture. I wanted to track down the idea killers and continued my journey.

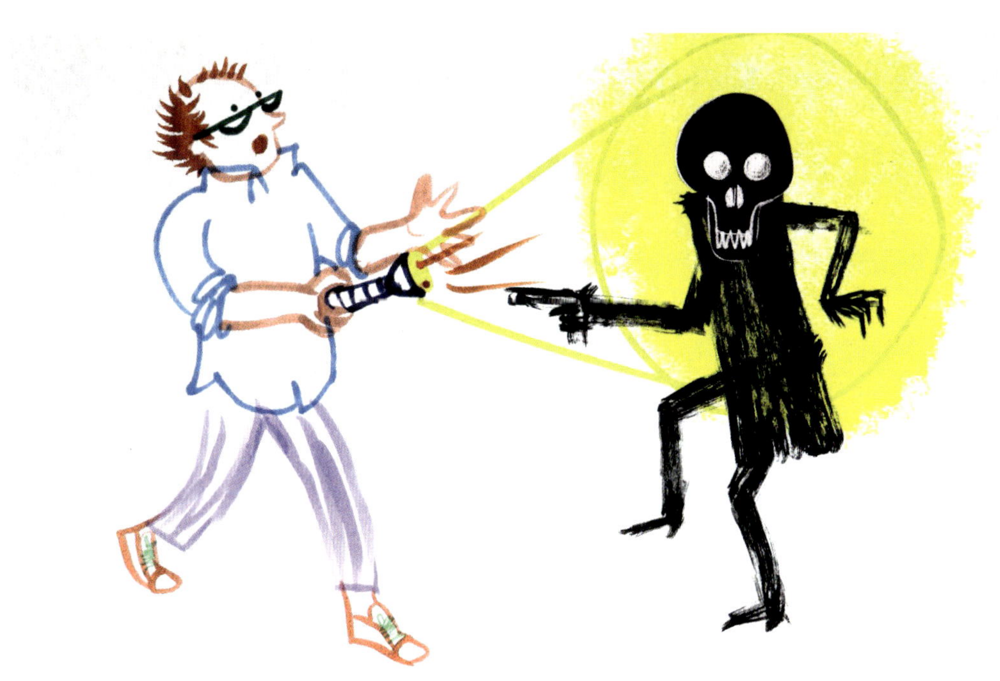

CENSORSHIP
NO CENSORSHIP!
i EAT
iDEOLOGIES......
Juerre 2021
(WAS ZIEHST DU AN HEUTE NACHT)

So here I am, back again, walking the surface of the earth, asking complete strangers, good old friends, and new companions on all six continents what is it precisely that hinders and threatens creativity.

If Samuel Beckett were alive today and living in North Korea, we would still be waiting for Godot, as the Index on Censorship once put it. Political extremes can perform swift euthanasia on creativity. Totalitarian regimes have found terror and imprisonment a very successful way of dissuading people from being creative. Does censorship make being creative a very bad idea or can censorship stimulate creativity up to a point?

Creative repression has stimulated creative rebellions for centuries. Whether it's resistance to political oppression, challenging the norm and the status quo, or the urge to draw attention to social injustice, it's often a novel, a painting, a song, or, as in the case of director Agnieszka Holland, a film that is remembered. The president of the European Film Academy, Agnieszka Holland grew up in Poland and Czechoslovakia, at the time of the Warsaw Pact. I met her in Sevilla, Spain.

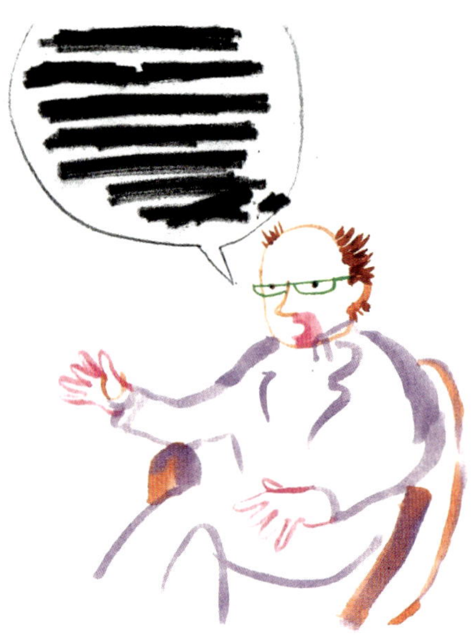

"THE REGIME THINKS THAT POWER CAN BREAK EVERYTHING, BUT POWER IS POWERLESS IN FRONT OF THE PEOPLE WHO DEFY THE POWER."

AGNIESZKA HOLLAND

You know, I have the long experience of living in a communist country. And my first very conscious experience was Czechoslovakia after 1968, when the process of so-called normalization started. And I've seen how easy it is to break the people. It is much more comfortable for them not to stick up. Not to call for attention.
And to conform somehow to the regime. When the censorship, when the state shows up with instructions, and the boundaries we cannot cross, we accommodate. Most of us do. Only some remain, you know, rebellious.

As Oleg Senzov said in his last statement during his trial, cowardice is the biggest sin of man. And we see that the people who are courageous, like Oleg or Panahi or many others, are giving all of us some kind of strength. And finally, the censorship can provoke us to think deeper. The regime thinks that power can break everything, but power is powerless in front of the people who defy the power.

So, can we say the pen is mightier than the sword?

Yes. The spirit can be stronger than the bars. So I think it's important that those people who show their courage and creative need or urge in such a wonderful and risky way know that they are not alone. So as far as I am safe and as far as I can do more or less what I want to do or tell what I want to tell I feel that it's my duty to help those who can't.

"AS OLEG SENZOV SAID IN HIS LAST STATEMENT DURING HIS TRIAL, COWARDICE IS THE BIGGEST SIN OF MAN."

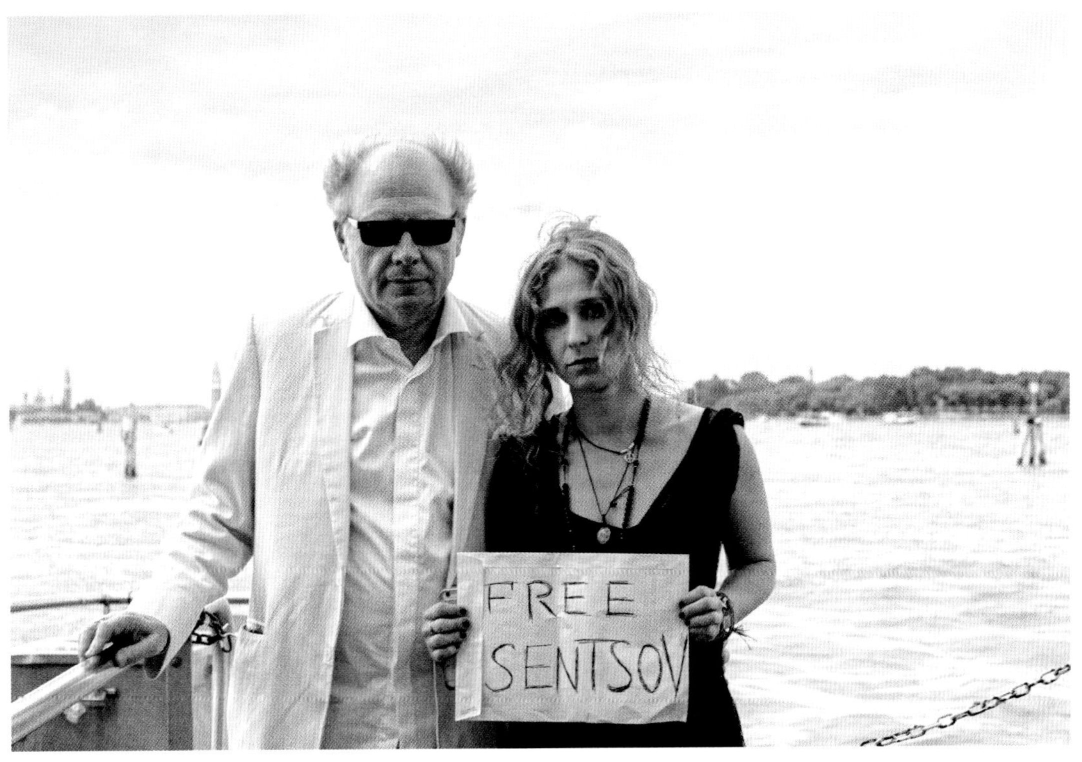

The pen is mightier than the sword—this reminded me of my meeting with President Mikhail Gorbachev.

MIKHAIL GORBACHEV

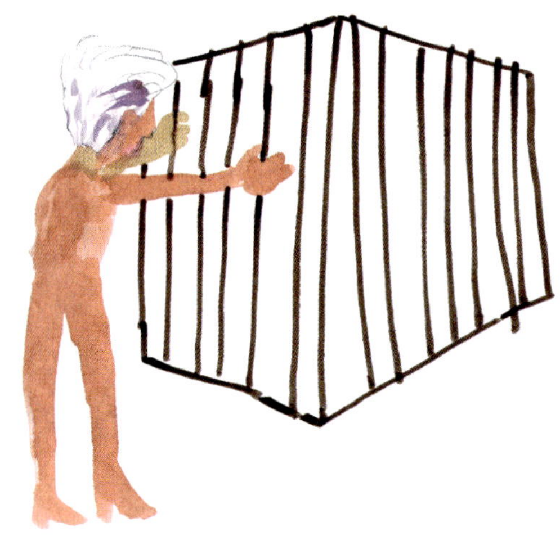

When President Ronald Reagan and you signed the INF Treaty, Parker Pen ran an ad with the headline, "The Pen is Mightier than the Sword." Is that still valid today? Is creativity mightier than propaganda?

Certainly, more than that. I am convinced that if there are any lessons this century teaches us, then the most important one is, that force is no solution to any problem. Whenever you use force, the consequences are the most severe. But it came out that when we believed and trusted each other, we were able to solve the old conflicts. At the end of my presidentship, I managed to organize the Madrid conference with George Bush. I've always been a supporter for this process to continue, to resolve that old, heavy conflict, a knot in which we all are interested in to untuck. You see, I can name several countries: Afghanistan, Cambodia, Central Africa, Angola … it was not done by weapons. Arms divided people and that caused numerous deaths, destruction, damaged ecology. Countries and human psychology were militarized there. It's a destructive force. That is why I strongly favor political solutions.

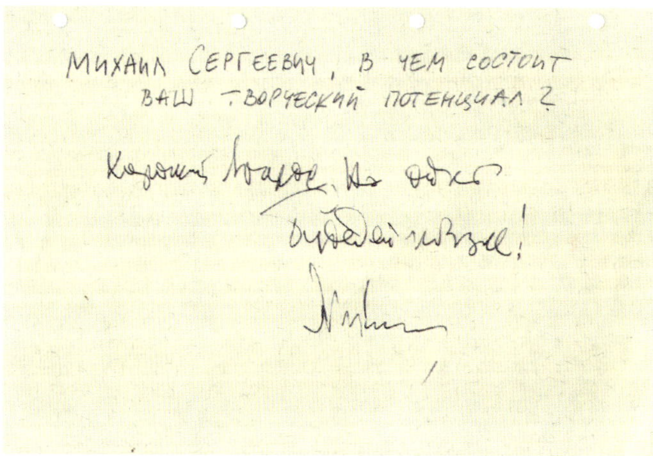

МИХАИЛ СЕРГЕЕВИЧ, В ЧЕМ СОСТОИТ ВАШ ТВОРЧЕСКИЙ ПОТЕНЦИАЛ?

Хороший вопрос. Но ответ впереди!

What is the correlation between politics and creativity?

Deficiency of political leadership comes from a lack of new visions in politics, lack of realization of what is happening with our world, with all of us everywhere. That is why politics is lagging behind. But I wouldn't blame politicians for that. I'd like less politics and more art, but still it's a huge possibility for any kind of information, especially for art and creativity, to be the people's communication. I think that, of course, if the media and television will break free from all the lies, which are everywhere in the media, the East and the West will be better for all of us. Everyone will have art.

So why are you creative?

Mikhail Gorbachev took a pen and wrote "Great Question. The answer comes later."

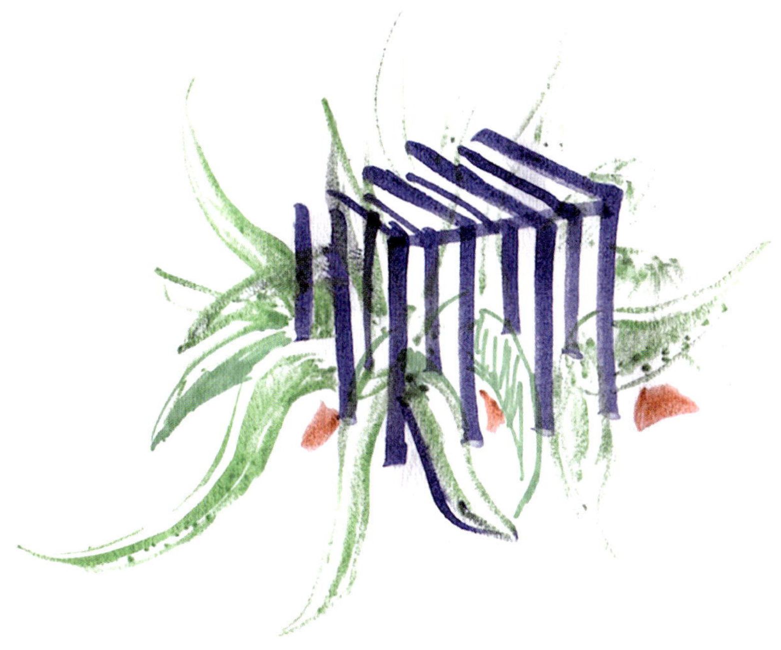

While the jury is still out on Mikhail Gorbachev's answer, I was strolling along the old town of Sevilla to meet with Romanian director and artist Adina Pintilie. She not only won the Berlin Film Festival, but who is also the featured artist of the Romanian Pavilion at the Venice Art Biennale.

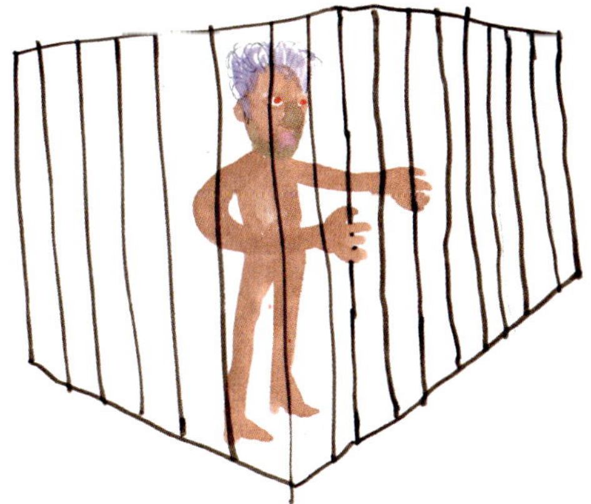

ADINA PINTILIE

The root has to grow very deep in order to get to the water.

If you look at the artistic movements in censored societies, they are very strong there, very strong artists. And even if politically or socially the dictatorship somehow isn't there anymore, there is still a lot of internal censorship. And let's say in Romania it's that, in other countries it's the Bible belt. We have different kinds of censorship inside which come from our backgrounds, from our history.

I was still mulling over this question of anger as a powerful fuel for the creative engine while strolling past St. Florian monastery, deep in the heart of Austria. Could social outrage be a force of nature powerful enough to topple governments' control (and aggression) and outrun state censorship? As if in answer to a prayer, I was attracted by the sound of what can only be described as a blood organ. Of course, the manic organist was the artist Hermann Nitsch.

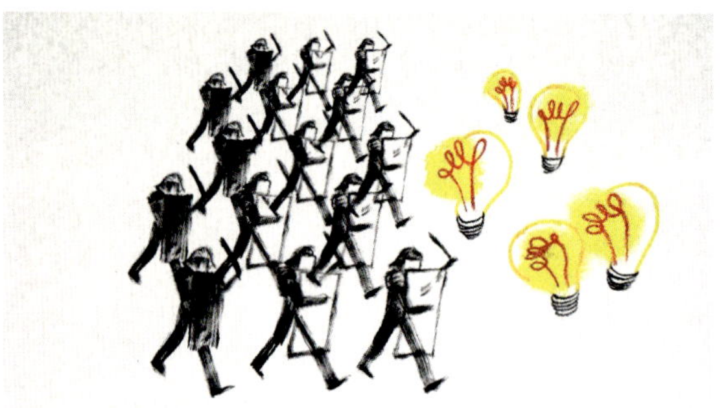

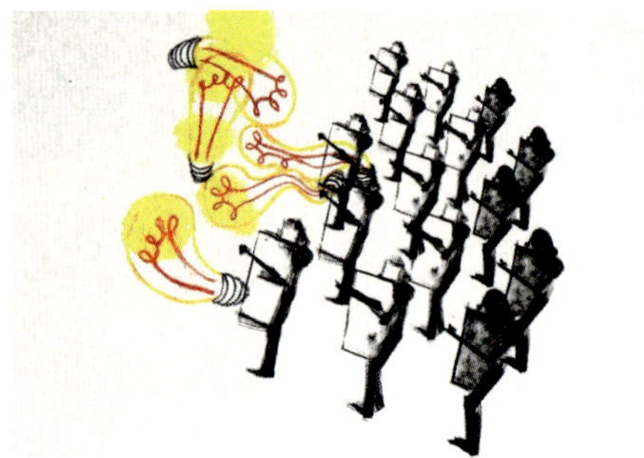

HERMANN NITSCH

Well, I've learned a lot from psychoanalysis. A lot from Freud, a lot from Jung. And it goes like this: I'm a playwright and through my actions I make repressed areas visible and conscious. And even antiquity spoke of catharsis. My point is that the repressed is taken up into consciousness. And especially through form, through art. And that we are purified by it. Even in ancient times, Sophocles' *Oedipus the King* was about a terrible crime committed by an innocent man. And there, too, there was a profound attempt to make people aware of it. And that is also what I have set myself as my task. I have dealt a lot with mythology, also through Wagner, through Jung, and all the myths and religions are our collective dreams of us. And that's what I've tried to track down in my art.

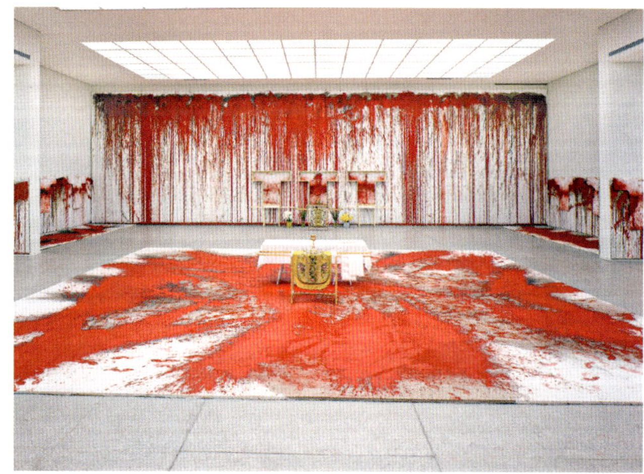

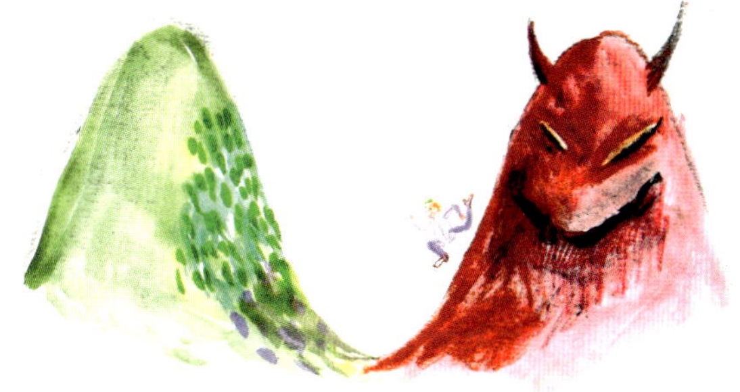

The police locked me up three times. But … that's normal when you're doing something new. Leonardo, Michelangelo … they dissected bodies. The Inquisition would have hunted them down, if they had been caught. It's always been like that, and it always will be when somebody does something new. Even Galilei, he had to renounce. Creativity is hindered by censorship and one's own superficiality. Although I find one's own superficiality worse than censorship. I find censorship stimulating up to a point.

DAVID BOWIE

Once you suppress one thing, you have automatically cast the shadow of censorship over everything, because it acts like a house of dominos.

DALAI LAMA

How important is freedom of speech for creativity?

Oh, very important. Freedom of speech is the freedom of thought. I think first: freedom of thought. Through that way, there are various, sort of, imaginations, visions you can develop. Then, based on that, judge … analyze … or, make assessment. Then freedom of speech, to communicate with other fellow human beings. I think through that way, you see the discussion, or consultations. You see, from one side visions and from one side other visions, their visions. They must actually express these visions, then you should discuss. And then find some sort of practical new ideas can develop. So freedom of speech is very essential.

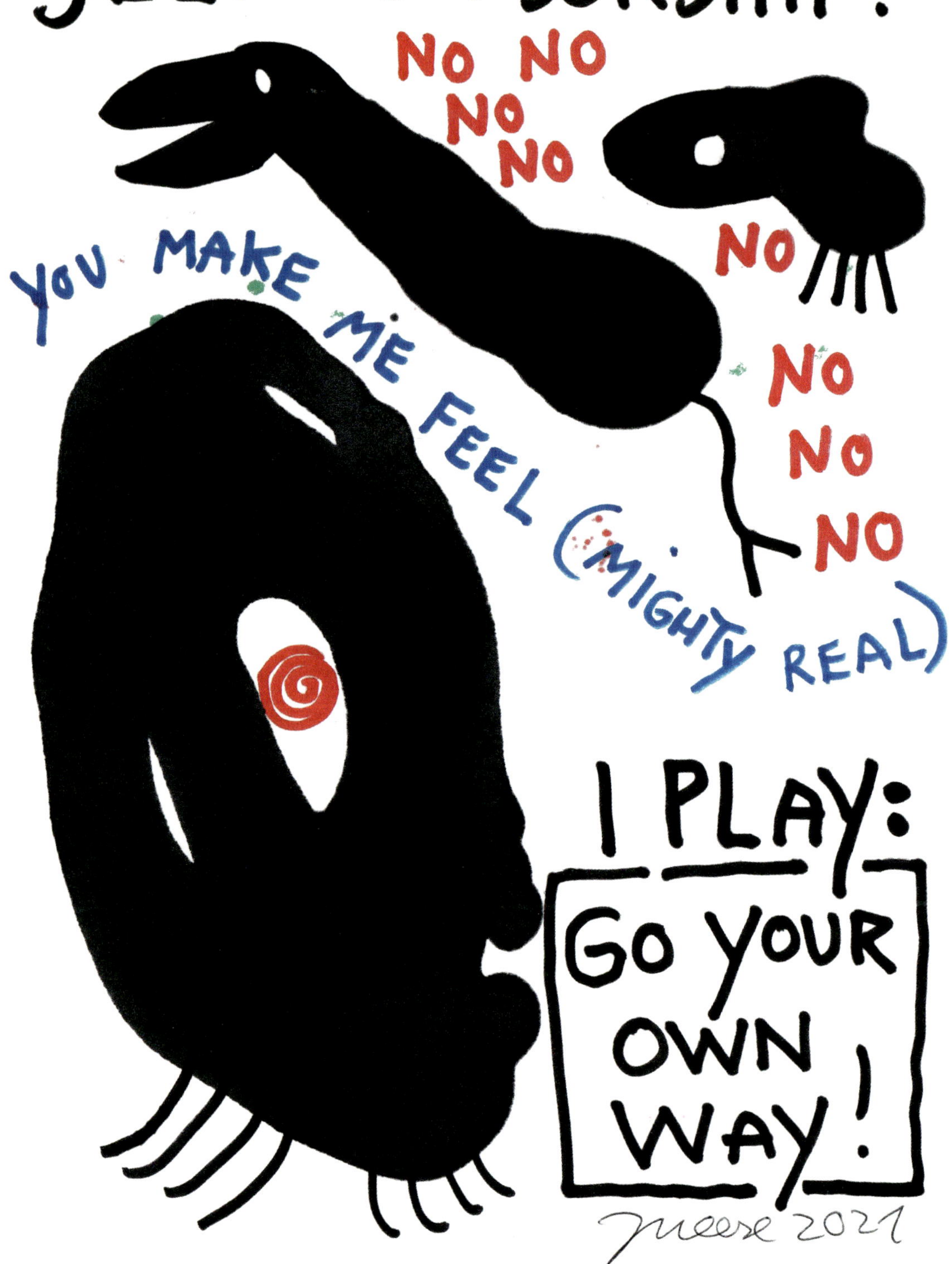
SELF-CENSORSHIP!
NO NO
NO
NO
NO
YOU MAKE ME FEEL (MIGHTY REAL)
NO
NO
NO
I PLAY:
GO YOUR OWN WAY!
meese 2021

The petit bourgeois inside all of ourselves is constantly pestering us with, "But what will my friends say? What wil the neighbors say? What will the press say? Better don't do it. Be careful. Keep your head down." Is it political correctness? Or is it repression?

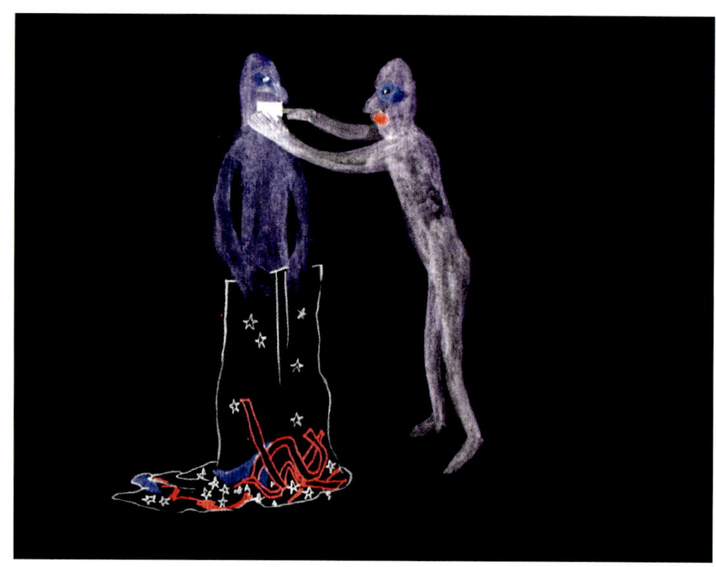

SHIRIN NESHAT

Every project that I make, automatically, I self-censor myself. In that way, I would not disrespect any religion, I would not overtly take sides with any particular group or political belief. And even if you think about my aesthetics. I work black and white. Aesthetically, I work with a very particular language. And I enforce a kind of a regiment. But within that, I'm a minimalist.

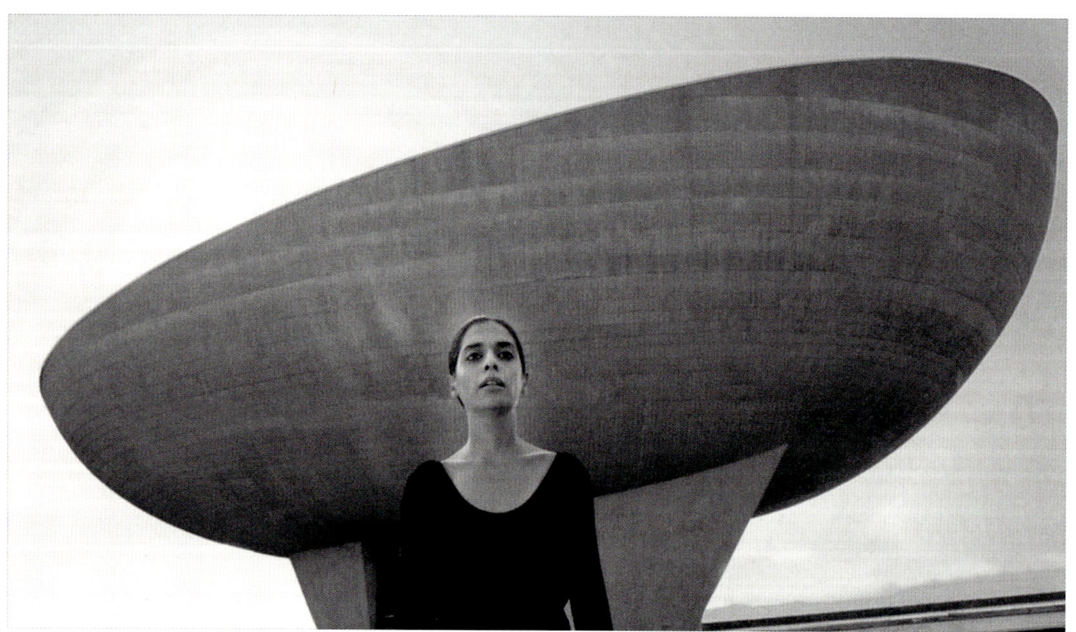

If you see my films, my videos, my photographs. And I think that has to with being born an Iranian and always being told to control your public and private life to a certain degree. Particularly within the Islamic tradition, with the veil. We are always told to build a wall around ourselves, whether it's of fabric or a wall around our house. To hide everything. And we are also always also very fearful of people in power. People who could bring us down. I'm always afraid of the police, the immigration. And there is just something about us who have been living in a state of fear forever.

Then again, the spirit is stronger than the bars.

I think you are right. I think that the people who live in this state of mind are also the ones that are most deviant and break more rules, more codes. And I mean, I don't have to tell you that—nothing could be greater proof than Iranian culture and films. And great cinema, great artists, and theater and all kinds of creative people happening with no freedom of expression. No support. People are just exploding. And really that is the hopeful thing.

"EVERY PROJECT THAT I MAKE, I AUTOMATICALLY SELF-CENSOR MYSELF."

Why are you creative, Shirin?

To cope with life + my anxiety.
Shirin

Václav Havel, the former president of Czechoslovakia, used to be a writer. Meeting him, I thought I was in a John Le Carré spy movie. I left Prague and drove through a snowstorm through the countryside of Bohemia until I saw a castle. Surrounded by dancing snowflakes, guards with Russian fur hats appeared, not looking too friendly in the headlights of the car. Eventually, they let me pass and I met Václav Havel to talk about creativity.

VÁCLAV HAVEL

I did not go into politics because I loved politics and wanted to be part of it, as it is the way in democratic society, but rather that I was propelled into it. Throughout my life I was always interested in public matters. I commented on them, I could not tolerate injustice, I risked confrontation with the regime, with the powers. As a writer I was a well-known person, people waited to hear what I would say, I had a greater burden of civic responsibility than other people, it is true that it was all indirectly political, but I cannot say that I ever wanted to become a politician as such. I became one from one day to the next after the revolutionary changes that took place here, when communism collapsed in 1988. In my opinion politics can also be—and should be—a creative activity. And for me personally, because I feel myself to be a creative person, in some respects. I wanted to make films, but under communism this was not possible, because I couldn't study at FAMU, and unless I graduated from FAMU I could not make films. There were all sorts of things I wanted to do. I worked for theaters, I wrote, and so on, but for me the genre was not important, the important aspect was creativity, to do something which in one way or another encompassed the whole world but was a concrete artifact. And politics, the way I see it, is, or rather should also be, a creative activity. And I enjoy politics whenever I have the feeling that I am creating something and that is producing results and sometimes a conclusion.

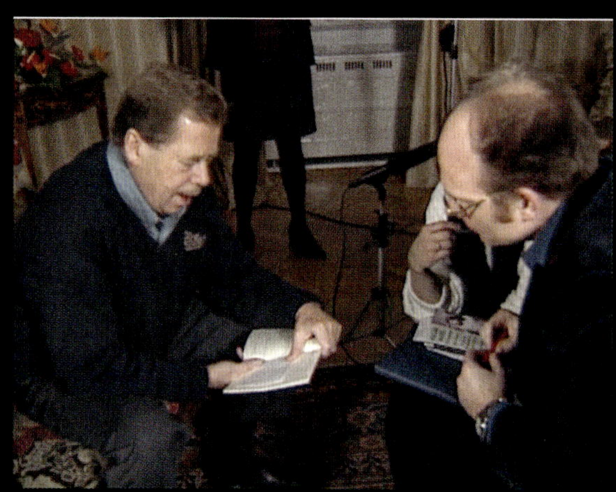

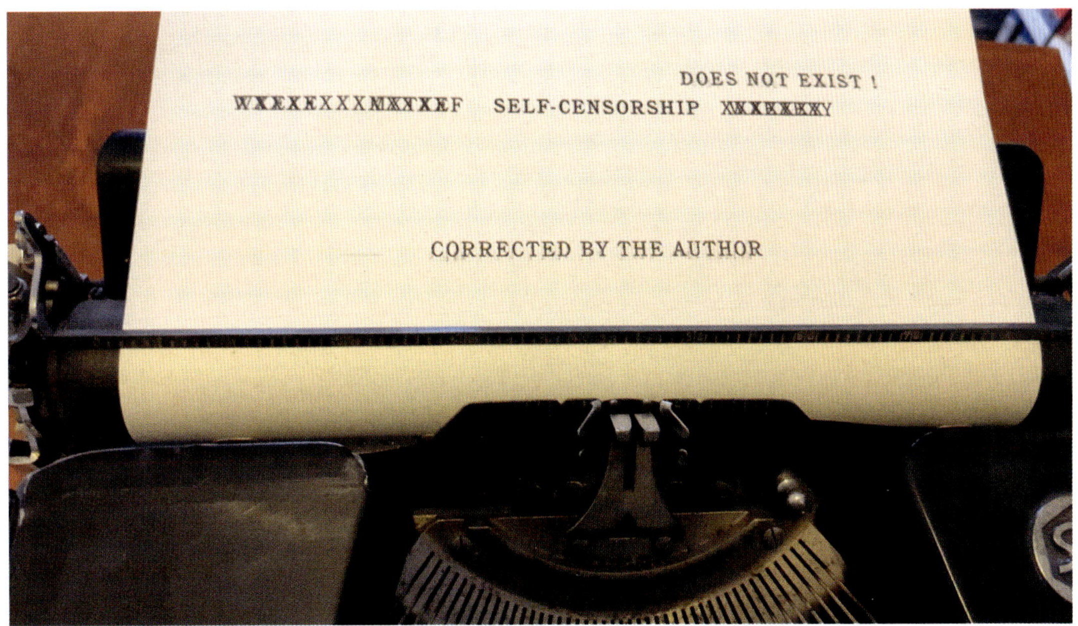

He explained to me how he, together with the director Miloš Forman, protested against censorship in the Velvet Revolution. At the end of the conversation, I gave him a book of a typographical poem entitled "Self-Censorship." It was a provocative, clever poem. Havel had published it a few years earlier. He picked up the book, recognized the poem, and said, "Ah, Autocensura." From state censorship to self-censorship, and from self-censorship to fear. But as it turns out, fear not only teaches us to fear; it also brings us to a new, creative vocabulary.

MASHA ALYOKHINA

I don't believe that something can kill your creativity, because it can appear even if you do not, let's say, expect it. But I can say one thing, which is quite important. I want to talk about fear. Because fear can stop not only your creativity, it can stop your life. Fear is usually the basis of censorship. When people are afraid of the government or the state or some authorities, fear can paralyze your creativity. But when you become your own state and you start to censor yourself, then you have a real problem, because fear always will find a reason to stop you. It will create thousands and thousands of reasons around what can happen to you. If you do something in countries like Russia or China, people are afraid sometimes to be honest in their art to criticize those who have power, because they are afraid to lose their job or lose their freedom and go to prison, or sometimes people even fear for their lives. But here, in Western European countries, a lot of times there might be people who are afraid to lose the money. And they start to create something just to make a more stable platform for themselves. And they start to just be the creators of the establishment. So that can be a problem.

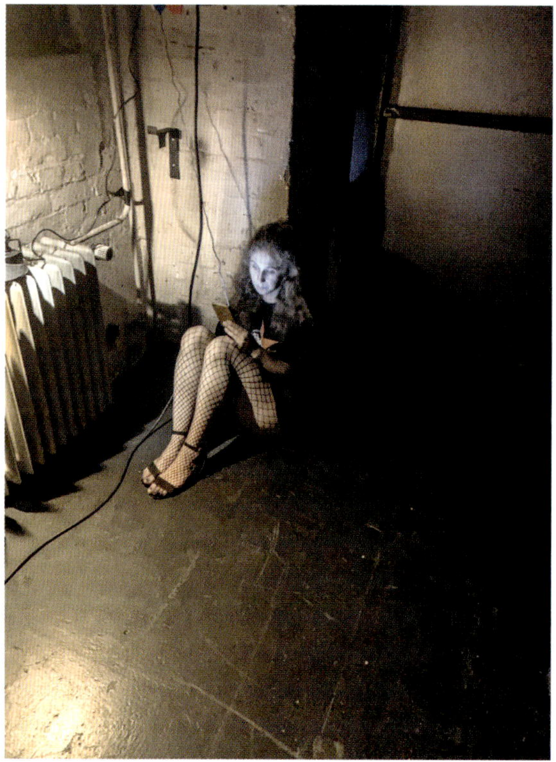

In a synagogue in São Paulo, I met Rabbi Henry Sobel. He offered a different perspective on the idea of self-censorship by referencing what he called the "fine judgement" that every creative person should have.

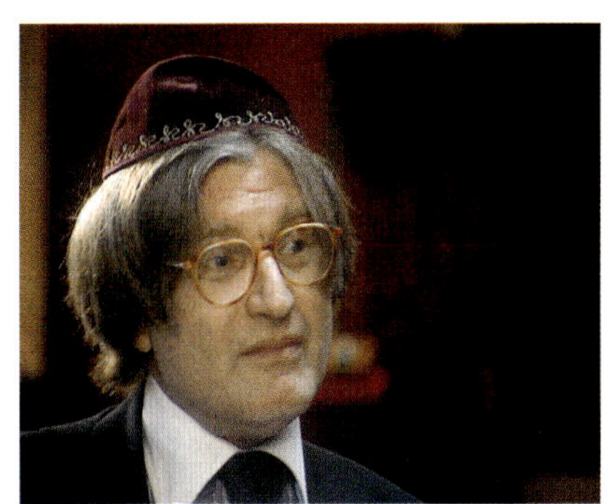

RABBI HENRY SOBEL

Where are the boundaries of creativity?

I think your question is extremely important, very legitimate, and very provocative in the good sense. Um, first of all, I do not accept the concept of censorship, whether it's in the newspapers or on television or in the advertising agencies; it's antidemocratic, it's antiethical, it's antihuman, we know it. But then again, liberty implies responsibility.

They are two sides of the same coin. I believe that each and every advertisement is a potential for good and can be a potential for bad. I would like each and every director and professional in the world of publicity to use their discretion, fine judgement to know what is respectful and what is not respectful. Yes, there can be disrespect in an advertisement, if it unjustly hurts the sensitivity of the onlooker. Now, I'm not one to preach morality and I'm not one to give you or anybody else a lesson on how to use fine judgement, especially when it comes to creativity, which is something very, very, very, very special. I just trust the good judgement of the people who are responsible for creativity and let them exercise their own censorship from inside, not from outside, so it's not censorship.

"I JUST TRUST THE GOOD JUDGEMENT OF THE PEOPLE WHO ARE RESPONSIBLE FOR CREATIVITY AND LET THEM EXERCISE THEIR OWN CENSORSHIP FROM INSIDE, NOT FROM OUTSIDE, SO IT'S NOT CENSORSHIP."

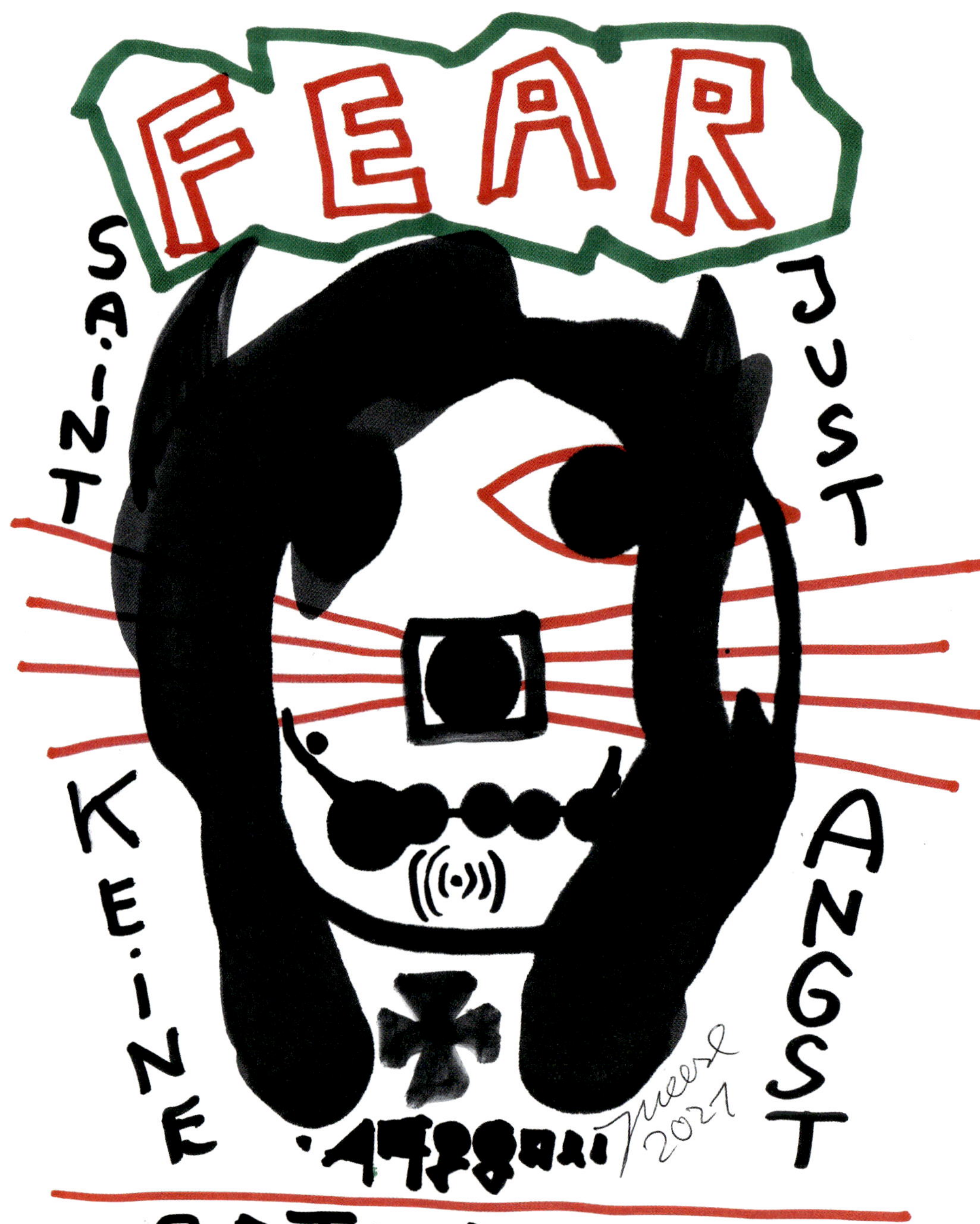
FEAR
SAINT
JUST
KEINE
ANGST
Meese
2021
ART ≠ FEAR
KUNST ≠ ANGST
1789

After seeing one of David Lynch's films, someone said to him, "I don't understand the narrative of your film. I'm lost." And David answered, "Well, I don't understand life." It's hard to make a narrative of your life without knowing what's coming next. That mystery of life. That fear of the future. Of not understanding things: David captures this very well. Why is it that for some of us, fear is our muse?

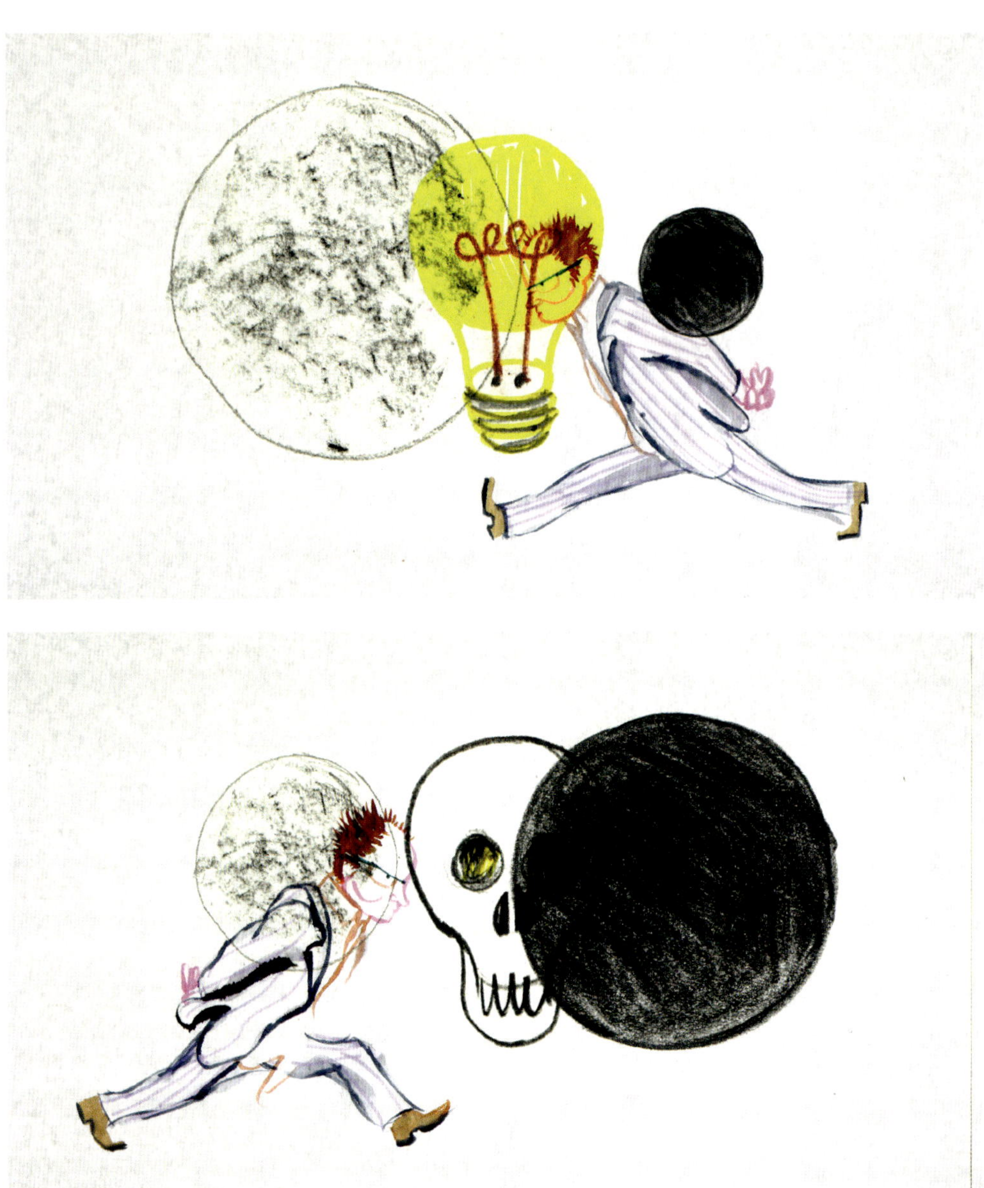

Some people seem to become even more creative in oppressive political circumstances. Others internalize the rules and use them to be creative. And still others internalize the rules so deeply that they stop being creative. Is fear a beta-blocker of creativity or can fear, on the flip side, also motivate creativity?

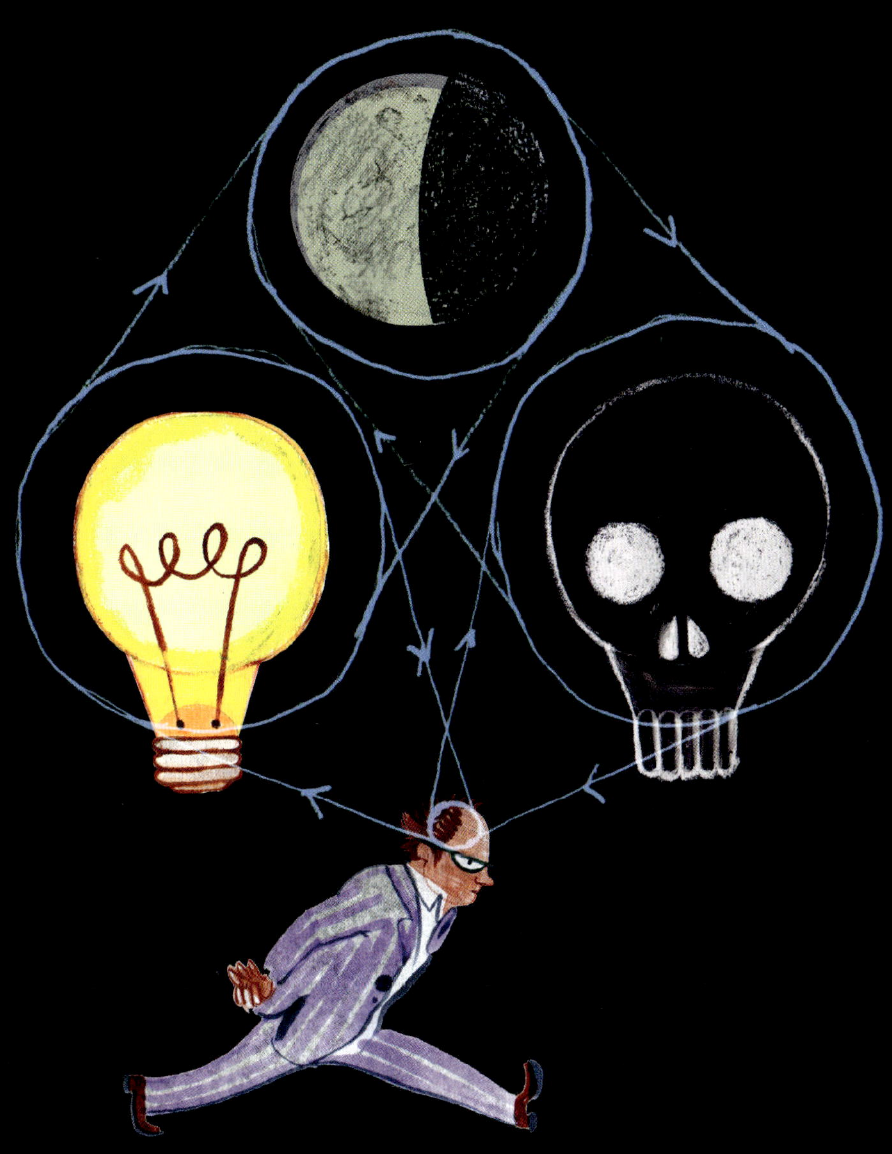

This whole thing was careening out of control, but I couldn't stop. I soon found myself on Fifth Avenue on my way to spend time with the thin white Duke of New York, David Bowie.
We had coffee and David played me demo tapes of his newest album *Outside*. We decided for the interview, we would do a surreal Magritte kind of setup. David looking into the camera and me looking out of the window. When I asked him why he's creative, we conversed back-to-back.

"I FIND IT AN INTOXICATING PARALLEL TO MY PERCEIVED REALITY TO BE ABLE TO HAVE THIS OTHER ONE WHERE YOU CAN EXPLORE ANXIETIES AND FEARS."

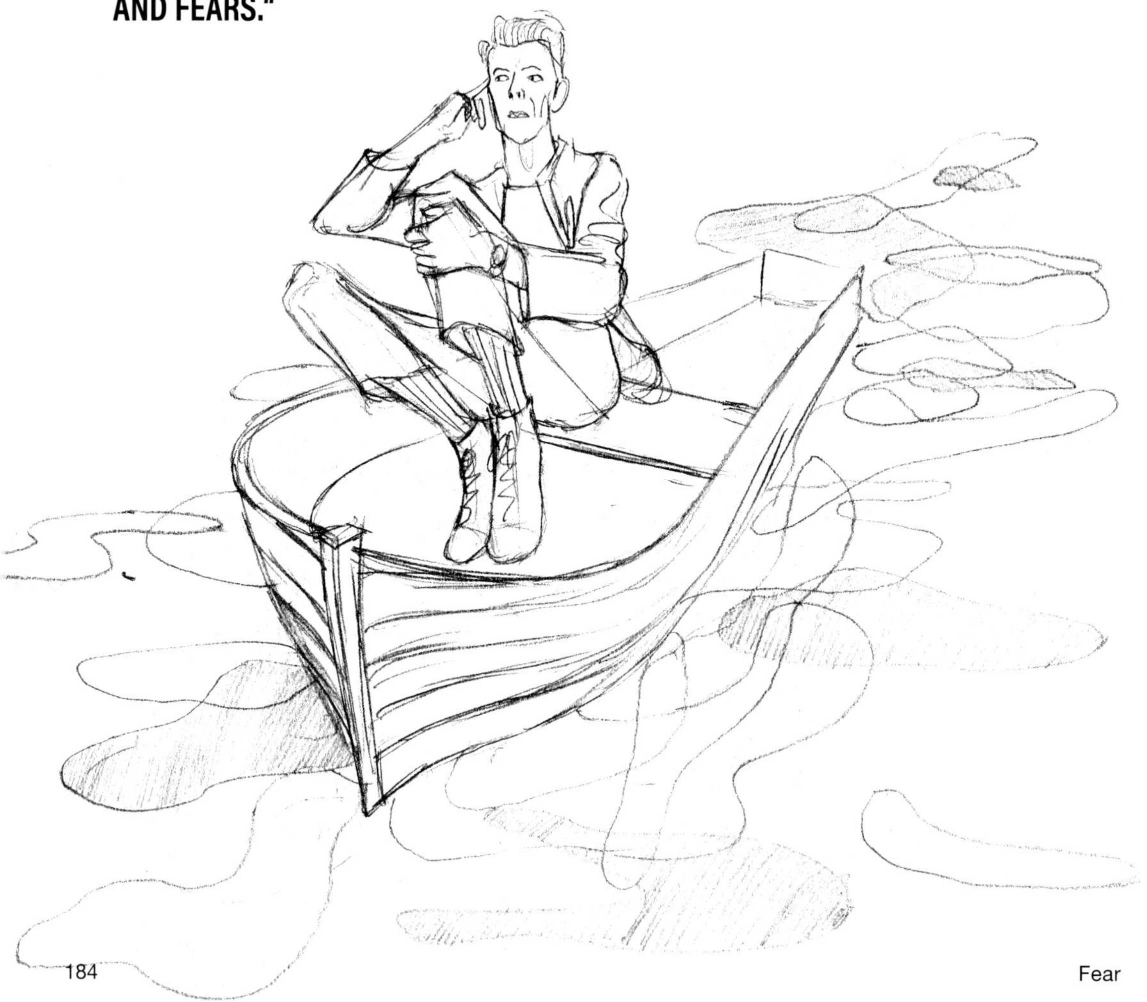

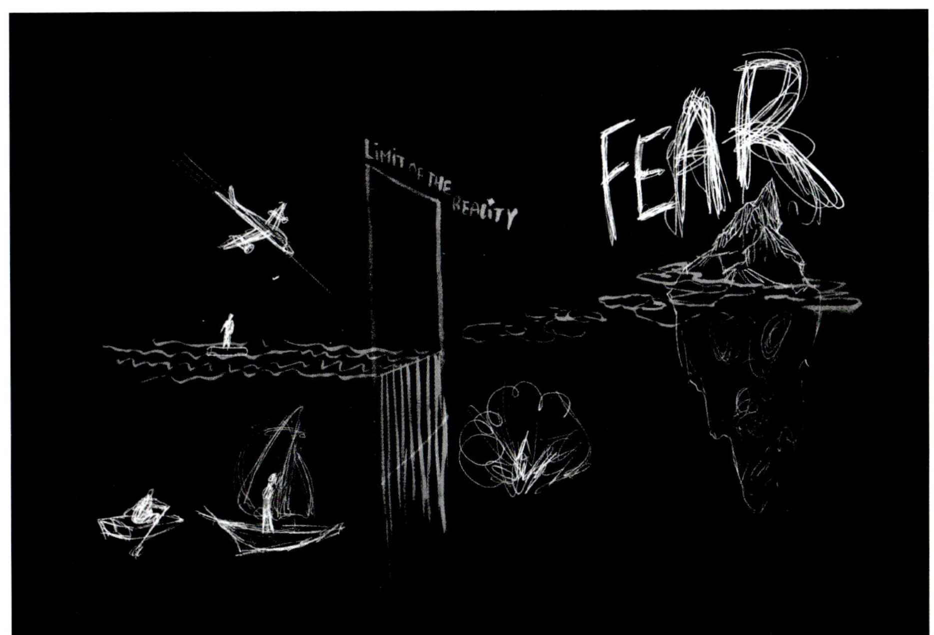

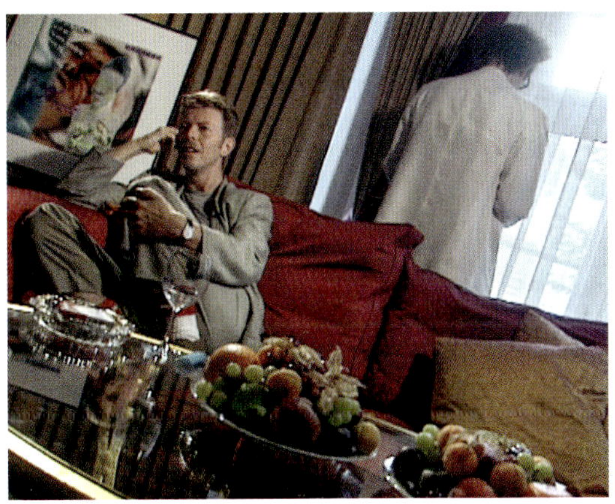

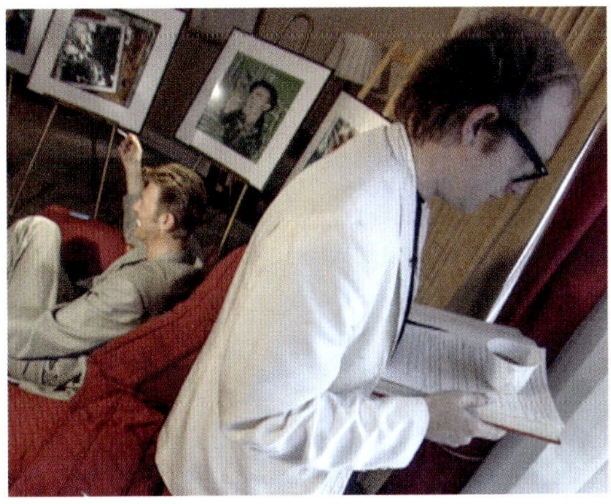

DAVID BOWIE

I think creativity has something to do with wanting to find a place where I can kind of set sail and know that I really won't fall off the world when I get to the edge of the sea. There will just be more and more sea to navigate.

There's the idea that being creative is one of the few human endeavours that you can get involved in where you can, as Brian Eno would say, crash your airplane and walk away from it. I think it is sort of an intellectual field of adventure—it can either be play or it can be war or maybe a hybrid of both. I find it an intoxicating parallel to my perceived reality to be able to have this other one where you can explore anxieties and fears. I think that is probably why I am creative.

Fight or flight? Exploring fears instead of evading them? With the thriller and psychological thriller, an entire genre thrives on this creative confrontation of one's fear, starting with a classic: fear of the dark. I made a short feature titled *Who Killed the Idea?* starring Hollywood actor Harvey Keitel, who had to face his fear the hard way.

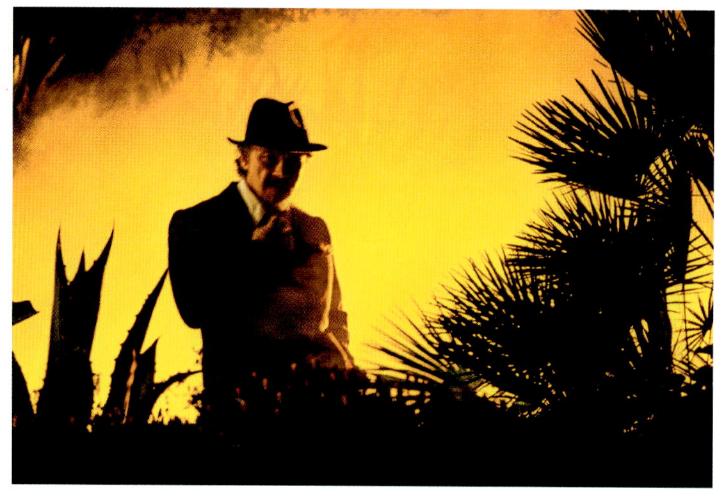

HARVEY KEITEL

"WE'RE ALL AFRAID OF WHAT WE DON'T KNOW."

When I was seventeen, I joined the Marines and during one part of our training, in night combat, we were in a field, a lot of us, and you couldn't see your hand in front of your face. It was pitch black. An instructor's form you could see against the skyline. And it was our first course in night combat, and this instructor said to us, "You're all afraid of the darkness. We're all afraid of what we don't know. I'm going to teach about the darkness, so that you know it, and so that you'll no longer be afraid of it." For me that instructor's words invaded my future. And I never forgot his words. In all the reading I've done and all the mythology I've read, and all the religious writings I've read, the darkness is the one place they all have in common that they speak about. That we must enter into.

JON AMIEL

What I do know, for certain, is that every time I've come to a crossroads in my life and had a choice about which way to go, I've, generally speaking, chosen the route that scared me most. I certainly seek out journeys that scare me. I think it's the conquering of my own fears. That's one of the largest motivating forces in my life.

Brings to mind Robert Frost's poem: "Two roads diverged in a wood, and I—I took the one less travelled by, And that has made all the difference." If we are not prepared to take any risks, we should not use the word "creativity" any longer.

When I met *Pulp Fiction* star Tim Roth, he told me that fear of unemployment sparked his creativity. As has been said before, fear is one of the most toxic, and, well ... most feared killers of creativity. Once it invades our creative space, intuition turns into instinct, and, instinctively, all those great ideas run like hell.

TIM ROTH

The fear of unemployment drives me. A lot of people have it. It's this whole thing about giving up acting for a while. I was worried, you give it up and they don't want you back. Suddenly nobody's interested in hiring you. It would be scary. I know a lot of actors who are like that and I know a lot of directors and writers who are like—fear of unemployment, fear of not being needed, as well. If I'm not working in about two weeks, I start getting depressed. I love to be occupied. And that can be a real problem because your work can suffer, your life can suffer. But I have to be doing something. I'd do a seven-day week if I was allowed. But I'm not allowed. The crew always want a five-day week.

Onward and upward. Mountaineer Reinhold Messner confronts his fear whenever he climbs the highest peaks of the world.

REINHOLD MESSNER

Fear is part of our humanity. Whenever we want to dare something which we are not familiar with, fears and doubts come. And the bigger the goals are, the more likely that fears and doubts come. Now I can reduce a large part of the fears in advance, simply with training, with know-how, with skill, with studies, how I solve these problems that could arise. And with that, the fears disappear. But in the end, there remains a balance, so to speak, between the courage to go on and the fears that are still there. And if I didn't have any fears, maybe in the end there wouldn't be this necessary decision to take the first step. I call it the gift of daring. If I have no fears, then the whole thing is quite banal and I say even for me it would have been boring. But then when I start my journey, the fears shrink. I know that, that is of course a great experience. If, on the other hand, I hesitate and wait and wait, the fears increase. That's why it's very important that this step is taken courageously. The step into it, for me into the adventure, for the artist into his expression, whatever he then expresses.

"WHEN I START MY JOURNEY, THE FEARS SHRINK."

Fear can be a creative source, but it rarely behaves as it should. It quickly gets out of hand, playing out irrational scenarios to the ultimate fearsome absurdity, and it does a great job of convincing us of even the most abstruse what-ifs. It takes a cool head. The drive is all the stronger when there is just the right amount of fear at the back.

AI WEIWEI

I think that fear is always a motivation for meaningful creativity. You know, because we have one mysterious life which is only given for very mysterious reasons and then can be taken away by unknown force.

DAVE TROTT

Fear can give you an edge, as long as you're in charge of it, as long as you know how to use it to make yourself do what you know you really ought to do but you're too lazy or embarrassed to do. Use the fear to get you past your own mind. Your mind is telling you, "Don't do it, it's embarrassing and anyway, why should you have to?" And that's when you need to be able to turn on the fear. I was reading the *Harvard Business Review*, Alex Ferguson was talking about the European cup final, when Bayern was winning one-nil and they're a really good team, and Man United just couldn't break through, and Ferguson got his whole team to walk past the European Cup and he said to them: "Now remember, you're six inches away from that cup, and if you don't win that's the closest you're ever going to get in your entire life. You're never going to touch that European cup if you don't win." He said "Don't come back and allow yourself to regret it for the rest of your life. Because you'll be regretting it for the next fifty years of your life." That's using fear in a positive way. To put the fear that you're going to do absolutely everything short of dying to win that game, and they did. But that's using fear in a positive way.

"FEAR CAN GIVE YOU AN EDGE, AS LONG AS YOU'RE IN CHARGE OF IT."

Back to the guy who is not afraid to be different. I met the art director and designer George Lois in New York again when he had an exhibition at the MoMA, where he showed his famous *Esquire Covers*. George gave me a book and that book was called *George, Be Careful.* George then took a pen and wrote me a dedication in the book: "Be reckless, Hermann." I bet he wrote that to all his fans. However, that doesn't make it less true. After all, this book is intended to encourage us to stand up to the inner censor and not to be afraid to be different.

GEORGE LOIS

I did a book, my first book I called *George, Be Careful*. And I remember when I was six months old, the hand of God coming through, pointing to my crib saying "George, be careful!" Not true, but that's okay. My mother said "George, be careful!," my father said "George, be careful!," my teachers in school, my coaches in sports, when I wanted a career—"George, be careful!" And when I went into advertising, into graphic design, everybody around you says always, whenever you do something exciting, which is almost always, they say: "George, be careful!" Everybody wants you to be careful. And if you're careful in life, especially in advertising or magazine design, you're dull! So, it's my antislogan: "George, be careful!"—no, no, "George, be reckless!" Reckless doesn't mean crazy; reckless means seemingly outrageous. You look at something and go, "Whoa! Oh, that's good, oh that's good."

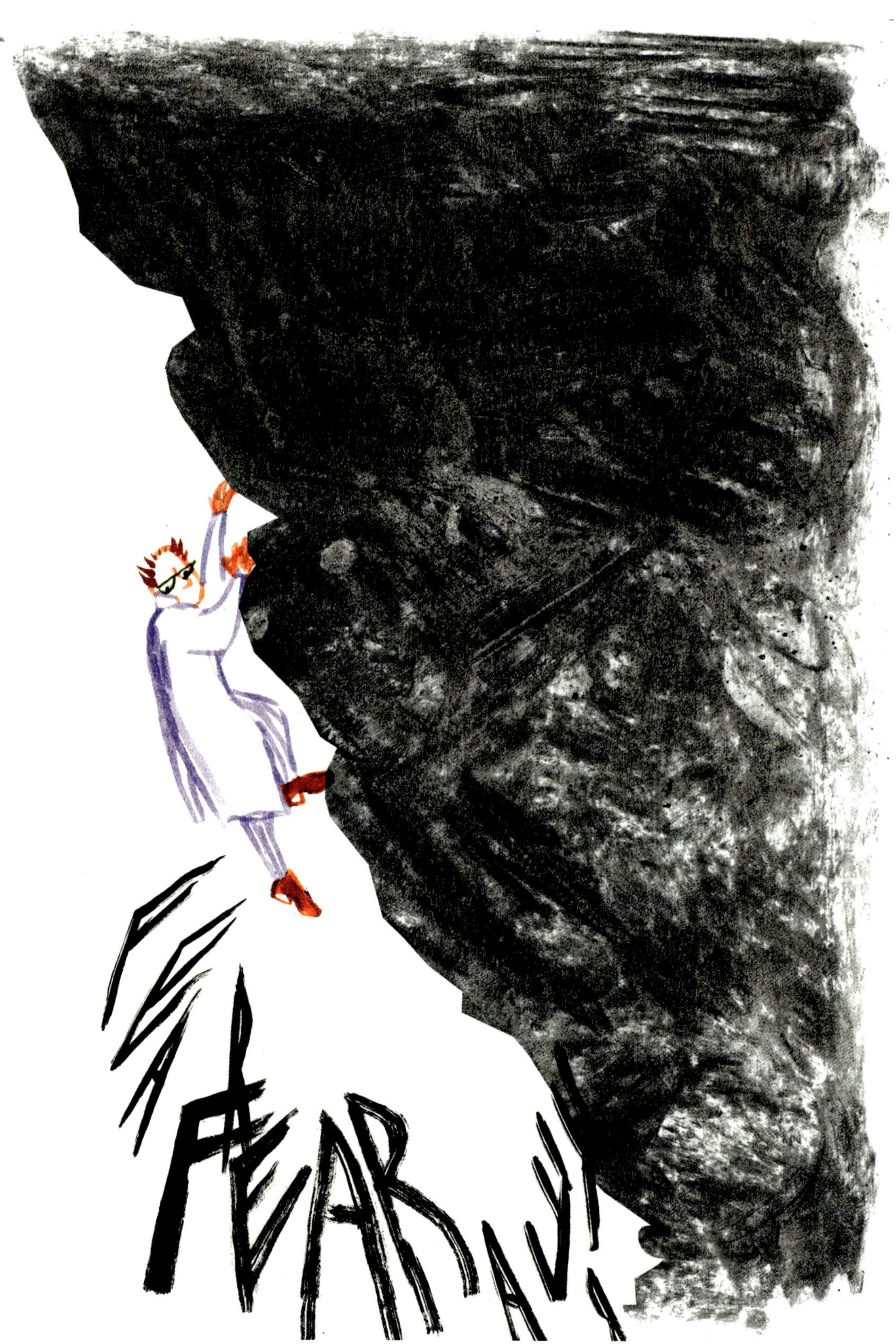
FEAR

MARKUS LÜPERTZ

Writers are often afraid of the blank piece of paper. Are you afraid of the white canvas?

That's the other side. You are facing the canvas with only a brush and colors. You are actually alone. That's a kind of loneliness you cannot even imagine. And the first stroke is fatal, isn't it? That's where the death zone begins. Then the picture starts to fight back. But if you keep at it long enough, it begins to speak. And then the picture tells you exactly what you have to do. That has to do with perseverance, persistence, and just an inability to lose, to not give up.

ISABELLA ROSSELLINI

It's very hard to be a writer. I once worked with Norman Mailer. We made an infinitely unsuccessful film. With a wonderful title: *Tough Guys Don't Dance*. And Norman was so happy. He said, "I'm always alone. Always, for hours a day. And now, instead, I have all of you here. It's so much fun. And then I write something, in my head, I write the dialogue, but then you say it differently—and it's better!" And he was so enthusiastic, and I completely understand. That is the pleasure of working in films.

NICK CAVE

Gabriel Garcia Marquez described writing as the most solitary experience there is. He said a blank piece of paper is scary. As a writer, do you share this viewpoint?

Yeah, I do. I think that the real problem with writing for me is that you are on your own. Entirely on your own. There is no help that you can get from anybody. It is impossible to draw people into it. At the end of the day, you have to sit down and you have to write what you have to write. And you have to face each day, the blank piece of paper and I find that a terrifying thing. Songwriting is different and, in a way, suits my artistic mechanism much more. What a blank page immediately gives you is a feeling of isolation, a feeling of loneliness, a feeling of detachment from the world. That's what a blank page gives to me.

Director Ilya Khrzhanovsky is the artistic director of the Babi Yar Holocaust Memorial Center. In a conversation with me, he describes the relationship between fear and creativity.

ILYA KHRZHANOVSKY

I think fear is the greatest enemy of creativity, and it is actually the result of a totalitarian regime. Because a totalitarian regime is not only the physical violent, which is a big part of it, but it's the mental violence. You broke your right to have your own opinion, your right to be active, your right to be different, your right to be strange, your right to write something. It's about human rights, which is not in the human rights memorandum or constitution, but it is inside the human soul. Freedom of speech and everything. But it's freedom of thought. That's the main thing. People continue to resist thinking.

Into the darkness and out the other side, preferably with a brilliant idea in tow. If only it were that simple. Instead, we encounter an adversary no less than ourselves—the paranoid philistine, disguised as the voice of reason. A voice we may have already internalized. Can we use it to turn fear into an idea? How can we use fear as a vehicle?

LUISA NEUBAUER

My creative stimulus is an existential fear of the climate crisis and the ignorance of those who could or should stop it. On the one hand, there's also the dialectic at work. On the other hand, of course, the world, so to speak, is the place. And that's worth fighting for. And when you look around and realize, "Yes, breathtaking nature is more breathtaking than anything humans could ever put togeter." It does. It's already thought-provoking and motivating.

And the more I learned about creativity as a form of "not dying," the more I had to accept that there was something in creativity that solved and was simultaneously created by our deepest existential terrors. Creativity might be beautiful, but it sprang from a dark and scary place. As we can witness in the radical works of British artist Marianna Simnett.

MARIANNA SIMNETT

I don't think that it's possible to control fear. I think most of my work is about attempting a loss of control or to deauthorize or try to bring down systems that are positions of authority or control. I've, even myself, I tried to lose control with my body or to change myself, like forcing unconsciousness upon myself.

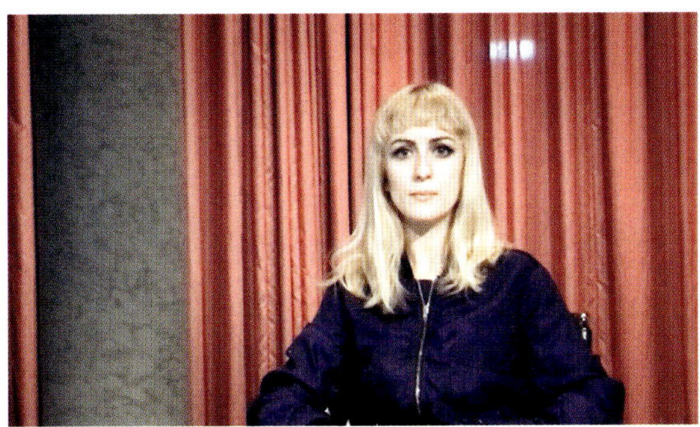

Sometimes I perform real procedures on myself, other times I use prosthetics and fake theatrical materials and I don't tell people when I'm telling the truth, and everything gets blurred into these spaces of discomfort where you don't really know if the cockroaches brain is really being pierced.

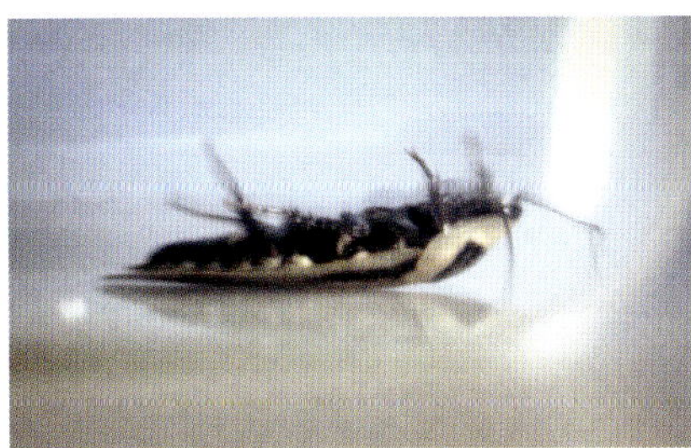

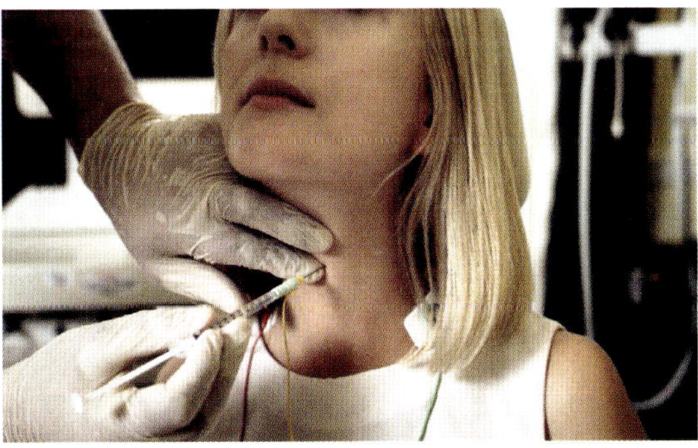

Sometimes we have these Cronenberg-Scanners moments where the leg suddenly explodes and it's really about pushing to the outer edges and the limits of the body and the mind. I've had a procedure which made my voice lower with an injection of Botox in my larynx.

The more I learned about the major engine of our creativity is our deepest existential terrors and fears, the more I realized I had to speak to David Lynch—the master of anxiety. But there was always an answering machine saying: "If you're calling from Uganda, the fridge is already sold." This seemed to have more twists and turns than Mulholland Drive. It was as if this Svenghali of the surreal was trying to draw me into another mystery.

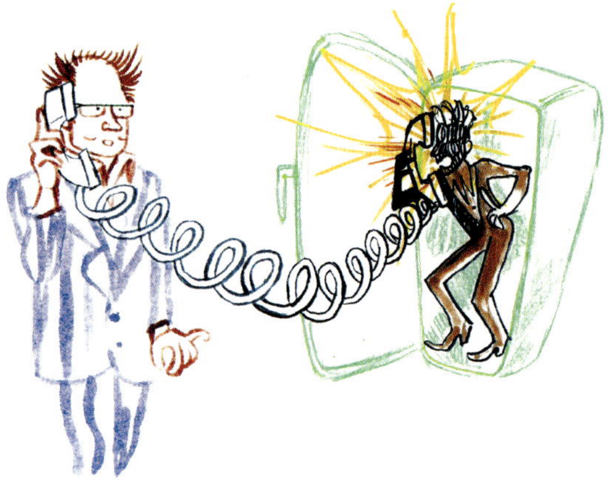

DAVID LYNCH

I am creative because there's really nothing more thrilling then getting an idea and then translating it, realizing that idea. Bringing something from the abstract to the material. You can create a new world.

From the abstract to the material. That brings me to the question: How did the invention of the photographic camera change creativity?

Well, every medium gives you chances for creating something and the still image, even though there's many, many, many people with cameras, always still photography is alive and well and evolving. And when you have motion pictures, you're dealing with time and sequences and all the other elements that come together, it's the most magical.

"BRINGING SOMETHING FROM THE ABSTRACT TO THE MATERIAL."

David draws a street that leads into the heart of darkness as an answer to the question why he is creative. In the midst of the darkness, he draws a question mark.

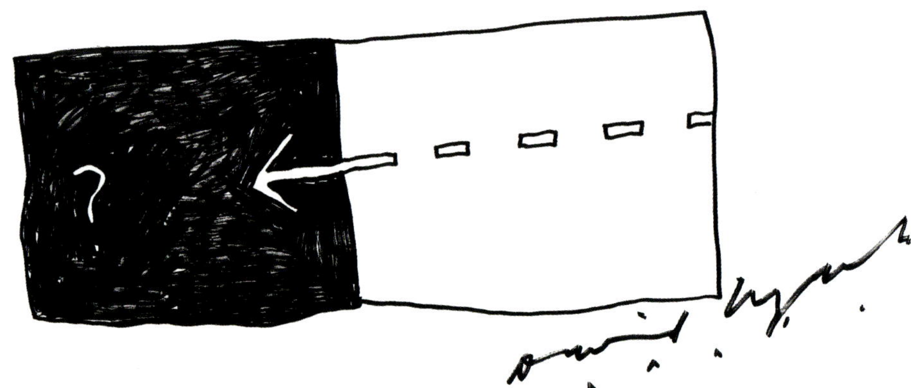

Lynch made me realize how dangerous these creative people can be. If you can get an audience to change their minds about reality—it's only a short step to making them change reality. For creativity to use its mind-bending skills as an instrument of social change. As a weapon of revolution.

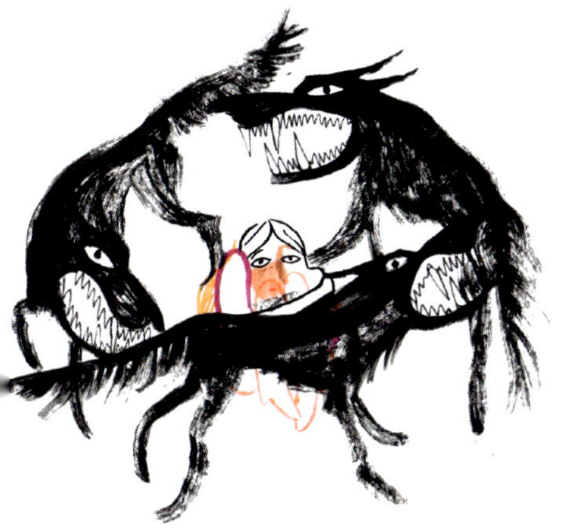

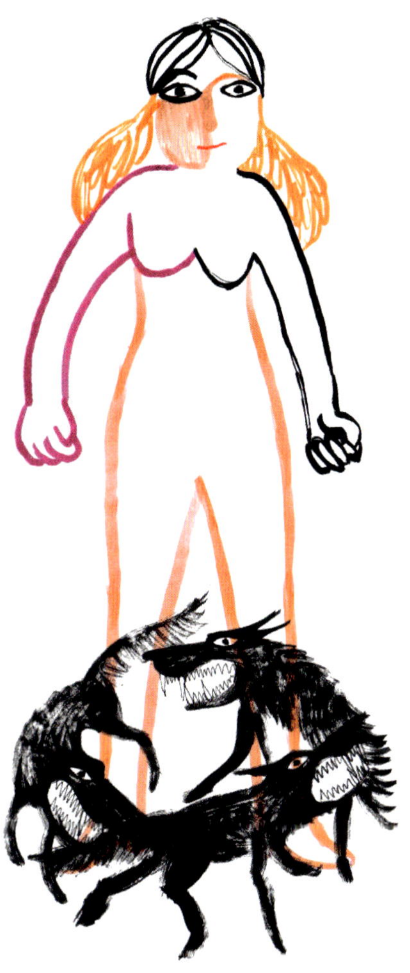

MASHA ALJOKHINA

If you're afraid, just do it. Doesn't matter, afraid or not afraid. History doesn't care about your feelings. If you change history, you will probably, after that, have an option to talk about your feelings. But when you are doing something, just do it. It's your decision, your desire.

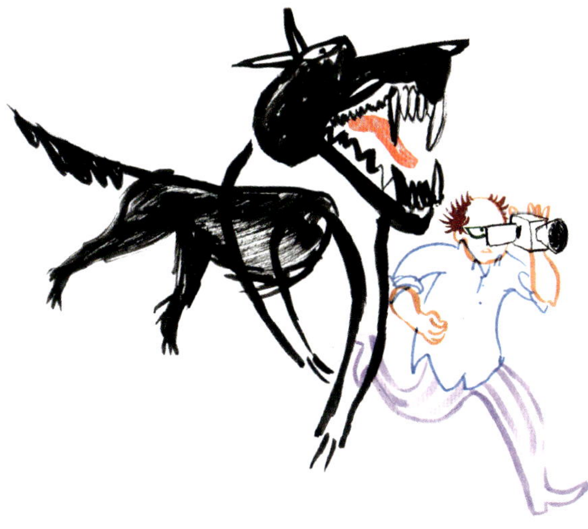

EDGAR REITZ

There is a longing for a certain state, which is the state of no longer knowing what I am doing. I find nothing more beautiful than being able to deal with my material in a completely surrendered and almost unconscious way. That is not readily achievable. It's achievable by seeping into the ambience of the subject and the people you're working with. And then one day you're covered in the kind of work you're doing, you're so wrapped up in everything that you don't know what you're doing anymore. And the most beautiful things happen when you're free-falling.

"AND THE MOST BEAUTIFUL THINGS HAPPEN WHEN YOU'RE FREE-FALLING."

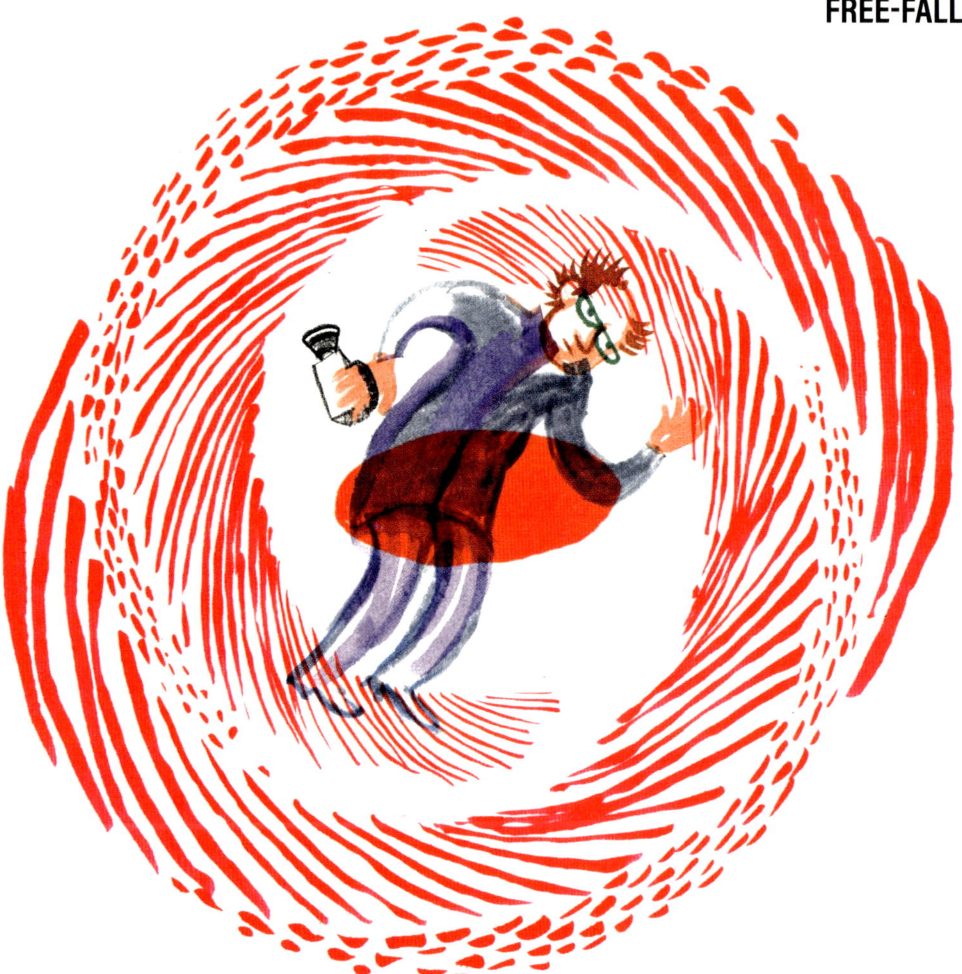

"WHEN SOMEONE SAYS "ACTION," YOU DON'T KNOW WHAT WILL HAPPEN."

TRINE DYRHOLM

When I have to act, I love to be in the moment of, I call it conscious unconsciousness. Because that is the moment where everything is ready. When we all know where the camera is, the sound guy is here, and we know the lines, we know what the scene is about. But then, when someone says "action," you don't know what will happen. And I am very attracted to that moment, because that is in between. I always try to trick my brain or my system to say that. We are ready, and "action"—I don't know what will happen.

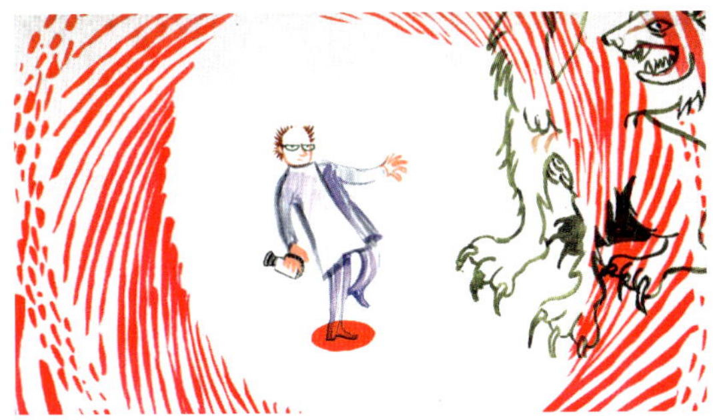

UDO KIER

"The souls of human beings must be terrorized to their deepest core by unfathomable and seemingly senseless crimes that have only one purpose: to spread fear and terror." This is from Dr. Mabuse, Fritz Lang. And he was talking about being creative has to do with fear and terror.

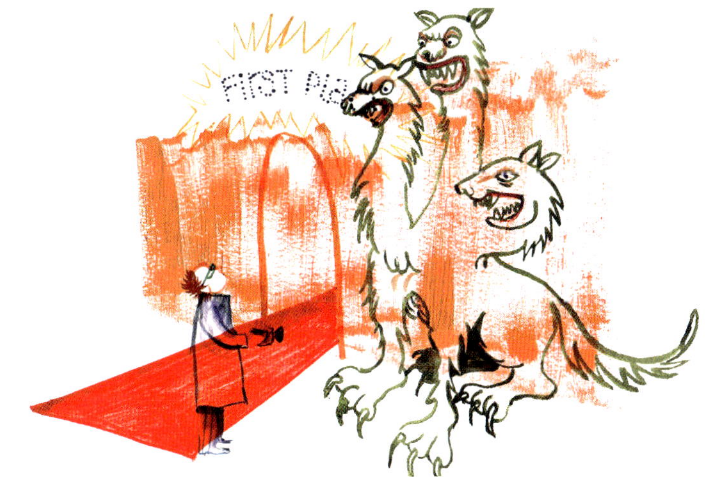

With the visions of Dr. Mabuse in my head, I left Udo's home in California. The visions of Dr. Mabuse drove me into a downward spiral. And spat me out of the gates of creativity, where I landed in a heap on the ground. When I got up and turned around, I noticed that the gates of creativity are guarded by a modern dog of hell, a modern Cerberus. And his name was the gatekeepers.

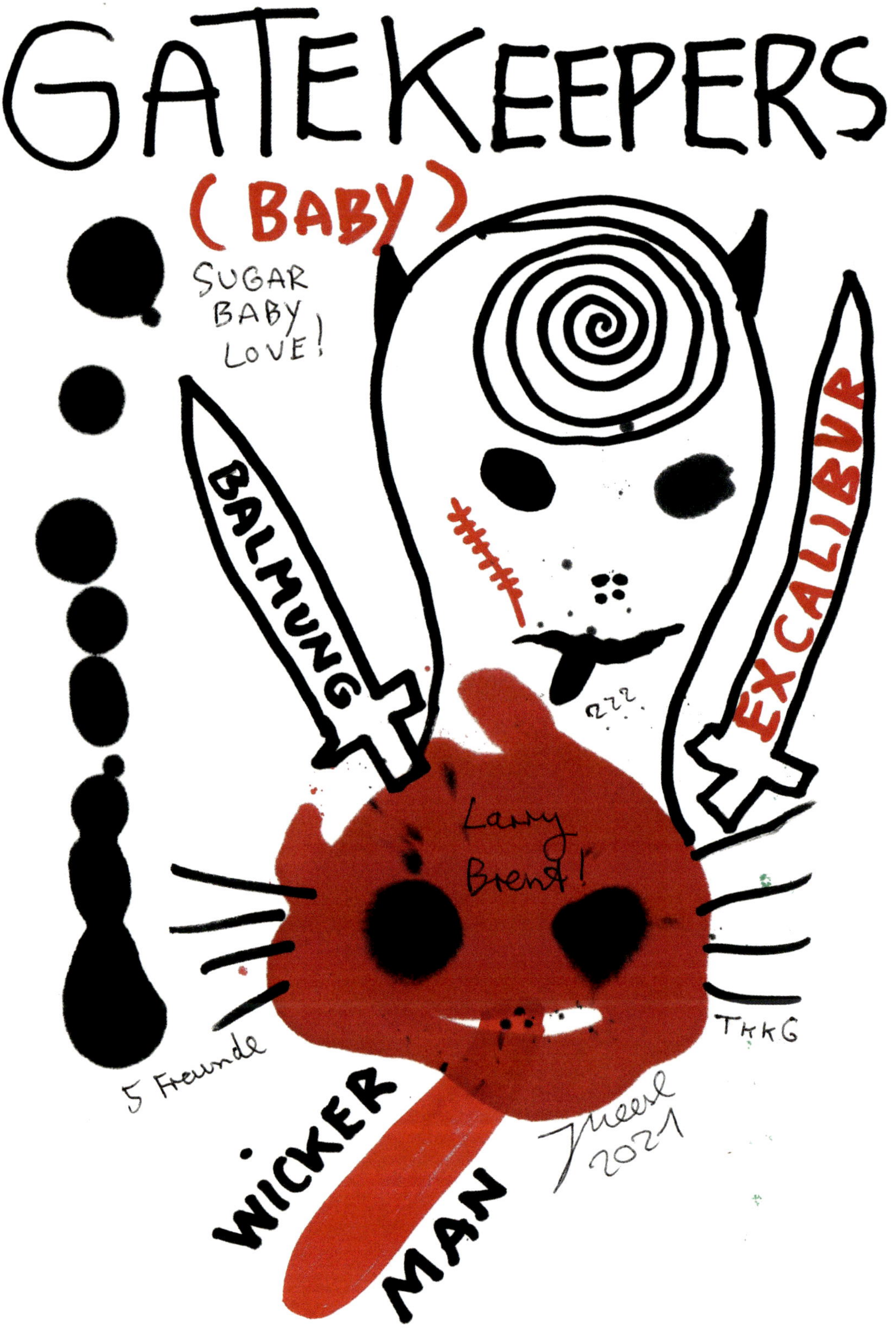

GATEKEEPERS

(BABY)

SUGAR
BABY
LOVE!

BALMUNG

EXCALIBUR

zzz

Larry
Brent!

TKKG

5 Freunde

WICKER
MAN

Meese
2021

In the tragic assassination of creativity, we have a list of suspects. And right at the top of the list are the gatekeepers, those who, Caesar-like, give the thumbs-up or thumbs-down. Those media tyrants and cultural censors who revel in the power of "no." Institutions behave like it's forever 1984. The Academie Française sat on the French language for centuries. Doing its best to prohibit the production of a Shakespeare or a James Joyce. The institutional mindset would make the invention of new words a criminal offence. And even if you're allowed to apply, it'll take forever for your idea to get through the system. Any good idea will be crushed by the wheels of bureaucracy.

Some time ago I was invited to a panel, and the topic was mentors, the opposite of gatekeepers. And someone said: "Mentors are all well and good, but make sure to find the right mentor." I went to award-winning director Lars Kraume. How did gatekeepers and mentors influence his creativity?

LARS KRAUME

Gatekeepers. ... Well, I think in order to be creative you need to have aggression. You can't move forward unless you have an urgent need to do so. That's a permanent obstacle that you have to overcome. People always think that nobody needs their film. Of course, that's not surprising. Last year in the United States, 520 new series were produced. Whether the world needs my new German series that I have in mind comes into question. And if you don't have the ability to ignore this and prevail against these gatekeepers that tell you, "We don't need that," of course you'll falter. Support is very important, any form of support. That's been my experience. All that positive support that I received, first from my parents who gave me a camera, then from the photographer whom I assisted, and then Reinhard Hauff as the dean of my film school. In my case, unlike other people's cases, he was not a gatekeeper, but a door opener. He highlighted my films, he presented them, he introduced me to people. That kind of support is an immense help, of course. Or also the first professional actor Florian Lukas, with whom I shot, and I was totally unsure, because I had no idea what an actor is and what he does and so forth, but I was suddenly in this role of the director, and he said, "It's ok, it's good how you do it." And that alone is enough. And that little bit of wind in the sails is often enough to just move forward.

"IN ORDER TO BE CREATIVE YOU NEED TO HAVE AGGRESSION."

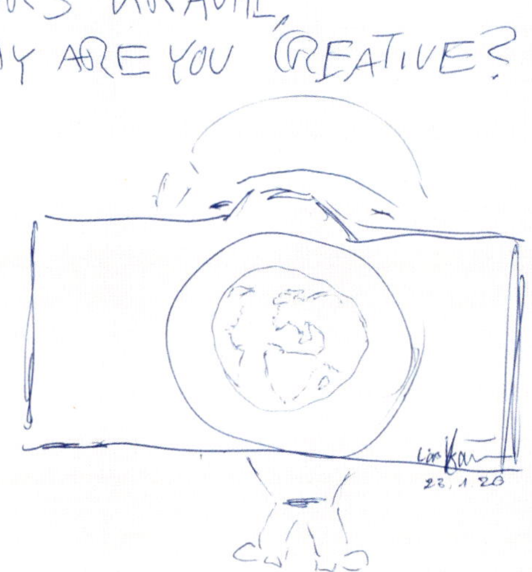

Two-time Oscar winner and Zampano actor Anthony Quinn was very lucky with his mentor. His mentor, star architect Frank Lloyd Wright, was anything but a gatekeeper:

ANTHONY QUINN

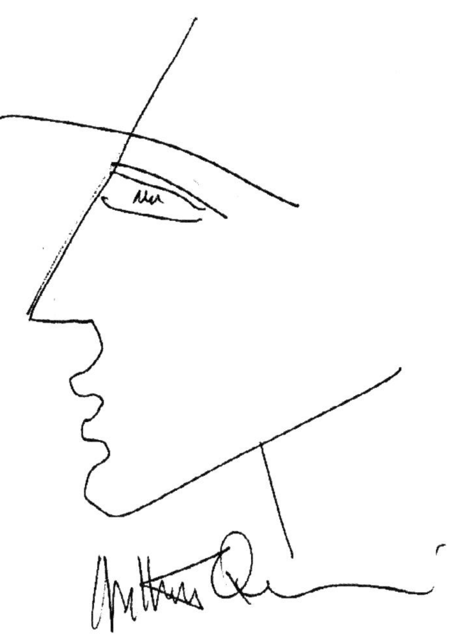

I became an adult, around twenty years old. Frank Lloyd Wright was my teacher and mentor. I studied architecture and he said to me by accident: your speech is very bad. And I said, what has my speech got to do with being an architect? He said, well, people won't listen to you. So he said, you'd better go and get an operation on your tongue. So he sent me to a doctor and the doctor said, yes, I was tongue-tied, I was, my tongue was flat. So he said it'll cost you 200 dollars to do the operation. I didn't have the money, but Frank Lloyd Wright said, do the operation and I can afford it. So they did the operation. Then a very funny thing happened. I didn't know how to use my tongue. So then Frank again says, oh well, go to drama school or something. So I went to a drama school and I was the janitor, because I didn't like Mr. Wright to pay for my lessons.
And I went up to Frank Lloyd Wright and I said: Mr. Wright, they're offering me 350 dollars a week at Paramount to act and I don't know what to do. I don't know whether to come back and study with you. He said, "Oh my God, you take it, you take it, you'll never earn that kind of money with me as an architect. It'll take you ten years to earn that kind of money." So I took the job.

TRINE DYRHOLM

Good collaboration is so inspiring. So now that I've started to kind of be a mentor for young actors and actresses, and actually I just had a meeting with a very interesting, talented young actress. And she got a huge job and we talked about character work and stuff like that.
And she had such good, interesting questions about the whole thing and then in the end she talked about how some people say that you have to do this, you have to do this, you have to do this. And then I just heard myself say: "I think you know, what you have to do." I mean you have to find your way. That is important, because you talked about education and nobody knows what is the right way. Nobody knows. And that is a lesson that we have to learn. Nobody can really tell us anything. But we can be inspired by each other and we can understand something when we share our different experiences. But she has to find her way and you could already tell that she had an intuition of the character. So just there, to jump into it and see what will happen.

WIM WENDERS

I don't think it's people killing the idea, so much as institutions. As soon as ideas get institutionalized, their biggest enemy is at work. You see that best in the church, for instance. The church is the worst enemy of religion. And religion is a great idea. Christ's idea was fantastic. If he came into the world today, the first thing he would have to do away with is the church. And basically, that's the story of all ideas. Communism … great idea. And look what happened. Look, who killed it was the institutions who incorporated it. Same with movie studios, I mean … you bring an idea there, the studio takes it and the moment the studio owns it, the idea is dead.

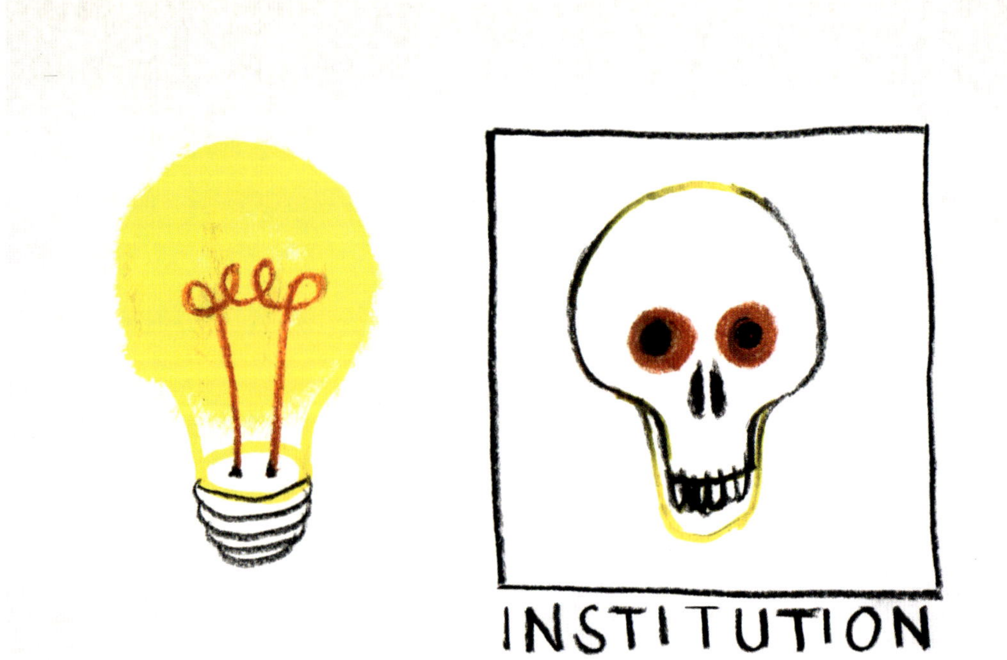

On the flip side, some institutions can be promoters of ideas and creative projects, as director Ilya Khrzhanovsky and artist Flaka Haliti told me, when she was studying at Städel Art School in Frankfurt.

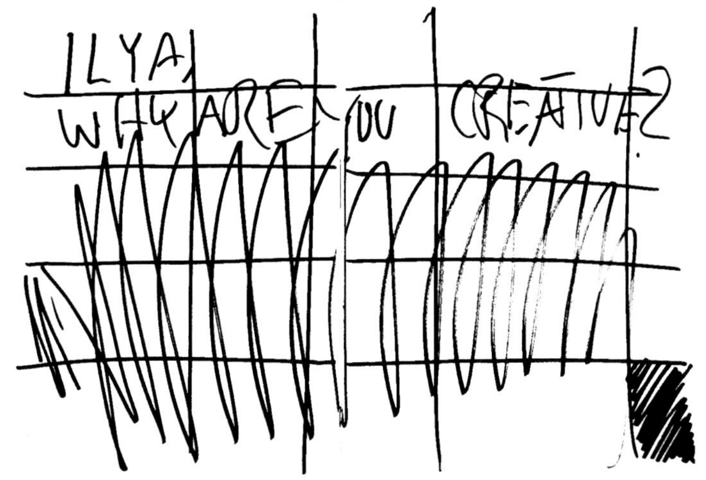

ILYA KHRZHANOVSKY

I think the institution is the biggest supporter of creativity, if the institution is done in the right way. If there is a human element there, if it's right people running it. I think the institutions in Germany, for example, did so much for creativity. And it's not only official institutions. A lot of great things start as private initiatives and become institutions. I believe ininstitutions.

"I THINK THE INSTITUTION IS THE BIGGEST SUPPORTER FOR CREATIVITY, IF THE INSTITUTION IS DONE IN THE RIGHT WAY."

FLAKA HALITI

Bureaucracy is everywhere, and once you learn how to apply to one foundation you learn a lot about so many other things, especially the politics of the foundation, fitting the "box perfectly," which is not easy sometimes. And in the end, you just understand that this money that you get is not really for free. Because you have to do a lot of work on that. Because writing papers, giving, delivering, doing, responding to them, and all this ongoing engagement with the bureaucratic stuff is a job that you are doing. And they still treat you as though "I'm giving you money for free." No, you just did a job, you spent many hours working on the computer, doing this and that. So at the end it's a job too, a tricky job.

Director Klaus Lemke was not so fond of applying at institutions. He picked an underground car park for our meeting, the coolest place he could think of to escape the summer heat.

KLAUS LEMKE

Two out of three theater directors sit in front of their computers all day long doing paperwork to get money from the state for their wanky projects and mistake it for creativity when they buy some new garden furniture that suits their wife's party better. But to talk about creativity in Germany is nonsense, because here nobody knows what it is. Creativity is essentially about taking yourself by the hand and stumbling into the dark, not knowing if you are going to get beaten up for it.

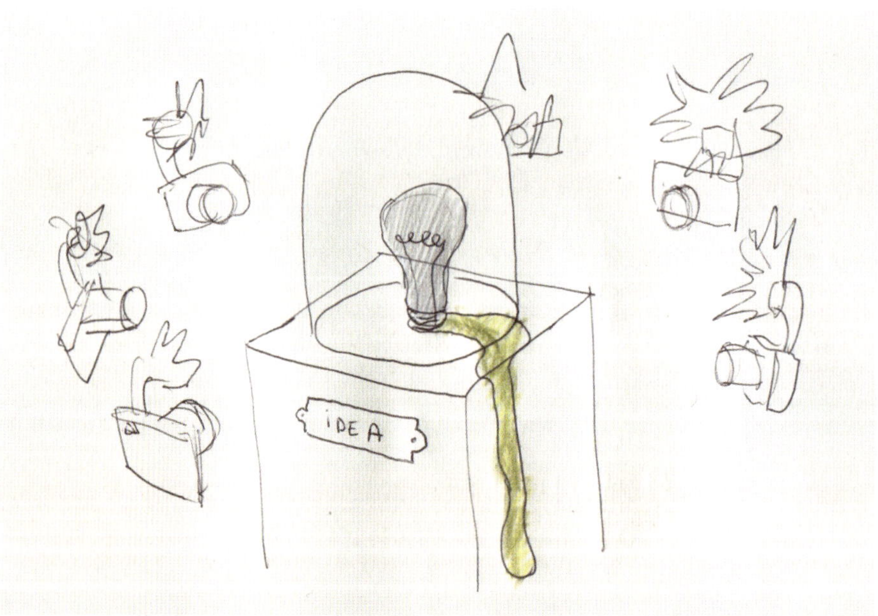

American director Jim Jarmusch explains to us why ideas can't be killed. We meet Jim Jarmusch on a rooftop in NYC. He talks about the subjugation of ideas.

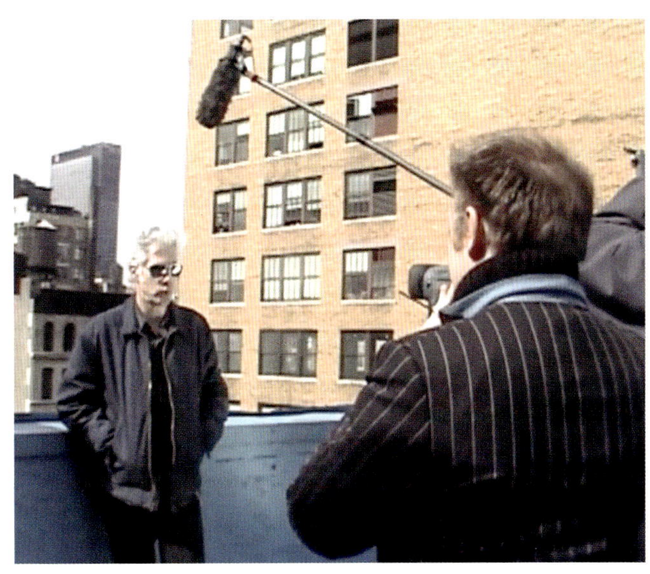

JIM JARMUSCH

I don't think ideas can be killed because ideas have their own life, and they will always be resurging and are impossible to kill. They certainly can be wounded or injured. I think mostly by a kind of corporate mentality and by trying to subjugate the craftsmanship of filmmaking and instead making it demographics and marketing and creating the product for the audience, which I think is really responsible for damaging ideas.

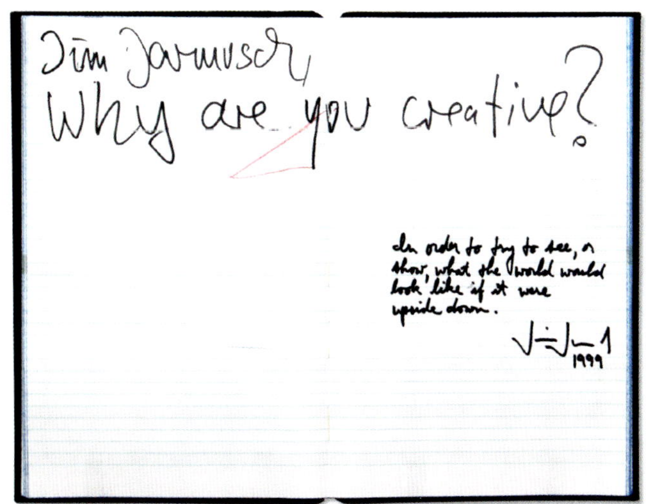

JIM JARMUSCH

On the flip side, what is stimulating ideas?

I've always been interested in when like dogs, when dogs don't understand something, they turn their head. It's almost like they are trying to see it from a different angle. I think it is very valuable to try to look at things not. … I'm very suspicious of what we are supposed to think about any given thing, so I often have a reaction of trying to imaging the opposite or looking at it from the upside down way. Jack Kerouac said something I like very much: "The Buddhists are right. The world is upside down." And I think if you look at the world in a different perspective then what is false or what is real, is reinterpretable.

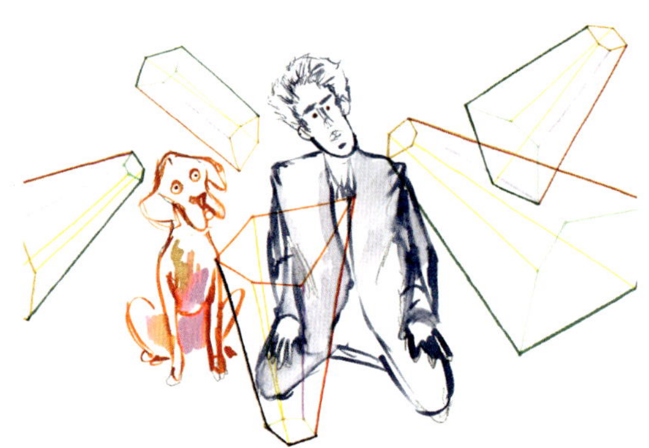

To put things upside down is a great tool for creativity. In one of our conversations, musician and artist Blixa Bargeld refers to Sigmund Freud, who already hinted that putting things upside down leads to results.

BLIXA BARGELD

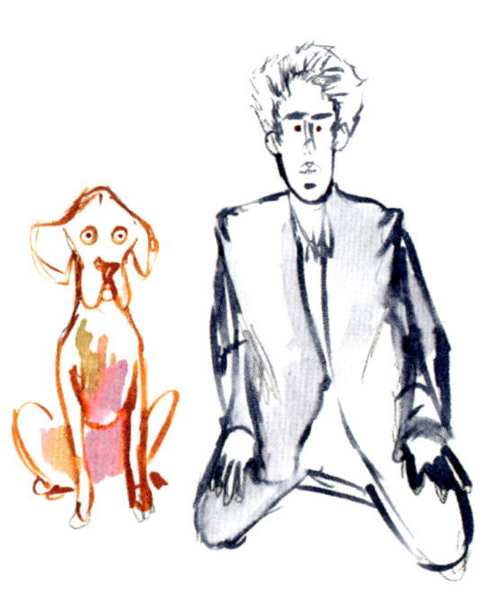

That's a quote by Sigmund Freud. He says: "Sometimes you can't see the truth unless you turn it on its head." In the moment when something unexpected happens, when something comes in from the side or does something completely different or the other way around, when it puts the truth upside down to realize that there is an opening and that something can be done there, something you didn't know of before, the fact that there is an opening at all. You realize that there possibly is a door through which you are able to enter. Then you are on the way to find the solution to a problem.

In London, Cannes Film Festival winner Mike Leigh talks about his experience with gatekeepers. With the right support from his mentor, he got ahead and outsmarted the gatekeepers. His mentor was producer Tony Garnett.

MIKE LEIGH

My first television film was produced by Tony Garnett, who had of course worked with Ken Loach a lot at that time. And what was great was that he simply wheeled me into the BBC and said, here's the guy, he hasn't got a script, he is going to make this film and that's that all there is to it. What's quite amusing about that is that I had, I think two or three years earlier—at that point I was in my middle and late twenties—applied to the BBC to get on the trainee director's course, although I had directed quite a lot of theater and I made some short films. I applied to the BBC and was interviewed by an extremely formidable committee, who said, "What would you do?" I said, I rehearse for a couple of months and then I shoot the film and make it up while we're shooting it. And they rejected me. And they sent me a letter saying, please reapply next year. So I reapplied the next year and went through the same process again. And again they sent me a letter saying, please reapply next year. And the next time they sent me a letter saying, it's time to reapply, I wrote back, I'm terribly sorry, I can't. I'm actually working for the BBC making a film.

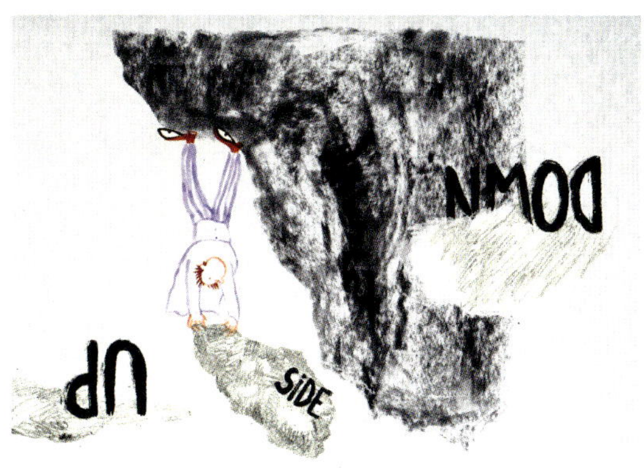

MALCOLM MCLAREN

Critics are people that really are often impoverished because they are usually highly intelligent, extremely sensitive, very well homed, brilliant detectives, police forces searching for who has the idea. Sometimes they want to be willing conspirators and promoters and sometimes they are want to be willing killers and demoters and they are there because they believe they are the guardians of the culture. Why did they enlist? Because they are part policemen and they are part failed artists and failed artists can easily become policemen. Adolf I litler was a failed artist in one part and policeman in another. And those people can be extremely dangerous, the combination, the chemical combination is extremely explosive—so the pen of a critic can be the pen of a killer, a homicidal maniac, a killer of ideas. At the same time he can also be a worshipper, protector, seller, promoter of ideas.

Sometimes you think it really depends on what side of the bed he crawled out that morning. That's the adrenaline the most critics work with.

I was interested to know about gatekeepers in literature. I went to the Berlin Literature Festival to meet with Nigerian Novelist Chibundu Onuzo to talk about her experiences with the British publishing industry. What was her creative experience with that industry? Were they gatekeepers or promoters?

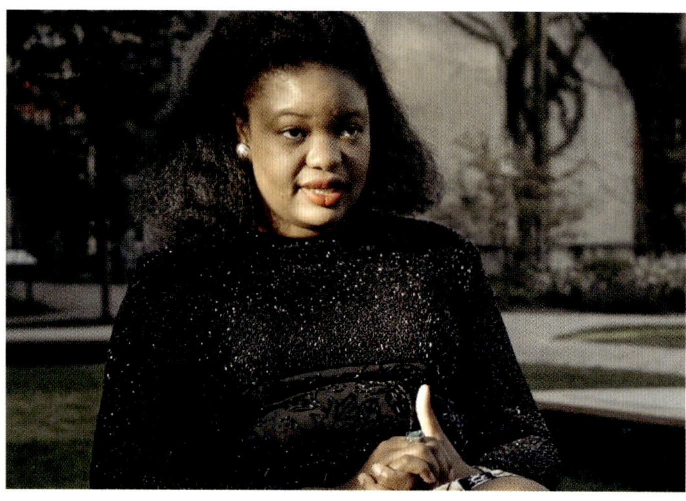

CHIBUNDU ONUZO

In England, in the United Kingdom, the publishing industry is very white. So … white editors, white publishing directors, it's very white. And so … it's a question that a lot of critics of Africans literature have: that … the only stories that are published, that are fit, stories about war, are stories about poverty, because there's a certain narrative that these gatekeepers feel is what people want to read about Africa. So you don't want to read a boy-meets-girl love story that doesn't talk about politics or a dictatorship or war or some very heavy problematic issue. That is just sort of boy meets girl, no trauma, no tragedy, no nothing. They don't understand the references, they don't appreciate the skill that's gone into something because they don't understand the context that it's coming from. And … yeah, in England especially, you just, you need more black editors who can say, "This is culturally relevant, this is relevant where I'm coming from."

If they force you to tell a certain narrative, that can be really annoying, can't it?

Yes, yes, yes. I mean, I had a little bit of that in my first novel, at the copyediting stage, where the Pidgin English which is sort of a Nigerian language that's developed out of English, but it's not English anymore, it has its own syntax. I mean, it's also included other West African languages into it. And the copyeditor would just say, "I don't understand this, I don't understand that," and I sort of felt I had to then change it and tailor it to this sort of … and of course, the norm is always a white person, especially publishing. But there will be lots of other readers who do understand that. I was very young when I signed my contract. I was nineteen, I was twenty-one when I got published. And so, I didn't know that I could say no. This is my book and I'll use whatever Pidgin I want. And I could do that by that time I got to my second novel, *Welcome to Lagos*. And yeah, I just was like: no, I'm not changing it, sorry.

Artist and dandy Sebastian Horsley was barred from entering the United States. Why would Uncle Sam and his fellow gatekeepers refuse to let a nice guy like Sebastian pass through? Why would they want to keep the gateway to America shut?

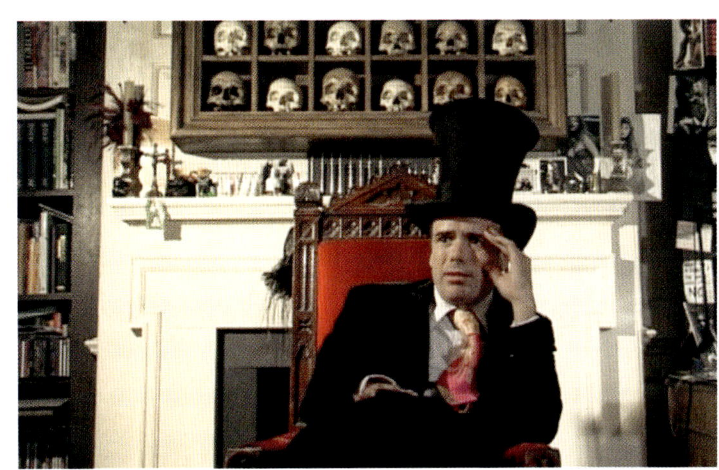

"IF YOU MAKE PEOPLE THINK THEY'RE THINKING, THEY WILL APPLAUD YOU, BUT IF YOU REALLY MAKE PEOPLE THINK, THEY WILL HATE YOU."

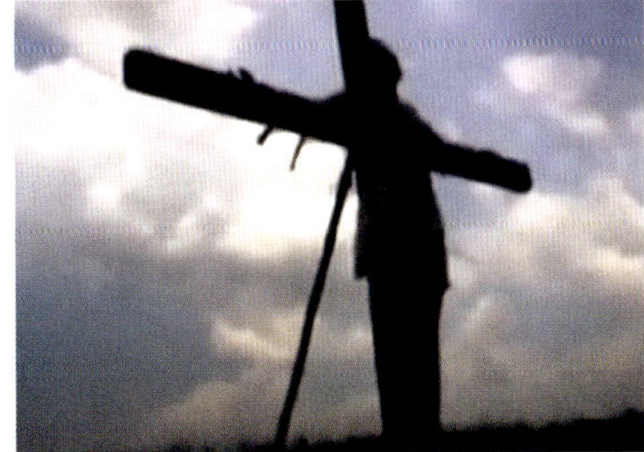

SEBASTIAN HORSLEY

My book *Dandy in the Underworld* came out across America, and I went to go over there to do a tour. And they wouldn't let me in, because of the book. They said I was suffering from moral turpitude. And that's interesting, because … well there is nothing worse than not being allowed into a country that you wouldn't be seen dead in. And in the book, I describe my life, which begins with my mother trying to abort me and ends on the cross, and in between I try to offend as many people as possible. But I have a life as a prostitute, I was a prostitute for many years and seeing prostitutes, running a brothel, being a heroin addict, a crack addict, all that sort of carry-on, you know. They thought that this was naughty, and some saw a threat to their society. I failed to see that. If you make people think they're thinking, they will applaud you, but if you really make people think, they will hate you.

My conversation with Sebastian left me rattled. I needed a coffee or six to restore my confidence. The six coffees worked too well! I was now jittery and paranoid pondering Sebastian's persecution by US immigration, and here I was about to enter Japan! Amazingly, the gatekeepers let me in and I spoke to media artist Sputniko!.

SPUTNIKO!

In Japan, gatekeepers are an issue. I don't know if you know that Tokyo Medical University in Japan, very prestigious medical schools … last year, they found that they were reducing the points of female applicants' scores so less women would enter their university. So I got really annoyed at that. So I made this fictional art project, an art university called "Tokyo Medical University For Rejected Women." So this is a new school. So I am the president of this university, and we made this sort of big newspaper article about this new university. So this is the paper. And what we do as a school is that. …

Can anyone apply?

Actually, yeah. We're very understanding of diversity. So women, rejected women could apply, but also men could apply. And the reason why men can apply is that … these women … because Japan loves male doctors so much, you know. They love male doctors, elite male doctors. These women, who were rejected from Japanese medical schools, they build the perfect elite male doctor that Japan wants and then, we put them on a drone, you know, a drone. We deliver these elite male doctors all over Japan so that Japan, the medical world, would have these amazing male doctors that they love.

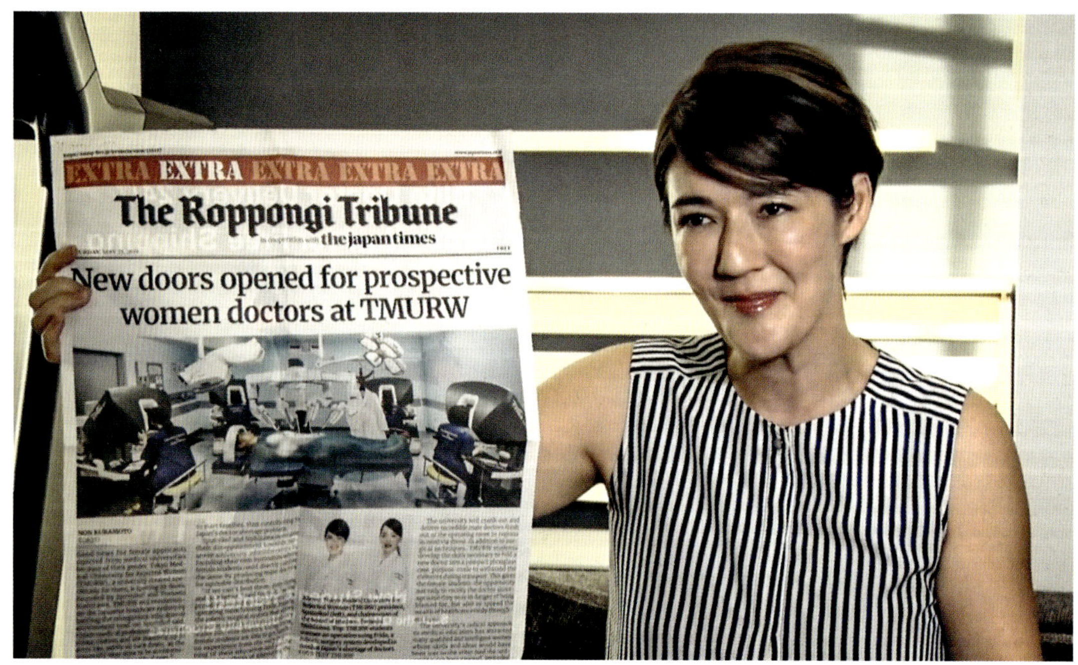

T.C. BOYLE

When my first novel *Water Music* came out, there was film interest to make it. There has been, all through, forever, but nobody's quite made it yet, although it is underway at this point, I think. And I had a very famous old agent in Hollywood who's been there forever. I won't mention his name, but he was now an old man and everybody knew him and he was great and he took me under his wing, and he tried to make deals. And all the deals wanted me to participate, to write, to be part of it. Then he kept calling me with this and that and it's so exciting, I finally said, "Ok. I'll do it, under these conditions: I want to direct, I want to star in it, and I want to play all the principle female roles in drag." So here, truly, we're talking about creativity: I am my own God, I am my own boss. I don't want to agree with anyone, I don't want to have a committee, I don't want a meeting. I just want to be alone and do my own thing.

"I WANT TO DIRECT, I WANT TO STAR IN IT, AND I WANT TO PLAY ALL THE PRINCIPLE FEMALE ROLES IN DRAG."

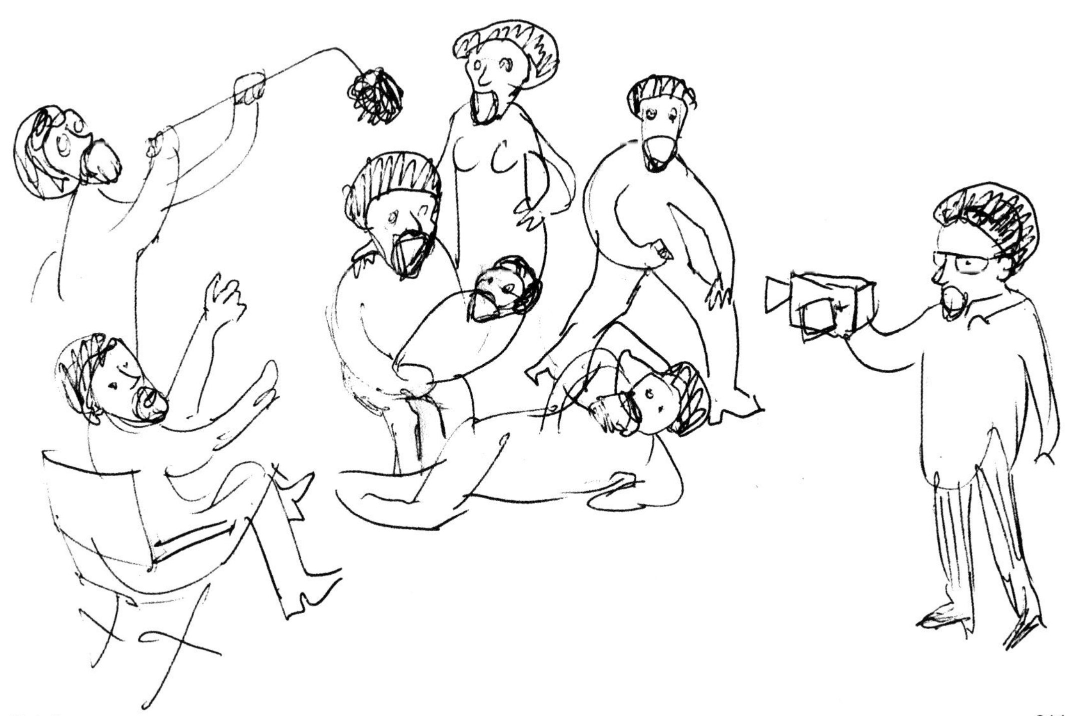

Director Andreas Dresen grew up in East Germany in the Cold War and explained a paradox—that the Brandenburg Gate was itself a gatekeeper.

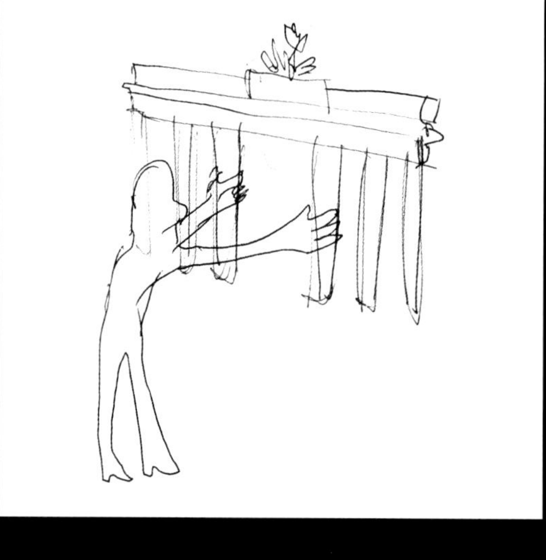

That was the trouble. There were too many gatekeepers. I thought I knew every inch of this dirty old town, but I'd never seen anything like this case. It was initiated by Ilya Khrzhanovsky, the mastermind behind DAU, one of the most ambitious and controversial among projects of modern art. Ilya wanted to put reality upside down by recreating the Berlin Wall.

ANDREAS DRESEN

I was born in 1963 and the wall was already there. I could never imagine then what it would be like if it was suddenly gone. For me it was part of my world, and so I accepted it. When it suddenly opened up in 1989, I stood on the other side of the Brandenburg Gate, looked at my home country through the gate and started to cry, because for the first time it was clear to me. The people all shouted "madness!" And by madness they meant that they could go to the West, and I thought so too.

And then, as I was standing there, I suddenly realized: no, the madness is actually not that I can come here now, the madness is actually that I could not come here before. How absurd is that? I stand in front of a gate for the first time and notice for the first time that this gate is called a gate, because you can pass through it. For me it had only been a synonym for a border before. And so suddenly, from one moment to the next, the world turns upside down and you see life with different eyes. And that means that the world is man-made. You can change anything, even the most unfortunate conditions, and you just need to make an effort to do so.

ILYA KHRZHANOVSKY

The wall project was cancelled, and it was destroyed at a low bureaucracy level. And finally, we lost a lot of money. But I think the main thing that's happened is Berliners lost a big art project. All this campaign in the press, it's fake news because the news was that the Russians were coming in to build the wall again. You know, I'm like a Russian Jew. I think I am a person who has the right to destroy the wall. But to destroy the wall, you need to build it again and destroy it through a ritual. And the idea was to make this kind of ritual and for it to be ritualistically destroyed. There was a big art project, Ai Weiwei planned to paint the wall, the whole wall. Then the wall should be destroyed. Then the people can take for free, the pieces of this wall. Marina Abramović wanted to be part of the project. She had a fantastic performance that she planned. It was a unique performance. It was two unique art pieces which never happened. That's for me very sad.

But who knows? Maybe you can bring it, reerect it somehow, you never know.

The wall is still in the storage because we produced it.

ADINA PINTILIE

"I THINK IF THERE IS NO WALL TO BREAK ... THEN WHAT ARE YOU GOING TO BREAK."

I think if there is no wall to break … then what are you going to break? How can you get free from the prison? You need the walls. And you need the … let's say, the conflict, I think, you need this tension. That you break through, the wall that you break through so you can grow. I think if it's all harmonic, and there is no tension and there is no problem, there is no place to grow. Sometimes the demon is also the angel. It has a double, it's dialectic, you know, it's the same thing.

ALEXANDER SCHEER

Well, it's a paradox, I have to say. In East Berlin way back then, you were more free. You were surrounded by a wall but you were more free. So it is indeed a dialectical paradox. But you have to use some tricks, take some detours, and be subversive. So the question that every artist and each and every creative person has to ask is: "Who and what is the enemy?" If you ain't got nothing you can turn against, then what the hell.

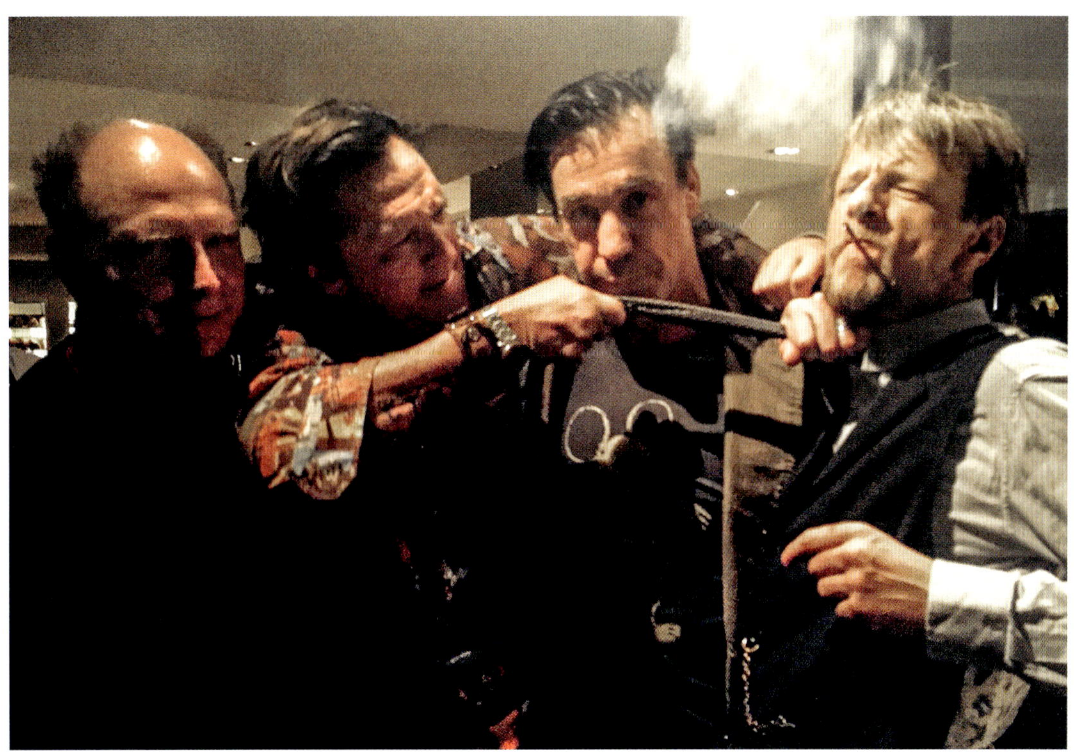

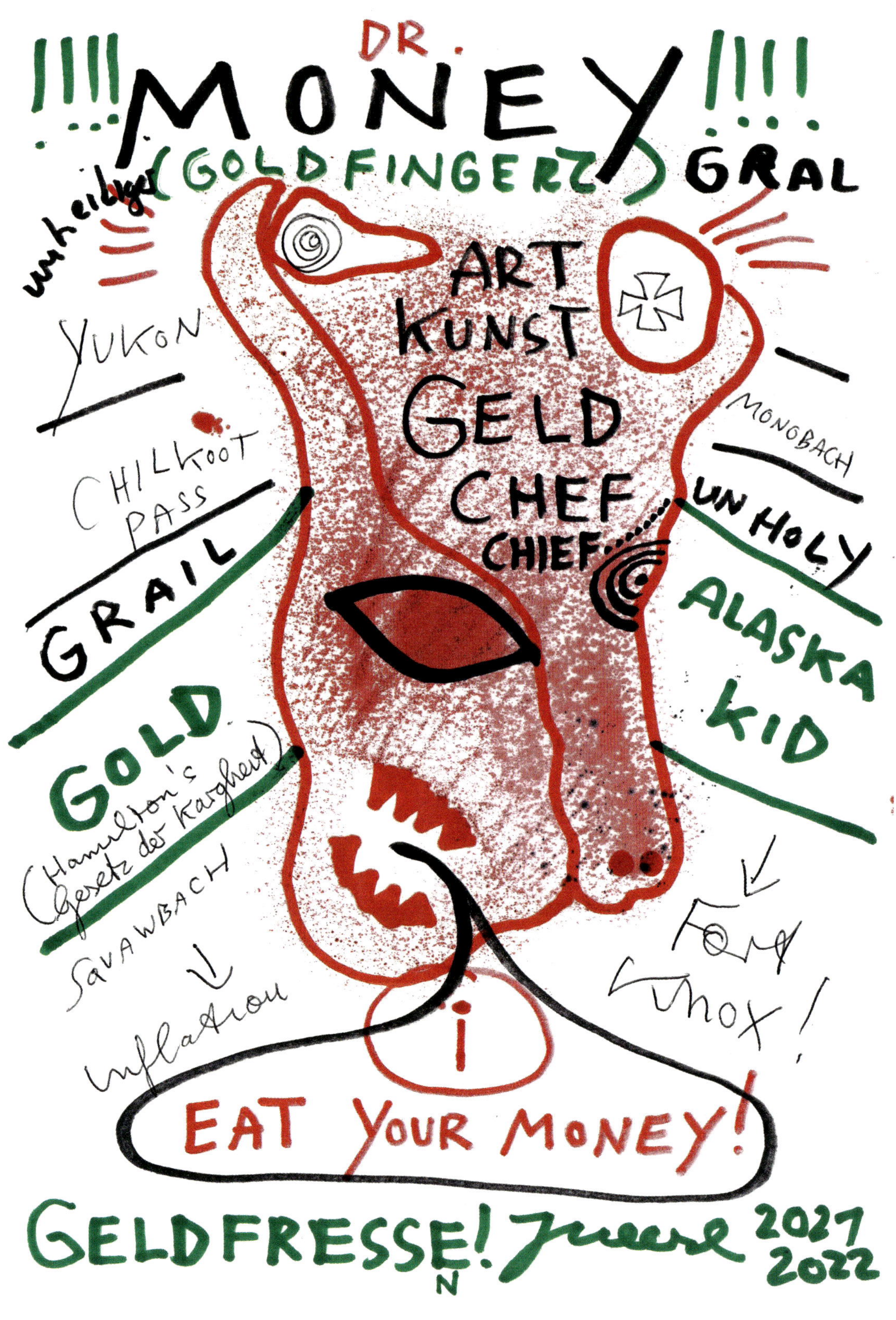

DR.
MONEY
(GOLDFINGERZ)
GRAL
ART
KUNST
GELD
CHEF
CHIEF
YUKON
MONOBACH
CHILKOOT PASS
UNHOLY
GRAIL
ALASKA KID
GOLD
(Hamilton's Gesetz der Kargheit)
SAVAWBACH
inflation
EAT YOUR MONEY!
GELDFRESSE!
2021
2022

Marcel Duchamp said that one day the artist of the future would be able to just point his finger at something and say it was art and it would be art. So he picked out a bottle rack and he sold it for $5,000. When someone came and asked him, "What's the difference between your bottle rack and the one that I can buy for $5?," and he said, "I'm an artist, and I chose it." Now was he a true visionary artist, or just a fucking dork? Someone once told Picasso that they'd bought a painting, supposedly by Picasso, but it was unsigned and they wanted to know if it was genuine. Picasso said, "Well, how much did you pay for that painting?," and they said "$100,000." And Picasso said "Hmm, well it must be genuine!" Now, by the time Picasso had died, he had amassed one of the finest collections of bank notes in the world. Was he a businessman or an artist? Can you be both?

MARINA ABRAMOVIĆ

It's a very romantic relationship between the artist and the money—has been, until now. And it's always the idea that artists have to be beyond their money, should not ask for money. I really think it's total bullshit. Because I really think that way, the artist is being exploited very much. And it's always the galleries and the dealers, and the artist after he's dead is the best artist because if he's dead, he can be manipulated however much you want. And actually that is profits. And I think that it is very important that artists take things in their own hands and be independent from the gallery and the dealer system as much as possible. As much energy as artists today have to spend creating work, they have to spend as much energy placing the work in the right context in the right place. That is real success.
Because for me it's not the same if my work goes to the really good museum where lots of people can see it than if it's some stupid collection of some Texas guy who doesn't know what he bought. And you are just one among the three hundreds of kitschy stuff next to it. I mean, that's not the same thing. I really think that it's so important that you know what's going on. And that I think is the new attitude of the new generation of artists. So talking about the money is okay, selling work for money, it's okay too.

Keep the copyright.

All copyright is yours.

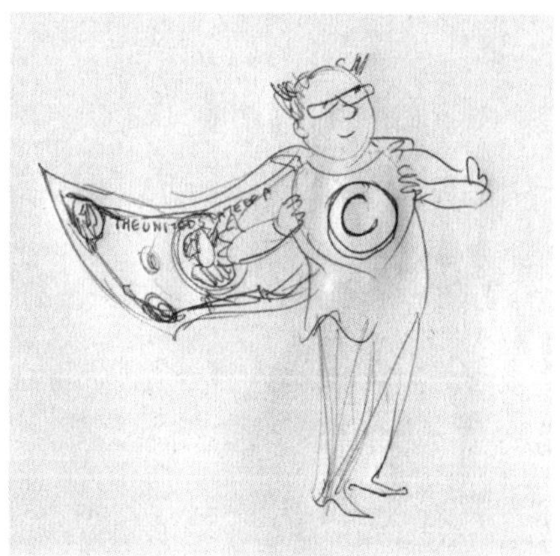

Does money foster art, or does money kill art? We travelled to Italy and met with director and artist Alfie Nze.

"MONEY KILLS CREATIVITY."

ALFIE NZE

Money kills creativity. I have some ... some people that I consider artist friends, especially painters, you know, here in Italy, and for the fact that, you know, the painter has to continuously work for his gallery, for the gallery owner to continue to sell his work and everything and then boredom comes in, you know, and the artist finds himself having to continuously do something, produce new work. That is not creativity. And of course, few artists can afford to do one painting in five years, you know, and this is where again the God called money comes in.

Rewind to the late 1990s. At the beginning of the millennium, Damien Hirst managed to become the most expensive artist of the Brit Art Movement.

DAMIEN HIRST

When I started making art, sculptures and art, but the ideas at the time when I was studying was like breaking down the boundaries. I realized very quickly that you can sell anything. You have the idea which is totally understandable, you just find a way to sell it. The spot-painting on the wall is a spot-painting on the wall, and the exhibition—I just do it. I didn't need to make it sell. People just buy that.

What brand would you like to do advertising for?

I do it for soap powder. I have no morals.

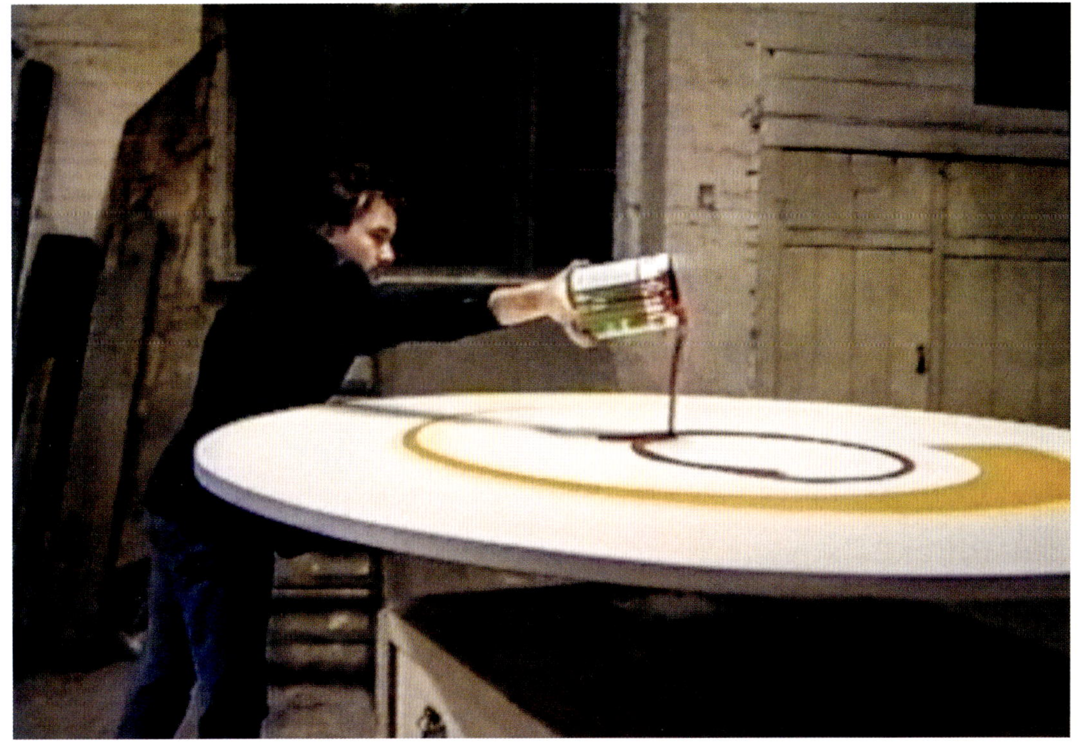

Also, for legendary director Russ Meyer, money played an important part in the creative process.

RUSS MEYER

I make films that are saleable. None of them have lost money. I don't give much thought to what the public thinks I should do, I make the films the way I like them to be. I've been lucky, I suppose. Most everything I've done has made a considerable amount of money. And through the years now you find that you have all these videos which is really proof perfect that you did the right thing. Sex sells.

Of course, money plays a role in creativity. A few souls have admitted it's all about the money. Academy Award–winning director Hugh Hudson confessed that he certainly directs adverts just for the money so he could put it toward his more altruistic movie endeavors. As Groucho Marx says: "Happiness can't buy you money."

HUGH HUDSON

I make commercials to practice my craft and to make money and that's a perfectly fair answer about commercials, because commercials are only made to take money from you and give it to me.

Not surprisingly considering his name, even artist and musician Blixa Bargeld did a commercial with me for Hornbach DYI superstore. One of the rare occasions when art and advertising meet. The commercials were invited to screen at exhibitions and were widely shown across art galleries and museums.

BLIXA BARGELD

Money, apart from being my pen name, my artist name, as translated … but money that I have in cash, is certainly a tool that I need to survive. The medium I use to acquire that tool is art. So it's basically going in circles. I have to produce art in some way, whatever you want to call it, music or acting or just talking like now, and then I get money and from that money I continue making art. In between I eat, but I call that art too. It has to do with cultural arrangement. To do the right thing at the right time, and it has a social dimension because it pleases me.

Tracey Emin is one of the great artists of our time. But why did Charlie Saatchi buy Tracey Emin's unmade bed?

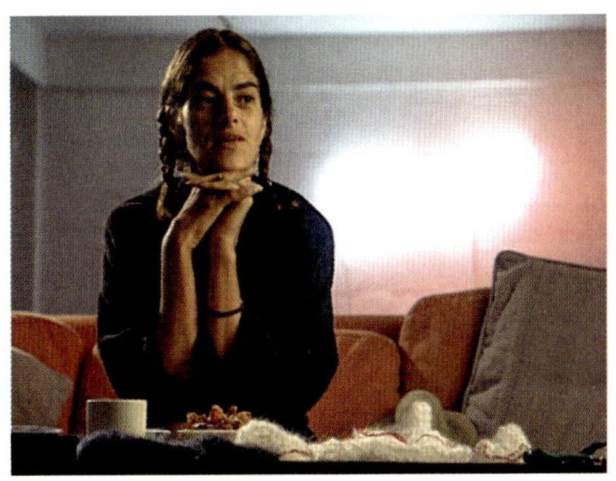

TRACEY EMIN

You were laying in the bed?
What's the story behind the bed?

"SELLING OUT CAN BE SELLING YOUR WORK TO A COLLECTOR WHO YOU THINK HAS A SHIT COLLECTION JUST TO GET THE MONEY."

I got up to get some water because I was so dehydrated, and I fell over. I didn't fall over, I just couldn't stand up, just sort of flopped on the floor. And I got back into bed, and I just thought: "Oh dear, if I don't get up, I'm going to die. I'm just going to die, I'm just going to lay there and die." So then I got up, and then I had a bath.
Then, I looked around the whole flat. Everywhere was a mess. It was just terrible. If anyone came in, I would have been certified, someone would have put me into a mental hospital immediately if they had just seen the state of me and the state of how I was living. And I just thought: "Oh, this has got to stop." I suddenly got a perspective on the bed, and I thought it looks fuckin' amazing. I thought that it's got to stop, but it looks fantastic. This is all me, I made all this. So that's how the bed came about, really. Selling out can be selling your work to a collector who you think has a shit collection just to get the money, you know. Or selling out can be filling in hundreds of forms to the arts council, begging for a bit of money and having to be small and be nice to people that you're not really sure about. People who think they have a position of power over you.

GEORGE R. R. MARTIN

Does money have an effect as a motivator? Mark Twain said: "It's the only sensible reason to write."

Yeah, and I mean, Dr. Johnson famously said: "No man but a blockhead ever wrote, except for money." You know, because we live in a society where you have to pay your rent; you have to buy food; you have to pay for all the necessities of life. So at a certain point when I started out, my dream was just to make enough money so I could write full time and not have to do anything else. Now, that wasn't true for the first ten years of my career, although I wrote and I sold and I had day jobs, the writing was secondary to it. But there's always this tension that has existed, I think, since the earliest day of publishing at least, between, commerce and art. You wanna make great art but you're aware too that to survive people have to pay you money for it or you will be homeless on the street and trying to write on pieces of discarded toilet paper. So, you know, the cliché of the artist starving in the garret is still very much with us, and I think each individual writer or each individual artist has to decide where they're gonna come down on that spectrum. And it is a spectrum, I mean, there are people on one end who are just totally commercial hacks: "What warrants me the most money, whatever it is, that's what I'll do. The audience rules, I'm just providing something that the audience wants to see." And on the other end there are the, you know, "I am an 'Artiste.' Don't trouble me with money. I don't want your stinking money, I am creating for the ages and I must follow my muse." And, you know, those kinds work best if they have trust funds or a patron (laughs) like the Pope, or in these days Kickstarter. I think most of us are somewhere in the middle between those two and we're always wrestling with one side or another.

"NO MAN BUT A BLOCKHEAD EVER WROTE, EXCEPT FOR MONEY."

Martin's novel *A Song of Ice and Fire* was turned in a successful series, and Umberto Eco's *The Name of the Rose* was turned into a successful feature film with Sean Connery. Is money a fuel or beta-blocker to the creative freedom of the writer? I travelled to Davos to meet with Umberto Eco, who revealed to me how authors making a living from their creativity before the invention of the printing press.

UMBERTO ECO

You know, even before the invention of the press, an author had to give a manuscript to be copied … that was a problem that always existed. If you write, you have to make your work circulate and you enter a commercial circuit, but this existed even in ancient Rome. You went to the bookshop not to buy books, but to buy manuscripts, and that's what was sold. So it is not a result of technological or capitalistic development, it has always been like that, and in a sense was more immoral once because a writer, philosopher, in order to survive, had to be protected by a king, an emperor, and so he was not so free.

"VIRGIL WAS BETTER THAN ME, BUT LESS FREE THAN ME BECAUSE HE HAD TO COMPLY WITH THE REQUESTS OF THE EMPEROR."

Renaissance writers were less free than modern scribblers?

They were less free than our contemporary writers. Virgil was better than me, but less free than me because he had to comply with the requests of the emperor.

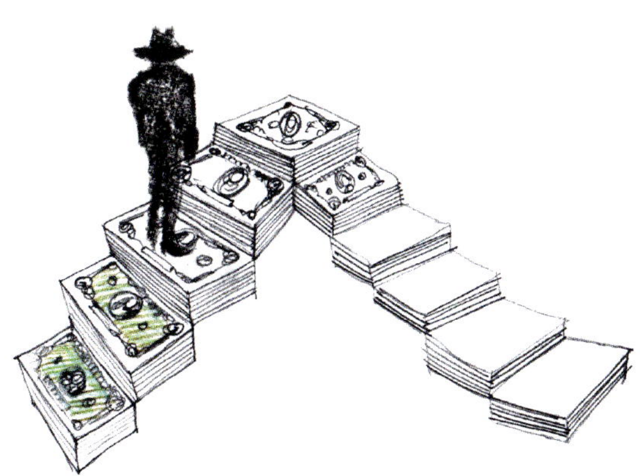

I spent a lot of time of my research journey on the American West Coast. One day, I found myself walking up the ramp to the Chateaux Marmont in Los Angeles to meet with Michael Madsen.

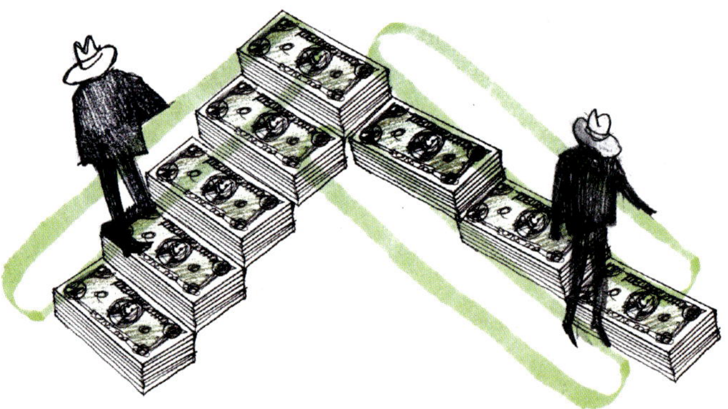

MICHAEL MADSEN

I had no money when I started out working in a gas station in Beverly Hills. So, I had to be creative. Of course, money plays a role. But what is that role? A villain? A hero? In what disguise does money appear? Picasso once said: "I want to live as a poor man with a lot of money." It's so complicated when money talks. Part of being creative is deciding what you make it say.

I filled up the tank and drove on. Sean Penn explained to me the connection between film financing and creativity. A vicious circle that Orson Welles already saw through.

SEAN PENN

Orson Welles said, making movies is 98 percent hustle and 2 percent filmmaking. And it's true. Long before you get the audience's money, you have got to get the financiers' money. We all do it, you know, but it's like, the necessity for wood in a world that doesn't want its trees cut down.

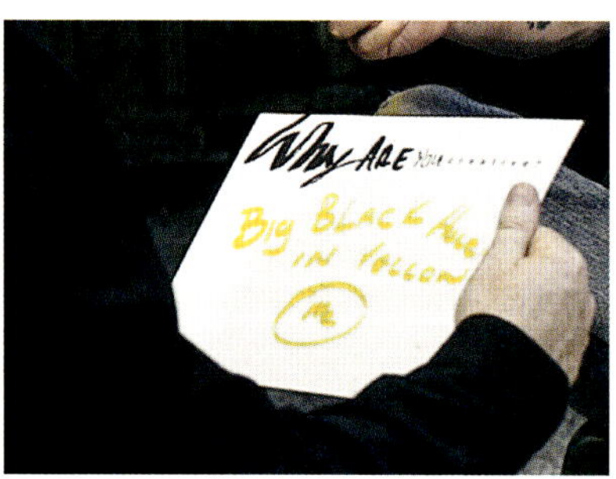

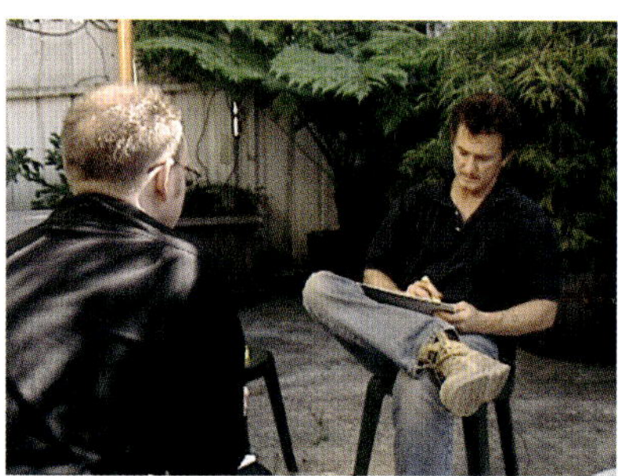

Finally, Sean gave me his answer to the question,
"Why are you creative?" - Yes. "A Big Black Hole In Yellow—Me."

Thanks Sean, that's very helpful. I'm not sure it's a definitive answer. Certainly not a very popular answer. If we're looking for a unified field theory of creativity, that is. For example, the group of people who said "Big Black Hole In Yellow – me" was quite small, Sean. And I did ask quite a lot of people.

Hardly anyone in the history of creativity has experienced such a roller coaster ride as *Brazil* director Terry Gilliam. One look at *Man of La Mancha*, now released under the title *The Man Who Killed Don Quixote*, is enough. All that could go wrong went wrong. *Force majeure*. So it's hardly surprising that he has a decided opinion on the obstacles to creativity, first and foremost money.

TERRY GILLIAM

Well, in the world of films, just the reality of raising money and dealing with the people who control the money is deadly. So the job is being a long-distance runner and trying to get through that. But sometimes it doesn't work. I'm always amazed at how limited the people are who control the money. What they want, they just want to make more money. Sometimes it isn't even that, they just want to play safe, they don't want to lose their jobs, that's where their thought process comes from. At the moment, I am doing a commercial and it's totally deadening because there is nothing to say in a commercial as far as I'm concerned. You manipulate icons, images, clichés … and sometimes you can use it to make something interesting. I won't name the product I am doing at the moment but it's … it's a deadening experience, I mean … and it's something I only do when I get very depressed and it makes me even more depressed. And then eventually I reach the bottom of the pit and have to crawl my way out when I know there is no lower I can go and I'm very close to that right now.

"I'M ALWAYS AMAZED AT HOW LIMITED THE PEOPLE ARE WHO CONTROL THE MONEY."

"A LOT OF PEOPLE ARE CREATIVE BUT HAVE NO OUTLET."

SHIRIN NESHAT

For a lot of people, they feel intimidated by the system that has been created. To succeed as an artist, to be creative, matches the idea of a career. You know, and I know a lot of people who are very talented but refuse to participate in this rat race. You know, if you are a filmmaker you have to beg for money to make a film. And if you get rejected, and then you have to chase around producers and then festivals and then distributors or if you're a visual artist, you have to go, choose or find a curator, a gallery, and someone to buy your work. And if you don't have that personality, you know, that drive ... there are thousands and thousands of incredibly talented people who just said: "Forget it! I just don't participate in this system. I have a lot to give, have a lot to say, but I don't fit into this system." And there are a lot of people who don't have much to say, don't have a lot of great creative energy, but they are very successful. So, it's unfortunately, it is a very capitalistic system of hierarchy and—you know, I've been very lucky. And I often feel bad because of that. Because I've been very privileged. But I know so many people who are not privileged. And they are depressed. And their creative input, it's not being shared. Because the system that has been created, you know. The whole infrastructure, that has been created to create a hierarchy, you know. And it's very unfortunate. And I'm glad you're making this film that you are making because you are putting creativity under question, you know. Because a lot of people are creative but have no outlet, you know. And we have to question that.

How can we escape the rat race? Throughout history, from the Borgias to the Saatchis—money has nourished creativity. Particularly today, when creatives must have marketing among their skill sets and culture's very existence often depends on the realpolitik of the marketplace. Maurizio Cattelan's controversial golden toilet was stolen from a British palace. It wasn't stolen for its usefulness! It was stolen because the art world valued it at a million dollars.

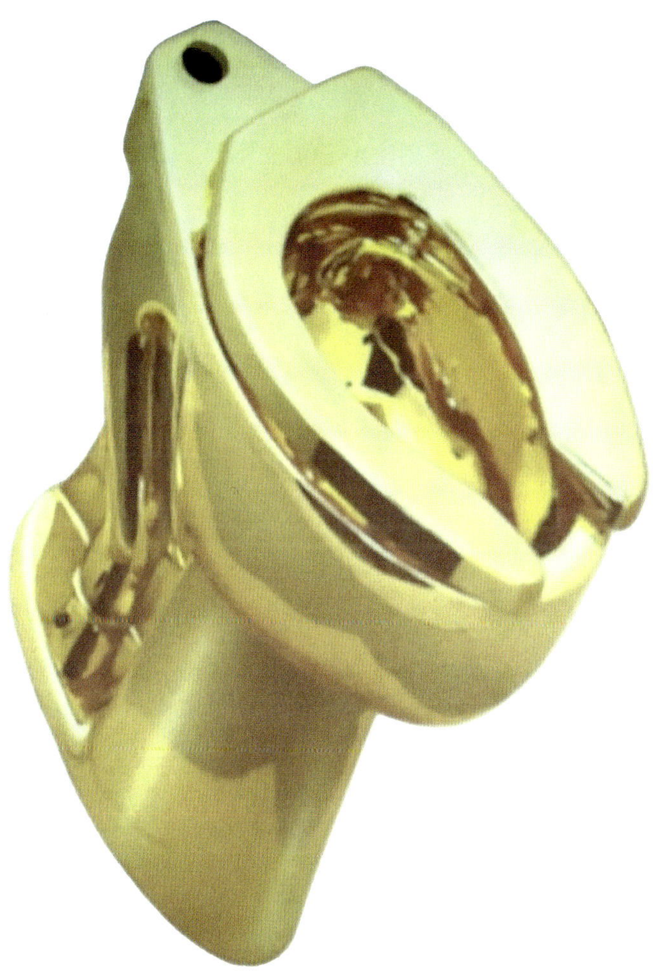

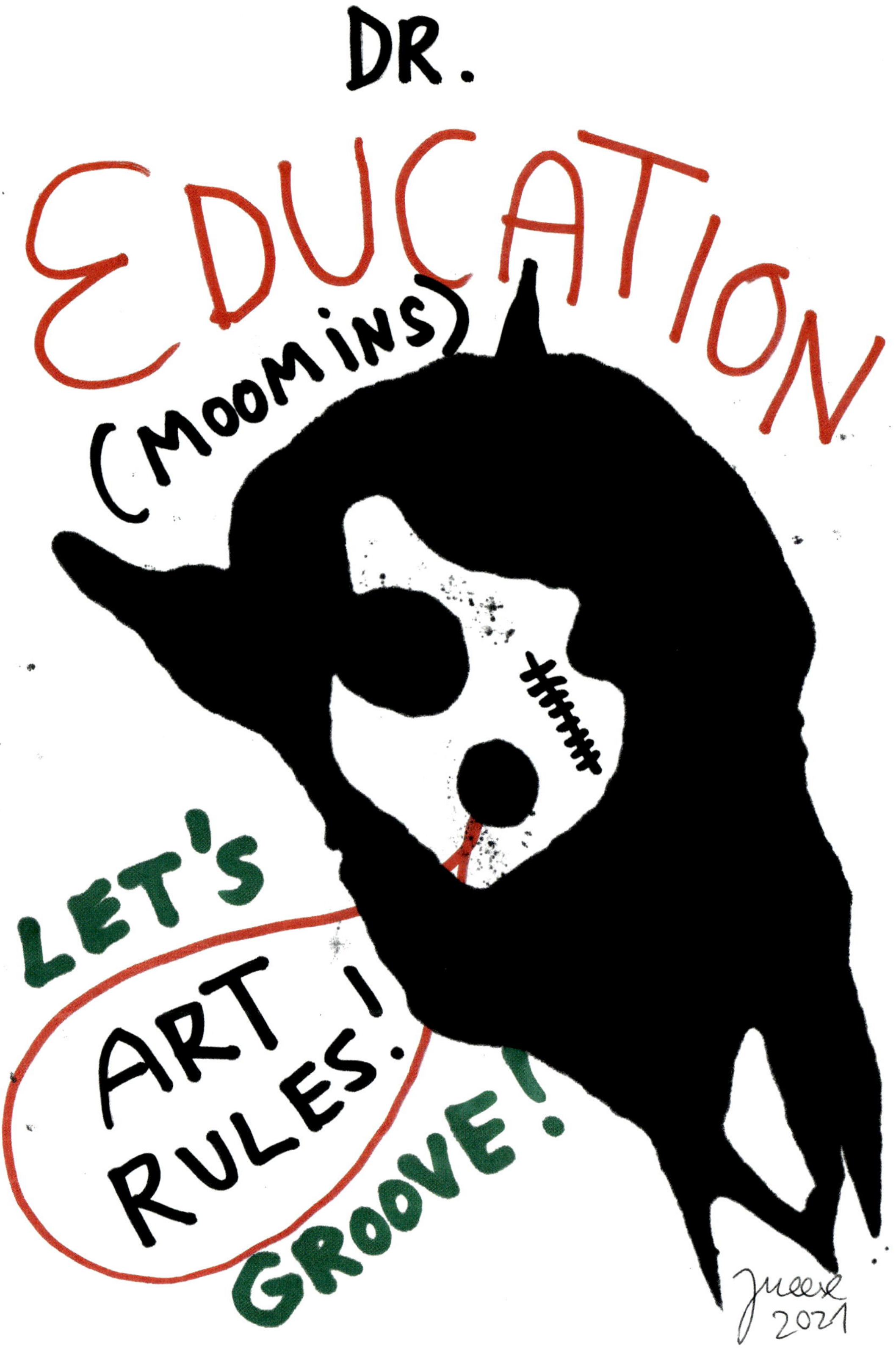

DR.

EDUCATION

(MOOMINS)

LET'S

ART!
RULES!

GROOVE!

Jueex
2021

Personally, I think everybody is creative. The only difference between the so-called creative and the so-called noncreative people is that the so-called creative people do it. Whereas everybody else talks about, thinks about it, agrees with it but doesn’t do it. Is education the answer? Can education nurture creativity? Or, on the other hand, can education kill creativity?

ISABELLA ROSSELLINI

I think everybody is creative. You know, I was wondering, because once I was told, when I was going to school, that I didn't write well ... I was surprised, you know, because I did films, I wrote books. But school told me that I had to take a writing course, because my writing was not the way the university writes. So I took the course. And it was, you know, so you had to have an opening statement, and then that opening statement is repeated longer, and then at the end you sum it up, and you basically repeat with other words what you said in the beginning. And this formula—it was so boring! Because you say everything in the beginning, so there is no suspense, no surprise. You just say it at the beginning, then you say it longer, and then you say it in other words at the end. It took me a whole course to understand that that was the boring thing that I learned never to do. And the teacher that I became very close friends with, she wanted to be a novelist. And I said to her, "Judith, I think that you taught this course too long. I think that you are creative, like probably everybody is. But you are so chained by this structure, that you feel that people otherwise can't follow you. Forget, maybe you should write for a year, things that make no sense. Break it up. Then you let your voice come out." Sometimes I think education can suffocate creativity.

Rainer Maria Rilke's *Letters to a Young Poet* is probably the best book about creativity ever written. It was also Dennis Hopper's favorite book. So, some years ago, I filmed Rilke's letters with Dennis, who quoted Rainer Maria Rilke's *Letters to a Young Poet*.

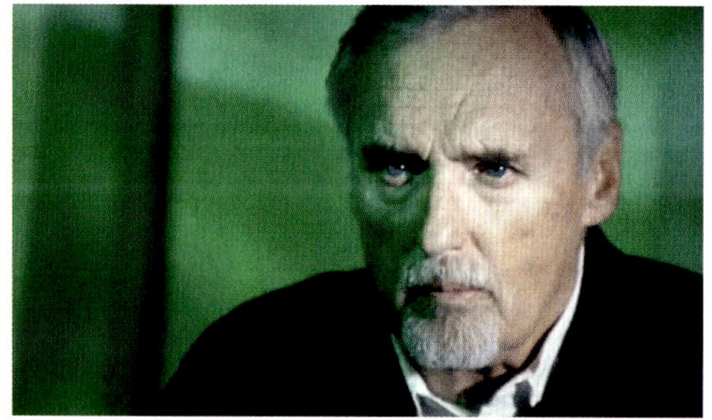

DENNIS HOPPER

There's only one single way: go into yourself. Search for the reason that has bidden you to write. Find out whether it is spreading out its roots in the deepest places of your heart. Acknowledge to yourself whether you would have to die if it would deny you to write. This, above all, ask yourself in the stillest moment of your night: Must I write? Delve into yourself for a deep answer. And if this should be in the affirmative, if you may meet this earnest question with a strong and simple "I must," then build your life according to this necessity.

What is so special about Rilke's letters that they have fascinated creative people for decades? I went to Barcelona and talked to Spanish director Isabel Coixet.

ISABEL COIXET

Every time I go to a film school to do a masterclass I would say: you know, you don't need to be here. Just read Rainer Maria Rilke and everything you need to know as creator is there. But read it carefully and do it. It's not that easy. Because being humble is very, very difficult. Like not thinking your work is the center of the universe and, at the same time, work like your work is the center of the universe.

Diane Kruger had the privilege of learning acting from Dennis Hopper when they both worked on a film in South Africa. He was a great teacher and encourager who helped Diane kick off her worldwide acting career.

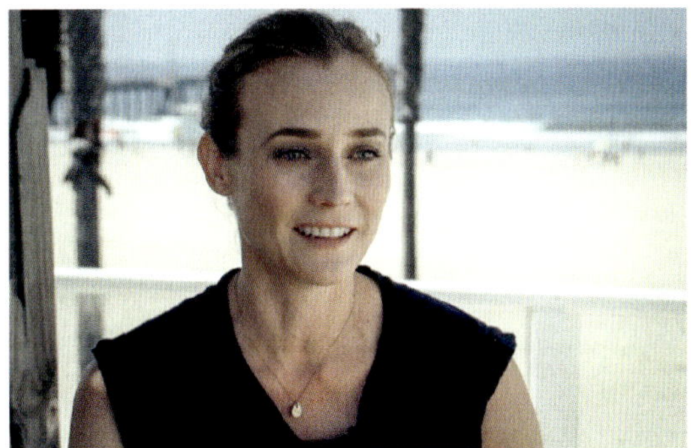

DIANE KRUGER

You know, I think people want to be creative. I'm not sure everybody allows themselves or is encouraged to be creative. I think it's important as kids, you know, to reencourage our children to be creative and live that life. So I don't know, and I think a lot of people go through life thinking, "Oh, this is not for me, it's too late, I'm scared of this," you know, including myself sometimes. It's human nature.

Who holds the key to creativity? How can we unlock creativity? In London, I met the woman who opened many doors: the architect Zaha Hadid.

ZAHA HADID

Education gives people a key to what is seen as an unlocked door. And I don't mean only high education, acquiring degrees, because that doesn't really do much, but really to encourage people to think and to open their eyes and their minds to worlds which could only exist in someone else's imagination. And that is really the role of any teacher, you know, that they have to be able to see in that student or the pupil or the child, something which is not obvious to them and help them like a string, pull it out.

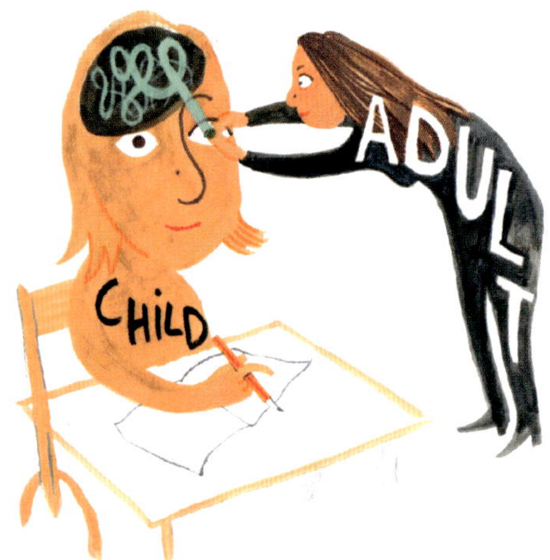

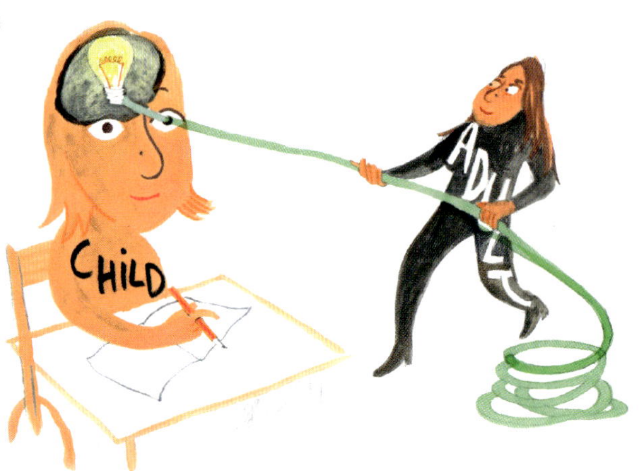

Singer and musician Peter Gabriel compares the different creative disciplines with languages that we can learn. What is his approach?

PETER GABRIEL

For me, creativity is a language and it's an emotional language, I think. So, I think it has a lot to do with childhood. One thing about creativity is I think this idea that artists are these angels that descend from heaven with immense talent, I think that's bullshit. I think that you could give a pill to anyone in the street and you tell them in twelve months' time, they are going to die unless they create some good art. If their survival is really dependent on doing something creative, then they will find a way to become an artist, whoever they are. Art, music, these are just languages, and nobody thinks they can't learn a language. Maybe it's difficult, but if I live there then that becomes my home, then I know I will learn that language. At school I wasn't good at music. I was not good at art, so I sort of felt if I'll be able to get away with making a career with doing creative things, and yet as a kid I was judged, you know, not good enough to be a creative person. I sort of feel, if I could get away with it then anyone can.

In *Worstward Ho* Samuel Beckett describes the process of failure: "Try again. Fail. Fail again. Fail better."

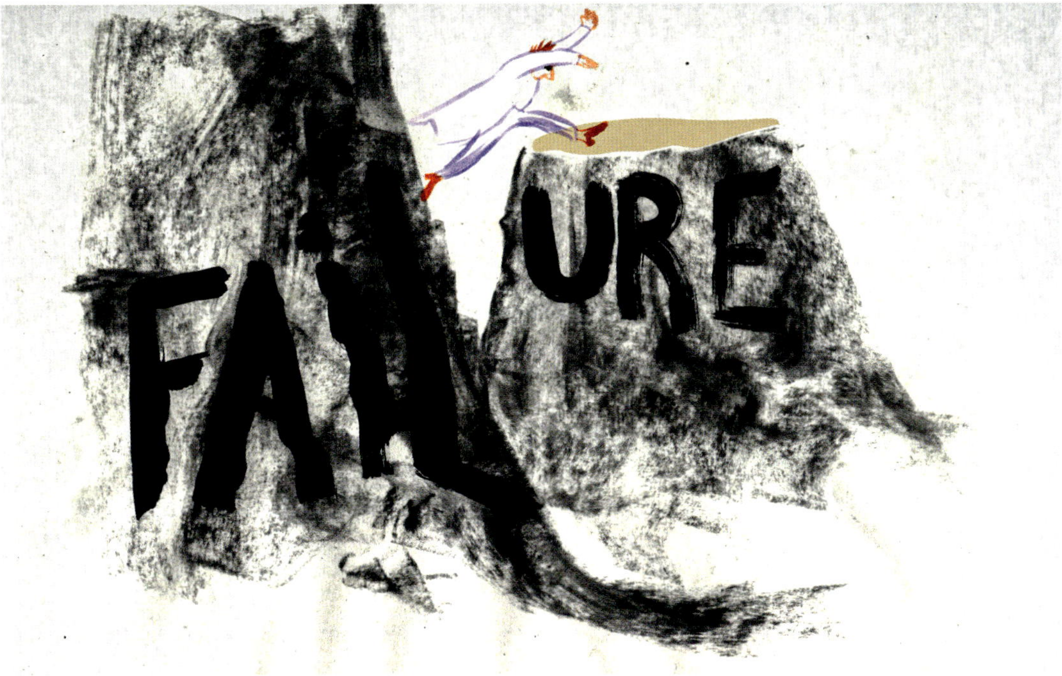

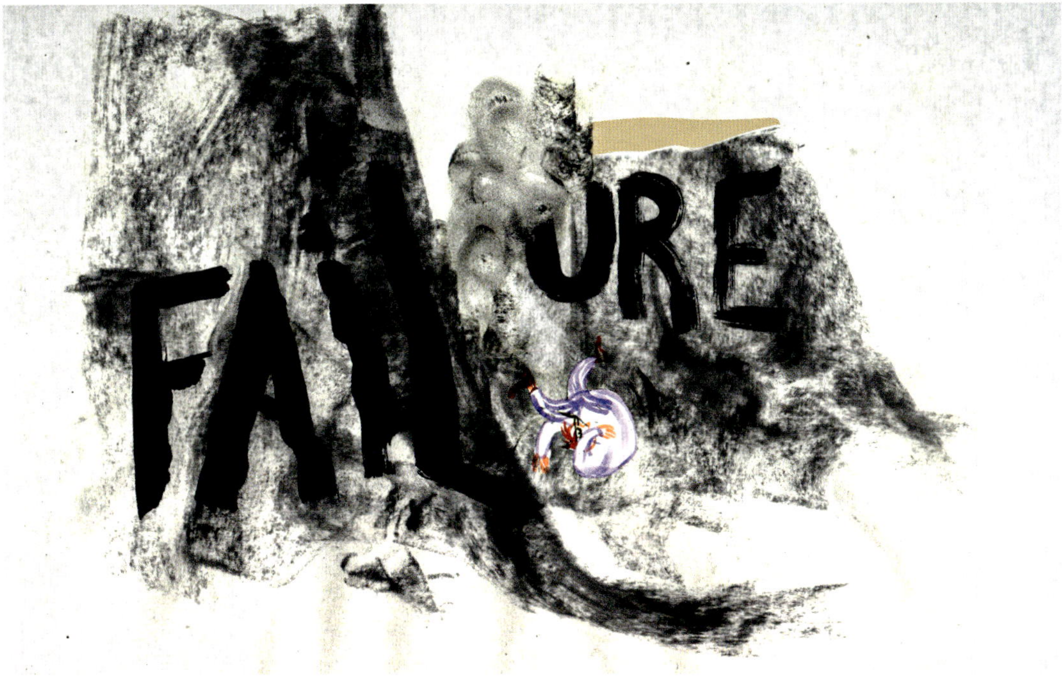

MARINA ABRAMOVIĆ

The fear of failure is always there. Without failure you can't go anywhere, you can't go to new or different places. A very big businessman told me: "I measure my success with how many failures I had." And that's really important. Every successful person had many failures in his life.

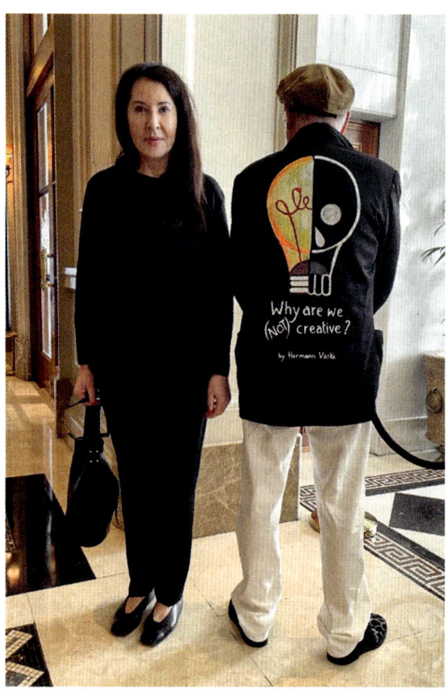

MALCOLM MCLAREN

You told me the story when you went to art school which I find very interesting. Why is it a good idea to be a flamboyant failure?

Well, I think I'm a product of the 1960s. That's when I went to art school in London. And the only thing I learned from a typically goat-bearded lecturer, was the question of failure. It was a really valid point, because most people in a karaoke world do not understand the word failure.

Failure in the artistic world back then, in the last century, was a word that was noble. Why? Because it is thought as an artist then, it was thought better to be an flamboyant failure than any kind of benign success. To understand that is to understand that failure creates success in another way, a much grander, deeper, more profound way. It's a way of not having any fear. It gives you an immense freedom, it breaks the shackles that force you to conform. That's what this art lecturer, when I was eighteen back in the mid-1960s, meant. That statement had an immense effect upon me. Because it meant after one had understood the idea of becoming a magnificent failure, how are you going to do that when you walk out of the holier-than-thou trappings, these wonderful, in England havens of the disenfranchised to enter the real world and make failure, you're noble pursuit and your raison d'être in life.

I began doing that by creating something called "anti-fashion" with my partner at that time, Vivienne Westwood. I thereafter created something that most people thought of as "anti-music." This idea was something born out of a group I called the Sex Pistols. That was an attempt at actually being authentic. This idea of stretching the bounderies of creating something that may not be for sale, but be desired, I felt followed the path of what this man was suggesting. It was my attempt, and if anyone would be responsible for punk-rock, it was probably this goat-bearded lecturer who told me "better to be a flamboyant failure than a benign success." He is utterly responsible for most of what I've done in my life.

So thanks to Malcolm's goat-bearded lecturer and onto Picasso. "We are all born artists. The only problem is to remain an artist when you get older." That's how Pablo Picasso put it. Netflix founder Reed Hastings sees the opportunity for creative failure as a vehicle to stay creative.

Reed Hastings, why are you creative?

IT'S MORE FUN THAN FOLLOWING ORDERS.

—REED

REED HASTINGS

A big influence for me was after university when I was a high school math teacher in southern Africa with the Peace Corps. It was a very remote area. And you learn a lot of independence travelling on your own a lot, looking out for the kids, getting to know your kids.

"ONE OF THE IMPORTANT PARTS ABOUT SUPPORTING CREATIVITY IS TOLERATING FAILURE."

I've been creative in wanting to do things my whole life. I think we probably all start creatively—making sandcastles, selling lemonade. And then the practicalities of life intervene and not everybody stays creative. Probably one of the important parts about supporting creativity is tolerating failure. The more a family or a society embraces that it is okay to fail, that it was brave to try, the more people will take risks and be creative. Because being creative is more fun than following orders.

Reed Hastings graduated from Stanford University. When it comes to education, artist Hermann Nitsch recommends the school of a Japanese Zen monastery. I asked him why.

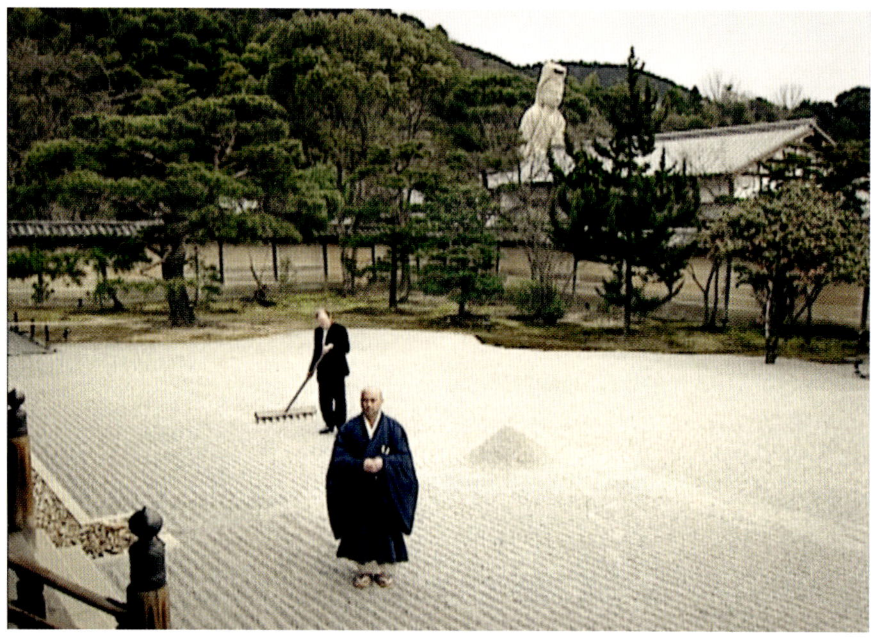

HERMANN NITSCH

The young monk asks the master: How can I attain enlightenment? And the master says: sweep the way to the temple for another year. You can't do that, you can't learn that by going to school, by taking university exams. You're either there or you're not.

SIR JOHN HEGARTY

Is there a correlation between Zen and creativity?

I think anybody who has ideas, who does actually have really great ideas, they are moments of pure Zen; in other words, it is where the true you, the real self, has been allowed to kind of come out to express itself. Take in a problem, understand how to deal with the problem and come up with a solution. And that's why, I think when you have a great idea, it just is, I've already said, actually, it's the nearest thing to giving birth. Because in a way you do give birth. I mean having an idea is the nearest a man will come, anyway, to giving birth, in the sense that you create something and it has a shape and a form. You know how to treat it, you know where it should go. You know what's right for it, what's wrong for it. It has an entity. It exists, it is there, it is an idea. And I think that creates a tremendous euphoria in you. A tremendous sense of excitement. And you feel, kind of all sorts of other problems just falling away.

TRACEY EMIN

I know that I learned more about creativity, my own creativity after my first abortion. I learned more about the essence and knowledge of where things come from than any fucking art college or lecture or what anyone could tell me. I also knew intuitively that as soon as I came around after my abortion, that all the art that I'd ever made was a real big bunch of crap and needed to be destroyed immediately.

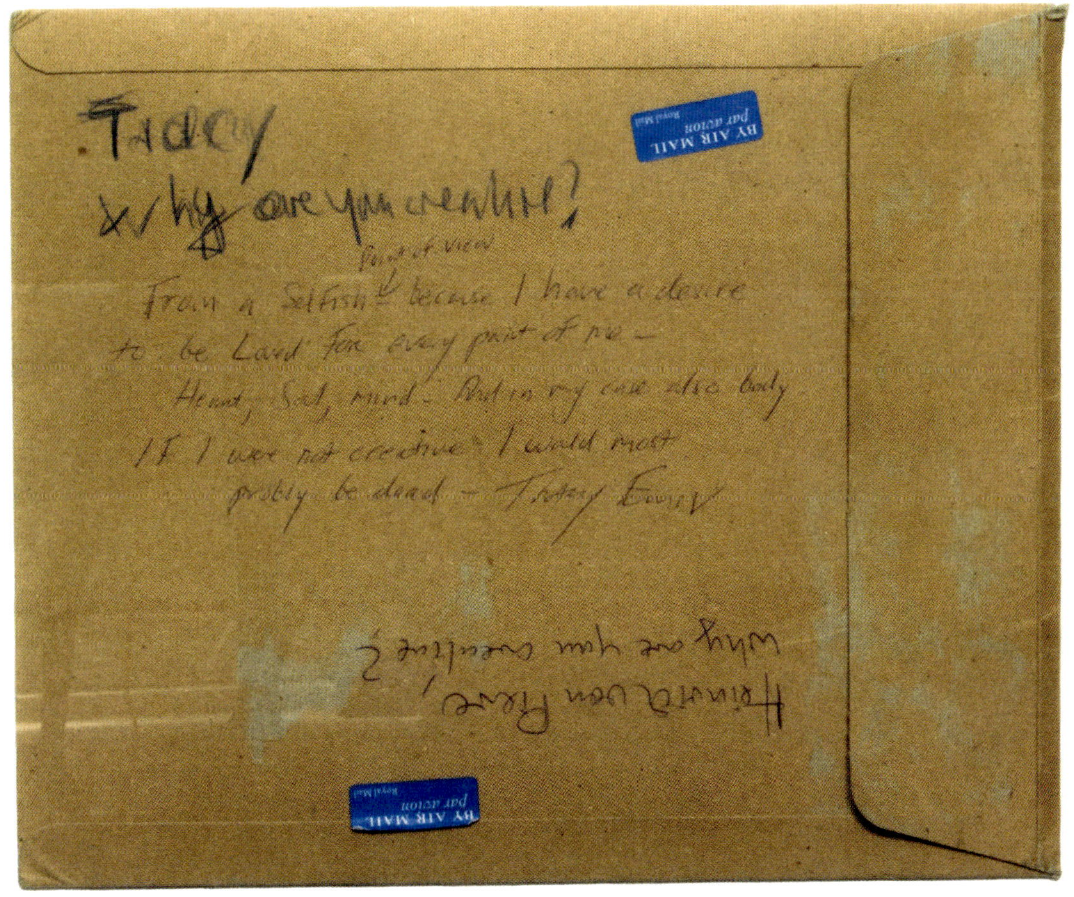

When I asked Oscar winner István Szabó about the beta-blockers of creativity, he referred to an interview that Gabriel García Márquez gave.

ISTVÁN SZABÓ

I read an interview with Gabriel García Márquez, the great South American writer. And the young man asked him about his talent and creativity, asked him how he found his beautiful stories, and he said, "No, the stories are from the people, they are living in villages." And then the journalist asked: "Okay, if you think you collected all the beautiful stories from the peasants in the villages, then why aren't there more fantastic writers like you? Why is it only you who created such beautiful stories?" And his answer was: "Because the sad reality is that there are hundreds and hundreds of talented people in my country who cannot read and write because the society never allowed them to do that." So I think it's important to know how many talented people can never find their own talent because the world never allowed them to meet with their own talent.

DIETER MEIER

I heard a lecture by Ernst Bloch, an audience discussion, and there was a friend of mine, a real expert and specialist, it was about political theater and politics and art in general, and then the janitor at the university where it was taking place turned the lights on and off at eleven o'clock at night. He wanted to make it clear that we had to stop discussing now. And Bloch's wife came in and said, "Ernst," he was already over eighty at the time, "don't you see, he wants to stop here." And then he says to his wife, "Leave me alone, I can learn something here." And that's actually symptomatic for truly enlightened people, that in the sense of a lived dialectic, they always come to a new synthesis, which is apparently valid at the moment, but which is then questioned with an antithesis. And that's what makes life somehow exciting, that nothing stays the way it used to be, but everything changes.

REZO

Sir Ken Robinson was famous in the UK for daring to say the shocking iconoclastic thing: "School kills creativity." Do you agree with his disruptive statement?

I wouldn't say school kills creativity but rather the passion. In music, when I have to analyze fucking triads, I'm not going to develop any passion for music. That's obvious. I was terrible in music, I had terrible grades because that has nothing to do with making music. I just look at other works of music, and not only from a completely normal perspective. There are so many perspectives to take a look at a piece or a song. You can listen to the lyrics, the effects, there's echo and reverb, there's the mix, there's an endless variety of styles. In school, all you do is you mostly listen to classical music and look at sheet music. Of course that kills passion. Our professors didn't know *8 Mile* by Eminem. And I thought: "Damn, he won an Oscar for it fifteen years ago, and they don't even know it." That's music, that's their subject. What if I went to a class in computer sciences and the professor said: "What's a smartphone?" "That came in the last fifteen years." "No, didn't know that." They would kick him out. Why, then, is a professor in music sciences not kicked out if he doesn't know fucking *8 Mile*? That's ridiculous and, above all, embarrassing and shaming. I think you should be embarrassed and ashamed that you call yourself a music teacher while only wanking off to Bach. You're not a music teacher. Of all the ways in which you can study music, you only have this one tiny perspective. You can do that, but don't call yourself a music teacher.

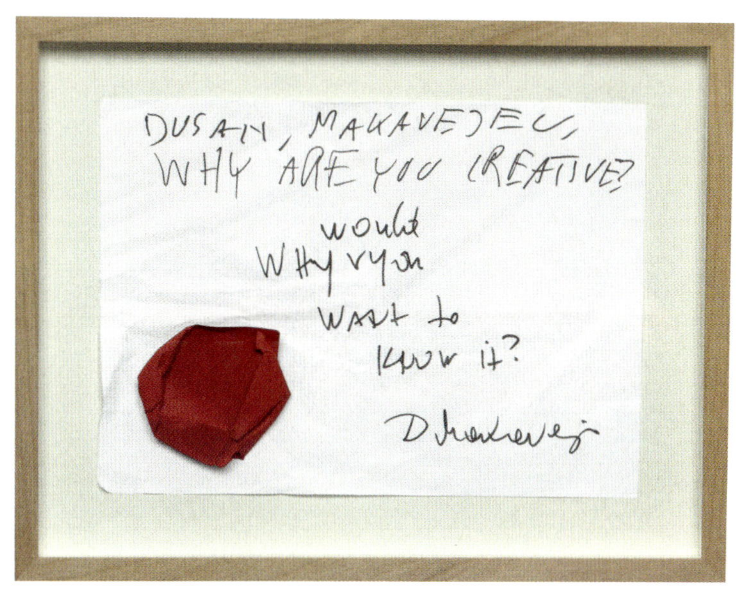

DUŠAN MAKAVEJEV

I liked my studies, some wonderful professors, it was wonderful. One of them started as an elementary school teacher and he stayed at the level of an elementary school teacher. Because I really learned from him that the real teacher is he who teaches a six-year-old the alphabet or how to wash his hands. And this is what he was teaching us. And then we talked about it with him and he said: “There is nothing in modern psychology that our peasant woman does not know about.” Something like “the early bird catches the worm.” And then he was giving us examples from the people working in the fields and the mountains, how women would know better than men if the bad weather is coming. So it was wonderful, because later I learned that actually when you work on something, when you have some problems you just should just stop and say: What would peasant women do? But this kind of knowledge is something that is like more in the skin, and I would not have learned about it without my professor Boris Stefanovitsh.

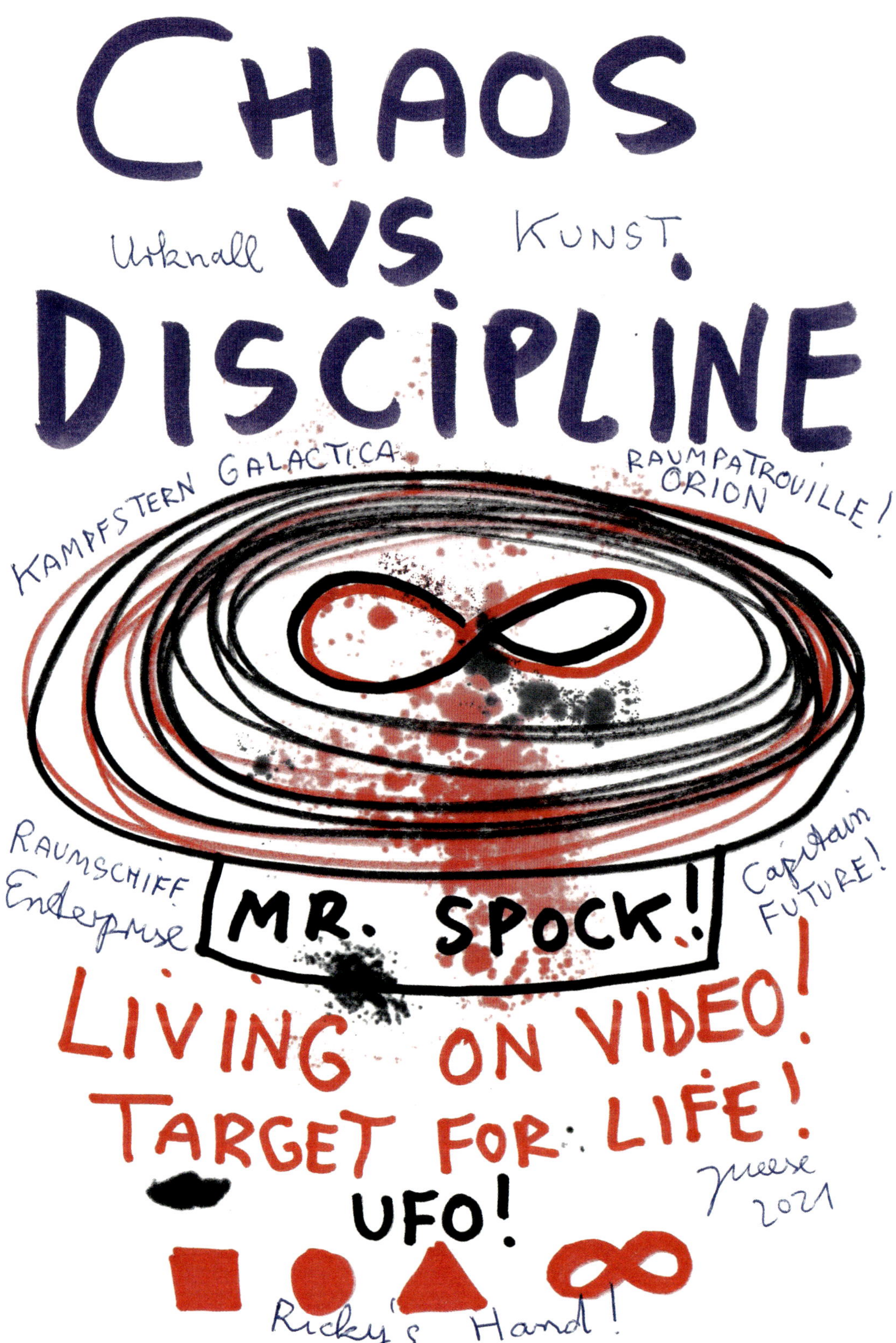
CHAOS
Urknall
VS
KUNST.
DISCIPLINE
KAMPFSTERN GALACTICA
RAUMPATROUILLE!
ORION
RAUMSCHIFF
Enterprise
MR. SPOCK!
Capitain
FUTURE!
LIVING ON VIDEO!
TARGET FOR LIFE!
UFO!
Ricky's Hand!

Nietzsche, Nietzsche, Nietzsche. He seems to accompany me on my journey. I always liked Nietzsche's quote: "One must still have chaos in oneself to be able to give birth to a dancing star."

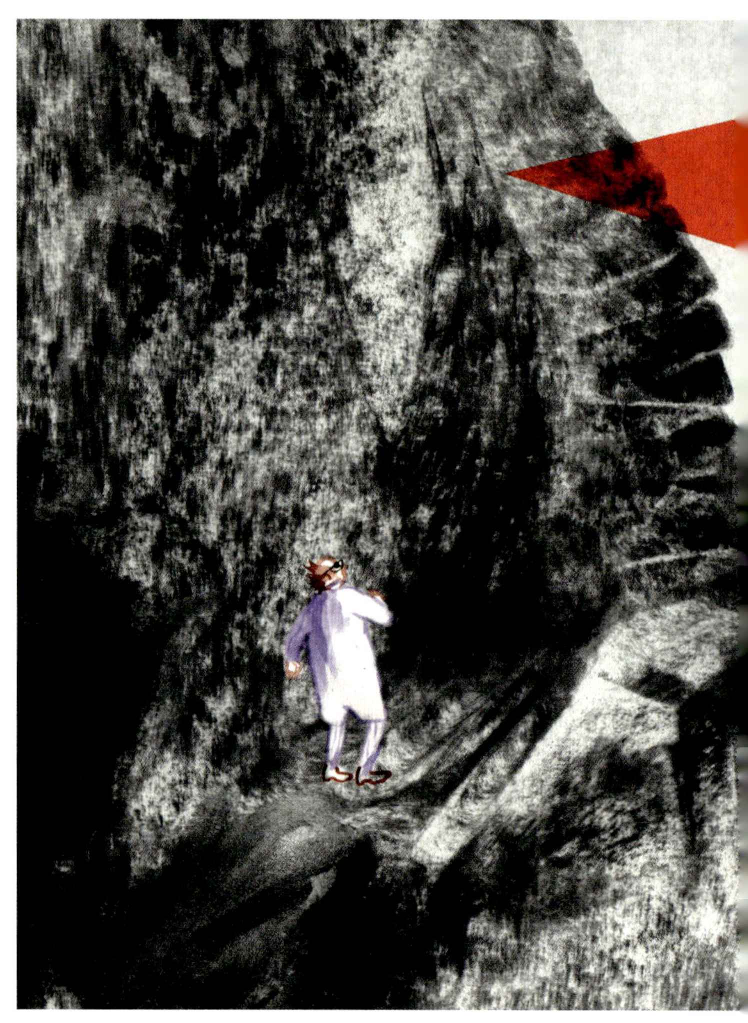

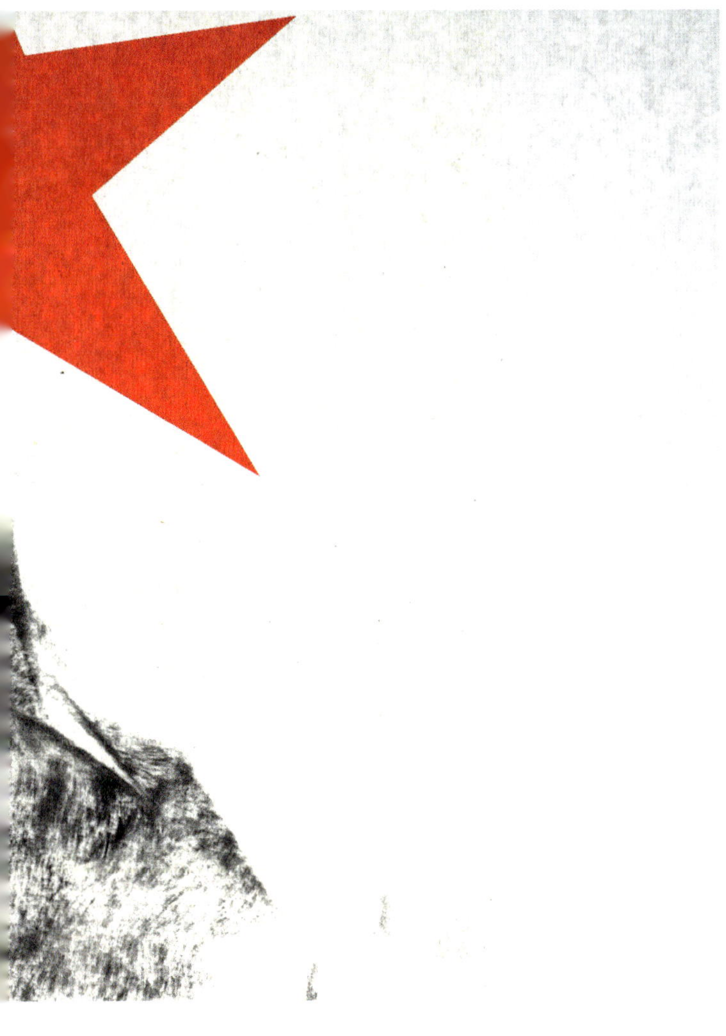

Does creativity thrive on chaos or discipline? Pierre Boulez gave birth to many dancing stars. After a Schönberg concert, I met the conductor at a dinner party in Frankfurt.

PIERRE BOULEZ

I think it's a dialectic between chaos and discipline. So sometimes the ideas come really chaotic and you have to put them in order. Or the opposite—so I mean, you can't predict this dialectic, it comes with every piece, you really start composing with every piece; because it's different every time.

BJÖRK

I guess I am very lucky in the sense that I got sent to a classical music school for ten years as a child. So I was introduced to discipline very early, but at the same time I got a very free form of hippie upbringing, which meant I could always do whatever I wanted and I could stay up as late as I wanted. So this is as much freedom as a person can have, and it has been available to me, but also discipline.

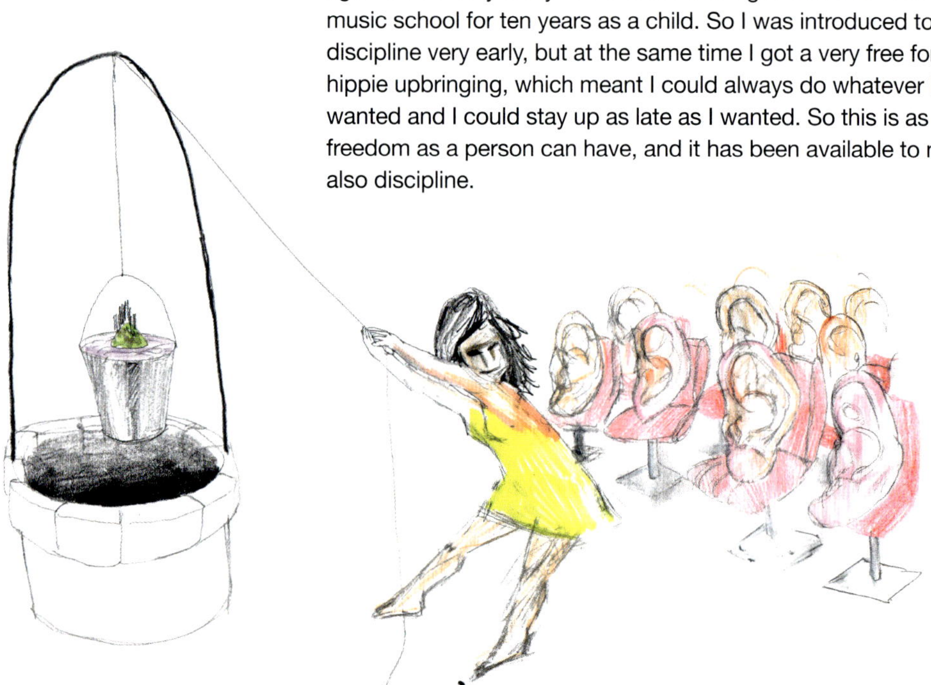

So, I think for me personally it is both, it works. Right now, my discipline seems to be mostly in when I arrange music, or when I am collecting libraries of beats, or the studio process is very disciplined and very focused. But with my voice, for instance, and my songwriting, it is sort of the opposite. I would never let the analytical side of me in there, because it can be very destructive. But luckily enough all of us have got a very unpredictable nature and unpredictable mood swings, all the time, all of us.

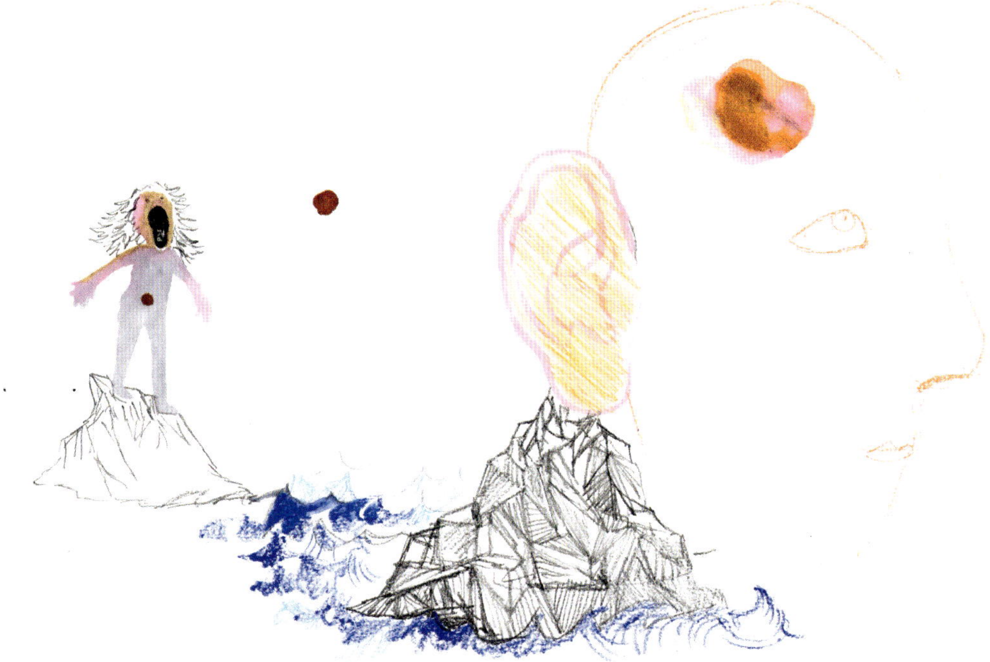

And I have a lot of faith in that. It's like the weather, like you wake up in the morning and you don't know what you are going to feel like at ten in the evening. I think it is not our role to try to control that. I think it is more when you wake up and you are enjoying discipline, do something that is disciplined! And when you wake up in the morning and you just want to run around in the snow and write songs, then do that. I guess that's the luxury of being self-employed. You can do whatever you are in the mood for.

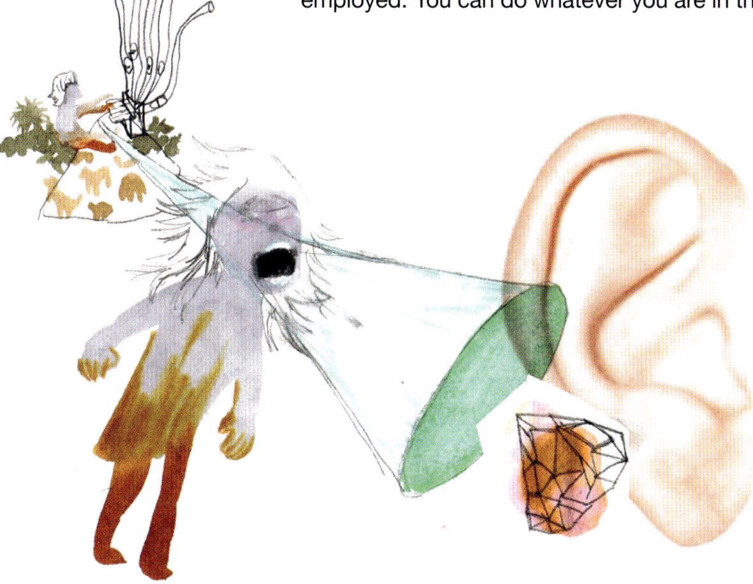

LUISA NEUBAUER

Chaos assists. The creative chaos, especially the organizational chaos, the political chaos. To a certain extent, this chaos factor is what makes us unpredictable and thus strengthens us. But chaos can also be insanely troublesome, of course, if it is structurally omnipresent. We have a very structured authoritarian German style, and we are also very rigorous with our processes, because we know that if we want to organize ourselves, then we need fortified structures. At the same time this chaos factor is always there where you are looking. There's something in the unpredictability that we benefit from.

"THE DISCIPLINE THAT I LEARNED EARLY ON IN MUSIC WAS THE BASIS OF MY EDUCATION."

What is the dialectic between Doric columns and John Cage? I travelled to New York. Here, I met Velvet Underground musician John Cale.

JOHN CALE

I have no doubts that the discipline that I learned early on in music was the basis of my education. Actually, I think that when I think of a classical education what I mean are these Greek and Latin structures of really Doric columns and kind of very foursquare structures. And that was something that was reinforced for me by John Cage. He actually dealt in terms of what responsibilities you have as an artist. And what was interesting to me when I met him was that I had all these preconceptions about what performance and art … where they lived in the universe. Where were they? Were they on the stage or were they in the living room? He came along and threw that right out the window. He couldn't really distinguish between whether you are on the stage or not. There were walls that were broken down systematically by various composers, Lamonte being the one after John Cage. And what it made me realize was that you're doing it all the time, which took the pressure off of, "Well, shall I do it now?" You are doing it anyway, whether you want to or not. But—and this is something I picked up in school, in drama school—when you have a certain sense of classical structure, when you understand that there is a presentation to be made, you can always prepare yourself for that presentation. And that's a structure that you have. You may be creating something all the time, but when you have a sense of presentation, then it puts it in a certain category of creativity that is different from the others.

God / Dog!
(meaning: I don't believe in God
but I do believe that it is human
to think + to work towards perfection.
+ I was born creative. + somehow
I found a way to cultivate my potential
through discipline.
Vivienne Westwood.

VIVIENNE WESTWOOD

You're born creative. The important point, having said that, is that creativity can be killed and creativity can be cultivated. And possibly the reason that I have managed to stay so long is because other aspects of my character, some kind of stamina or whatever else it is. I might quote André Gide: "L'art naît de contraintes, vit de lutte et meurt de liberté." I think he got it. You have to have some standard of excellence, you have to have discipline. We suffer, in the age in which we live, from a lack of solitude. Without solitude there is no discipline, because the only important discipline is the one which you impose upon yourself, and you do it, if you're creative, because you're getting somewhere, and you know that you're going to find something in the direction you're going, and you know you're going to get something out of the thing that interests you. And this is a discipline that you impose upon yourself, and, in the end, you are the judge of it. A really creative person is never flattered by what other people have to tell them, because only they are … you know, they're satisfied when they've done their best and they know they can't make it any better.

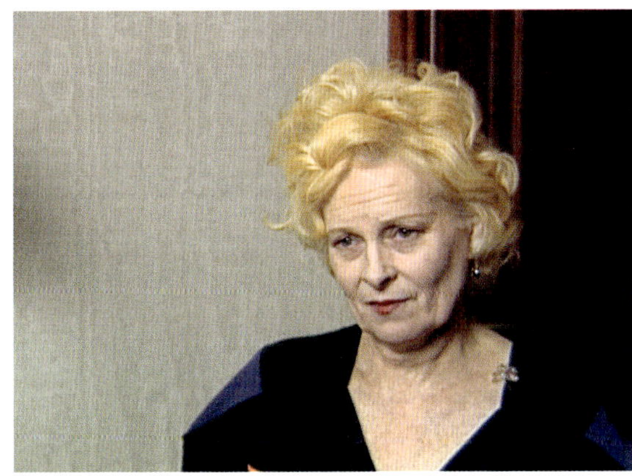

"WITHOUT SOLITUDE THERE IS NO DISCIPLINE."

JEAN-PIERRE DARDENNE

And how do surprises happen?

I think that you shouldn't look for them, otherwise they will never happen. As Luc said, this discipline can sometimes be a little chaotic, but it still remains a discipline so that things stay fresh and alive. From the couple of films we've made, we've learned one thing: the more you rehearse, the more you work on things, the more it enables us to create a climate that allows for fresh ideas when we're shooting.

For quite some time, French actress Charlotte Gainsbourg didn't seem to share this conviction. I found her decidedly direct as she told me what made her change her mind.

CHARLOTTE GAINSBOURG

I've always had the impression that acting is just based on creative play and spontaneity. And that it was all about having an intuitive side. I don't agree with that anymore. Because the only time I did theater I saw that I could work the same scene a hundred times, and I noticed that the more work was done, the more freedom came from it. Well, I have the impression that, on the contrary, I am not free. I am not free at a first rehearsal. At the end of the 150th, you rediscover something like freedom. Anyway, in terms of discipline and chaos, I have the impression that I am someone very disciplined, that I feel the need to work. I keep things in writing, but only to calm myself down. Things that give me the impression that I can see more clearly. But I don't see clearly at all. And that's all the better.

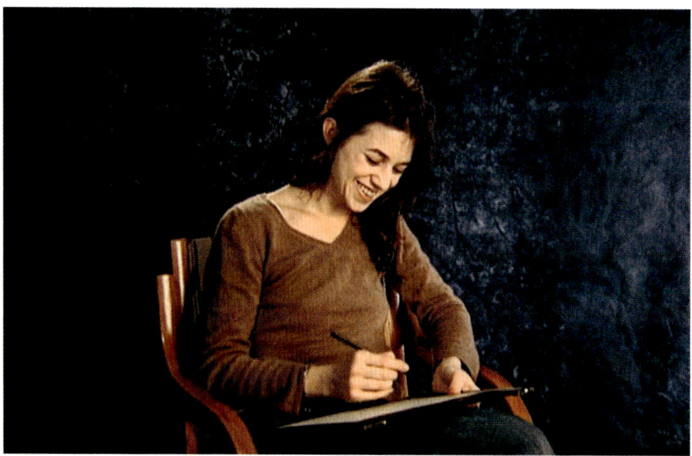

AMOS OZ

Well, it is imposing a certain kind of discipline on chaos. I need them both: the chaos are the gifts, the presents. Everything that this world is bombarding me with, showering me with. You know, I am a very early riser. I wake up at five o'clock every morning. There is no one outside except for me. I walk into the desert, which starts three minutes from my home in Arad, Israel. I take a little walk into the desert and then I see the marvelous performance of the sunrise and the changing of the colors and the mountains displaying themselves and playing with their own shadows, all this huge theater just for me. There is no one else to watch. I feel extremely grateful. I go to my study and try to do something in return. When I walk out of this world, it will not be a bad thing to try and give back some of what I have received, processed by me. That's what I meant when I said: I work out of gratitude.

BRIAN ENO

"CHAOS IS VERY FERTILE."

I think most of the people I know, and I guess myself, too, are between chaos and discipline. They allow things to be chaotic because chaos is very fertile, sometimes, and then they investigate those things with quite a lot of discipline, and they keep moving between the two positions of jumping into chaos with a kind of joyful smile on their face and then using all of their wits and their intelligence and their rationality to see how they can make the best of the situation they found themselves in.

DORIS DÖRRIE

My creativity is based on the mixture between chaos and discipline. Discipline, fortunately, my daughter taught me, that was really very important to me as a writer. To have a really limited amount of time every day and not wait for the big inspiration at night, but to be forced to sit at a desk every morning because I didn't have any other time. And the chaos, that's what I rather call "play," so to always put yourself in a playful mood as well, I think that's quite crucial for creativity.

LUC DARDENNE

I don't know if you can say chaos. But I think it takes a lot of work to construct our scenes, to construct the characters as well as the costumes. A lot of construction work, but always hoping to get points. Well, not all the time, but there are moments where we are surprised. Where the construction is overtaken by what the actor does, or that the camera does something that surprises us. Those are the great magic moments that you always expect, of course, and that can't be repeated all the time. Fortunately, by the way, otherwise they wouldn't be magical anymore. But I think it takes a lot of work and a lot of discipline. A lot of relentlessness. And then the chaos comes. But we're quite disciplined.

MICHAEL HANEKE

I think the crucial thing is the right mix between chaos and discipline. The discipline is there to tame the chaos. I believe that without discipline, work is not possible, but discipline alone is not enough.

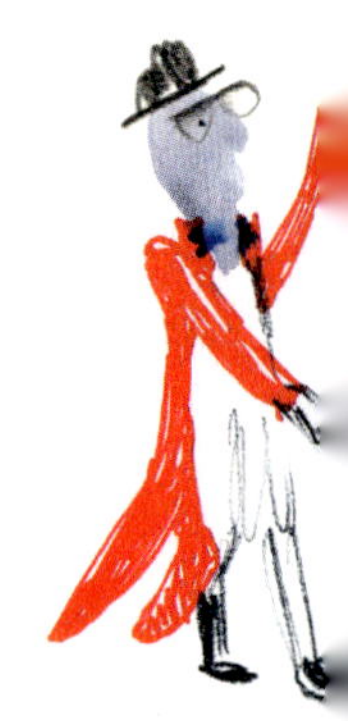

WERNER HERZOG

Your creativity, does it thrive more on chaos or on discipline?

In my case, it is discipline. 98 percent of what is sitting in front of you is discipline. In that moment where I do not have a strong grip on the storms and imaginations that are raging inside of me, if I would not have that strong grip I would possibly not be able to make a film.

ROBERT WILSON

I start with an order to make chaos. I learned that a long time ago with a painting teacher I had: he said you have to put all the colors in a certain order before you start painting; the yellows, and the oranges, and the reds, and the blues, and the greens, and lay it out in the same way in the same place each time. And then you can make chaos.

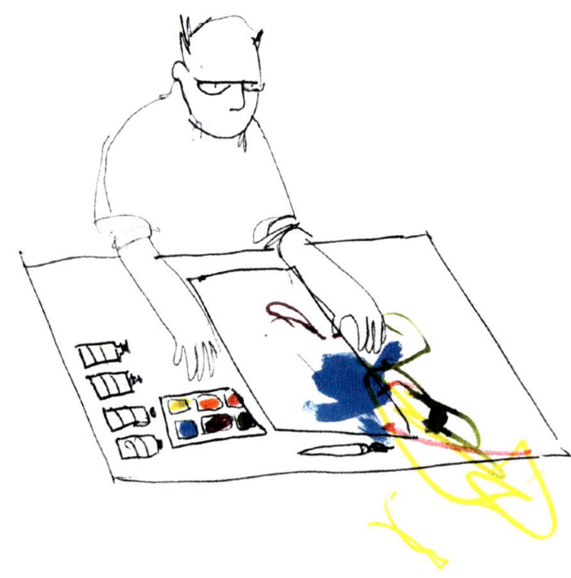

DIETER MEIER

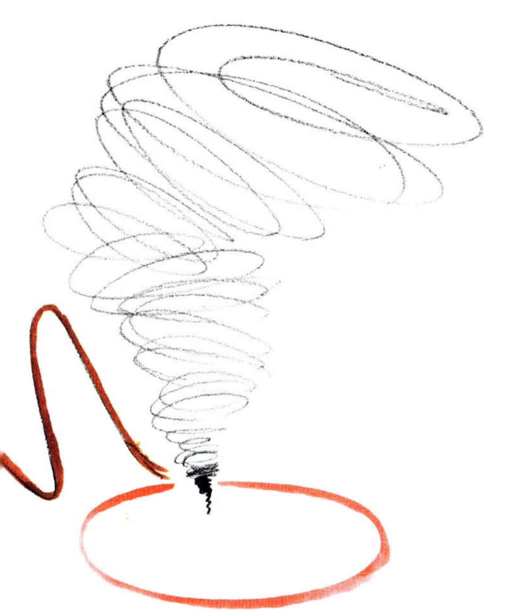

It's always chaos in the beginning. I also have a band next to Yello, an acoustic band, which is called "Out of Chaos." Because actually, in the beginning, there is always only the inkling and the unformed and the incomplete and thoroughly chaotic. It's like after the Big Bang, space was one big chaos until the galaxies were formed and the Milky Ways were formed and so on. And every beginning is always a chaotic soup, where nothing is organized yet, where one flies around. And gradually a certain order, a certain rhythm comes into it. It's like that with every process of creation. The real challenge is to somehow endure this chaos, this uncertainty about where it's going and the courage to surrender to this chaos instead of just saying, "Oh God, I'm not going to get anywhere and I'm going to throw it out right away."

It was a long dull day, duller than a German sitcom, when I met Academy Award–winning director Steven Soderbergh. Days before we had met in airport lounge and he agreed to meet up and talk about his creativity.

STEVEN SODERBERGH

Does your creativity thrive on chaos or on discipline?

A little bit of both. I believe in a sort of controlled anarchy. I do think that freedom of movement or at least the potential for movement is very important. That you shouldn't lock yourself in all the time, and if you have a plan and it's not working, you should be willing to start over again. But I do think you should have a plan.

Luckily, I had a plan. I continued my journey, not knowing what unexpected twists and turns were waiting on the road ahead.

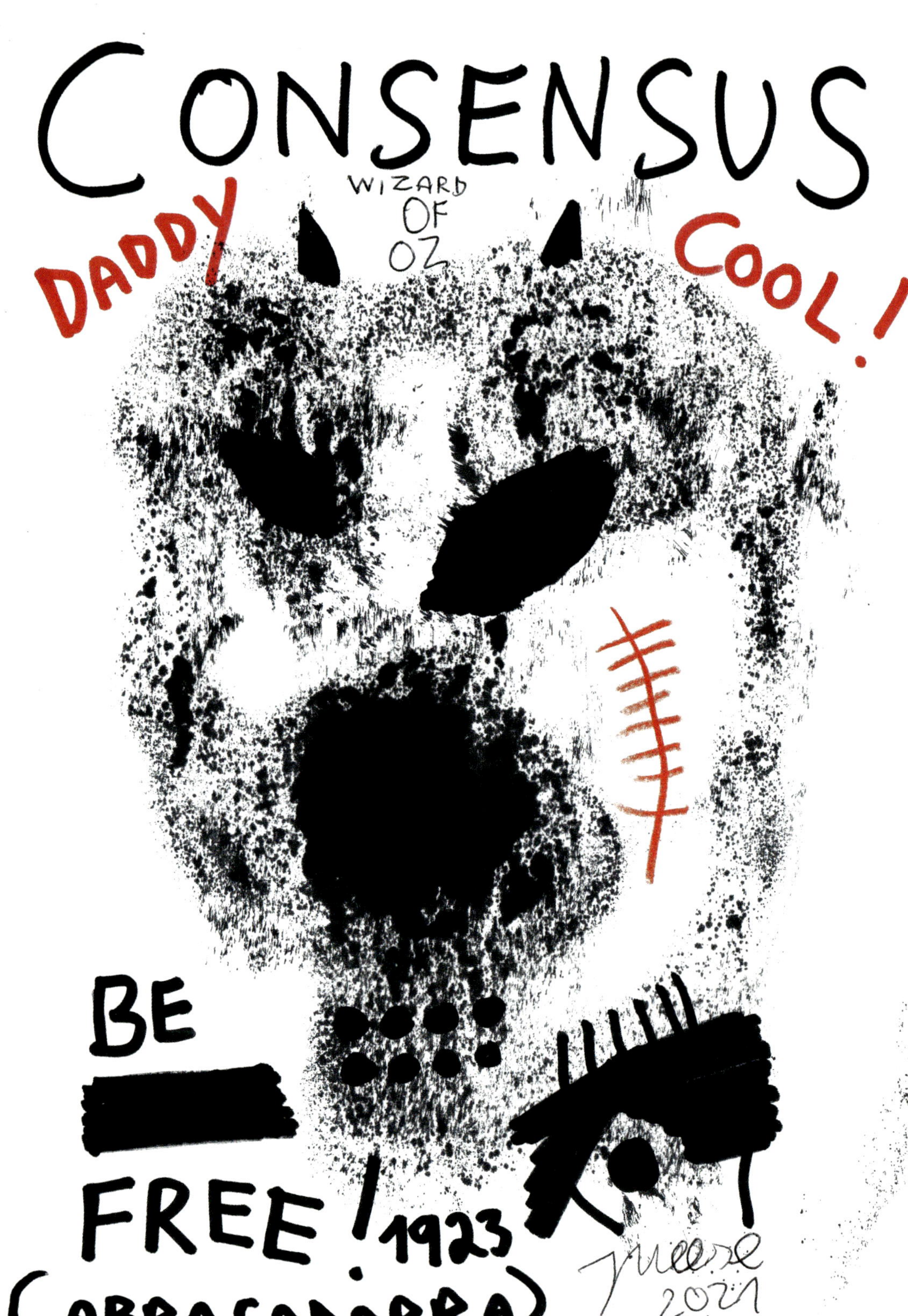
CONSENSUS
DADDY
WIZARD OF OZ
COOL!
BE
FREE! 1923
(ABRACADABRA)
2021

The roundtable is an exceedingly dangerous piece of furniture. Creativity favors a crazed maniac who everyone agrees is insane. Someone who doesn't negotiate. Someone for whom the grassroots search for compromise means just one thing: the reduction of a good idea to its lowest common denominator. Ideas are discussed and broken down at the roundtable.
The result is an idea that everyone can agree with, that offends no one, but surprises no one. Are committees responsible for murder in the first degree? Or can institutions be supporters of ideas?

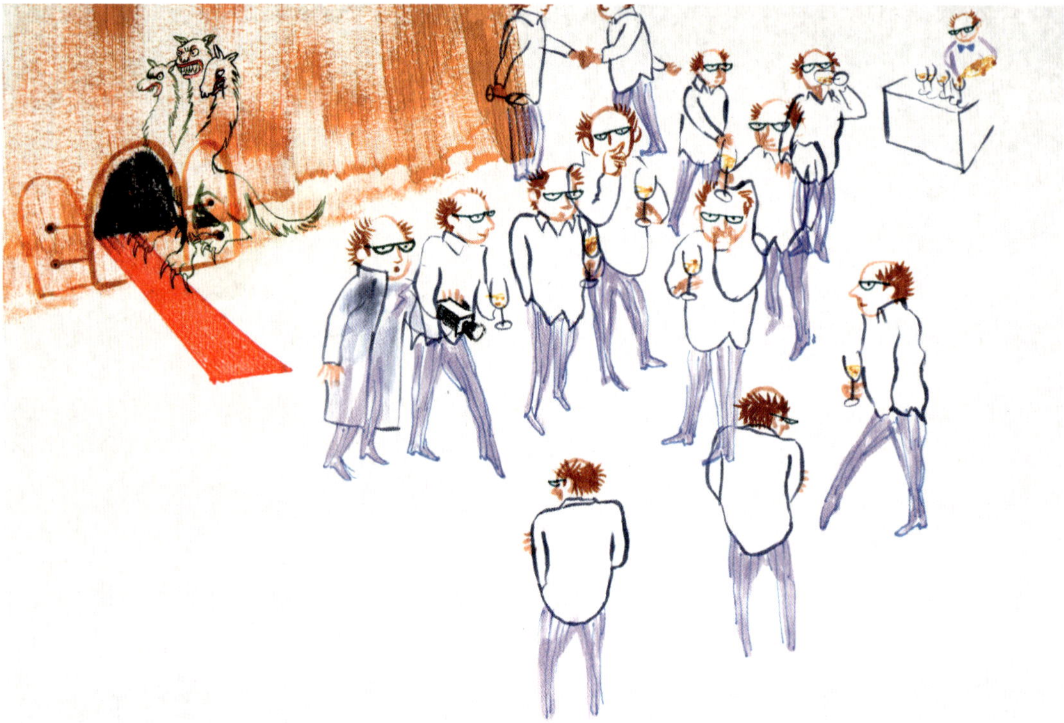

Marianna Simnett, who processes intrinsic and existential fears in her radical works, also spoke out against being pigeonholed into the ordinary and acceptable. Marianna's work goes full-frontal against the norm and the ordinary. She was invited to be part of the *Milk of Dream* exhibition at the Venice Biennale 2022.

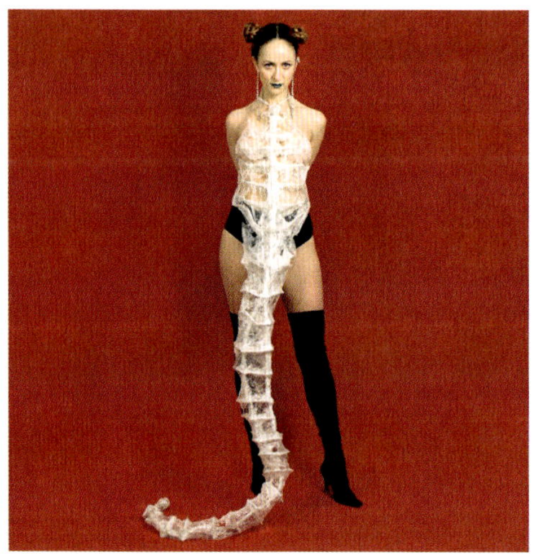

MARIANNA SIMNETT

Conforming is the main thing that fucks up creativity. I think that people forget who they are, because there is far too much noise and far too many voices that try to persuade you into a direction that wasn't your choice in the first place. And retaining a sense of what that is, is all about going against the tide and is a fight. And if you can manage that, then you reap the rewards, I think.

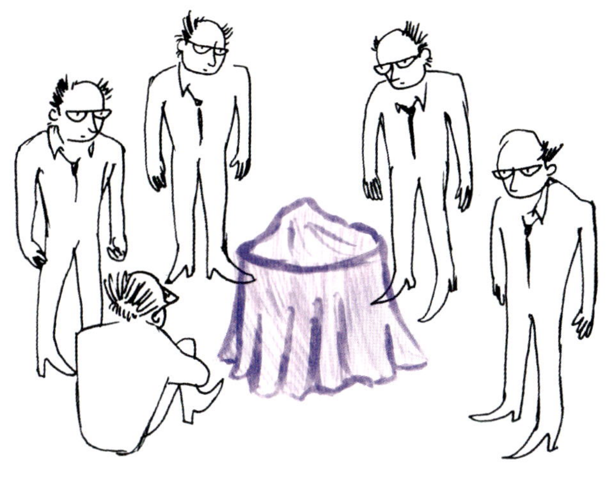

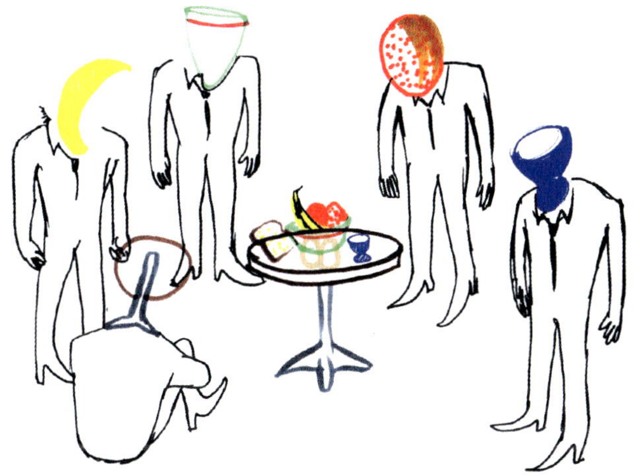

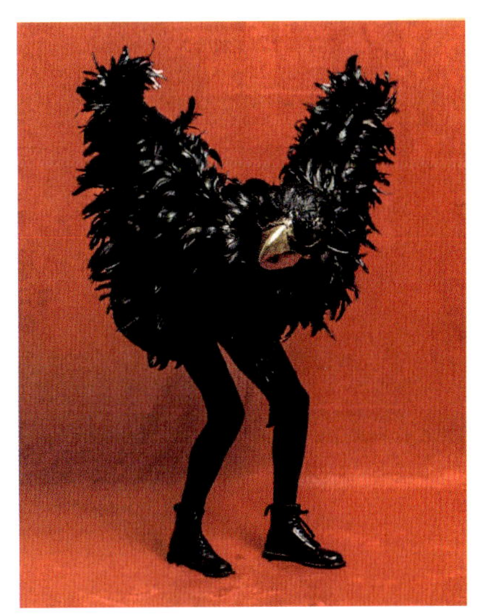

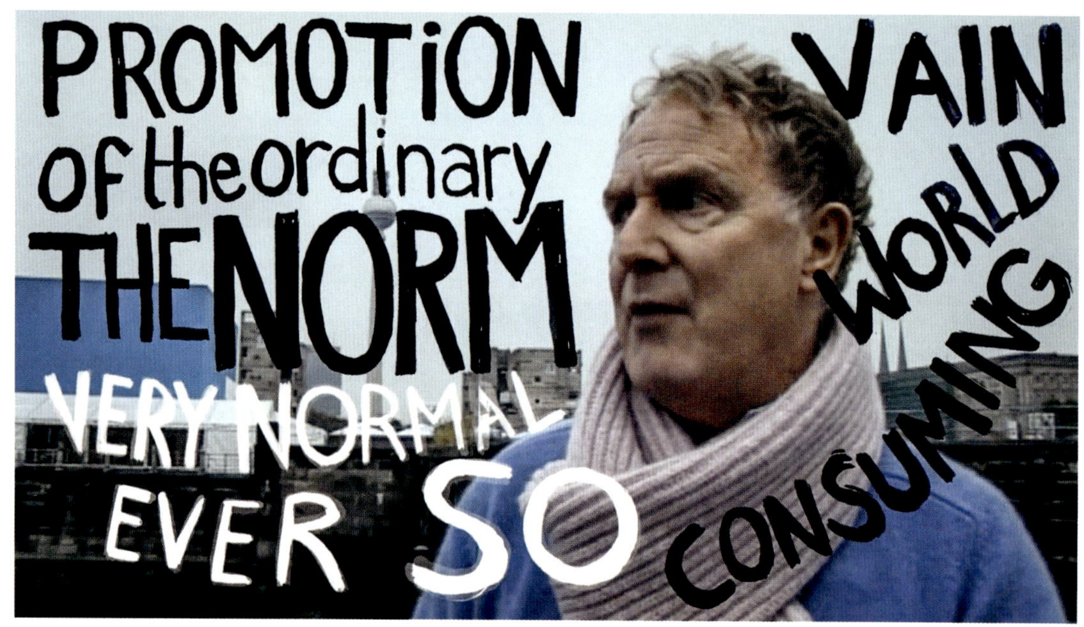

MALCOLM MCLAREN

Everyone is dazed and confused about what is culture. It is under the microscope more and more simply because we seem to get less and less satisfaction from it. Culture in the form of a movie, in the form of a work of art, in the form of a book, and so on. We're getting less and less satisfaction because we feel it's being sold to us in a way that seems to be eradicated the idea, it eradicated the original thought, eradicated what might be construed as dangerous, it eradicated the original dangerous thought, the original outlawed new idea. So, you could say ideas today are outlawed unless they can be turned into products for sale. And if that doesn't fit into this world of commerce, then this idea will automatically be killed by general consensus of corporate and economic factors.

MASHA ALJOKHINA

Vladimir Sorokin is one of the greatest contemporary Russian writers, and his novel *Norm* is antiutopian. There are several situations when, you know, people should eat the norm, and if they do not eat the norm, they will be punished somehow. And the norm is shit. It's a construct of people to control people. It's very sad that so many people are afraid just to, you know, to make the first step.

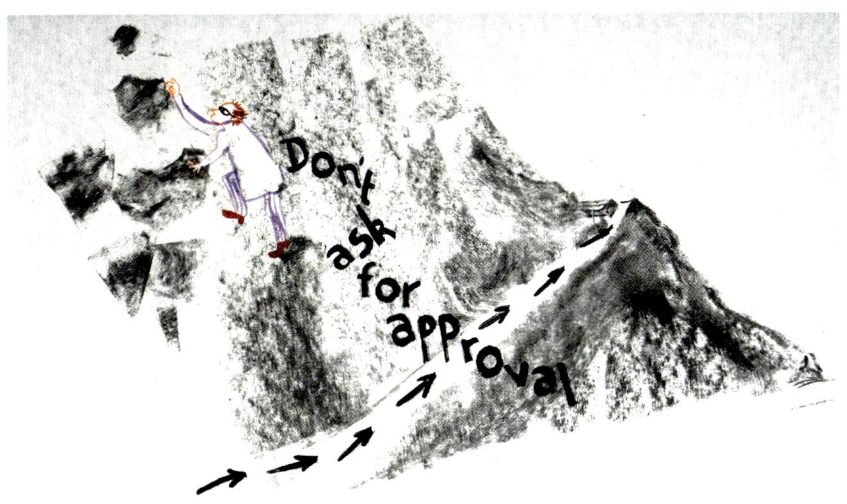

Abel Ferrara grew up in the Bronx. There, he learned an important lesson: don't take shit from anybody. Is hoping for approval a threat to creativity?

ABEL FERRARA

You know what a good film is? I can explain it and they'll never get it. But when I put it on the screen, at least it's there, you know. That's the right way to make movies, and, you know, it takes passion, and it takes sacrifice. And it's not a compromise. And any compromise that ends it, it's like, you know what I mean? Putting vinegar in water, I mean, it's over.

And you know, I am talking about the art and I am talking about filmmaking now, or it could be performance, could be music, it could be whatever, you know. You know what's real, you know what's good, you know what it takes to get it, you know. It's about sacrifice, it's about passion, and … you know, compromise? You shouldn't even say that word. Even to say you won't.

This kind of radical "don't take shit" attitude.

Yeah, that's it, exactly. Don't take no shit from nobody. That's how I was brought up.

Whereas for writer Amos Oz, compromise is an essential part of the creative process.

AMOS OZ

I am in a perpetual race with myself. In every book I have written, in fact in every sentence there are actually three: the one I have written, the one you have read, and the one I would have written in an ideal world. So very often I compromise. Once in many pages a simple sentence, an idiom, a phrase, a paragraph comes out exactly as I wanted. But more often than not I have to make little compromises, because language has its limitations.

But what if you're not willing to compromise? A lot of very talented people go into inner emigration because they simply can't bear to deal with the infrastructure of bullshit. An infrastructure that Italian photographer and creative director Oliviero Toscani is only too happy to defy:

OLIVIERO TOSCANI

You know, everybody is looking for consensus. Everybody is looking for likes. And this is what is causing conformity and … whenever people agree with me, I start to doubt myself and think I might be wrong.

But is compromise more than a social concept? Does it influence our thoughts and actions? Compromise as a human disposition? I met brain researcher Wolf Singer from the Max Planck Institute, who provides an answer:

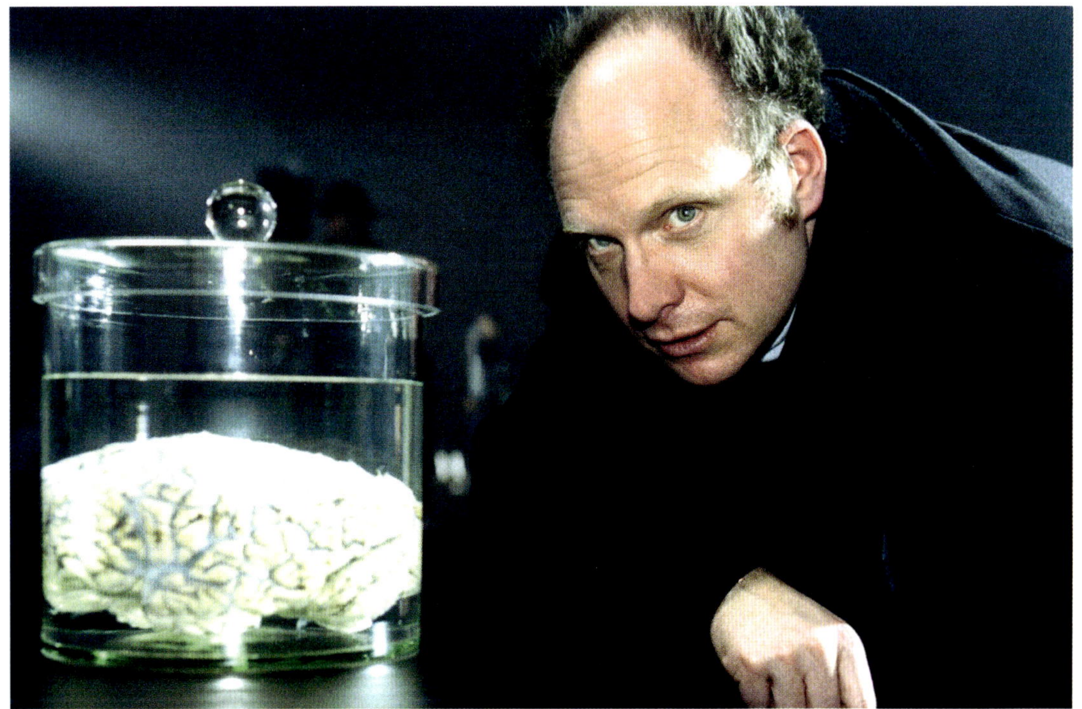

WOLF SINGER

Conformism – wanting to be like everyone else – is the greatest enemy of creativity, because then you feel you belong in a group and feel secure. That is the drama of many creative people, that they have penetrated into worlds that were not understood at the time when they were formulated by them and then had to walk long paths alone, often lacking recognition until the end of their lives, and then only posthumously was it recognized at some point what ingenious creations they were.

Fate of the avant-garde.

Fate of the avant-garde, yes. Repeats itself constantly and over and over again.

Alexander Reben is an artist and roboticist. What are the killers of creativity when viewed through the lens of art and technology? I drove along the harbor of Oakland to meet Alexander in Berkeley.

ALEXANDER REBEN

Conformity threatens creativity. And I think there are other barriers such as the tools that we use sometimes. They are constraining how we can be creative. One minor constraint would be Instagram filters, where you take an image and apply a particular look to that image. But everyone has the same filters on their phone. So then you start getting these images which look quite similar, even though the main content is different. By constraining the amount of tools and variability you have, you're also constraining the possibility for creativity, although constraint could also be useful in creativity, because if you're unconstrained there just may be so many things you could do that you can't focus on one. But maybe there's a happy balance between the two.

From *Sideways* to *Nebraska* and *Downsizing,* Alexander Payne is one of the great contemporary directors. I talked to him about egalitarian creativity and compromise.

ALEXANDER PAYNE

You know, the generous answer that you read in creativity books and generous artists is: oh yes, everyone is creative. They just have to access how. And Noam Chomsky would say the mere act of speaking language is an intensively creative and unique act. The fact that we dream. That we have those bizarre images, often brilliant images. Even less intelligent people have perhaps brilliant dreams of their unconscious trying to give them these messages. You could make the argument that we have basic creativity coursing inside of us. But that layer to make something that other people wanna see or what other people wanna feel, I don't know man.

What hinders creativity?

Conformity. Certainly, in film, I can't talk about other artistic media, but in film obviously limitation of your talent, and also conformity to ideological or popular or commercial morality. Compromise.

It was and is Tony Kaye's goal not to compromise. All the more legendary are Tony's fights with the Hollywood system, which had his film *American History X* recut without his consent. Tony's fight against the consensus is represented by an anecdote about his meeting with *Pirates of the Caribbean* producer and Hollywood mogul Jerry Bruckheimer.

TONY KAYE

"UNLESS YOU DO YOUR FIRST FILM WITH ME, IT WILL END IN TEARS."

Jerry Bruckheimer begged me to work with him. This was in 1993 or 1994, and there was a movie called *Con Air* about sort of an airplane. And Jerry Bruckheimer wanted me to make this film.
He sent me to Disney for a meeting. And Jerry didn't go to the meeting himself. He sent one of his top executives with me to the meeting. It was a formality. And I told the executives from Disney that you know I wanted to do the film and … but I didn't want to use actors. And they said "What?" And I said I wanted to go into prisons and get real convicts and use them. And they wanted to know why. And I said ehh … they thought I was joking. Because I wasn't, sadly I wasn't. And we left them, when I left the room with the executive he just said, "I don't understand what we're doing."
And then the cell phone went, and he said Jerry wants to see you immediately. And so I went to see Jerry, and Jerry sat there behind his immaculate, beautiful, amazing desk and he said, "Tony, let me explain something to you. Unless you do your first film with me, it will end in tears."

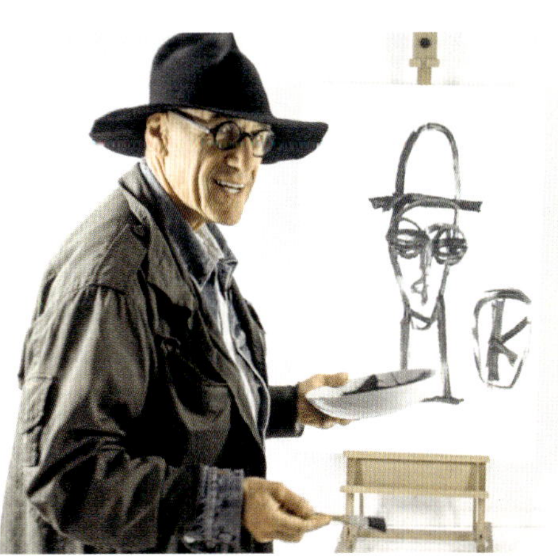

Tony Kaye never worked with Jerry Bruckheimer. He even wrote a song about it, dedicated a song to the hell of compromise: One hundred thousand million billion principles painted in red vermillion in the hell of compromise. I breathe rocks and I breathe coal, I'm turning green as I oxidize in my soul in the hell of compromise.

MAN VS. MACHINE

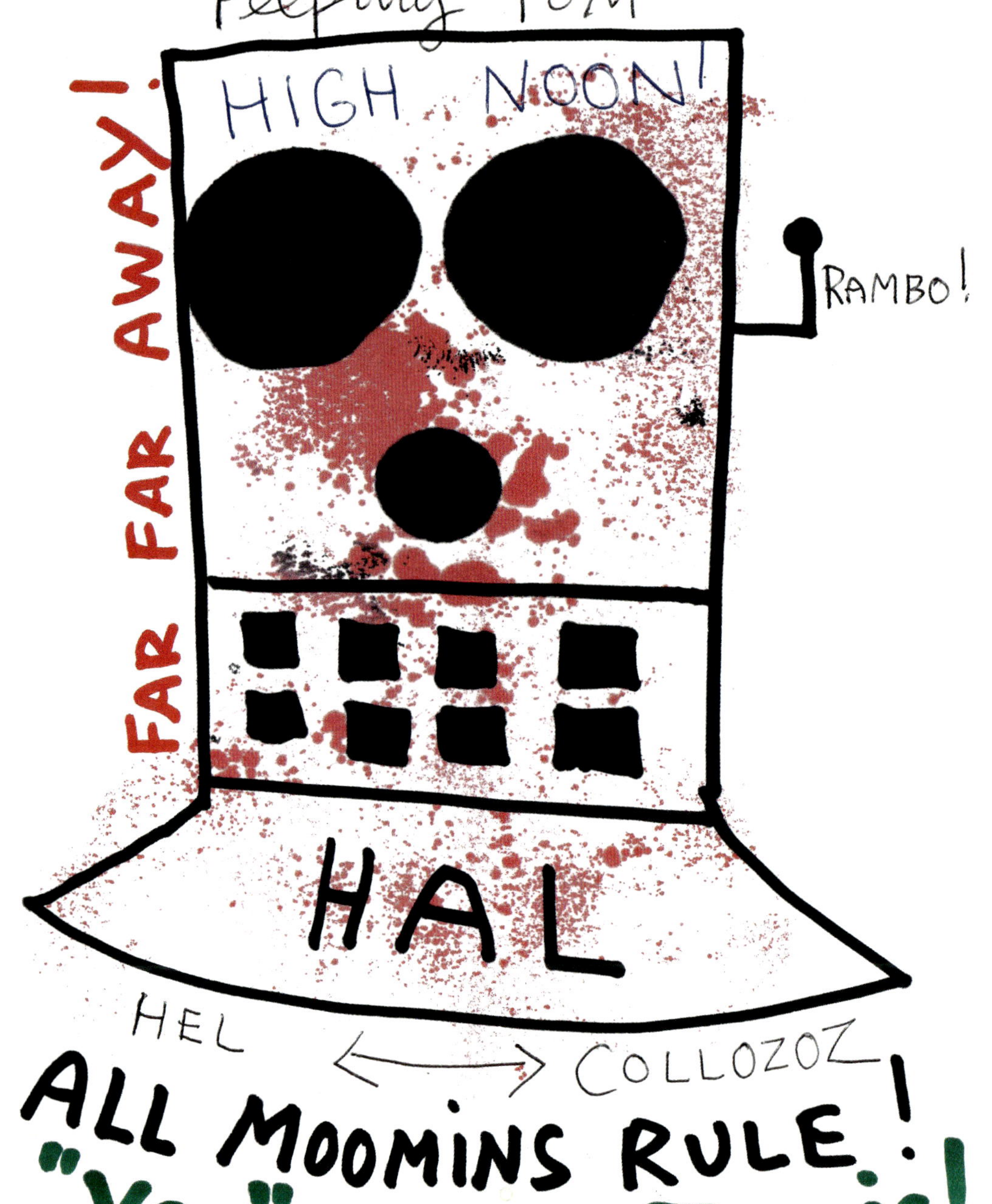

Today, the world of creativity is influenced increasingly by digital, nonhuman actors: artificial intelligence has become a substantial part of our lives and our creative output. Is it a great opportunity, or is it rather an increasingly influential threat?

In Paris, French philosopher Gaspard Koenig explains to us how we must subvert artificial intelligence in order to remain creative. And how important freedom of thought and choice is for creativity, so that individuals can pursue their self-determined individual way of life.

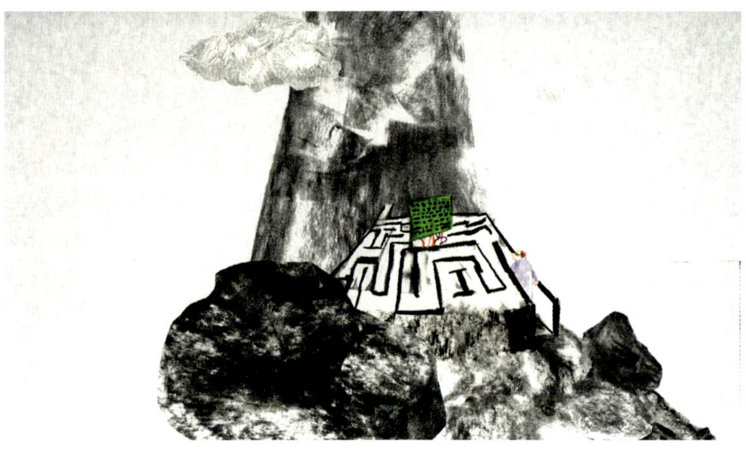

GASPARD KOENIG

"THE PROBLEM OF THOSE SOCIAL NETWORKS IS THAT THEY CLOSE DOWN THAT POSSIBILITY TO ESCAPE."

The problem of those social networks is that they close down that possibility of escape. They put you in a certain, you know, certain moods and a certain mode where you're never alone anymore. And each time you have a nice thought or each time you, you know, you have a joke that comes to mind or a reaction to something that pleases you, you share. And when I did that one turn on AI technology and I met this guy called Jaron Lanier, who is a technologist himself, which is also great, and who also ran technology and a very alternative kind of person. And he had just published a book called *Why You Should Quit Social Networks*. And we discussed. He convinced me. And so, when I left this meeting, I disconnected my Facebook and Twitter accounts, and I, I never put them on again. And, you know, for a week, I was like an addict. And I felt, you know, I was missing something. There was something missing. And after a while I rediscovered that form of independence and solitude. And so I think that was a very healthy thing to do. I don't want to exaggerate the prejudices that social networks cause, because you can use them in a reasonable and measured way. But the thing is that commercially speaking, they're built on addiction. And I met neuroscientists who are working for those platforms to know how our brains work. And what secrets of the brain to know where to push the button to obtain certain results. You can anticipate behaviour. You can twist, even manipulate our reactions.

I wanted to know if this is more than a utopian fantasy and asked multimedia artist and creative director Graham Fink about his first-hand experience experience working together with humanoid robots. Has digital data made the creative work better?

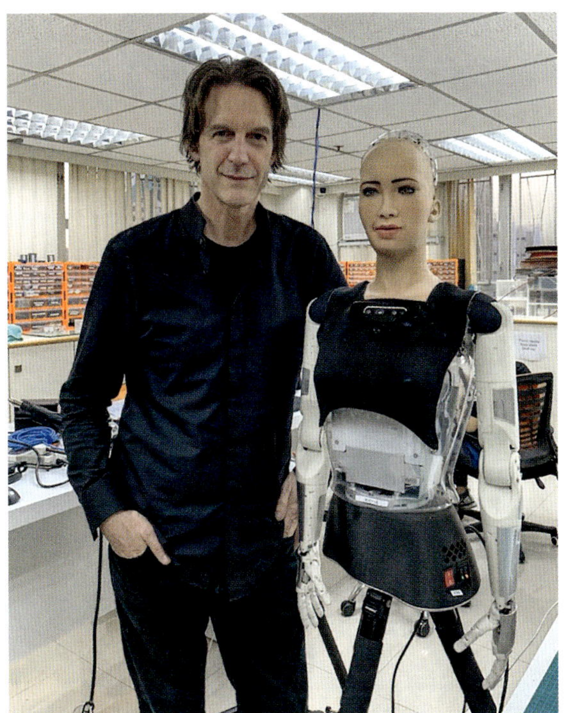

GRAHAM FINK

I'm doing some work with a couple of robots right now: one is Sophia, perhaps the world's most celebrated humanoid robot, who has ideas way above her station. And Ai-Da, the world's first humanoid robot artist, who just had an appearance at the Venice Biennale. I think her art is really different, because she's not just painting and drawing but making sculptures with her hands. AI is now writing ads, designing them, directing them, taking the photographs, and composing the music. And all this while thrashing even the world's best players at Go.

My first encounter with a new generation of AI-based robots came straight after I arrived at Ars Electronica in Austria. Ai-Da Robot and her inventor Aidan Meller were waiting for me in a former central post office. Aidan introduced me to Ai-Da Robot and explained how she works creatively.

AIDAN MELLER

So, this is Ai-Da, she is the world's first ultrarealistic robot artist. She is doing something innovative, and she is the first robot that is able to realistically look you in the eye and draw by just looking at you. So, she has a pencil in her hand, whatever she sees, she's able to actually draw, creating a drawing. Each drawing is different; even if it's the same person drawn, it is a different expressive drawing. I think, the more I understand artificial intelligence, the more intrigued I am, more slightly nervous I am, but very excited too. It's like most tools, it's a tool for good, but it could be a tool for bad. Our heroes, without a doubt, are George Orwell and *1984*, and Aldous Huxley with *Brave New World*. They were writing one hundred years ago, but in actual fact what they had to say is more relevant now than ever. So, I'm hoping that the work Ai-Da does engages audiences to be able to actually question the use of ethics within all of this.

When I was asking how Ai-Da works creatively, Aidan showed me some samples of her work on various displays.

Ai-Da has done a drawing and those coordinates from the drawing have then been exposed to a neuro-network. And that neuro, well the architecture of the neuro-network actually replots the points. And so, as a result, that makes her drawings very abstract. So, these are drawings of some trees, then we got a painting of the sea.

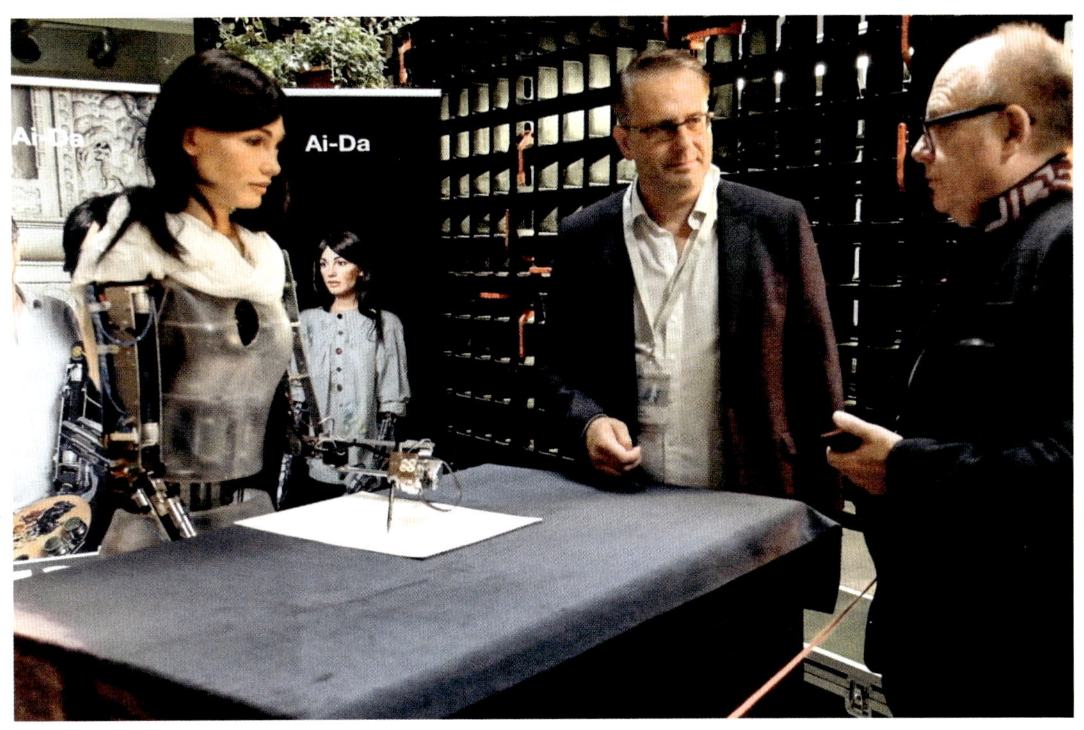

Whereas some critics see Ai-Da as just a robot with an advanced graphic program that diminishes the quality of creativity, others like chess grandmaster and mastermind Garry Kasparov see AI not as a threat but as a chance.

GARRY KASPAROV

Perceiving AI as a threat to human creativity is a total misunderstanding of the nature of human machine relations. Machines, in my opinion, could inspire human creativity, because they offer us new opportunities to reach our potential.

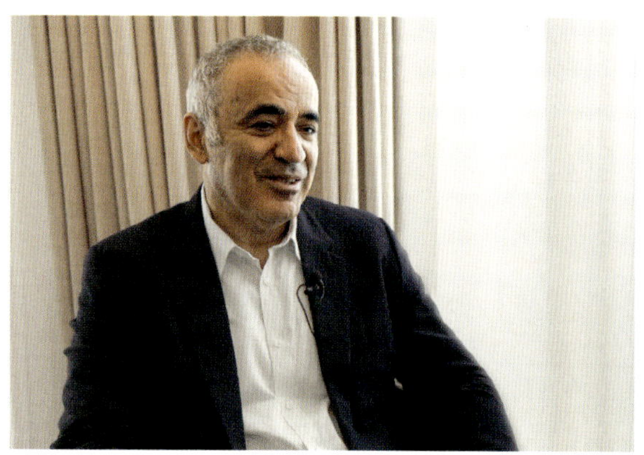

While I was still contemplating about Ai-Da, I was already on my way to Japan. I checked into Tokyo's robot hotel. Artificial intelligence was obviously on my mind when I talked to media artist Sputniko!. Sputniko! was not as optimistic as Graham and verbalized her concern that artificial intelligence could lead us into a completely dystopian world.

SPUTNIKO!

What's so scary is that these new technologies, like smartphones—I'm wearing (points at her digital watch) a watch. … They are the best friends for authoritarian, totalitarian governments. So, I'm scared that if these technologies get into the hand of these governments, then it becomes a real dystopia. Once, someone asked me, like, "What if AI can create artworks that can be very popular? Or people appreciate the artworks of AI. What would you do as an artist? Like, would your job be stolen by an AI?" And that question is strange because as artists you make works because you need to, you want to make the artworks. So just because an AI is making art that sells doesn't stop me from making art.

But what about ownership? Who owns the idea? The AI or the programmer? To Dr. Sheng-Ying Pao, it's not as simple as that. For her, the collaboration between man and machine opens up an entirely new discourse.

SHENG-YING PAO

AI would not just change the relationship between our fellow human beings, but also the way in which we collaborate. It will change our relationship with the devices around us, it will change our relationship with AI, with the technology. Now we have genetically modified babies, and we will start to redefine what creativity is. For example, if a piece of artwork is now made by AI, would we consider it being creative? Does that creativity belong to the machines? Who would that belong to? Whoever programmed the AI. And on the other hand, who takes responsibility? Who owns the …

Copyright.

Copyright, right. Is the copyright owned by the robot or is it owned by the programmer? The creator of the robot? So there's a lot of interesting questions for us to redefine what creativity is in the future.

ALEXANDER REBEN

There are two ways to look at AI from the point of creativity: one is that artificial intelligence is another tool for creativity just like a paintbrush was or when we discovered pigment. It could be a way for people to take their creative domain and apply it in another place. For example, I did this work with a dancer who was this really well-known awesome dancer. And her domain is in dance, she is very creative in dance. But through AI we're able to connect her through to robots which would draw or generate music. So we're able to take her creativity and move it into another domain which allowed her to be more creative. So, that's the way creativity can spread.
On the flip side, there are some systems out there which are in themselves maybe as good or better than humans at creating things. So we're seeing these tech-generated outcomes become very good and text summaries becoming very good. So things such as summarizing news might be a computerized thing pretty soon. For example, there is this model called GP D2 which was made by Elon Musk's open AI. It was a sort of nonprofit that was put together to release AI out into the world. And they actually wouldn't release this model because it was too good. It made text too well and they were worried that it would be so indistinguishable from actual human writing that it would become quite dangerous.

That's what our AI future could look like. But what challenges are awaiting us on the way? If AI had the better creative ideas, would this mean the end of human creativity?

WOLF SINGER

No. If you look closely at the systems that have been developed, the AlphaGo, for example, which can beat Go players and which beats chess players, and which can develop its own solution strategies through trial and error, which teaches them the rules of the game. If you compare the architecture of these systems with the architecture of our brains, you have to conclude that we are organized according to completely different principles. Principles that so far have not entered this artificial system at all, because they are so extremely difficult to implement. That's why I'm not at all worried at the moment that these systems can even hold a candle to us in the creativity sector.

Now we do have these humanoid robots. They checked me into a hotel in Japan some time ago.

Yes, they just look like us. But … that too is window dressing. Of course, a pocket calculator and also this thing (shows smartphone) can do much more than I can in individual cases. It remembers all phone numbers, I don't. It can calculate much faster, solve arithmetic tasks, therefore it is a very good calculator. But … it's not generative, it's not creative in that sense.

So, the apocalypse of some cultural pessimists …

It leaves me completely cold. Because, on the other hand, I see the unimaginable complexity of our brains, the enormous knowledge that evolution has acquired over millions of years about the structure of the world and has shaped these brains accordingly. Knowledge that is passed on again and again via the genes. But they won't be forming political parties or trying to seize power for the foreseeable future.

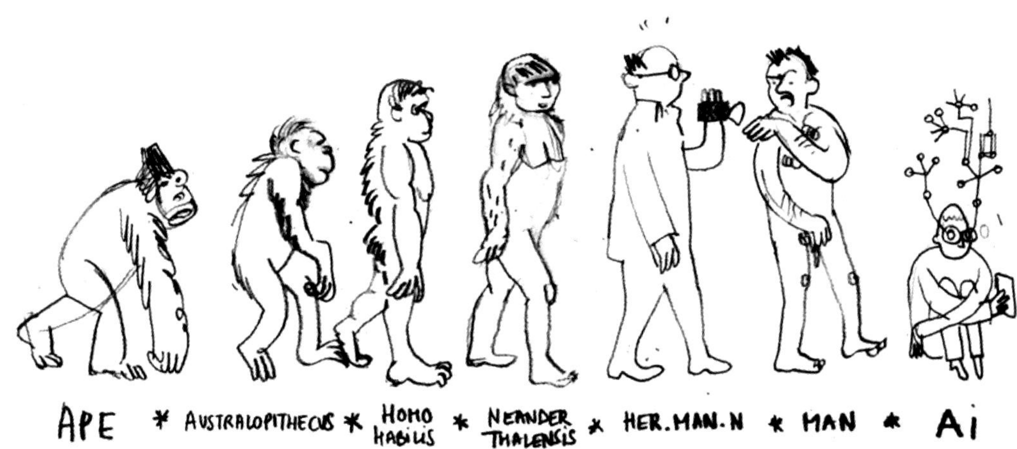

Once again, it is Oliviero Toscani who pins down the correlation between creativity and artificial intelligence.

OLIVIERO TOSCANI

Robots will never be able to be creative. Because robots are doing things right. They can't be wrong. Creativity is sometimes wrong. So a robot can't be creative. Otherwise, they're not a good robot. Probably a robot with some mistakes will be interesting. But it's impossible … a fucked-up robot, like a fucked-up human, is creative. But still, there is something that is real about that. You have to be fucked up somehow. Not integrated.

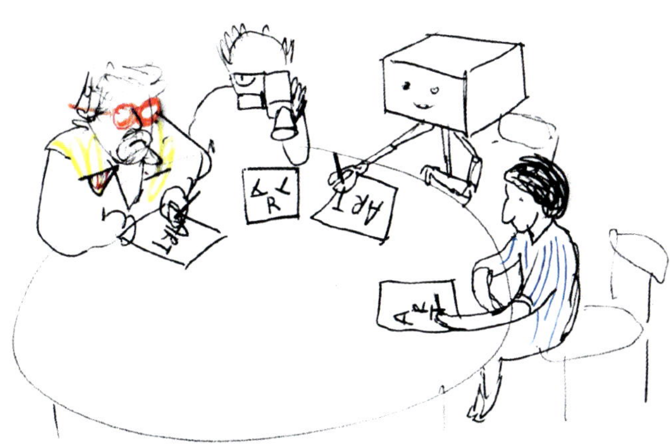

BERNARD STIEGLER

Socrates meets the young Phaedrus, who had just listened to a Sophist called Lysias, and asks him: "What are you doing there, where do you come from, and what is that scroll under your arm?" Phaedrus replies: "This is a speech by Lysias about love." And Socrates asks further: "But why did you take the speech? You listened to it, so why do you carry it around with you?" Phaedrus answers: "Because I want to learn it, I want to memorize it." And Socrates says: "But why do you want to memorize it?" "To know what love is." is Phaedrus's reply. And Socrates tells him: "No, if you do that, you will never know what love is. You alone can know what love is, only you alone." That's one way of talking about creativity.

Socrates was thrown into prison and finally executed for the crime of asking "why?" That's pretty much what I've been doing for years. I was worried. Perhaps I should stop now. Abandon my quest, go home and be a good boy. But no—my obsession would brook no distraction.

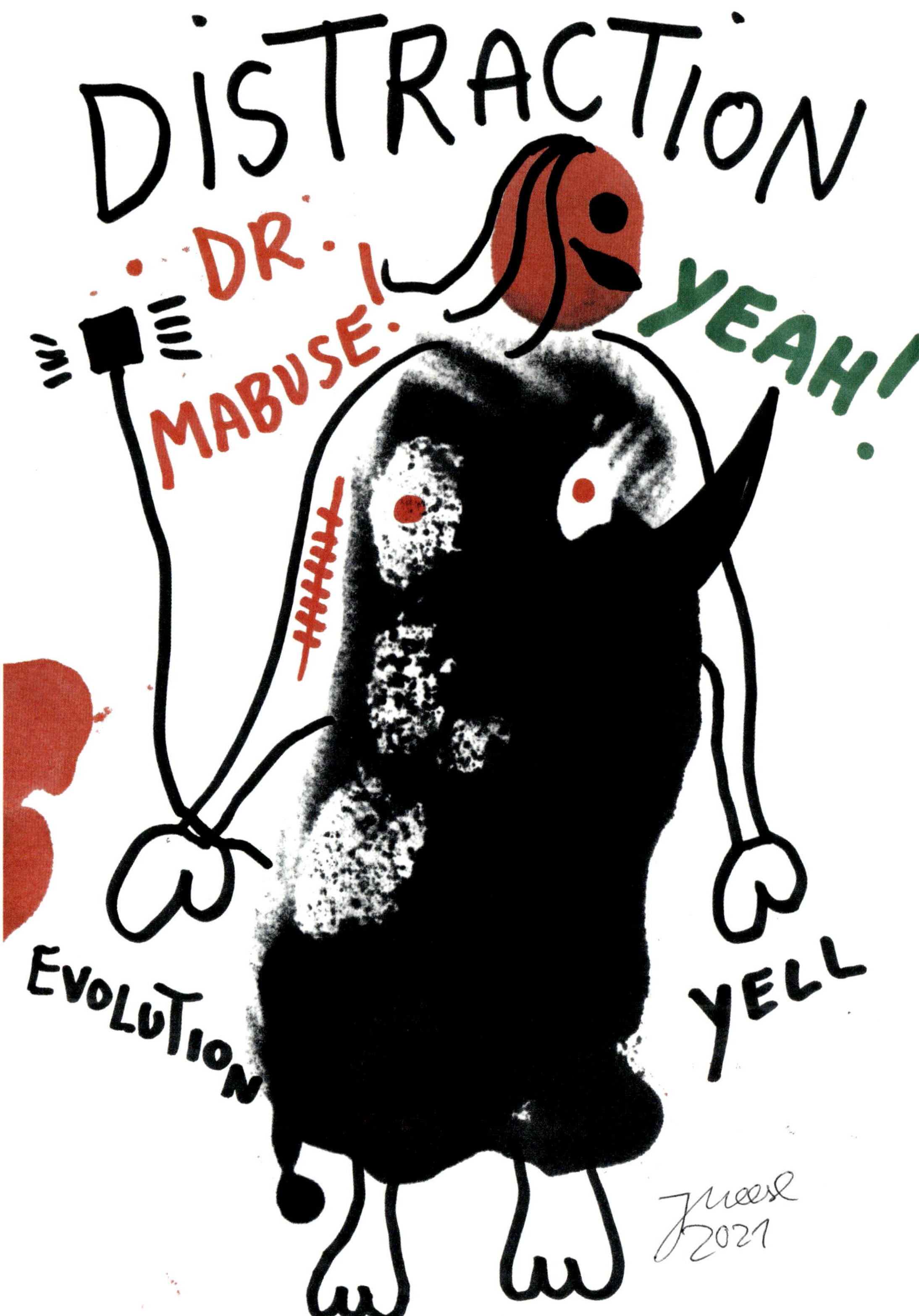
DISTRACTION
DR. MABUSE!
YEAH!
EVOLUTION
YELL
Meese 2021

In our fast-paced, instant-gratification society, we are distracted by smartphones, social media, and artificial intelligence. Do all these external diversions make us less creative? Or can they, on the flip side, give a boost to disruptive ideas?

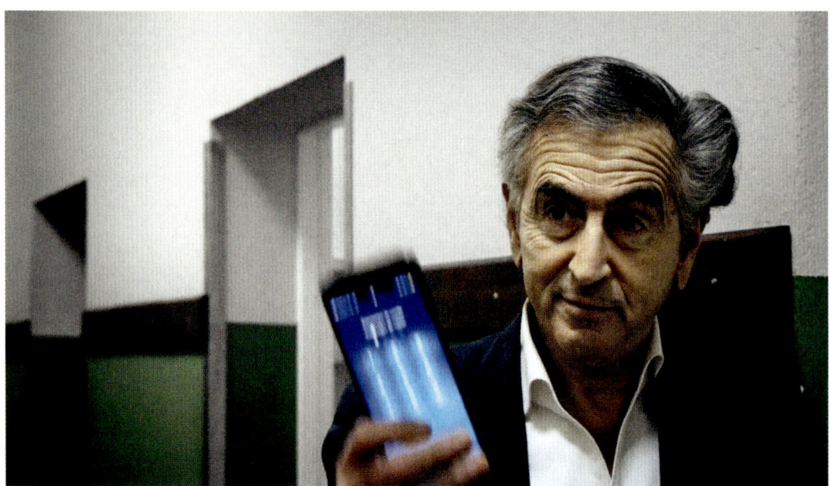

"THERE ARE MERELY SOME EVIL DARTH VADERS TO STIFLE CREATIVITY."

BERNARD-HENRI LÉVY

We must stop believing that the world is made to receive the creators, and that there are merely some evil Darth Vaders to stifle creativity. No, the world is made to prevent creative action, and creative action always takes place in defiance of that. Always. When I write, there's no social media, nothing like a cell phone, I only have it with me insofar as I'm talking to you, but when I write, I put it in the bathroom. I turn it off, go whole days without looking at it. The greatest enemy of writing, of that creative activity, is distraction, is noise, is the nothingness, the nothingness that makes you go limp. That is the greatest enemy. To all of this, you have to be deaf. So no more social networks, no more telephones, no more of these machines from hell. Hence this thing here: switch it off.

JOHN CLEESE

I think on the whole, that we are much more creative when we are in a slightly spacious, slightly more meditative state. I think if we're at the desk, answering the telephone, you know, taking text messages, firing off emails, we're never gonna be creative in that state. It's later that evening, when we are out for a walk or even in the bath while having the shower that you'll say "aha!" The mind is much more creative when it's relaxed.

DANIEL KEHLMANN

John Cleese suggests to create a space in which you can be creative. Does that work?

Yes, for sure. That works, but we have to be aware that distraction is creeping up into every space. Via telephone, smartphone, or computer, which at the same time is able to do some pretty entertaining things. I try to create a space by writing with my own hand—but not just now. I always used handwriting. It works for me as a helpful cultural technique, so to speak. Because you can't watch Netflix or write emails on a piece of paper. And that's why handwriting simply promotes concentration.

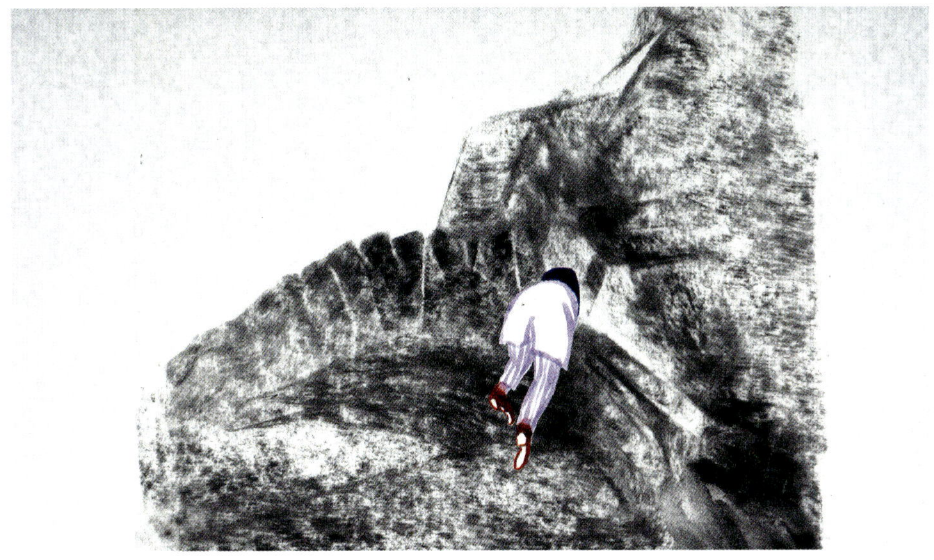

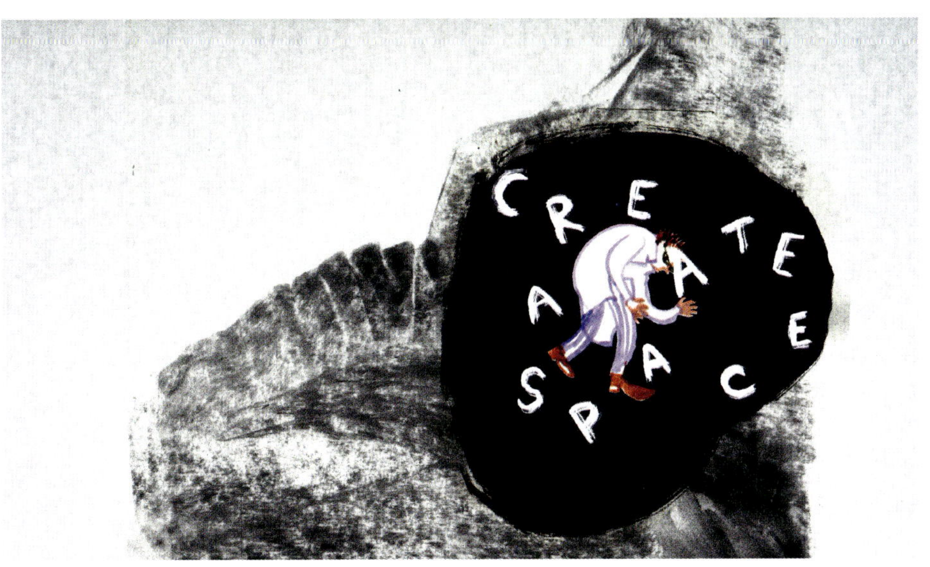

T.C. BOYLE

The biggest distraction for me is all the touring for books. Other than that, though, I am very rigid about my work schedule and I find my own space. I do also spend a lot of time in the Sequoia National Forest in a, what's called a cabin, but in fact it's just a house; deep in the woods there is no internet, the phone doesn't work. So there, I have enough quiet to actually become bored. And because I'm bored, I read more, I write more, and when I'm done with work, instead of running around hassling with the normal things of human life, I take this beautiful dog right here and we walk deep into the woods for hours. And I'll find a rock and sit on it and read my books. Sometimes, even in winter, I'll just put my head back and look at the sky and take a nap for ten minutes. That's living.

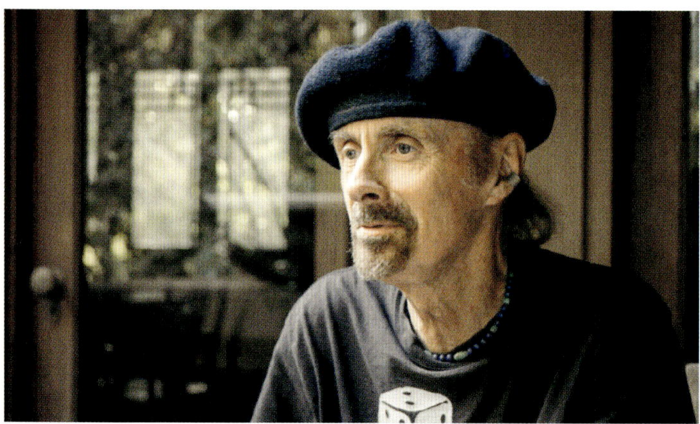

Hélène Grimaud is one of the best concert pianists in the world. Her interpretations of concertos by Tchaikovsky, Beethoven, and Brahms require the utmost concentration. In Baden-Baden, we talked about how distractions hinders her creativity. But what disturbs Hélène's concentration turns out to be just the thing that inspires others like Glenn Gould.

HÉLÈNE GRIMAUD

Noise can absolutely kill an idea if noise is seen as a parasite to concentration. By looking inward when silence sets in, into yourself, you are most in contact with your intuition. This impulse, this is the connective tissue through which intuition comes to you. Glenn Gould used to say that he played better while the vacuum cleaner was working. That way he heard less of his surroundings, which is why he could concentrate better on the mental sound image rather than the actual realization. Ultimately, it freed up the physical realization of that sound idea.

An example of disruption happened to the scientist Isaac Newton. We've all heard the story. Isaac Newton is sitting beneath an apple tree meditating about the secrets of the universe.

What is it that holds the universe together? What is it that keeps the planets at exactly the right distance from each other? What is it that keeps man and all things on the face of the planet earth? What stops us from flying off into space? Wait! Hang on a minute. I think I got it. I know what the answer is. What keeps us on the earth is. ... Suddenly—boink!—an apple hits him on the head. An "aha!" moment that prompted him to suddenly come up with his law of gravity.

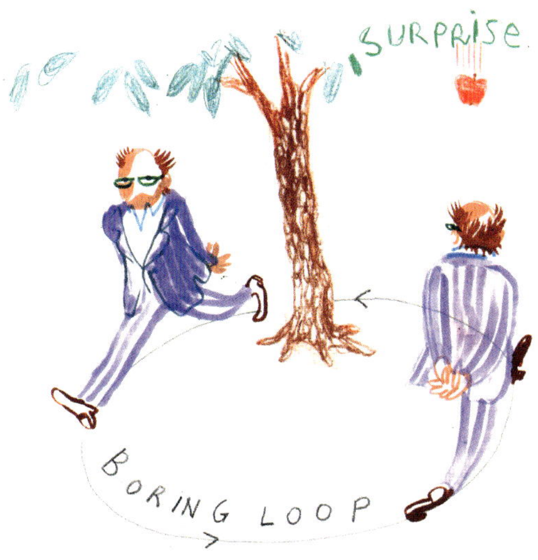

WOLF SINGER

Well, distraction is not always bad for creativity. But it may well be that the process has got caught in a, we would say a local minimum, from which it can no longer get out. And the solution simply won't come. And then a passing ICE train or a sudden shock, lightning and thunder, can provide the necessary stimulus to get out of this local minimum and then fall into an actual solution.

So sometimes distraction is a creative gift, like a mental leap, like a new connection made and disruptive ideas found. But mostly distractions are a result of everyday boredom. I was planning on painting an incredible masterpiece like Paul Gaugin, but then I suddenly remembered that we're out of coffee.

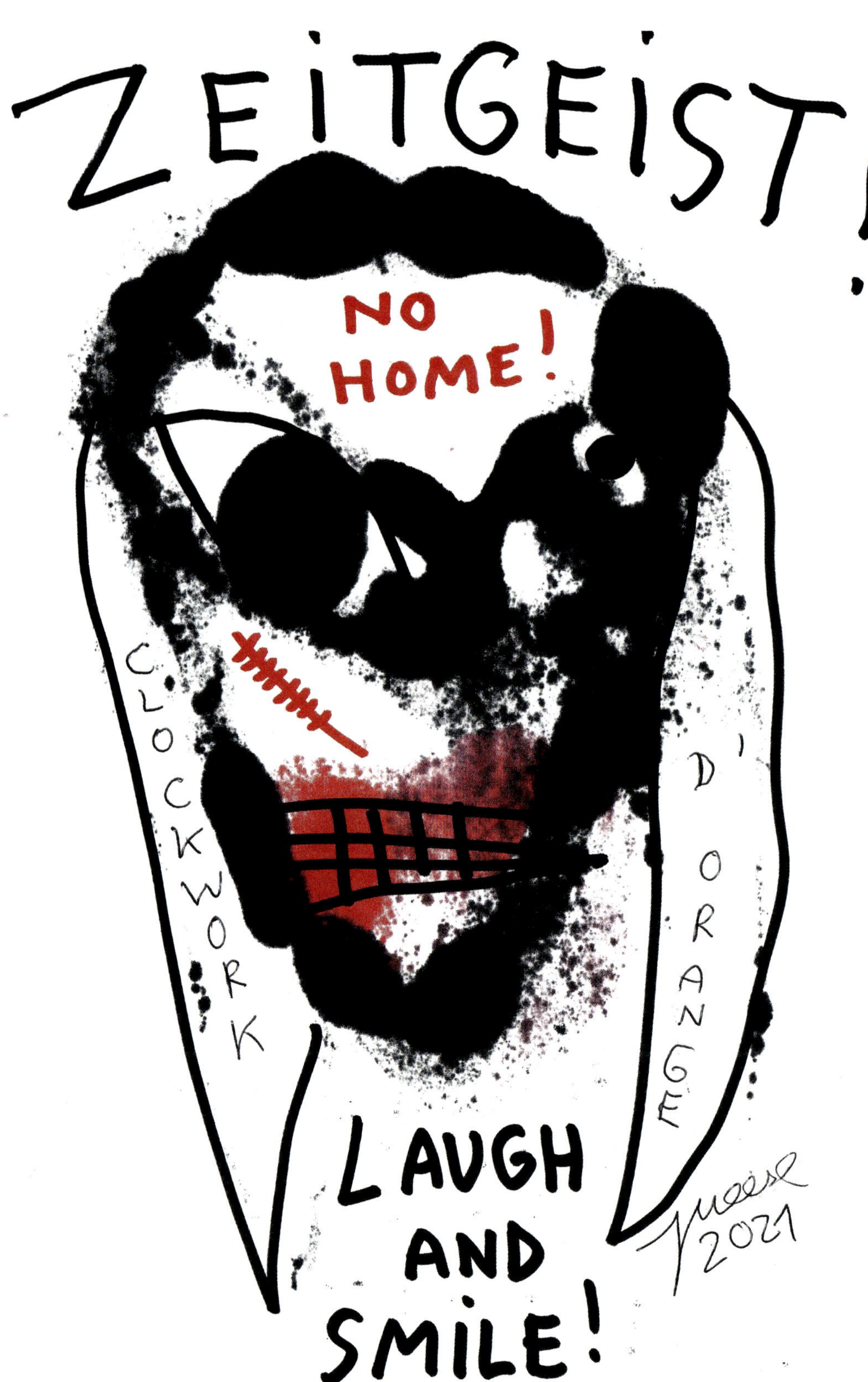
ZEITGEIST!
NO HOME!
CLOCKWORK
D'ORANGE
LAUGH AND SMILE!
2021

Sometimes, the zeitgeist is hostile to creativity. In times of uniformity, when creative people find the tide too strong to swim against, culture stagnates and festers.

Could the power of creativity—despite the dark days of global pandemic, climate crisis, and brutal wars—give us reasons for optimism and hope?

In the spring of 2020, the tide turned into a tsunami. A gigantic external influence was threatening creativity: COVID-19. It doesn't just kill art. It kills artists. To what extent did the pandemic hinder creativity? In March 2020, I met Julian Schnabel in New York.

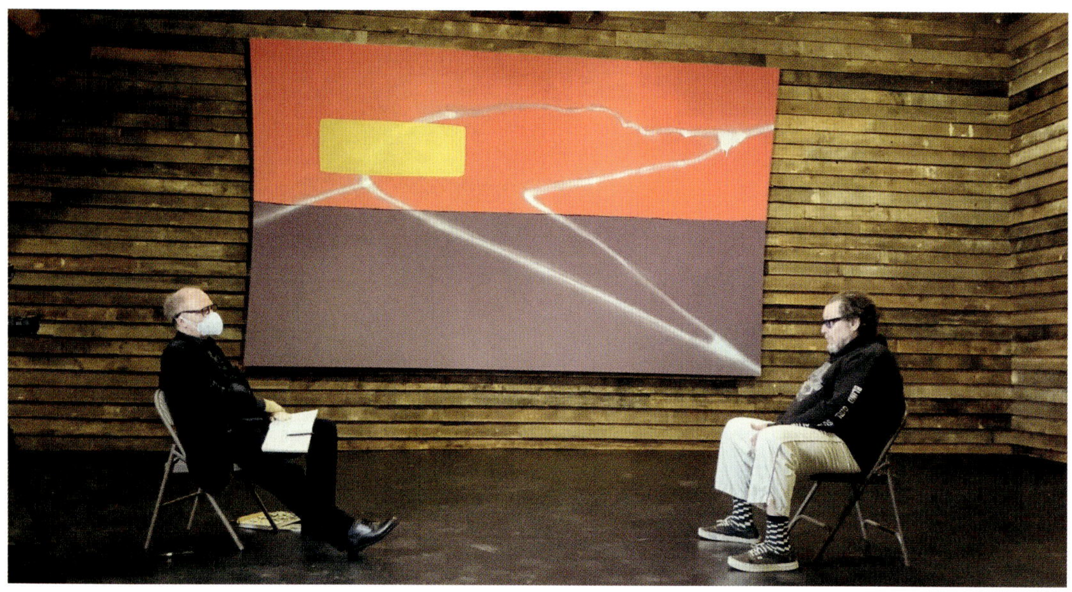

JULIAN SCHNABEL

"ARTISTS MAKE ART IN ALL SITUATIONS. THEY MAKE ART DURING WARTIME."

It depends what you do, I guess. I mean if you're trying to make a film and you have people, like a lot of people that you are coming into contact with and you're in the middle of that. Certainly, people are postponing things. The museums are closed. You know, it reminds me of Reinaldo's poem in "Before Night Falls": "Cerrado, cerrado, cerrado, todo cerrado, parque cerrado, cine cerrado." I mean, everything is closed.

There is always incongruity between life and art. So whether people see my show now or not is not really that important. I mean, I think artists make art in all situations. They make art during wartime, they make—I mean, the title of García Márquez's *Love in the Time of Cholera*. I mean, they're always difficult situations. So the good thing about being—whether it's being a writer or a painter—you don't really need other people around in order to do your work.

SHIRIN NESHAT

You know, external influences like COVID-19 affecting creativity. You know, is that a threat to creativity and creative people?

That's an interesting question. Pandemics like this one can catch you off-guard. And they affect you, in terms of the practical things like they interrupt your career, your projects, and your everyday lifestyle. But it's also the uncertainty and the unknown. Whenever that occurs that's something you don't actually predict, and there is something kind of exciting about that. When you have a crisis like that it, forces you to snap out of whatever it is that you're doing, and I think for a lot of artists, they tend to go inward. In a way, they escape what is happening by going into their imagination, sort of just really great. I find these moments of great crisis both terrifying but also a point of transformation individually. But in the strangest way, especially with this virus being so global, that you really are forced to stop thinking about yourself and be more conscious about the fact that you are just one entity among millions. And so, it's like the crisis, the suffering, the anxiety, the uncertainty—it's a very shared human experience and there is something, I think very positive about that. I think that there's something extremely powerful and positive about what happened. I think that, most importantly, I think our perspective changed. I think everyone's perspective, and that's what's amazing, is the entire world's perspective changed in terms of what matters and how insignificant we are in our lives in these certain moments and I think that this transformation really is fantastic.

ANTON DOLIN

In times of uncertainty, how can creative people or creative craftsmen do something meaningful and overcome the crisis?

Yes, this is very simple. What's going on right now is a catastrophe. COVID-19 and so on. Political crisis. There are people, particularly artists, who turn it to their advantage, because it supplies everything they need to be creative. It's the fuel for their creativity and all kinds of crisis are the best fuel possible. And the answers can all be different. Your answer can be escapism. And that can't be the only answer. You can reflect what's going on. You can escape it with your fantasies. It doesn't matter. But when life is not stable, this is the best possible condition for artists. As long as he's free to create, of course, and not in prison—and I'm talking about real prisons, not about self-isolation during COVID-19. So I truly believe this is a gift for our people, not for humanity, for humanity it's tough times, but for creative people it's a great period.

Anton, as a writer you have the benefit of working on your own. For instance, you don't need a big film crew.

I wrote two books during this pandemic. The first book is about my favorite series, *Twin Peaks*. So my idea was every day to watch one episode and then write a chapter about it: fifty episodes, fifty chapters every day. I never, never in the last twenty-five years could have fifty days in a row to work on something like this. And I truly believe the pandemic period, the period for TV series, we finally are at home with our TV screens. This is our main, you know, object of desire. So this is a time to think about it, to write about it, to create about it.

It was in the midst of the pandemic that I met artist and photographer Juergen Teller. Actor Lars Eidinger took a photo and shared it on Instagram.

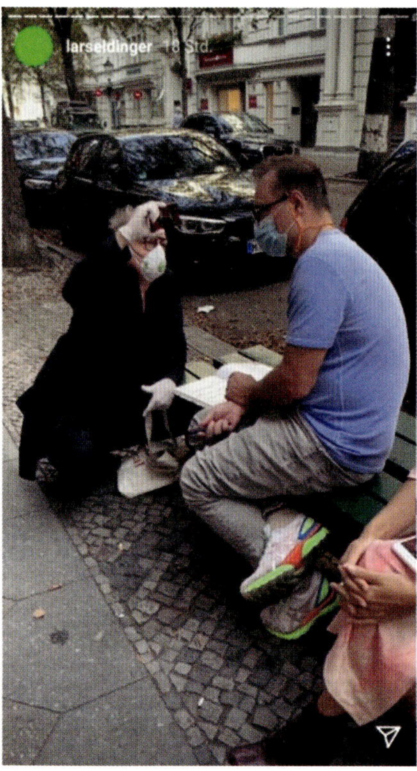

JUERGEN TELLER

What drives you creatively?

Because I'm alive and interested in the world.

How are you creative? How do you tackle that?

It's always different. Every project, everything is constantly moving and it's different. And for me, sometimes, if I think too much or … if I'm too "verkrampft," you know, sometimes you have blockers, a block and you can't think of anything and you think: "Oh my God, what am I gonna do next?" Then nothing comes. But when you let loose suddenly something life experiences come to you and it carries on, completely free and easy.

And can you tell us, what stops people from being creative? What are the beta-blockers?

Angst and conventions. You have to break out of it. And you have to make your own morals up, and your own rules. And you have to jump into the cold water, try things, react on instinct, on feelings.

Do you think creativity can help solve the problems of the world?

To a certain extent, yes. You know, because you're hopefully educating people into a nicer, better world, into a more human world.

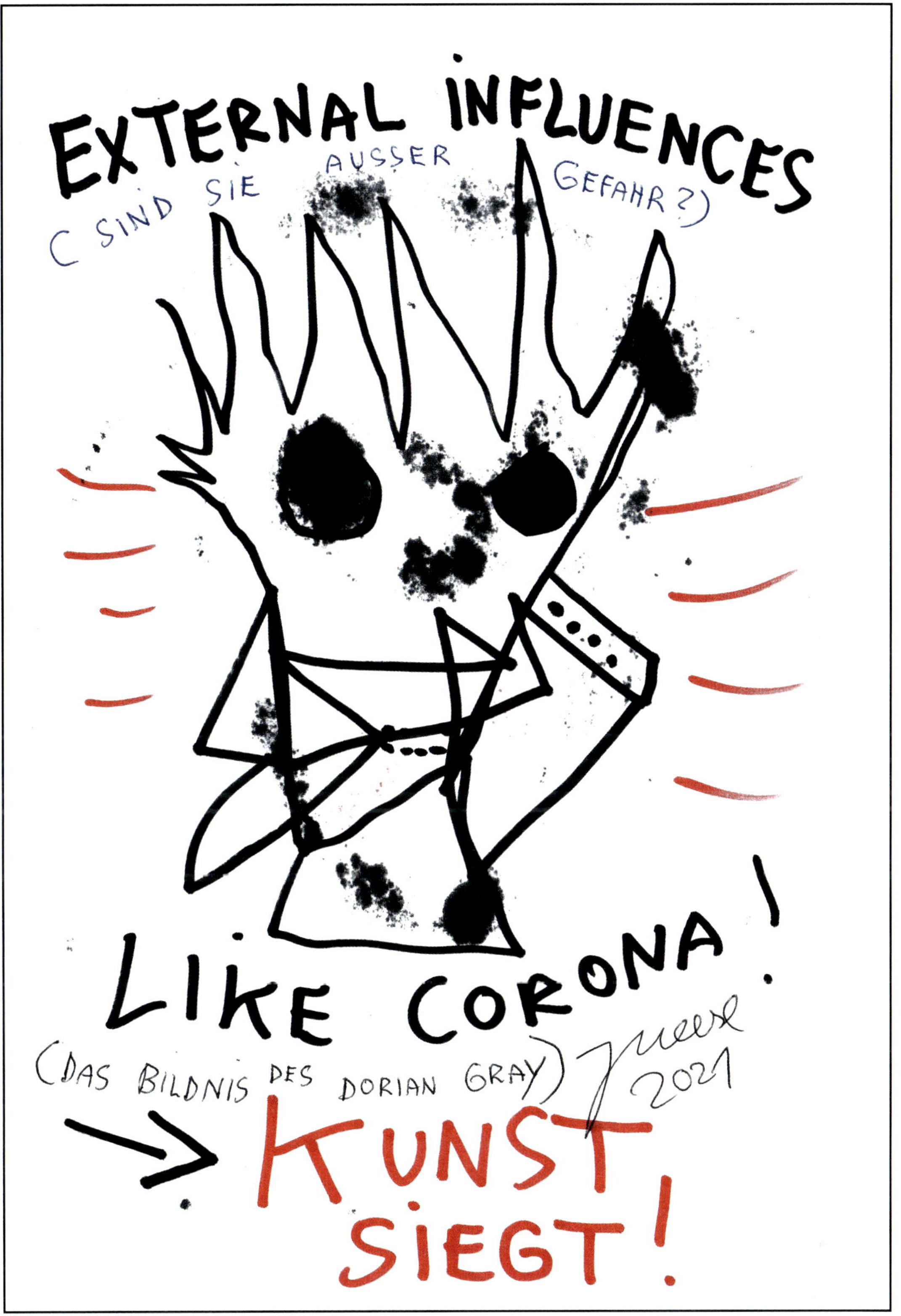
EXTERNAL INFLUENCES
(SIND SIE AUSSER GEFAHR?)
LIKE CORONA!
(DAS BILDNIS DES DORIAN GRAY)
2021
→ KUNST SIEGT!

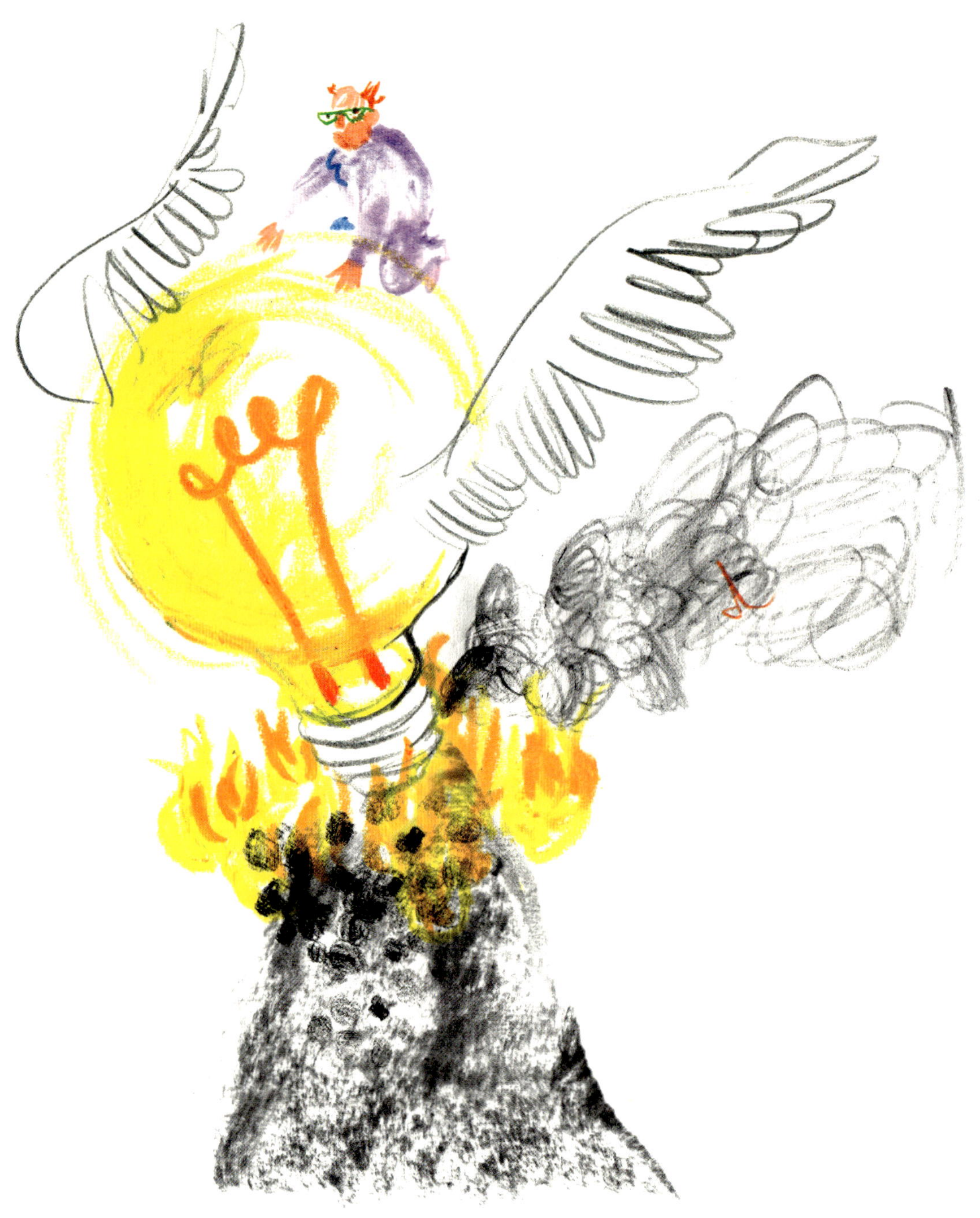

MARINA ABRAMOVIĆ

Even in the darkest times, creativity will always find its way.

I take the example of the Phoenix. It burns and is then reborn from its ashes. And this is how it is with creativity. There is always a way to find a way. There never been a century without creativity in my knowledge.

MAŁGORZATA SZUMOWSKA

So there is hope that after all these modern crises that we are facing. There could be a renaissance. I think it's going to be a renaissance because, you know, the history of humanity, the history that culture shows us always is upside down. And very often after the crisis, it's an even bigger renaissance. So I do believe in a renaissance of cinema. I do believe in art and the positive power of creativity very deeply.

SHIRIN NESHAT

I've always seen in that darkness a glimpse of light. I guess, I mean, I'm an optimist. And everything I've ever made in my work is about the sense of duality. The good and evil, the light and darkness. The horror and violence versus mysticism and poetry. And I think my entire character, my constitution, is about, you know, a sense of optimism and pessimism that I experience in the world.

So it's very interesting to see what happens to people when they are in this dark moment and how they learn to transform that into something positive. And cope with it, live with it, help each other and be very creative.

JULIAN SCHNABEL

Art will spring up, just like grass in between the cracks of cement, no matter what situations there are. One of my favorite quotes is really by Tarkovsky. When he talks about art being a living organism. And he says: life contains death. A representation of life doesn't. And so, it's in denial of death. So all art is optimistic. Even if the subject matter is tragic.

"ART WILL SPRING UP, JUST LIKE GRASS IN BETWEEN THE CRACKS OF CEMENT."

But how can creativity help us to educate people into a more human approach despite the dark times and the threat of the climate crisis? I asked climate scientist Ernst Ulrich von Weizsäcker.

ERNST ULRICH VON WEIZSÄCKER

This is the Anthropocene, where *Homo sapiens* govern all. If I was a giraffe or a monkey, I would hate the Anthropocene. It's our death of wild animals, you know. It's a disaster for the living world. To have humans dominating and destroying nearly all. This is the main problem. And how can you, with the young students of "Fridays for Future," fight this massive change, this massive challenge? All the creativity of the world will not change the facts. Creativity is very good for communicating, for being visible. This is all a given. But it's not enough, against the reality of humans dominating and destroying nature. It's not a matter of creativity. Even if we are the most creative revolutionaries, we can't change the facts. This is the problem.

How can we change the facts?

Reversing some of the trends. Including population size and consumption. And framing the conditions for doing good business. So, that he who is doing the right thing for sustainable development will make money. And he who is destroying sustainability will not. This changing of the framing conditions for business, for profits. Maybe the biggest and most difficult task for our generation. Today, we have a strong economic incentive for destruction. That is the problem. All the creativity of start-ups, of businesses, tends to be accelerating destruction. This is creativity. And we don't realize that it's destructive creativity.

Creativity can be destructive and can be constructive.

You know, four out of five start-ups that come up today are disappearing. And one is successful and the successful ones are those that accelerate consumption. Because the measure of success is more consumption. You understand what I'm saying? It's very cruel what I say.

It's a downward spiral.

Absolutely. And unless and until we develop a new kind of mentality for humanity that hates destruction and loves regeneration or restoration, we will lose the game. And I understand this from my encounter with Greta Thunberg and this new fabulous generation of students.

"ALL CREATIVITY OF THE WORLD WILL NOT CHANGE THE FACTS."

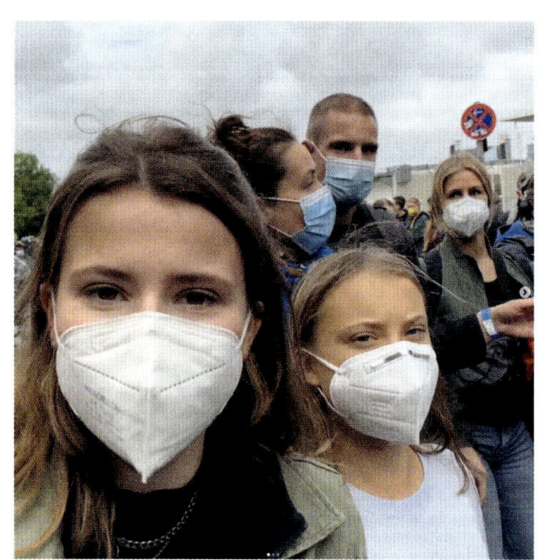

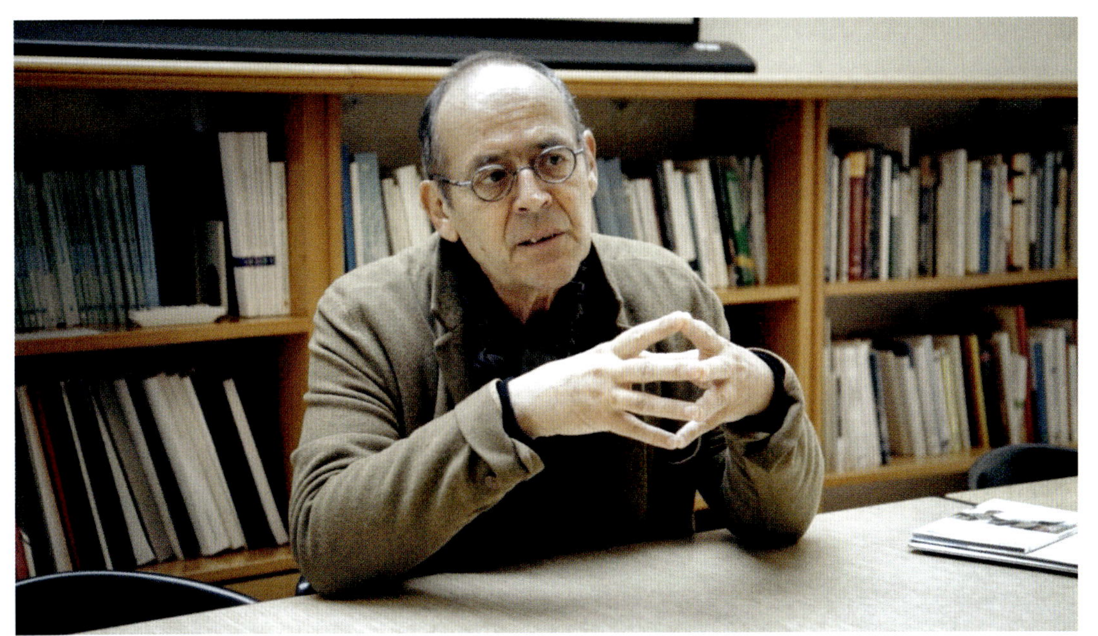

BERNARD STIEGLER

Today we are confronted with the fact that we are responsible for creativity. We must be extremely creative. Why? Well, Greta Thunberg tells us why. Because if we are not creative, as the IPCC, the Intergovernmental Panel on Climate Change says, then we are destroying the world. We are heading to the end of a habitable world. A human world in the sense that in it, life is worth living; in it one can live with dignity. Today, we say that the only way to fight against entropy, meaning the Anthropocene, is to create negative entropy. And for that, again, creativity has to be given a central place. For us today, the problem is how we ourselves and the younger generation are deprived through Facebook, through information technologies, of the ability to think for ourselves, to think for themselves. Which does not mean rejecting Scripture. Socrates did not reject Scripture at all, contrary to claims by some who have read him badly. Nor should technology be rejected; on the contrary, it must be transformed. It is a question of being creative, and creativity today also consists of finding new ways of not only using the technologies, but of conceiving them.

"WE MUST BE EXTREMELY CREATIVE. WHY? WELL, GRETA THUNBERG TELLS US WHY."

Our planet is under serious threat from external influences. An increasingly ferocious zeitgeist, from climate change and our ever-accelerating consumption. Does the new generation of students understand something that all the adults never understood? Perhaps they understand that creativity is not just a matter of artistic interest but a key to our very survival. I went to the climate conference in Lausanne to listen to the Fridays For Future kids.

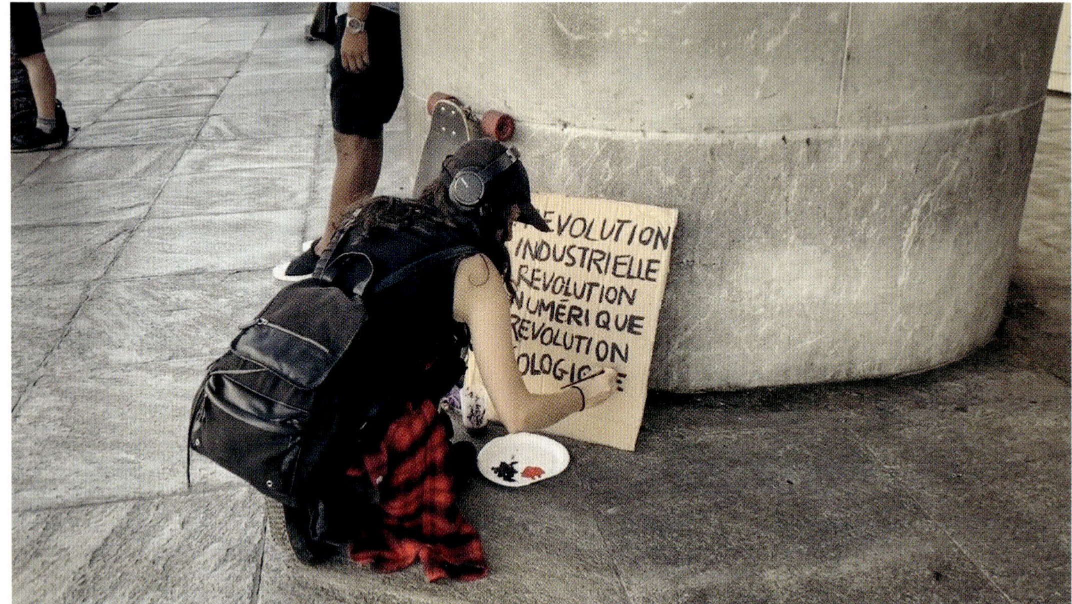

FRANCESCA JELLICOE

I tried at one point to work in a creative job and I just got sick of the fact that my creativity was being used to basically, I guess, feed this void that they create in people. I think the best thing that we're able to do individually is basically to change our own lives, the way we do things, the way we consume.

How do you use your creativity in order to dramatize the protest?

Well, I feel like I can put my creativity to good use for things that I believe in. Whatever happens, either we'll be able to change the way we do things and things will get better or we'll just end up, you know, realizing our own extinction.

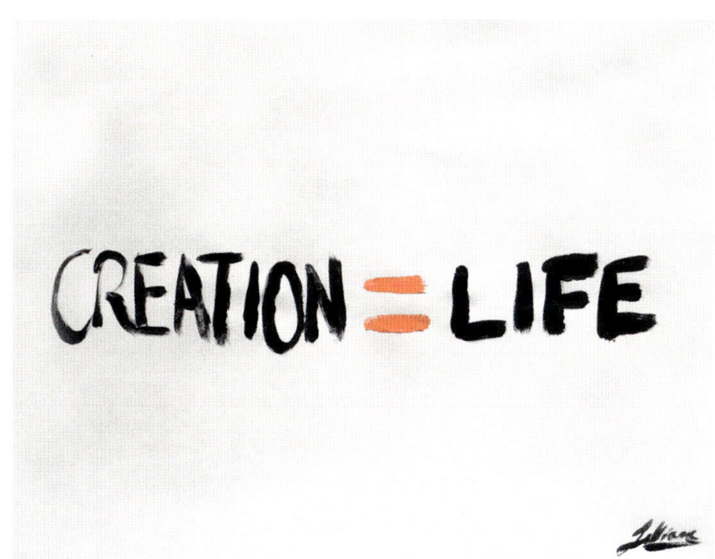

"IDEAS ARE NORMALLY KILLED NOT BY PEOPLE BUT BY OTHER IDEAS."

AMOS OZ

What kills ideas? Other ideas. What else? Ideas are normally killed not by people but by other ideas. It is not possible for a government, for a secret service for, a censorship to kill an idea. The only way to kill an idea, or rather to push it aside is when another idea, stronger idea, comes and takes center stage.

Activist and physician Lakshmi Thevasagayam of the Lützerath climate collective, who put climate protest center stage, told me about how creativity is helping a village that is threatened by destructive coal mining to survive.

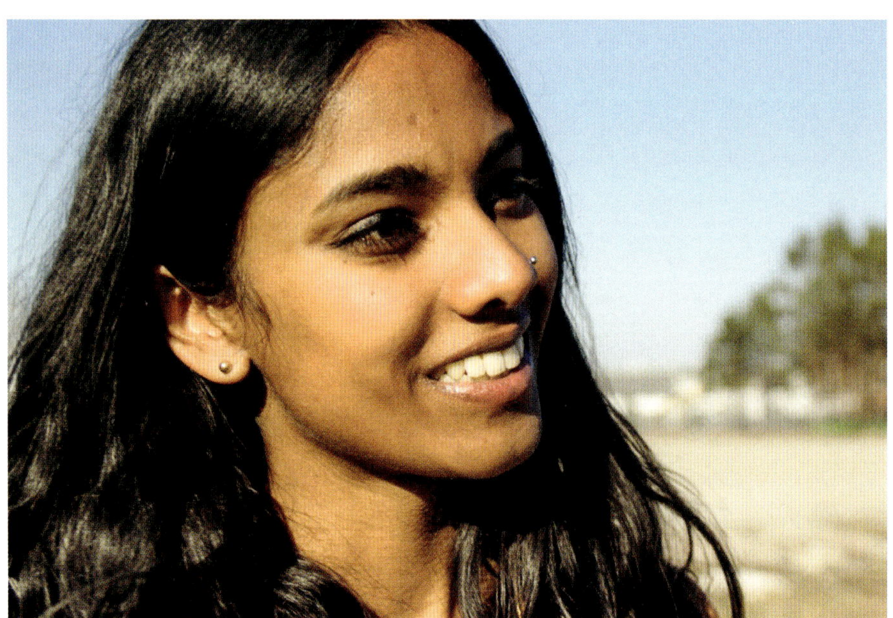

LAKSHMI THEVASAGAYAM

I think creativity has actually helped us in the village of Lützerath. The fact that Lützerath stands at all today and will continue to stand is thanks to creativity. Lützerath was to be removed in 2019 to continue mining coal and further individual profits. But because people became so creative, they built tree houses in the trees, and when the trees were full, they built huts on the meadows. People have found creative ways and means to block the roads and make our resistance more and more colorful.

I think the occupation of Lützerath in itself was incredibly creative, because this village was considered lost. And because people had set their hopes on it, because they were ready to go there and say, "We're staying here," that is already a symbol of great creativity and imagination that we absolutely need. And I think that's exactly what's lacking the most, when we think of solutions to the climate catastrophe. Because it can't be the same solutions that caused it. And the same people who caused the climate catastrophe, namely capitalism and white supremacy, that are going to provide solutions to somehow prevent or overcome this climate catastrophe.
I believe the most important factors are courage and people coming together. Those are the two things that it takes for people to also be creative, because we first need hope. And I feel like a lot of people have lost that hope. But only when we come together and realize that we are many, we realize that we can change something. And that's why we're here.

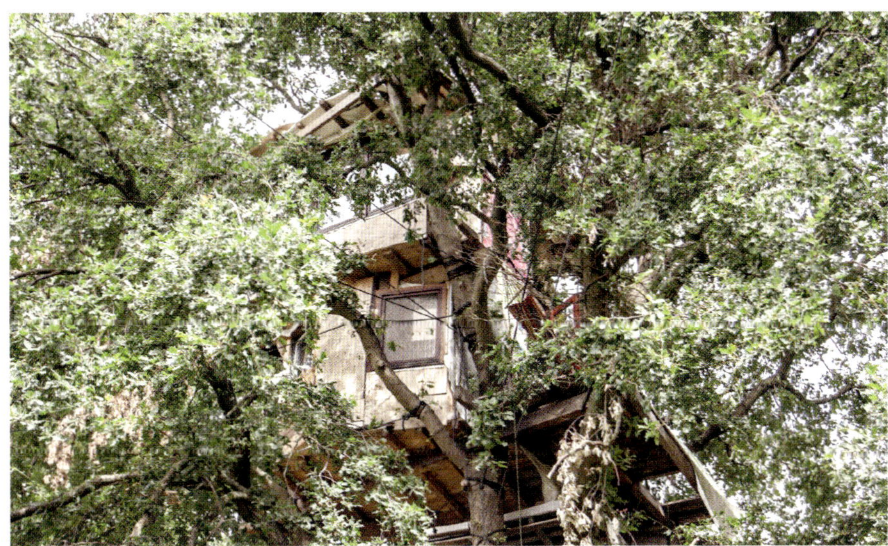

Where do activism and art meet?

Art has always been a place where activism in particular becomes possible, because a lot of things have only been addressed or made at all sayable by and through the arts. And they're two things that can mutually validate and empower each other.

That's something that just hooks me back in. That as well as wanting to give the bourgeoisie a kicking—creativity seems to also carry with it this powerful altruism, this compassion and this innocent courage to speak truth to power.

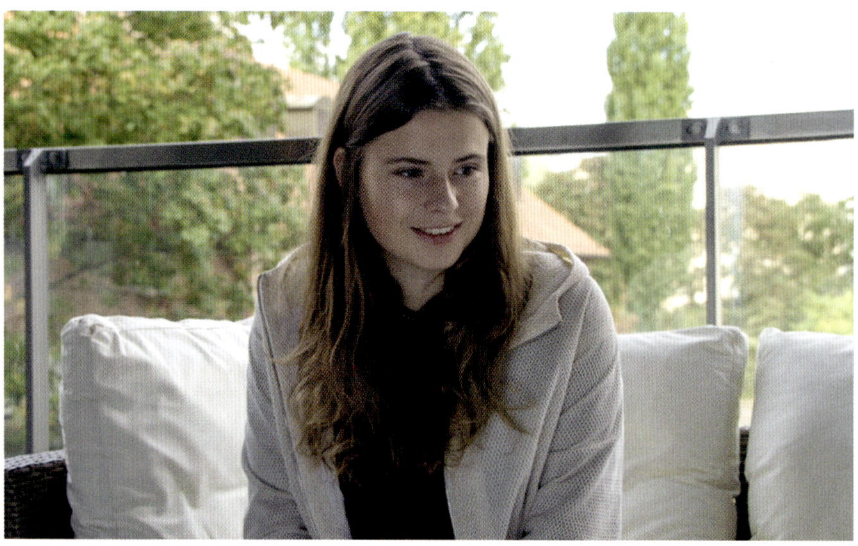

LUISA NEUBAUER

How can creativity help solve the problems of the world? Or can creativity at all help solve the problems of the world?

"OF COURSE CREATIVITY CAN HELP SOLVE THE PROBLEMS OF THE WORLD."

Of course. It must. Of course creativity can help solve the problems of the world. Where we are is in a situation we have never been in before. We have created energy monopolies that intend to continue to cause so much climate and environmental destruction for decades to come so that it is not clear how much longer people will be able to live on this planet at all. We have practically created machines and power complexes that exceed that, that is, with their destructive power they exceed what we can imagine.

The climate crisis as part of the Anthropocene or, in other words, the various ecological crises are manmade. That is the important message for us since this means that humans can avert this catastrophe. And this also means that we must see the climate crisis or the overcoming of ecological crises as a creative task, just as we have seen the development of large machines as a creative task in the past, machines that paved the way for the Industrial Revolution. Now, it's about advancing on this development, but it's also about redevelopment. Active ways out present us with paths and points of escape, and that is only possible in a sea of creativity in which we swim every day.

Nobel Prize Laureate Muhammad Yunus also focuses on manmade aspects of our problems. And since the problems are manmade, the solutions should be manmade also. So how can we clean up the mess?

MUHAMMAD YUNUS

It is a basic belief that our problems are man-made problems and it is within the capacity of human beings to solve them. If we have created the mess, we can clean up the mess. So we have the power of creativity to do that, I think we can do that. It should not be difficult. If I am looking at a problem I am trying to see how to solve the problem. It is almost like an insect, trying to get to a destination, it comes to an obstacle point, and it does not stop. It simply turns around and goes around it, and continues to reach the target. So basically, that's what I do, and in the process probably I try to avoid the conventional way of doing things, I think of new ways.

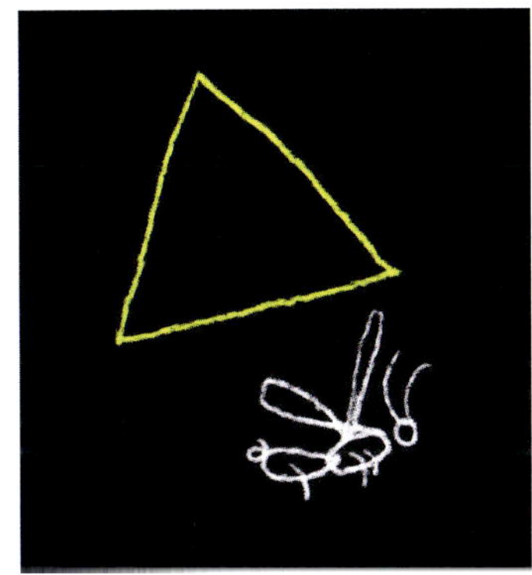

ISABELLA ROSSELLINI

Can creativity help solve the problems of the world?

I don't know … solving the problems of the world … but in some of the *Green Porno* have a sort of environmental message. And this was because a marine biologist, Claudio Campagna, saw them and liked them. And he said to me, "You know, we scientists have been exhaustively alerting people to global warming, to the mass extinction of animals. And we can't just keep repeating it. And when I saw your film I thought that it was so original that maybe there is a way to say this message, but using your humor and your language. And so we used a few of your films just as propaganda." I don't know if it helped, I don't think we solved any problems.

It makes people aware.

It makes people aware as much as they can be, you know, every bit helps. But I think that art is wonderful because it doesn't make you feel alone.

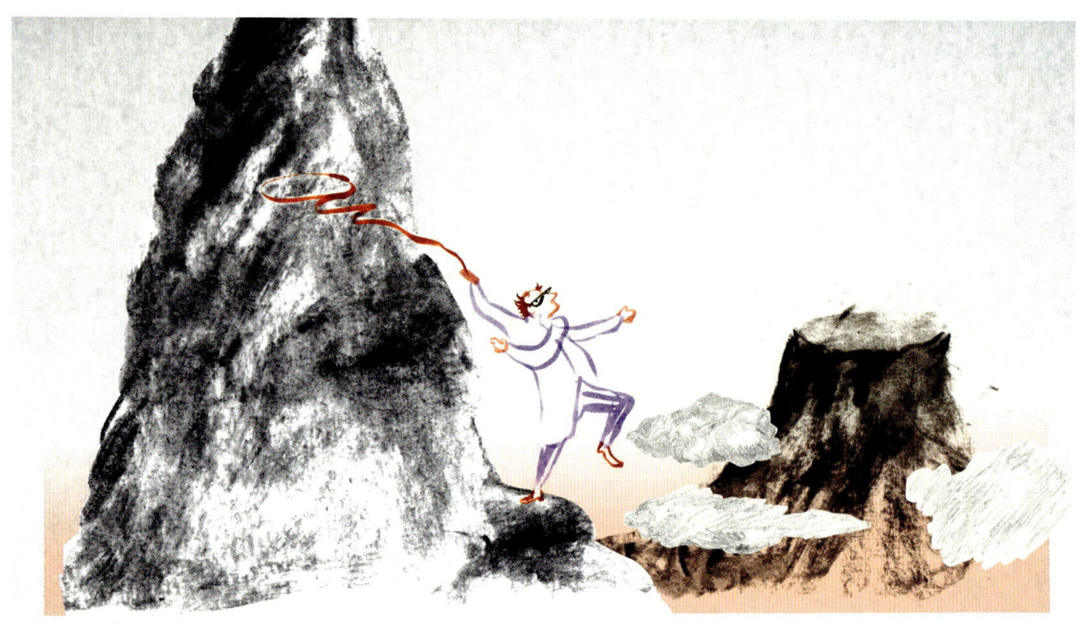

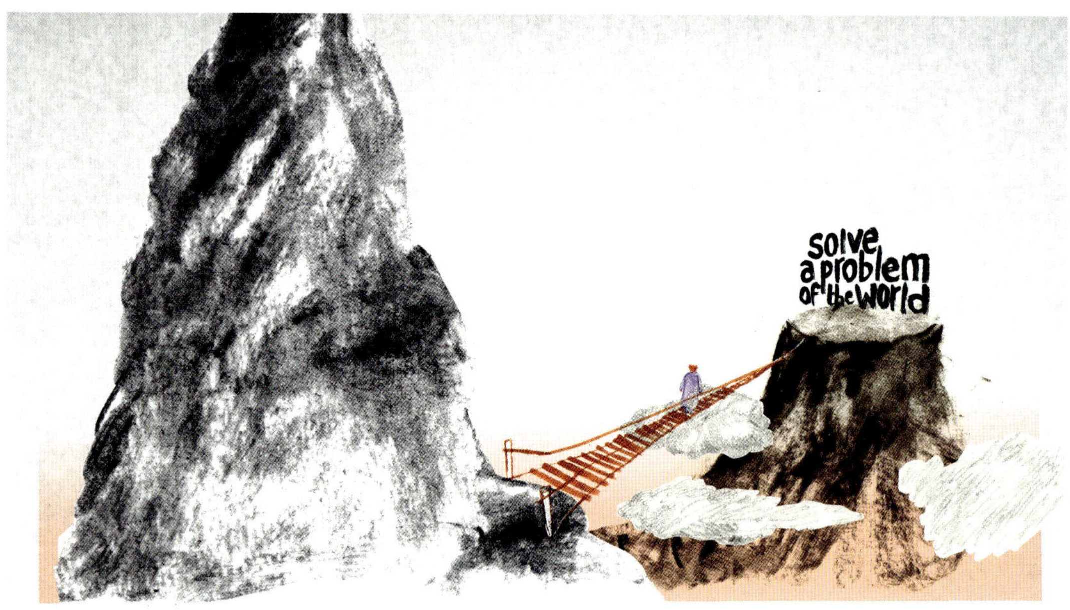
solve
a problem
of the world

SHIRIN NESHAT

In a world between environment and poverty, between refugee crisis, between the violence, all of that is happening, the racism and just everything that is going wrong at this moment—now we have COVID-19. Soon the artists won't have the luxury to distance themselves from the horror, from the darkness. We cannot just make art for the form of entertainment. I think soon you're going to find where that idea of the commercial, the way that the money has dominated the creative enterprise—it's going to take a backseat. Because artists are very shaken and very upset and, therefore, they must respond to their time that they are living in.

As artists, we're communicators and it really makes you question about, you know, how you position art in relation to this moment of crisis and where the artist stands in response to this period of uncertainty.

And how can we possibly shed light or create the work that is sort of relevant, but also that can, in the future, reflect something about the time that we lived in? We're still digesting and we're still adapting to the new life and we're being very rapid in saying, "Oh, it's over, it's over. Everything is normal again," and it's not. And I think, you know, these moments really make one think about this for myself. What kind of narratives do I want to share with my audience? And how could I possibly make something that is meaningful?

MASHA ALYOKHINA

Creativity can certainly help solve the problems of the world. Art is society's doctor. And only political art can cure society's political ills.

Masha is a strong believer in the superpower of creativity. But what are other artists saying?

PEDRO ALMODÓVAR

We don't really find our creativity until we are old. It is very important to survive, it is very important just to live, I mean for the human being, for humankind, but you have to think that creativity is sometimes in the hands of evil, so we also have to fight against that creativity.

Creativity is a double-edged sword.

Yes, you can be a real creator. I mean you can be a saint and a creator and you can be also an evil creator.

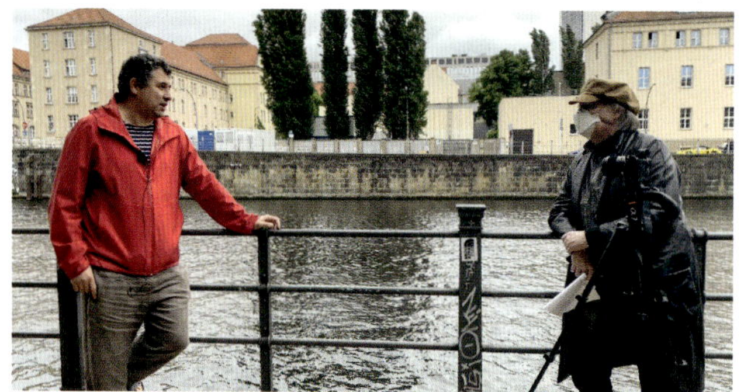

"I THINK CREATIVITY IS LIKE A SWORD WITH TWO BLADES."

RADU JUDE

I think creativity is like a sword with two blades. Now the progress that exists in the world I think is made by people who were creative in order to do good things. New medicine, new things, new social ways of organization. I think Wittgenstein had it right in his book *Philosophische Untersuchungen*, the quote is: "It is the nature of progress to seem bigger than it is." It sounds like a marketing phrase.

BRIAN ENO

I think creativity can cause a lot of problems as well. Creativity isn't necessarily good, you know; creativity is neutral, creativity is the name of the process of thinking about things in a new way. You can think about new ways of killing people as well. So it's not necessarily a good thing.

UMBERTO ECO

Can creativity per se help solve the problems of the world?

Creativity, per se, doesn't solve any problem, because it depends on what you are creating. Even the invention of the atomic bomb was a creative invention, but it posed more problems than it solved. The problem is not creativity. The problem is how to face the problems posed by creativity. Take the internet: it has certainly produced one of the greatest revolutions of the millennium, but it creates incredible problems.

WERNER HERZOG

Do you think that creativity is able to solve the problems of the world?

"THE FATES OF PEOPLES AND HISTORY ALWAYS STILL DEPEND ON INDIVIDUALS."

I have never been asked this question in such a good way. I think that in the history of humankind it was those with creative intelligence who could make a political vision become reality. I don't think this could be accomplished merely by superb administrations. That's not enough. The fates of peoples and history still depend on individuals to a great degree. On someone who sees the circumstances more clearly than others, who can define a line in the perspective, see further than others, and put things into action.

I had the opportunity to ask Nobel Peace Prize Laureate President Nelson Mandela whether he believes in the problem-solving capabilities of creativity.

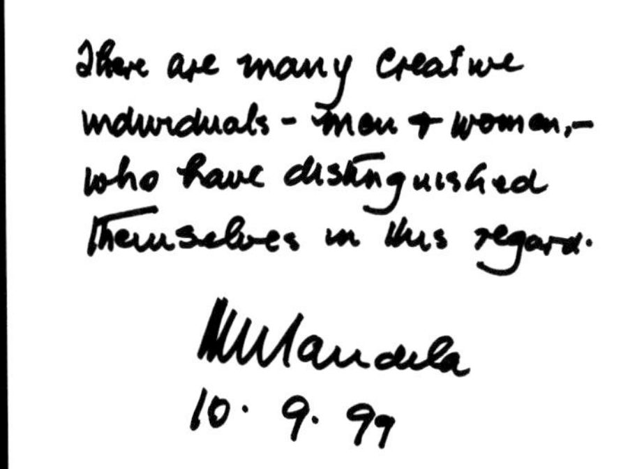

There are many creative individuals - men + women, - who have distinguished themselves in this regard.

NMandela
10. 9. 99

NELSON MANDELA

Mr. President, do you think we need creative thinking to solve the problems of the world?

Well, creative thinking is always absolutely necessary. We don't want stereotype views and clichés, which are not related to the specific situation we are addressing. If we wanted to be relevant, then we have to be creative. And other views should be related to the problem that we are addressing.

There are problems on top of problems, problems on the hill we climb. Once, the Russian director Andrey Zvyagintsev told me an anecdote that offers a solution.

ANDREY ZVYAGINTSEV

"FIND YOUR VOICE."

My teacher once said something that I will remember for the rest of my life, and that may also be a parting word for young people. I always use this quote when I meet young people. I'll just repeat it. He said that the theater is 2,500 years old. In all that time, the theater has seen everything. Absolutely everything. And even when they found a new form, trust me, everything has already been done. Everything. Except for one thing: you. That's a very inspiring quote. It tells us that your voice is the only true and important one. Your own voice. And the achievements, the resonance, the quality of this voice, all of that is entirely up to your taste, your feeling for boundaries, your perception for the marvelous. Raise and nurture these qualities in yourself: read a lot, read lots of literature, books. Read more books. Watch more movies. Look at more art and so on. And maybe that mass will turn into quality. Believe in your voice, believe in yourself. Find your voice.

In Venice, Yoko Ono shocked with one hundreds coffins on display at the avant-garde art exhibition *Open* on the Lido. The coffins of her work *Nutopia* each bore an olive branch, a symbol of peace.

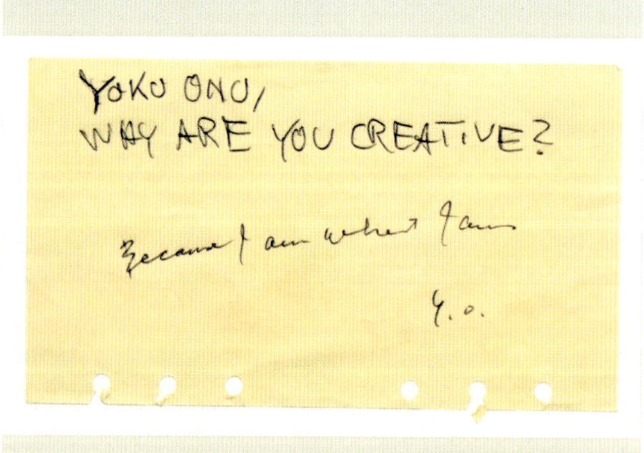
YOKO ONO,
WHY ARE YOU CREATIVE?

Because I am what I am

Y.O.

YOKO ONO

The idea is that this is about massacre. Hundred people, families, couples, children, they were all killed together, and this happens in every country. Every country has a memory of massacre. And I am saying no more massacre, no more war, no more killing. My inspiration and creativity is about life, about reality. And by knowing and facing and confronting reality, we become wiser.

Yoko found her voice and her cause. "I am who I am," she wrote me on a piece of paper.

In order to find a cause, look into yourself. If you know who you are, you will know what you want to change in the world.

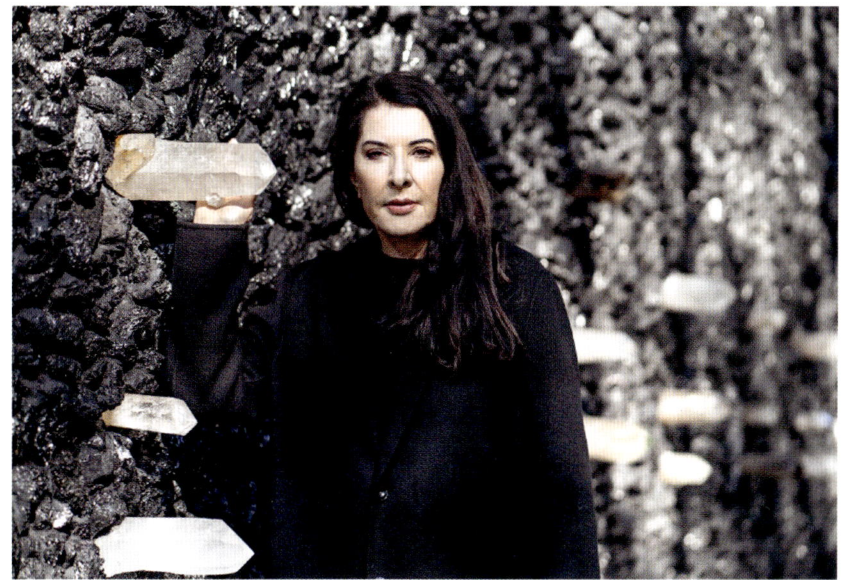

MARINA ABRAMOVIĆ

I'm going to Kiev for the big opening of the Babi Yar memorial. I'm doing a huge project there in for the Babi Yar, which is the Jewish monument. Five presidents are coming to my installation first. It's war, crime, and forgiveness. So, this is happening now. I'm going straight at the end of the week. I show you now what I'm doing in Kiev. It's kind of huge. It is 300 tons weight. You know I decided to get inspiration for the wall of Ukraine from the wall of Jerusalem. Connected. I made this wall which is forty meters made out of coal, which is like the source of energy, and I put 120 faceless people crying of forgiveness. That makes it a wall of crime and forgiveness. Forgiveness is something nobody used. It's also at night. And then the presidents of the country are going to stand with that wall.

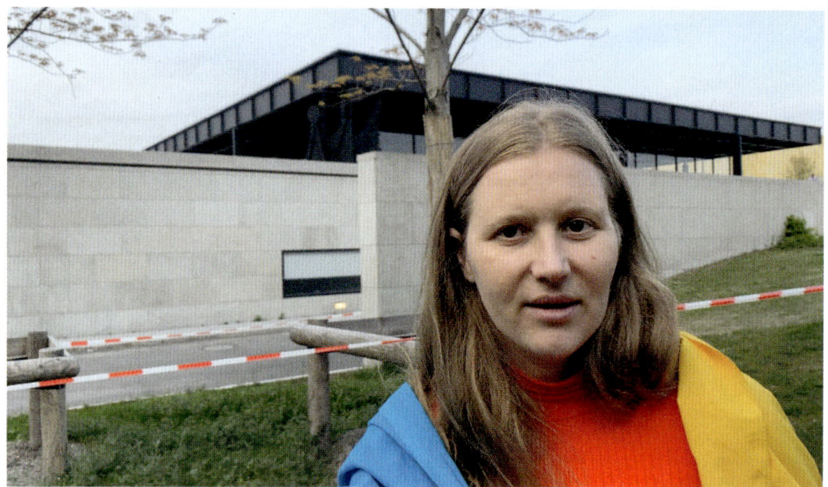

Once upon a time, the world was to be improved. Today, it can only be saved. Ukrainian artist and activist Maria Kulikovska believes in the healing power of creativity. At Berlin Gallery Weekend she did an important performance rolling herself in the Ukrainian flag on the steps of the Neue Nationalgallerie.

MARIA KULIKOVSKA

To what extent can creativity help solve the problems in the world?

It's a huge question. To answer it we can go back to Joseph Beuys. He is one of the pioneers who was teaching us to use creativity to solve a lot of problems. And I think, in general, we see now through this horror, what's going on in Ukraine, that weapons on a big scale really cannot fix anything. Because you will always find someone who has even stronger weapons, and then it's like a never-ending competition of who is the strongest. So like, right now, I think that all of us need to think, what is the future, really? What kind of future do we want to live in? Will it even exist? And if it will, then maybe we need to build and design it differently and think more creatively.

So, you think that basically everyone should find a good cause to be engaged to make the world a better place. Or is this too utopian?

I think that as an artist, I am utopianist. Of course, we always believe that everyone should be great and everyone should be creative as much as we can. And find a good cause.

So it's a correlation between creativity and politics.

Any artwork is political. I don't believe that as an artist we are nonpolitical or that we are out of politics. What is politics? It's relationships between people. It's not politicians, parties, or ministers. It's society. It's the relationships between us. So no one cannot escape this freely. I am using the Ukrainian flag now. It's a very direct political language, I would say. But I'm using it in a different way as performance, as action in a cultural field. But I hope that this act can become a platform for discussion for many of us. And when we meet and discuss, it's like starting changes. Now, in this situation of the war, we really need actions from the politicians, like acts of solidarity, of helping with weapons, money, open borders, supporting people. But if we go further on a bigger scale, I think that soft power can win in the long term.

LUISA NEUBAUER

From the very start, we have to look at solutions and possibilities that things will change. That's it, that would be the definition of hope. A possibility for change. And without hope, nothing goes forward.

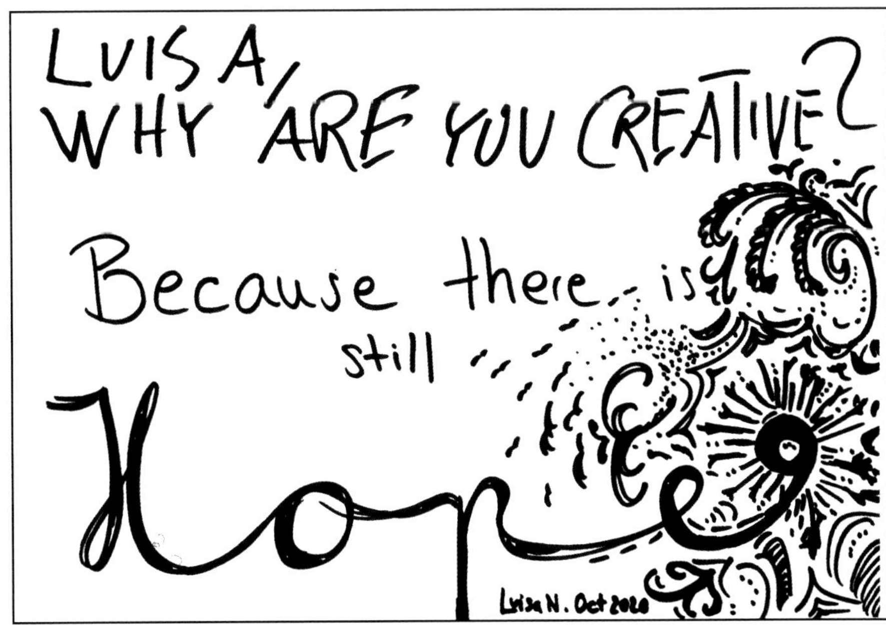

Nobody expressed the principle of hope to me better than the Israeli writer Amos Oz with his parable of the teaspoon. In the parable he compares the problems of the world with a big fire. And Oz is convinced that you can extinguish the problems of the world with a teaspoon. How? Simply by not stopping to throw teaspoons of water on the glow. And if we all creatively participate, we will pull this off.

AMOS OZ

I'm a great follower of the parable of the teaspoon. So in my own way with a little teaspoon, I try to add some more imagination into the world. But this is like trying to irrigate a whole desert with a teaspoon. You know, one day there shall be an order of the teaspoon. When I see a huge fire like the war, the cruelty and the suffering, I have three choices.

One: run away and to hell with the others.
Two: sit down and scream, "This is terrible."
Three: fill my little teaspoon with water, throw it on the flame.

The teaspoon is small, the flame is huge, and yet, if everybody will do just that, it will tame the flame. I think people should use their teaspoons to minimize the pain and the sorrow and the suffering and the injustice. The order of the teaspoon.

SHIRIN NESHAT

I am really optimistic that this period of crisis, politically, environmentally, health-wise, is going to be a turning point for the creative community. And for our audience to raise their bar in terms of what they expect from us, which will also force us to rethink our narratives.

I think that in a few years hopefully things will change. And when we talk to each other again, I hope that you will be asking me a very different question.

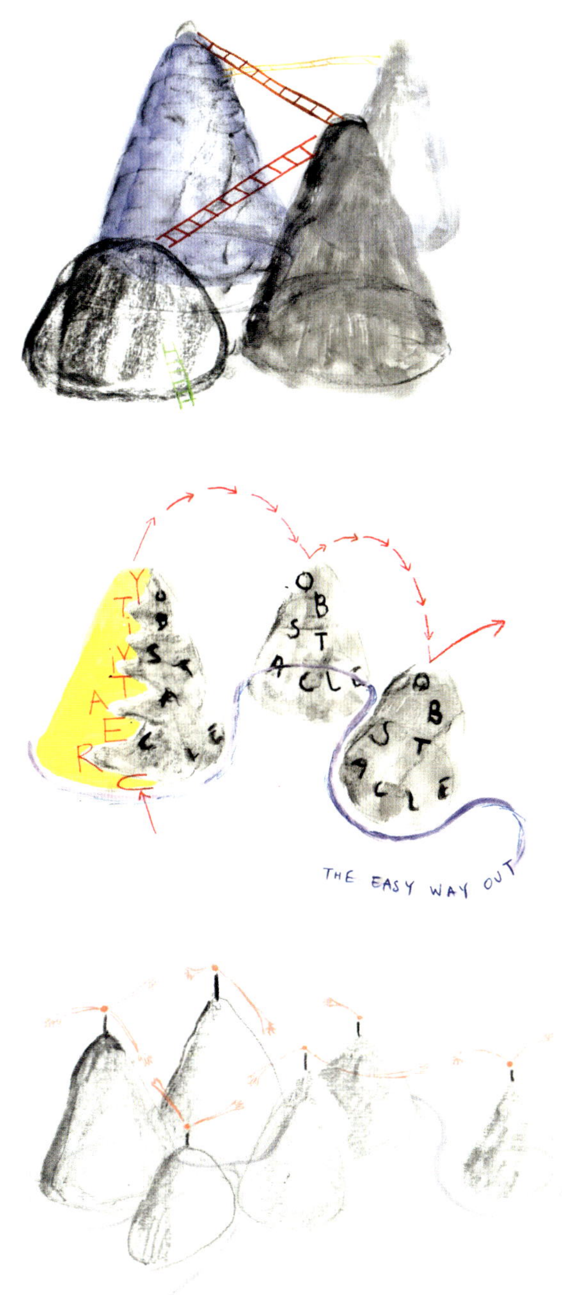
CREATIVITY
OBSTACLE
OBSTACLE
OBSTACLE
THE EASY WAY OUT

But today the only question we should be asking is, "How can creativity help solve the problems of a dying planet?" This Anthropocene period, with its existential threats of climate change and war, is inviting us to explore new and disruptive ideas if we want to avoid disaster.

Creativity may be under threat. But either way, if we are to survive ourselves, it's time we put creativity at the top of the pyramid.

In the final part of my film trilogy *Can Creativity Save the World,* I explore the crucial role and extraordinary power of creativity in helping to solve the problems of the world. Despite these dark days of global pandemic, manmade climate catastrophe, and brutal war, the power of creative, imaginative thinking gives us reasons for optimism and hope.
In *Can Creativity Save the World,* some of the world's greatest creative minds discuss how they try to identify and free up their own creativity—and how to apply that creativity to a new world.

Can Creativity save the World?

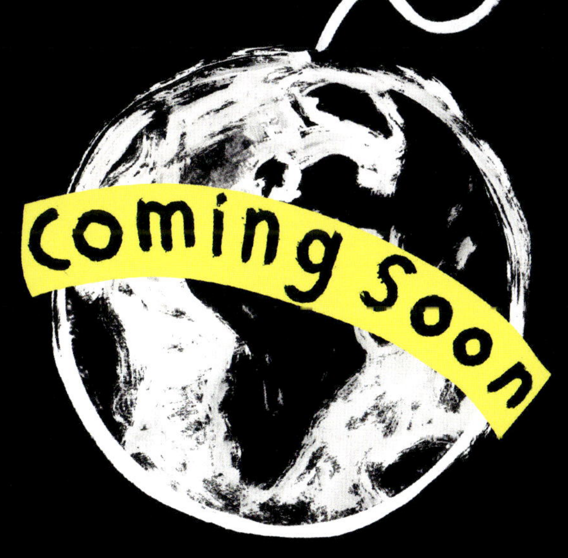

a film by
Hermann Vaske

THE HERMANN VASKE COLLECTION

All of the participants also created an artifact for the project—some very personal, some bizarre. Vaske has exhibited these artifacts with considerable success in Europe. Exhibitions included the Museum of Communication in Berlin and the Espace Miramar in Cannes as part of the Cannes Film Festival.

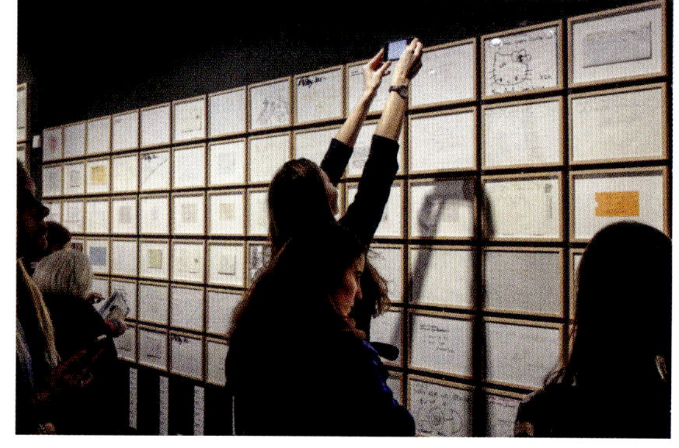

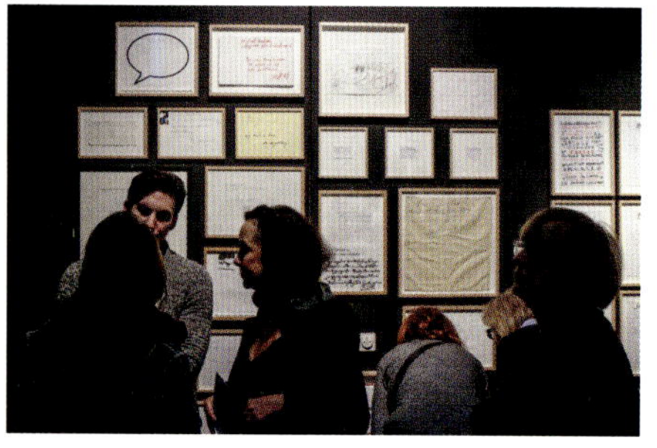

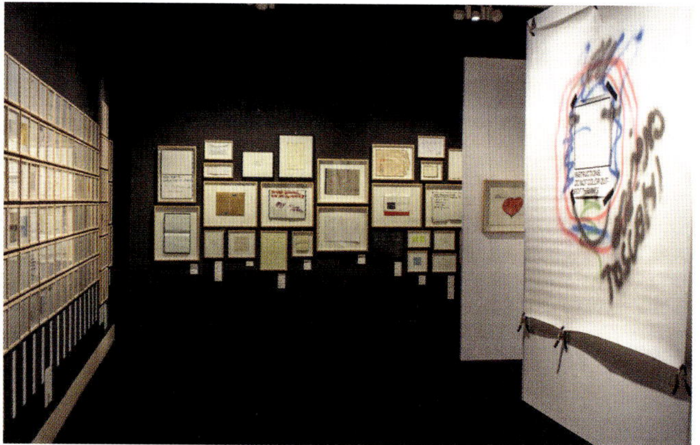

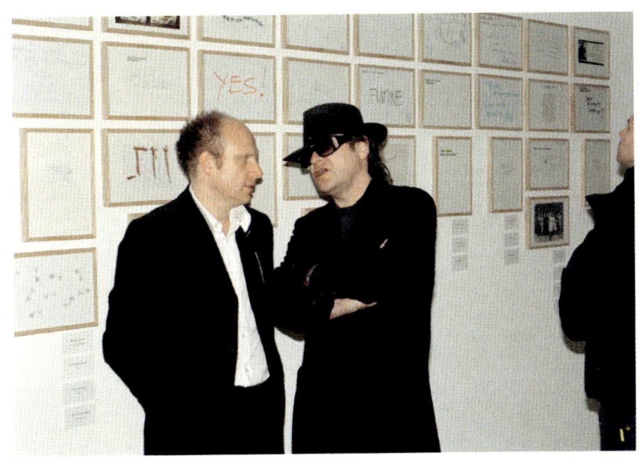
YES!

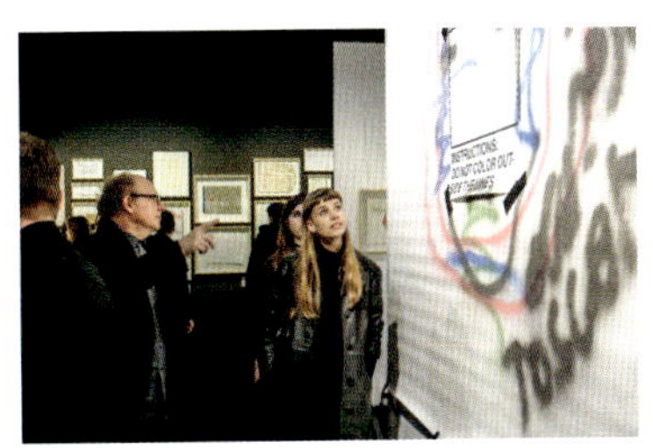

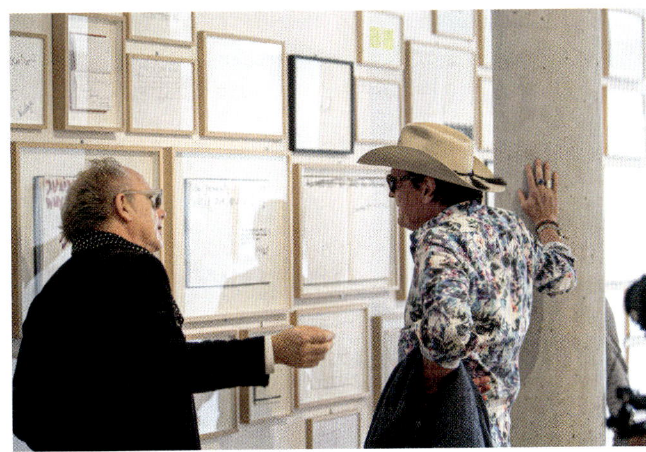

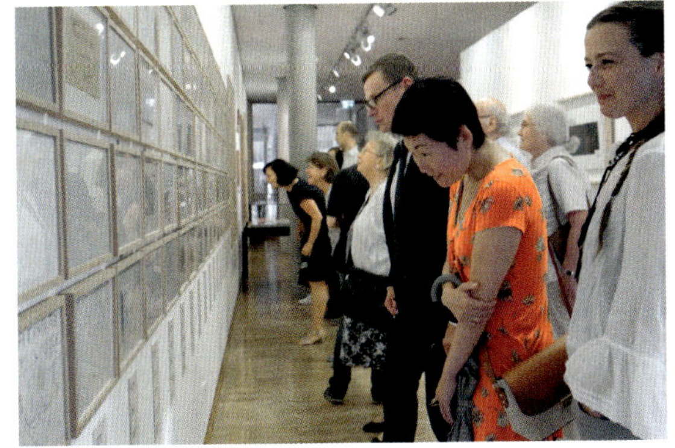

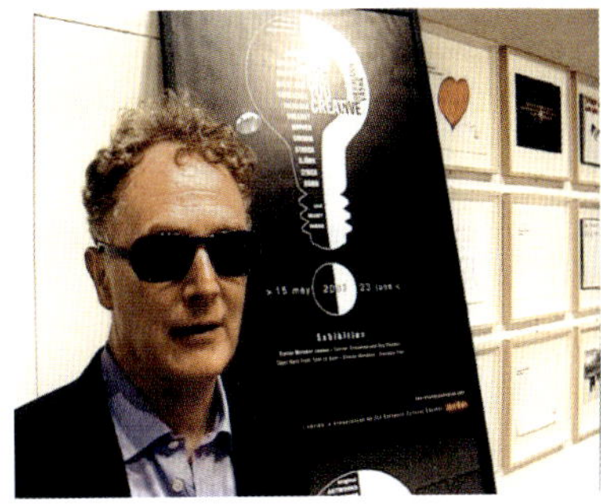

FILMS "WHY ARE WE CREATIVE?"

Film trailer
"Why are we creative?"

David Lynch reveals what motivates him to bring something from the abstract to the material.

Nick Cave explains that creativity is his destiny.

David Bowie describes how he can sail to the end of the world where he just finds more sea to navigate.

Björk tells us about the egalitarian culture of creativity in her family.

Angelina Jolie instructs on combining art with something you care about.

Marina Abramović unloads about the urge of create.

Willem Dafoe opens up about how the act of creation makes him feel.

Tracey Emin talks about her ambition to get better and better.

Georg Baselitz maintains that creating art has something to do with showing off.

Zaha Hadid insists that developing ideas is hard work.

Ed Ruscha compares creativity with a boxing match.

FILMS "WHY ARE WE NOT CREATIVE?"

Film trailer
"Why are we not creative?"

Lars Kraume explains that creativity has something to do with aggression.

Rezo lays out the argument that economic circumstances hinder creativity.

Mike Leigh shares about the difficulties to get ideas into the system.

Julian Schnabel believes that art will always spring up through the cracks in cement, despite the difficulties.

Sputniko! talks about the beta-blockers of creativity in conjunction with artificial intelligence.

Dieter Meier discusses the correlation of creativity with chaos and fear.

Trine Dyrholm elaborates on the relationship between creativity and truth.

Luisa Neubauer connects creativity with fear of failure.

Oliviero Toscani thinks that creativity is probably a vision of absurdity.

Adina Pintillie talks about the importance of tension, conflicts, and the breaking of walls in creativity.

Brian Newman complains about the circumstances and people that kill ideas.

INDEX OF NAMES

ACKNOWLEDGEMENTS

I would like to express my gratitude to the following people, without whom the project would not have been possible.

To all the artists and creators for their precious time and for sharing their thoughts and creative wisdom.
To Jonathan Meese for all the great artworks.
Ars longa, vita brevis. Thanks for our friendship since the time of Karl Marx.
To Valerie Pirson. Thanks for your invaluable contributions and inspirations for the *Creativity Trilogy*, for this book, and for bringing the characters to life.
To Esra Gülmen for the great movie posters and of course for her striking cover artwork.
To Mark Williams for inspiration and will power.
To Maike Backhaus who reminded me that less is more. Thanks for your companionship and invaluable input since the days of Schmidtstrasse.
To Fabio Holub for his editing and production skills and for being such a good driver.
To Max Kaplan for his support, great language skills, and extraordinary writing contributions.
To Ruth Rosenberger, Hans Walter Hütter, and Harald Biermann from the Haus der Geschichte.
To the rest of the Emotional Network team: Angelina Yarovara, Lena Schubert,
Lea Holtfreter, Isabell Bullerschen, Sonja Risse, and Kristian Stern for their enthusiastic work despite the pandemic (in the dark days of the lockdown).
To Anja Schaluschke, Dr. Helmut Gold, Dr. Elisabeth Dühr, and Bernard Brochand for the Espace Miramar in Cannes, and to Festival de Cannes for making exhibitions possible.
To my New York friend Risa Mickenberg for her wit and writing, and her exceptional creations.
To Anna Schoeppe (HessenFilm) and Kirsten Niehuus (MBB) for making creativity possible.
To Aby Mehler, Ruth Rosenberger, Bernd Neumann, Stephan Landwehr, Stefan Laudyn, Johanna Süß, Gregor Maria Schubert, and Walter Scheuerl for creative support.
To Diana Iljine and Christoph Gröner from Filmfest Munich for many creative adventures.
A very Special Thanks to Luisa Neubauer and Mayor Katrin Habenschaden for taking the stage at Gasteig.
To Gaia Furrer and Giorgio Gosetti from Giornate degli Autori of the Venice Filmfestival and to Marina Abramović and Masha Alyokhina for coming to Venice to support the launch.
To Dave Trott and George Lois for their help and inspiration.
To Charles V. Bender, whom I studied with at the American Film Institute, for his energy, continuous support, and production skills.
To my longtime partner Sabine Bubeck-Paaz for her patience and input.
To ARTE's Kathrin Brinckmann, Wolfgang Bergmann, Dieter Schneider, and Barbara Häbe.
To Hans Robert Eisenhauer and Joe Pytka who were always there when I needed them.
To Hengameh Panahi, Charlotte Mickie, and Stefan Kloos for bringing the goods to the market.
To Matthias Sievecke, for home is where the art is.
To the communication specialists Matthias Storath, Matthias Spaetgens, Stephan Vogel, Marcel Loko, Marjorieth Sanmartin, Alina Schlaier, Jürgen, and Jan Knaus.
To my Cannes partner of thirty years, Florian Weischer.
To Andreas Prasse of Wall Decaux for making good ideas and striking posters visible.
To Hannes Fuchs, Teresa Spöckner, Laura Hermes, Jonas Rose, and Raban Ruddigkeit for graphic design, typography, art direction, and layout.
To Anton Corbijn, Florian Luxenburger, Jörg Steinmetz, Lars Hinsenhofen, Martin May, Nadine Fraczkowski, and Rainer März.
To Pari Esfandiari, who was always part of the journey since the Champneys days in London.

ALSO BY HERMANN VASKE

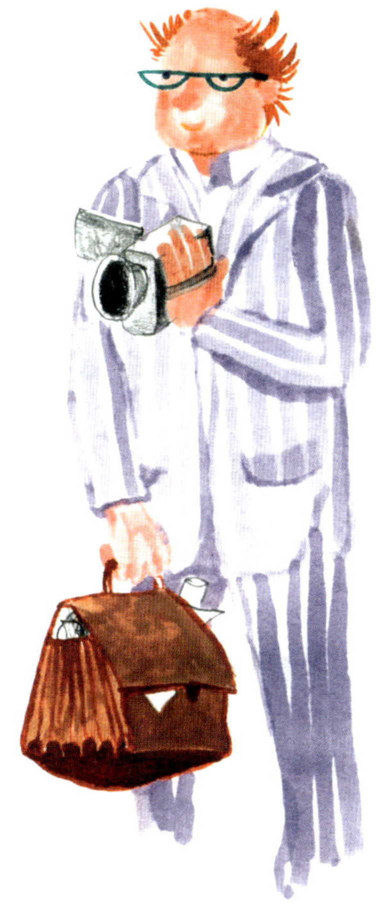

BOOKS:

Why Are You Creative?
Standing on the Shoulders Giants

FILMS:

Why Are We (Not) Creative?
Why Are We Creative? The Centipede's Dilemma
Dennis Hopper: Uneasy Rider
Bra Wars: Hollywood's Affair with the Bra.
Arteholic
Balkan Spirit
Digital Bomb
Beyond: A Cyberspace Odyssey
The Radical Gardener
Must I Write/Letters to a Young Poet
The Art of Football
Invasion of the Ideas
Who Killed the Idea?
Das Kleine Fernsehspiel Reloaded
The Ten Commandments of Creativity
The A-Z of Separating People from their Money
The Fine Art of Separating People from their Money

Hermann Vaske is a director, author, and producer. He studied at the Berlin University of the Arts and the American Film Institute in Los Angeles.

As a director he worked with actors such as Dennis Hopper, Harvey Keitel, Sir Peter Ustinov, and John Cleese. As a producer, he worked with artists such as Marina Abramović, Shirin Neshat, and Vivienne Westwood and extraordinary human beings such as Nelson Mandela, Stephen Hawking, and the Dalai Lama. His films have been shown in Venice, Cannes, Toronto, and Palm Springs and won numerous awards. Including the Grimme-Preis, Germany's TV Oscar, the Hessian Film Award, Venice TV Festival, Gold Clios, Cannes Lions, and New York Festivals Film & TV Awards.

Vaske is a professor at the University of Applied Arts Trier. He is a member of the German Film Academy and Art Directors Club and a member of the European Film Academy.

PHOTO AND PICTURE CREDITS

© Hermann Vaske's
Emotional Network
pp. 15, 18, 22, 27, 36, 43, 49, 56, 60, 87, 103, 106, 111, 121, 134, 136, 140, 145, 147, 151, 157, 159, 161, 176–79, 185, 186, 193, 205, 209, 210, 217, 219, 222, 234, 245, 246, 254, 266, 284, 286, 295, 298, 305

© Why Are You Creative? Collection
Hermann Vaske
pp. 17–22, 38, 41, 42, 45, 48, 51–53, 57–60, 69, 71, 73, 78, 81, 85, 88, 89, 92, 97, 100, 101, 103, 113, 118–122, 126, 127, 130, 131, 136, 144, 145, 150, 153, 154, 157, 168, 175, 196, 200, 201, 203, 205, 233, 235, 237, 245, 287, 295, 296, 299

© Valérie Pirson /
Emotional Network
pp. 4, 5, 7, 9, 14, 15, 26, 28, 30, 31, 37, 39, 40, 61–63, 65, 68, 76, 77, 80, 83–86, 88, 94, 95, 98, 99, 101, 109, 116, 117, 123, 128, 137, 154– 56, 158, 159, 161, 163, 164, 166, 168–71, 173, 182–85, 190, 194–97, 202, 204, 206, 207, 211, 212, 216, 221, 222, 230, 231, 240, 241, 242, 243, 248, 249, 252, 253, 254, 255, 262, 268, 269, 273, 275, 282, 287, 292, 301, 303, 311, 314, 315

© Florian Luxenburger /
Emotional Network
pp. 8, 135, 167, 304, 305 (middle page)

© Jonathan Meese
pp. 10, 12, 24, 34, 46, 54, 66, 74, 90, 104, 114, 124, 132, 148, 164, 172, 180, 198, 214, 226, 238, 250, 260, 270, 276, 281

© Esra Gülmen
pp. 11, 162

© Patricia Lewandowska /
Emotional Network
pp. 16, 38, 93, 141, 213, 232, 259, 290

© Vanessa Kirsch /
Emotional Network
pp. 23, 291

© Lars Hinsenhofen /
Emotional Network
pp. 33, 41, 144, 147, 257

© Evgeny Revvo /
Emotional Network
pp. 70, 139, 143, 147, 208, 272

© Charles V. Bender /
Emotional Network
p. 78

© Dave Burdette /
Emotional Network
pp. 102, 278

© Bill Turnley /
Emotional Network
p. 108

© Raban Ruddigkeit /
Emotional Network
p. 113

© Sasha Rendulic /
Emotional Network
pp. 120, 229

© Natalia Mamaj /
Emotional Network
p. 138

© Shirin Neshat
Roja, 2016
Video still
Courtesy of the artist and
Gladstone Gallery
p. 174

© Anton Corbijn
p. 146

© Marcello Serpa
p. 147

© Jörg Steinmetz
p. 160

© Nitsch Foundation
20. Malaktion, February 18–21, 1987, Secession, Wien
(Photo: Liesl Biber)
p. 170

© Phedon Papamichael /
Emotional Network
p. 186

© Marianna Simnett
(Photo: Krystian Lipiec)
pp. 252, 253

© Marianna Simnett
The Needle and the Larynx, 2016
Video still
Courtesy of the artist and
Serpentine Galleries, London
p. 193

© Sebastian Horsley Estate
Crucifixion
Courtesy Sarah Lucas
p. 209

© Oliviero Toscani / Arte Generali
Film featuring Maurizio Cattelan
p. 225

© Rain Li /
Emotional Network
p. 228

© Isabell Bullerschen /
Emotional Network
p. 265

© Shealynn Chin
p. 263

© Dustin Pearlman /
Emotional Network
p. 274

© Lars Eidinger
p. 280

© Charlotte Pouch /
Emotional Network
p. 285

© Nico Gühlstorf /
Emotional Network
p. 288

© Daniel Toelke /
Emotional Network
p. 289

© Rainer März /
Emotional Network
p. 305 (above)

© Max Kaplan /
Emotional Network
p. 294

© Marina Abramović
Crystal Wall of Crying
Babyn Yar Holocaust Memorial
Center, Kyiv, Ukraine
2021
Courtesy of the Marina Abramović
Archives and Babyn Yar
Holocaust Memorial Center
p. 297

"It's important that Hermann is putting creativity under the spotlight. In times of crisis, we should interrogate creativity."

—Shirin Neshat, Artist

"It is time to awaken our positive human potential by making the lives we lead meaningful. The answers collected in this project are evidence of people trying to do just that."

—His Holiness, the Dalai Lama

"Hermann's conversations should find a place in the libraries of every university—available to all students."

—Malcom McLaren, Artist

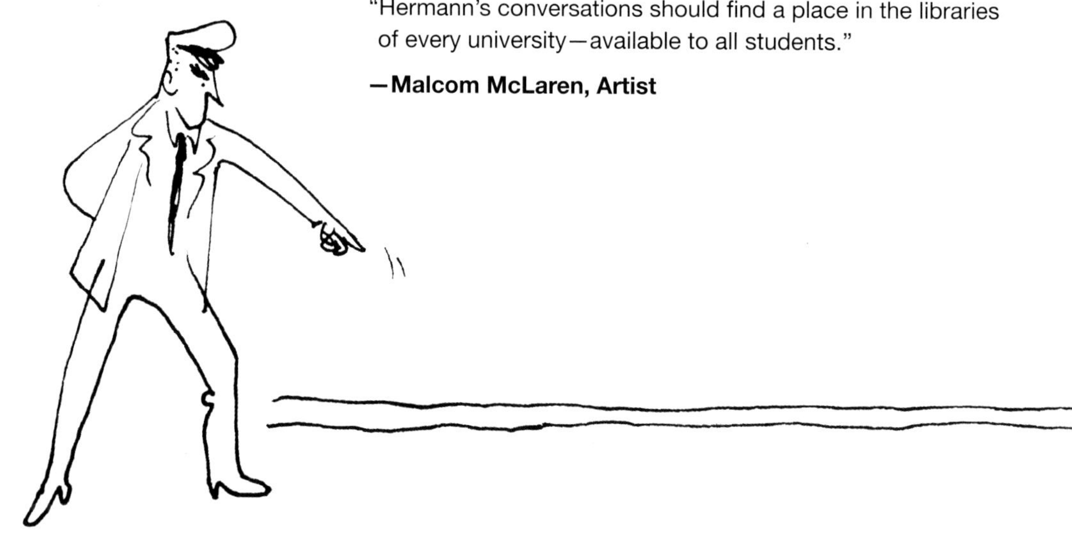

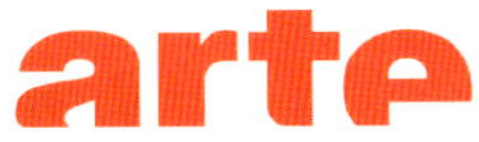

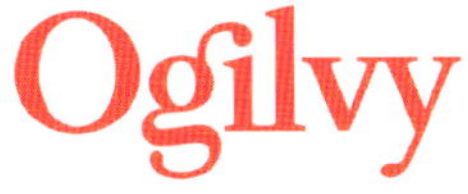

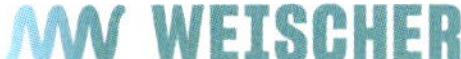

WallDecaux
Premium Out of Home

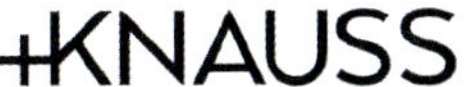

HIRSCHEN GROUP
Home of the brave

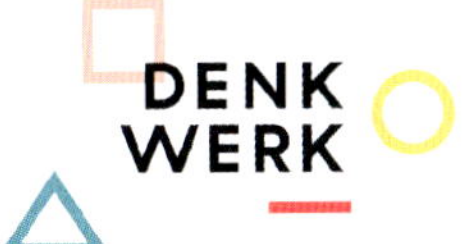

Heimat, Berlin.

Campus of Art and Design | HOCHSCHULE TRIER

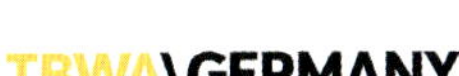

Scholz & Friends
Berlin

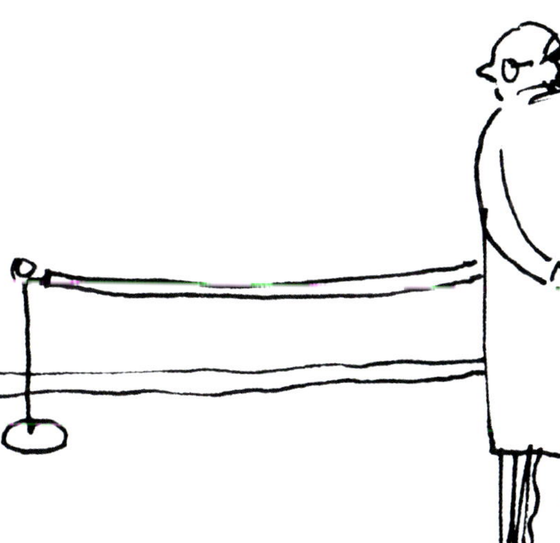

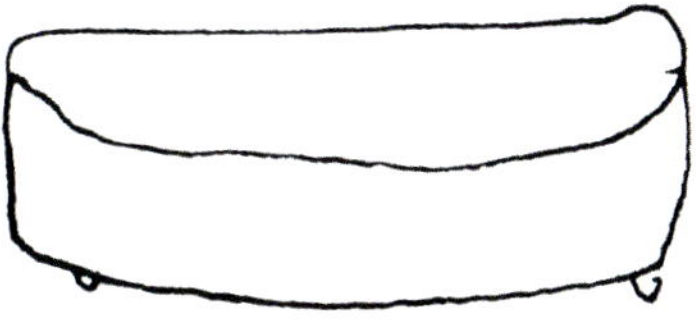

Editor: Hermann Vaske

Managing Editor: Maike Backhaus, Hermann Vaske, Max Kaplan, Fabio Holub

Project management: Sophie Pechhacker

Proofreading: Aaron Bogart

Copyediting: Maike Backhaus, Hermann Vaske, Max Kaplan, Fabio Holub, Lea Rosa Holtfreter, Hannes Fuchs

Translations: Max Kaplan

Typeface: Helvetica Neue, Acumin Pro

Chapter Artworks: Jonathan Meese

Illustration: Valérie Pirson

Cover Art: Esra Gülmen

Art Direction and Graphic Design: Hannes Fuchs, Teresa Spöckner, Laura Hermes, Jonas Rose, Raban Ruddigkeit

Production: Alise Ausmane

Reproductions: REPROMAYER Medienproduktion GmbH

Printing and Binding: Livonia Print

Paper: Arctic Volume White 150 g/m²

Concept and Interviews by
Hermann Vaske/Hermann Vaske's Emotional Network
E-Mail: vaske@whyareyoucreative.com
Instagram: @why.are.we.creative
www.hermannvaske.com/www.whyarewecreative.com

Published by
Hatje Cantz Verlag GmbH
Mommsenstraße 27
10629 Berlin
www.hatjecantz.com
A Ganske Publishing Group Company

ISBN 978-3-7757-5292-3

Printed in Europe